ESSAYS ON EUROPEAN LITERATURE

Essays on European Literature

++++++++++++++++++++++++++++++++++++

Kritische Essays zur europäischen Literatur

By E. R. Curtius

Translated by Michael Kowal

Princeton University Press
Princeton, New Jersey

Acknowledgments

I SHOULD like to express my gratitude to Frau Ilse Curtius of Bonn, whose kind hospitality enabled me to pursue research in the library of her late husband. Some of this material has been incorporated in the introduction. Professor Heinrich Lausberg of the University of Münster kindly furnished me with an advance proof of his biography of Curtius, which has since been published in *150 Jahre Rheinische Friedrich-Wilhelms-Universität zu Bonn* (1818-1968), Bonn, 1970, pp. 214-235. For the introduction I have further drawn upon two essays by American scholars, Alexander Gelley, "Ernst Robert Curtius: Topology and Critical Method," *Modern Language Notes*, LXXXI (1966), 579-594; and Arthur R. Evans, Jr., "Ernst Robert Curtius," *On Four Modern Humanists*, Princeton, 1970, pp. 85-145.

The essays "Friedrich Schlegel and France," "The Young Cocteau," and "George, Hofmannsthal and Calderón" were translated by Eva Schweizer Vogel, although the latter has been somewhat revised. I am also grateful to Professor Vogel for a partial draft of "Remarks on the French Novel" and for many helpful suggestions on the manuscript.

I owe thanks to my colleague Professor Martin Nozick of Queens College for reading the essays on Spanish literature and providing valuable criticism. For comments and advice I am indebted to Professor Ernst Fedor Hoffmann of Hunter College and to Professor Ursula Hoffmann of Lehman College. I should also like to thank my father for help in resolving difficulties of language and style.

The entire translation has been checked against previous translations into French and Italian. I have also consulted the earlier English versions of two essays, the second part of the essay on Ortega y Gasset by Willard R. Trask (*Partisan Review*, 1950) and the essay on Balzac by Harry Zohn

(*Modern Occasions*, 1971). I have profited from these translations and wish to record my indebtedness here.

It remains only to thank the editors of the Princeton University Press, and especially its associate director, Miss R. Miriam Brokaw, for their assistance throughout the preparation of this book.

M. K.

New York, July, 1973

Contents

CONTENTS

Introduction

ERNST ROBERT CURTIUS is best known in the English speaking world for his magisterial examination of mediaeval poetics and rhetoric, *European Literature and the Latin Middle Ages*. What is less known, what may even surprise, is that Curtius was not, in any technical sense, a "mediaevalist," that he turned to mediaeval studies relatively late, driven to them partly by inner necessity, partly by external pressures.

It is true that the ground for this development was carefully prepared. For Curtius entered upon the study of Romance philology when the split between linguistics and literature, which he was often afterwards to deplore, had not yet taken place. He had begun his academic career with a dissertation on an Old French text, *Li Quatre Livres des Reis* (published in 1911), and a study of the late nineteenth century French critic, Ferdinand Brunetière (1914). The two poles, mediaeval and modern, of his scholarship were therefore fixed at the outset. But for the next twenty years, Curtius' activities as critic and scholar were dedicated almost exclusively to modern literature.

While still a student he had formed associations in Berlin with the circle around Stefan George, and especially with the poet's chief disciple, Friedrich Gundolf, to whom he was bound for many years by a fast friendship. Whether for reasons of temperament or outlook, Curtius never became a member of the circle, did not publish in its journal, and, however strongly influenced by its efforts at intellectual and cultural renewal, did not share its aesthetic ends.

Curtius early discovered what he conceived to be his appointed task. It took shape in the book that carried his name across national frontiers, *Die literarischen Wegbereiter des neuen Frankreich* [*The Literary Pioneers of the New France*], which was published in 1919, but reaches back to lectures Curtius delivered at the University of Bonn in the summer of 1914 and, even further, to the experiences of his youth. Born in 1886, in Alsace, which had been ceded to Germany following the Franco-Prussian War of 1870, he witnessed during his student days in Strasbourg the nationalistic rancors and mutual incomprehension that divided France and Germany in the years before World War One. With his study of the rising generation of French writers, Curtius sought to promote an exchange of ideas between French and German intellectuals that should eventually lead to a new unity of the European mind. To mediate between the literary consciousness of France and Germany was, for Curtius, not a theoretical proposition but a cultural program. Because of the conjunction of circumstances, this program carried political implications. Curtius' conception of his task as a mediator, and the hopes and disappointments he met in executing it, may be read between the lines of his essay on Friedrich Schlegel, in whose efforts on behalf of German understanding of France he obviously saw a forerunner of his own.

During the 1920s Curtius established himself through a succession of books and essays as one of the outstanding European critics of modern, and especially of French, literature. The masterpieces of those productive years, the comprehensive interpretation of Balzac (1923), and the long and penetrating study of Proust included in the volume *Französischer Geist im neuen Europa* [*The French Mind in the New Europe*] (1925), also secured his reputation in academic circles, where until then his "modernist" subject matter and the cosmopolitan character and elegant style of his writing, designed to appeal to the cultured layman as well as the specialist, had aroused the misgivings of conservative colleagues. He had left Bonn for a professorship at the University of Marburg in 1920; in 1924 he was called to the chair of Romance languages and literature in Heidelberg, where he spent five happy and fertile years before returning to Bonn as successor to the celebrated Romance linguist, W. Meyer-Lübke. His appointment, which was not approved without opposition, was regarded at the time as a triumph of aesthetic modernism over solid professional competence. From 1929 until his retirement in 1951, and despite many offers, Curtius remained faithful to this university in the Rhineland. The significance to him of this region, with its many visible reminders of the ancient Roman-Germanic community, is touched upon in numerous passages in his essays. Rome, not only as idea but as living presence, came more and more to occupy the center of Curtius' later thought, and he died while on a visit there in 1956.

The *Essays on European Literature* constitutes an anthology, made by Curtius himself, of work composed over a span of nearly thirty years. It is a very personal collection, which to the attentive eye can reveal as much about the critic as about his subjects. The passionate engagement in the cause of a superpersonal ideal, a mind of Europe united through literature and represented by its eminent men of letters, is the essential factor in all of Curtius' life and thought. It determined the direction of his scholarship as well as the choice of his themes and his attitude toward them. For Curtius carried on his critical activity in close connection with the events and personalities of the era. He not only wrote on the leading authors of the 1920s but entered into association with them. These personal associations were of the greatest importance in shaping his outlook. He lived in the atmosphere of which he wrote. His contacts with Gide, Valéry, Eliot, Joyce, Hofmannsthal, Ortega, many of which ripened into lasting friendships, enabled him to maintain that immediacy of response, that living relation to the world of the mind, that characterizes his approach and imparts to his criticism its urgency and spontaneity.

In these contacts we may also discern another important impulse in the personal dialectic from which his production springs: the intuitive recognition of what belonged to him, of what he felt he could seize and appropriate. The recognition of related elements through spiritual vision, which is the principle of the comparison he draws between Emerson and Balzac, and which he defines as the law of *similia similibus*, is also the law of his own nature.

If the aspiration toward unity through the intuition of related elements is one aspect of Curtius' personal dialectic, the other is a rigorous intellectual discipline that has its roots in the positivistic traditions of nineteenth century German scholarship. His training under Gustav Gröber, the editor of the compendious *Grundriss der romanischen Philologie* [*Outline of Romance Philology*], a monumental survey that combines vast erudition with precise technical description, reinforced a bent for meticulous research and wide learning that reflects the influence of a family inheritance. His grandfather Ernst Curtius, one of the most famous classical archaeologists of the nineteenth century, was director of the excavations of the ruins at Olympia and author of a history of Greece that for many years remained a standard introduction to the subject. Ernst Robert Curtius always preserved a special fondness for classical philology, which with its long-established methods of textual, grammatical, and lexical analysis left a minimum of room for the speculations of *Geistesgeschichte*. The insistence upon accuracy of detail—he was fond of citing the art historian Aby Warburg's dictum "God is in the detail" and used it as one of the guiding mottoes for his *European Literature and the Latin Middle Ages*—is the positive expression of the love for concrete historical knowledge whose negative complement is the strong aversion to "intellectual constructions." He particularly mistrusted the tendency that he found in late nineteenth and early twentieth century developments in German humanistic studies to replace the empirical account of phenomena with abstract categories and theoretical explanations. Curtius' antipathy toward this procedure is the source of his pleasure at finding in Goethe the exemption of the "true classical scholar" from the conceptual system of philosophy. He saw in it a verification of his own attitude.

Vitalism and dynamism—but shaped and controlled by broad erudition and scholarly discipline—these are the postulates of Curtius' criticism. It is what he means when he speaks of the cooperation of intelligence and intuition. The antipathy toward *Geistesgeschichte* is not to be viewed merely as an ideological skepticism toward a method which he considered of dubious validity, but must be regarded as an intimate constituent of what Curtius likes to describe as a writer's "form of mind." The various designations Curtius finds for this phenomenon, "intellectual constitution," "spiritual person," and others, are all meant to signify the same idea: an integration or totality, composed of intuition and intelligence, which manifests itself in the author's work as his intellectual figure (as opposed to the empirical person), and which it is the task of the critic to apprehend, disengage, and dispose in its place in the hierarchy of manifestations of a similar kind. This act of sympathetic apprehension, in which related elements grasp each other, is, for Curtius, the fundamental act of criticism. In a well-known discussion of method in the essay on Proust, part of which is cited in the appendix to this book, he writes: "the spiritual form-elements of an author . . . those individual traits that matter, cannot be sought out—they must flash upon the mind. Critical talent is nothing but the capacity for being struck by such individual traits." Hence he can quote with approval T. S. Eliot's saying that there is no method. For the act of apprehension, which is at the same time an intuition of value, arises from the critic's own sense of life. In a letter written in 1927 to his friend, the Swiss editor and critic Max Rychner, Curtius explains the connection between the process of criticism and the sense of life very precisely: it may be cited here as a contribution to the "biology of the scholar," the problem of how the life and work of the investigator are connected that in his later years Curtius proposed as a task for criticism. In answer to why he keeps aloof from professorial "gatherings" he states: "I have a nervous need for independence like an unruly nag. I want to be free to bathe in the Neckar on bright summer nights or to see friends, even if a thousand gatherings or congresses are meeting that evening. But I also feel inwardly quite remote from the outlook of *Geistesgeschichte* (in which I include

Dilthey, Troeltsch, Max Weber, and many others). The world is not there to be historically understood but to be lovingly apprehended. The cosmos of the mind is, for me, not a museum but a garden in which I wander and pluck the fruits. Science is always *in suspenso* and in order to remain true to itself must always rest in the problematical as an aggregate condition. I am a radically believing person and feel happy in the definite. It is enough for me to know certain archetypal forms to which I have been born—to know them again—in love, from love. I know what I believe and affirm. To realize these things, not in a literary but in a vital fashion, would be my fulfillment. Vital, that is to say, in the substance of my life, not in action. 'Participation in the ideas,' says Plato. Nevertheless, I have a certain *curiosité intellectuelle*. I can 'leap' at the new, but only if and because it belongs to my domain. Not Faustian, insatiable and *per definitionem* dissatisfied. Not Faust but the *Divina Commedia* is for me the highest fulfillment. In Dante there is infinity and order at the same time."

Intuition was then, for Curtius, already a primary form of knowledge. It was the response of the person to the phenomena of the intellectual world, but valid only insofar as these were likewise nourished by energies akin to those of the knower. This means that the role of that vast erudition which Curtius brought to bear on his subjects is also a vital one. To be sure, Curtius shared with every great scholar the "antiquarian impulse," the love of collecting facts for its own sake. Without such a love of minutiae, detailed scholarship on so large a scale would hardly be possible. The reading, and the writing, of compendia presupposes it. But for Curtius the compilation of highly diverse instances could also be made subordinate to intuition and hence vitalized. The use of research is only to ensure that the initial grasp, the loving apprehension should be adequate to the total intellectual configuration that it is the critic's business to trace. To demonstrate configurations, to delineate patterns—that for Curtius is the object of criticism. Criticism reveals itself not as a process of analysis but of synthesis. It is the restoration of a primary unity, perceived in a moment and pursued through all its significant manifestations, in the work of an author, of a country, of an age, until the original vision has been recovered—but now illuminated, as it were, from within. Curtius' criticism marks the conversion of positivism into Platonism.

Such a view is, of course, essentially unhistorical. Was it a generational phenomenon, this alienation from history and the attempts to transcend it that we find in Curtius and his contemporaries, the writers born in the 1880s, in Joyce (1882), Ortega (1883), Pound (1885), Curtius (1886), Benn (1886), Eliot (1888)? And is the attraction of Toynbee (1889) for Curtius that he succeeds in reducing the contingency of history to a sequence of timeless recurrences surmounted by a scheme of redemption? Be that as it may, Curtius' development exhibits a movement away from history in proportion as he occupies himself more deeply with the past. Perhaps that is why an investigation into the sources and resources of tradition like *European Literature and the Latin Middle Ages* can remain at the same time, to a remarkable extent, a work of personal synthesis.

From this perspective the place of the *Critical Essays* in Curtius' career may also be illuminated. His early years in Strasbourg were lived under an acutely felt tension between German and French civilization. The young Curtius determines to mediate between the intellectual currents that were gaining ground in both countries: in Germany, renewal and revision of poetic and intellectual values in Stefan George and his circle; in France, rise of a cosmopolitan spirit and new forms of consciousness in the work of Gide, Claudel, Rolland, and the writers of the *Nouvelle Revue Française*. The results of this effort are comprised in five books and many articles on France and French culture published between 1919 and 1930. Of the activities of this period the essays on Friedrich Schlegel and Stefan George provide a summary and a retrospect.

During the same period Curtius also begins to explore the literature of two other European countries: England and Spain. The letter from T. S. Eliot inviting him to collaborate on *The Criterion*, which is mentioned in the essay on Hesse, dates from 1922. Curtius contributed three times to Eliot's review: in 1923, a section from the book on Balzac that he was then writing; in 1924, an analysis of Proust's style, later incorporated into the long study of 1925; and, in 1927, a programmatic piece on the tasks of the literary intelligence from a culturally—but not politically—conservative standpoint, entitled "Restoration of the Reason." With that Curtius' association with *The Criterion* ceased. He did not write the series of studies of modern English authors, a parallel to the French *Wegbereiter*, that Eliot frequently urged him to undertake and for which he even proposed the names. They included, at various times, Lawrence, Woolf, Pound, Joyce, Wyndham Lewis, and Lytton Strachey. Nor did he carry out the intention, announced in a letter to Ortega, of a similar book on the literary pioneers of modern Spain. Of these plans and projects the study of Joyce, which was issued as a brochure in 1929, is the fullest realization. It was recognized immediately as a landmark in the appreciation of Joyce's work and remains even today a fundamental demonstration of the interaction of theme and technique in *Ulysses*. By 1930, however, the crisis in German politics had forced Curtius into a polemical stance. The essays that originated around this time, on Virgil, Ayala, Schlegel, are all dominated by a single concern. It is to reaffirm the German intellectual inheritance without abandoning the commitment to a cosmopolitan ideal of culture. A strong emphasis on the indigenous values of nation and soil, as sources of productive strength, now holds the balance with the attitude of cosmopolitan receptivity that Curtius had previously recommended to his countrymen. The anti-Nazi polemic of 1932, *Deutscher Geist in Gefahr* (*The German Mind in Peril*) invokes the German humanistic tradition as a defense against the politicizing of the mind by doctrines of race, class, or party. But despite the strongly national—rather than nationalistic—orientation of this appeal, it could have little effect on the steadily deteriorating social and political situation. When the politics of culture confront the politics of power, the results are usually predictable. After 1932 Curtius took no more public positions until the end of the war. He had recommended in his polemic, as a positive program, a return to the Latin unity of the Middle Ages and to the foundations of the Christian West: he called it Humanism as Initiative. And in the years between 1933 and 1945, he set about singlehandedly to formulate its bases.

In 1948 Curtius brought out the book on the Middle Ages that had enabled him to sustain the dignity of the intellect during the Hitler regime. Like Erich Auerbach's *Mimesis*, which had appeared in 1946, *European Literature and the Latin Middle Ages* represents at once a summation of the great German philological tradition that descends from Herder, Goethe, and the Romantics through the historicism of the nineteenth century, and a testimony of intense personal pathos, wrested from solitude and despair in a period of unmitigated catastrophe. Auerbach's concept of figural realism and Curtius' vision of the topoi, the commonplace themes and devices of rhetoric, are principles that, however different for the understanding of history, contain an aesthetic of conservation. That Curtius thought of the topological method as a new foundation for an objective science of literature affects only the scholarly exterior of his book. Its inner core, as a work of the preserving memory, remains inviolate. Curtius had become in those years "a bitter and sarcastic man," as Willy Haas wrote, and he added, "magnificent in his bitterness."

The change in attitude wrought by the war and its aftermath is reflected in the essays written after 1945. Noticeable is the turning away from modern themes. A letter to Max Rychner in 1949 announces: "I have now finished my Eliot . . . but this should be my last work on modern literature. . . . I have had enough of interpreting modern spiritual and formal problems." Now the permanent heritage of European literature and its ordering in a hierarchy of values becomes the main concern. Three of the late essays are devoted to Goethe, another to a theme related to the topos principle; in still others, subjects previously discussed are treated reminiscentially (Borchardt on Virgil, Balzac, George). Although the years between 1947 and 1952 show a production more intense than any but the most fertile years of the 1920s, the bulk of this output is devoted to problems of Romance philology and hence accessible mainly to specialists.

Nevertheless, he did not entirely keep his promise. The introductions to Curtius' own translations of poems by Guillén and of Goyen's *House of Breath*, as well as the feuilletons collected in the *Büchertagebuch* (*Book Diary*)—fortnightly reviews of his reading that Curtius, at the suggestion of its editor Max Rychner, contributed between 1951 and 1952 to the Swiss newspaper *Die Tat*—reveal his undiminished capacity to keep up with and pronounce authoritatively upon a wide range of contemporary developments.

Yet it is undeniable that the essays from this period differ from those written in the twenties. Curtius says that they are more detached. But this is an official explanation designed to cover a withdrawal from modernism that had not gone unnoticed. There is a shift of accent that corresponds to changes in the climate of Curtius' soul. This change cannot be fully accounted for short of a biographical inquiry, for which all the materials are not yet available. But indications of it may be detected in the second parts of the essays on Ortega and Eliot, both of which date from the same year, 1949.

Among Curtius' habits was that of tenacity. He would not only worry a subject from many different angles but would take it up at intervals until he had found the sufficiently ample context in which it could be definitively encompassed. Cursory comparison of the essays with their first versions in periodicals discloses that nearly all were subjected to revision, some of it quite extensive, before being republished in the present collection. Readers of *European Literature* may recognize sections of the essay on Hofmannsthal and Calderón that Curtius adapted for that book. Sometimes these revisions are only in the interest of a more attractive presentation or to bring the material up to date. At others, they betray a shift in attitude toward it. The revisions undergone at various stages by the essay on Joyce are indicative of the oscillations in Curtius' feelings toward Joyce's work. The study of these changes throws important light on the process of evaluation in Curtius' criticism. It can only be glanced at here.

In 1927 Curtius published a translation of Eliot's *The Waste Land* to which the first part of the essay included in this book served as the introduction. Curtius himself calls it a fragment. It was followed in 1929 by a brief piece on Eliot as critic, in which the tenability of Eliot's position of royalism and classicism is questioned by a comparison with its models in Charles Maurras and the *Action Française*. In an essay on Virgil in 1944 Eliot tried to deny Goethe the status of a European classic. In 1946, broadcasting to Germany on "The Unity of European Culture," he conceded that while he knew of no standard by which the relative greatness of Wordsworth and Goethe as poets could be measured, he was certain that Goethe was the greater man. Curtius' nettled reaction to these statements, which he believed to be motivated by political rather than literary considerations and regarded as an instance of a general postwar hostility to German culture, forms the starting-point of his contribution to the volume honoring Eliot's sixtieth birthday in 1948. These conflicting and contradictory ingredients—love for *The Waste Land* and Eliot's early poetry, years of common association, postwar politics, and Curtius' defensive attitude about Germany's place in the culture of Europe—make up the complex and perhaps not entirely settled mixture that is the summarizing essay of 1949. It is masterly; but one feels at times that the critic, far from being detached, is not detached enough. And with the decline in sympathy there enters a certain formulaic harshness, a caustic irritability that constantly threatens to disrupt the polished surface of the presentation. Something unresolved seems to cling to the features of this portrait, but it is in the feeling and tone rather than the lineaments, which are drawn firmly and with sensitive discrimination. The serenity of spirit, to which Charles Du Bos had paid tribute in his "Approximation" of 1930, seems also to be troubled in the second part of the essay on Ortega, to whom Curtius had been bound by ties of friendship even closer than those to Eliot since the early 1920s. In 1924 Curtius' response to the thought of the young Spanish philosopher had been, with slight reservations, overwhelmingly enthusiastic. In 1949 the note is interrogative, even skeptical. A dissatisfaction, more implied than expressed, now makes itself felt. Ortega noticed it and in an exquisitely tender letter complained to his friend: "this article is, like all those you have written, but especially the more recent ones, excellent as an article. Your style has become more lucid, it is purer and at the same time more nervous." And yet, Ortega observes, the article "did not leave a pleasant aftertaste." Curtius replied in terms for which many echoes may be found throughout the later essays: "One writes differently at 63 than at 39. It is not from you that I have become alien but, to a certain extent, from philosophy. On the other hand I have moved closer to history; an extra-philosophical historiography whose masters for me are Goethe, Ranke, Burckhardt. I am quite conscious of this change; it signifies an unfolding of my entelechy. I have to express it. These are divergences in our natures; but nothing that could or should be considered as negation."

The withdrawal from philosophy, the turning toward history, represents an attitude that has its model in Goethe. But it also represents a reaction on Curtius' part to a controversy over Goethe that had become a burning cultural-political issue. In 1947 the philosopher Karl Jaspers, on being awarded the Goethe Prize of the city of Frankfurt, pronounced a discourse in which he raised some carefully worded doubts as to whether Goethe, with his harmonious world-view and avoidance of a tragic absolute, could still serve as a guide for German reconstruction after the total breakdown of moral and spiritual values that the nation had just experienced. Jaspers' discourse was a plea for conscience; but Curtius, construing it as yet another attack on German culture as embodied in its greatest figure, in a vehement rejoinder denounced the presumption of philosophy's claim to legislate in matters of poetry. The repercussions of this debate, in which curiously enough Curtius wished to see a renewal of the ancient quarrel, deriving from Plato, of poetry and philosophy, are evident not only in the essay on Ortega but also, especially, in "Fundamental Features of Goethe's World." Viewed in the light of the foregoing controversy, this essay reads almost like a declaration of principles. Here the answer to Jaspers' arguments is given not with the harshness of the cultural censor but with the clarity and balance of the custodian of a great heritage.

Curtius was a great affirmer. He was an optimist by disposition and by belief. Charles Du Bos, admiring the air of security diffused by his work, called him an "esprit spatieux," and compared the sensation of dwelling among his books to that of wandering in the vast cortile of an Italian Renaissance palace. Such criticism, born of intuitive sympathy and carried on by wide and profound erudition that has been absorbed into the very fibers of the temperament, depends for its effectiveness on the continuance of a positive impulse. Where Curtius is negative, he can be harsh and dismissive. He hated nihilism in all its forms—including that of existentialism—distrusted Flaubert, and ultimately came to dislike the work of James Joyce.

The three strains that we have noted—intuitive sympathy, broad erudition, and immediate contact with the historical situation—also constitute the basis for Curtius' evaluations. From the initial intuition the critic proceeds to a vision of the whole that is tested, in all its particulars, by the instruments of observation and knowledge. But this vision is itself placed against an horizon of themes, motifs, techniques, expanding to embrace larger structures, larger forms, until the intellectual constellation or figure has been defined and delineated within a field of forces theoretically as broad as the centuries of Western literature from Homer to the present. There are resemblances here to the view of tradition of T. S. Eliot. But for Curtius, more than for the poet, the "monuments" of the European tradition embody energies that can spring to life whenever and wherever they are brought into contact with another work or another mind that releases them. Hence, Curtius' conception of tradition is vital and dynamic, and does not run the risk of petrifaction into classics. Any work may spring to life, may unfold its energies anew, through the encounter with the historical person of the observer. Balzac receives new energies by being viewed through Proust, Emerson by being related to Balzac, and so forth. In this way a system of correspondences evolves that is mobile and alive. This sense of the unique potential vitality of a work of art Curtius kept to the very end. It prevented him from becoming fixed in his own preferences and prejudices, and permitted him to acknowledge and occasionally even to welcome new works, when he found that they could be accommodated within the spiritual system whose currents animated for him all the literature of the West. The metaphor of breath in Goyen's novel, the revival of the mediaeval jongleur in Cocteau, but also a motif such as the astonishment of men at seeing the first ship could be the trigger to set off this current of vital connections. Thus the problem of value is itself transformed and becomes a dimension of continuity.

Continuity—Curtius stresses it again and again. It functions in his criticism as a dialectic between originality and imitation, tradition and individual talent. At the meeting-point, where the fusion occurs, there the critic sets up his gauge. Yet the process of evaluation is never merely a mechanical weighing and measuring. Description, analysis, and judgment are aspects of a single act originating in and determined by the critic's own "sense of life." No moral, social, or political prepossessions are allowed to interfere with the final aesthetic estimate. In the essays on Hesse and on Du Bos we may observe this moment of the critical act at its purest. Hesse is situated between two generations of moderns, yet slightly apart from either. Though *The Glass Bead Game* is the ostensible subject, Hesse's entire career is passed in review. The poetry, the novels, themes, techniques, are conscientiously examined and assessed. The result is not an opinion on Hesse that can be extracted and filed away, but a total picture in which the negative and positive features have been integrated with the ground of the personality and the personality with the tendencies of the age. Here, as in the essay on Du Bos, where a similar procedure, only heightened and intensified, is used, everything is in its place. There are no gaps, no transitions, no interruptions. The whole is set before us as a whole, but illuminated, fluoroscoped, as it were, from without and within. These are the perfections of the critic.

Curtius had the gift, which he shares with Edmund Wilson, of enthusiasm. He makes us actually want to read the books that he writes about. If he resembles Eliot in his view of tradition, his capacity for precise, rapid analyses, his aptitude for the telling quotation, he is like Wilson in the broad range of his learning, in his power of compressed, evocative narrative and summary, in his continuing ability to respond to the new. Yet the main motive is different in all three critics. Eliot's critical activity grew out of his practice as a poet and derives its authority from there. After the early work, with its intense, penetrating application of the method of analysis and comparison, Eliot becomes, as Curtius once called him, a legislator of Parnassus, a position that has its predecessors in Boileau and Johnson. Wilson is a critic in the tradition of Sainte-Beuve and Taine. His interests are historical, psychological, sociological; his writing is motivated by the universal curiosity of the cultured man of letters. Curtius has the broad, classical humanism, the authoritative knowledge, but also the polemical temper of a Lessing. Philological scholarship on a vast historical scale is put at the service of a transtemporal ideal of the permanence of culture. His work stresses continuity and tends toward synthesis. Evaluation is neither explicit and dogmatic, as with Eliot, nor submerged in the historical process, as with Wilson. It is contained in the act of cognition, in the dialectic established between the mind of the perceiver and the spiritual entities that he is called upon to integrate. Curtius' method is intellectual characterization, but its values are informed and guided by the critic's own immediate relation to the subjects which he contemplates.

Criticism, according to Curtius, is a province of literature. The ultimate judgment to be pronounced upon the critic will therefore be an aesthetic one. It will rest upon his qualities of mind and style, of the mind in style, which, Pater has said, is a form of the imagination.

In this respect Curtius' "festive" prose (Rychner), with its energetic compression, its aphoristic turns, its stately movement and sustained architecture, its capacity for suddenly illuminating widely separated spheres of intelligence and emotion and for equally sudden ironic juxtapositions and disjunctions, is the index of his vigorous, lucid, discursive mind. The form of these essays is circular, as befits their object, which is the grasping of totality. By his synthesizing power, his compact, deliberate argumentation, his security in evaluation, he imposes upon his work the unity of mind and matter, the wholeness and transparency that belongs to art. This unity, like that of all great art, must be sought beyond the personality in a realm of the spirit that can be indicated but not defined, and that is hinted at in Simmel's remark that the business of life is to transcend life. There is something Platonic, even mystical about Curtius' belief in the affinities of the world of the spirit, though it manifests itself in his work not as a conviction but as a radiance.

Preface to the First Edition

MY FIRST works were concerned with French literature. What poetry can be we learn from Antiquity, from Spain, England, Germany. But what literature is can be learned only from France. In the present volume, it is true, the reader will find little on French literature. My books and scattered essays on the subject I hope to present again elsewhere.[1]

For a German, especially for someone like myself born and raised in Alsace, France was a necessary complement. It was also a tension, felt nowhere so strongly as in Alsace. The poetry of my Alsatian contemporaries Ernst Stadler and René Schickele tells of it. In this tension Europe was experienced as well: more challengingly than in Berlin or Munich. It makes good historical sense that negotiations for a Federation of Europe should be going on today in Strasbourg. But the Europe of France and Germany was not broad enough for me. I knew London before I knew Paris. England had things to give that I did not find in France: England and the New England of an Emerson and a Whitman, which I was not to set foot on until many decades later. Soon, Italy took its place beside England and France, shaping the soul with the glories of art and landscape (from its modern literature I could derive but little). Rome was the mother of the West. *Teutones in pace* was inscribed over the entrance to the Camposanto by St. Peter's—a motto that I would know how to translate in my own way. Then my studies—whose development is related in the Appendix—and travels led me to Spain. From Madrid a line ran diagonally across Europe to the Vienna of the Hapsburgs. Hofmannsthal, whom I always held in the highest esteem, was situated on this diagonal. So Europe became ever broader and richer for me. But all the

[1] Cf. *Französischer Geist im Zwanzigsten Jahrhundert* [*The French Mind in the Twentieth Century*] (Bern 1952).—TR.

children of Europe, including Germany inside the *limes*, bore the impress of Rome. The Roman heritage of European litterature I tried to demonstrate in *Europaische Literatur und Lateinisches Mittelalter* (Berne, Francke, 1948; 2nd ed. 1954), English translation, *European Literature and the Latin Middle Ages* (New York, 1953). This book is not, as some of my critics supposed, a renunciation of my "modernistic phase" or of my love for France. My concern has always been the same: the consciousness of Europe and the tradition of the West. But with advancing years I was compelled to dig deeper, to reach out further in time and space. Continuity became more important to me than actuality, Virgil and Dante of greater significance than more recent writers since Goethe's death.

The arrangement of the articles follows, on the whole, the chronology of the authors. Each in its own way seeks to promote the endeavors of criticism. But they stretch over more than a quarter of a century. During so long a period the perspectives and evaluations of the critic change. Sainte-Beuve wrote in the preface to the first volume of *Causeries du Lundi* in 1850: "Depuis vingt-cinq ans déjà que j'ai débuté dans la carrière, c'est la troisième forme que je suis amené à donner à mes impressions et à mes jugements littéraires, selon les âges et les milieux divers où j'ai passé." ["In the twenty-five years now since I entered on my career this is the third form that I have been led to give to my impressions and to my literary judgments, according to the periods and the various milieux through which I have passed."] In the first period (1824–1830) his criticism was polemical and aggressive; in the second (1830–1848) "analytique, descriptive et curieuse." He adds that this second phase had only one fault: "elle ne concluait pas." He had deliberately avoided value judgments, or at least thought he had. When he took up his critical activity again in October 1849, both the bourgeois and the socialist revolutions had been suppressed. To the dismay of the politicians, Louis-Napoleon had been elected president of the Republic by a plebiscite on the tenth of December, 1848. Reaction had triumphed over Revolution and would soon put an end to the Republic. From this turn in the political weather, which he cautiously describes as "a recently undergone experience," Sainte-Beuve drew the conclusions for the third phase of his criticism: "Les temps devenant plus rudes, l'orage et le bruit de la rue forçant chacun de grossir sa voix, et, en même temps, une expérience récente rendant plus vif à chaque esprit le sentiment du bien et du mal, j'ai cru qu'il y avait moyen d'oser plus, sans manquer aux convenances, et de dire enfin nettement ce qui me semblait la vérité sur les ouvrages et sur les auteurs." ["The times becoming harsher, the storm and noise of the street forcing each one to raise his voice, and, at the same time, a recent experience bringing the sense of good and evil home more vividly to every mind, I thought that there was a means of becoming more daring without offending against good manners and, finally, of saying clearly what seemed to me to be the truth about the works and the authors."]

I too might describe my critical activity from 1919 to 1931 as "analytique, descriptive et curieuse," except that what drove me on was less the curiosity of the amateur than the enthusiasm of the explorer. I was writing about foreign authors. They were unknown in Germany. I had first to introduce them to my readers. Description and analysis were imperative. Evaluation was present too, of course—it lay in the choice of authors. There could not be many, for only the greatest among the living attracted me. I have never been a daily reviewer, have never paid much attention to the fluctuations of the literary stock market, and looked upon many a celebrated contemporary as a pseudoreputation. But I could consider myself privileged, for I experienced at first hand one of the great eras of European literature. To have been the contemporary and interpreter of men like Gide, Claudel, Péguy, Proust, Valéry, Hofmannsthal, Ortega, Joyce, Eliot (to name only a few)—I regarded this as a piece of good fortune that would not readily occur again and that indeed has not occurred again. The twenty years from 1930 to 1950—taken as a whole, needless to say—have nothing equivalent to set beside the years from 1910 to 1930. "And Pharaoh saw coming up out of the river seven well favoured kine and fatfleshed; and they fed in a meadow. And, behold, seven other kine came up after them out of the river, ill favoured and leanfleshed; and stood by the other kine upon the brink of the river. And the ill favoured and leanfleshed kine did eat up the seven well favoured and fat kine." Of course I am aware—and have it instilled in me by my students—that today many fat kine are feeding in the meadow. So I keep a sharp lookout and will not swear anything away.

But at sixty one has other perspectives, interests, joys, needs than at forty. The accents shift. One sees less well from close by, better from far off. One tends to look beyond the foreground at the mountains that encircle the horizon. Today everything that existed before 1939 already seems to have receded into a historical distance. But I like to return to it. One will find essays in this book on the same author that are separated by more than twenty years. They are different in tone. The later pieces are more detached. How could it be otherwise? What Sainte-Beuve judged to be the "fault" of his early phase—"elle ne concluait pas"—is the perfect right of critical youth, as it is the right and the duty of a later phase to measure and weigh precisely. To the reader such a glimpse into the transformations of a critic ought not, I hope, to be unwelcome.

> Ältestes bewahrt mit Treue,
> Freundlich aufgefasstes Neue
>
> [The oldest faithfully preserved,
> The new amicably accepted]

is to be found in this book. I should never have written on Virgil had Max Rychner not urged me to do so. Under his direction the *Neue Schweizer Rundschau* was one of the five or six best periodicals in Europe (the Eliot essay of 1927 also appeared there). Today I would write differently about Virgil than in 1930. But the essay was greeted by specialists with approval and so it may be permitted to stand as a tribute to the great Latin poet. To treat of ancient and modern was a matter of course for Lessing, the Schlegels, Sainte-Beuve, Pater, as it is for Rudolph Alexander Schröder. Criticism that forgoes this privilege may be answered with Saintsbury's sentence: "Ancient without Modern is a stumbling-block, Modern without Ancient is foolishness utter and irremediable."

The last piece in the book attempts to demonstrate the continuity of the European literary tradition by an example drawn from mythology. It picks up the thread of my mediaeval studies. Literary history and literary criticism are two different things, but they can inhabit the same mansion. They have much to give to each other. Without critical training I should not have been able to write my book on the Middle Ages; and my training in history has, I hope, stood my criticism in good stead.

Bonn, Easter 1950.

Preface to the Second Edition

THE NEW edition has been heavily augmented. In part, writings missing since 1933 have been included (*James Joyce and his Ulysses*), in part, products of the last few years—like the studies of Borchardt, Charles Du Bos, Jorge Guillén, and the young American writer William Goyen.

Bonn, Pentecost 1954.

ESSAYS ON EUROPEAN LITERATURE

Virgil

+++

Hac casti maneant in religione nepotes.

THE TOMB OF Virgil and that of the first emperor lie buried beneath the bricks and mortar of populous Italian cities, surrounded by the bustle of our modern life. Virgil is known to us through historical records even to the date of his birth. To be able to celebrate its two-thousandth recurrence must inspire every lover of Rome with a shudder of pious joy. This is no scholarly reminiscence; it is a day of living remembrance, a reverent solemnization.

It would often seem as if our present, hurried generation had lost time through tempo, the past through lust for contemporaneity. We divagate into the far reaches of space—only to pay for our truancies with an undignified, ignoble contraction or a chimerical, flimsy expansion of our sense of time. It is well, therefore, that anniversaries that move to the rhythm of millennia should exhort us to reflection: the six hundred years since the death of Dante, the fifteen hundred years since the death of Augustine, the two thousand years since the death of Virgil. The one hundred years since Goethe only make plainer the meaning and value of millennial dates.

Virgil's anniversary is not popular, and for that reason doubly significant. Rightly understood it could be a landmark in the great mysterious movement of Western self-consciousness: in the dim unfolding of a process that would be memorable even if its struggle to be born occurred only as the dream of our highest, as the ineffable word of our best spirits—a process of integration and restoration of the Occident such as was envisaged by the profound and intuitive

3

mind of a Hofmannsthal, whose meditations spanned centuries.

That the Virgil Festival impinges upon such connections, that it evokes or can evoke such reverberations should be enough to declare the uniqueness of the name in whose honor it is being held. And how inexhaustible is that uniqueness! We shall never be able to fathom what the Fourth Eclogue meant to its author. It enjoys the mystic privilege of inexpressibility of substance as does that Eastern book of erotic mysticism which has entered our Holy Scriptures as the Song of Songs. And nevertheless it may be permitted us to confirm the mediaeval legend in our own sense; to believe that in the synchronicity of the divinely human revelation and the poet of the Roman Empire a European mystery lies concealed and waiting to be rediscovered. For this belief we possess the time-honored testimony of Dante. And we may account it one of the happy auguries of our history that an indissoluble bond unites Virgil with Dante, the great Roman *paganus*, the singer of flocks and fields, and the great Roman Christian, the pilgrim of the next world and the institutor of order in this one.

No one who clings, consciously or unconsciously, to the outmoded aesthetics of original genius will ever understand Virgil. Virgil's greatness and importance, his irreplaceable and unreplaced mission through all our ages, does not, or does not solely, derive from what he was personally. It can only be grasped if we are aware of what the *kairos* is able to impart to the individual.

That Virgil could be taken up and enhanced, after thirteen hundred years, by a Dante, that his message could find a response in the Florentine of the Trecento as it found a sanction in the last poet of the collapsing temporal Empire[1]—that is part of the very element and definition of Virgil's greatness. To appreciate this one has to break with all modern criteria and practice counting in long intervals of time. It is a way to

[1] Phocas (c. A.D. 500): "O vetustatis veneranda custos . . ." ["O guardian of Antiquity, who are worthy to be revered . . ."].

which we are not accustomed. But might it not be wholesome and necessary for that very reason? What has lasted two thousand years will last another two thousand. That much at least we can know precisely—and should we really refuse to correct our current perspective in the light of this knowledge?

For previous ages the *exempla maiorum* were a confirmation; for us they are a confrontation, and tradition is reversed into a corrective. We are so far removed from tradition that it appears new to us. Periods like these are perhaps the dawn of all renaissances. Thus our present German estrangement from Virgil might be reinterpreted as a preparation and a guarantee. A deeper understanding of *Romanitas* seems to be awakening among us—and can it have a representative more valid and more binding, mightier and milder, sweeter and more sonorous, than Virgil?

He is the most official of poets, for it was his poetic task to trace the eternity of Rome from its primitive origins even as Augustus, with the founding of the Principate, elevated it to the highest realization of its power. Here, on the plane of world-history, is demonstrated that realism, that irrefutable solidity rooted in and bound to the soil, that is part of the Roman Genius, like the Travertine marble, hardened by time, of which the tomb of Cecilia Metella and the dome of St. Peter's alike are constructed.

There is scarcely a building material so resistant to the erosion of time as this stone of the golden patina. It has its intellectual equivalent in the material of which Virgil's work is constructed: in that Latin speech the source of which is the swamps of Mantua and whose stone flags support a universal poem and a universal empire. The passionate self-abnegating will to permanence has hardened this substance. It is deeply significant that an early poem of Virgil's contains a renunciation of rhetoric. Cicero's Atticist prose could still appeal to our forefathers; today its formal ostentation pales beside the cadences of the patient craftsman, who began with jesting, satirical poems and, in unparalleled fashion, worked his way free to ever stricter, ever greater tasks (*paulo maiora*[2] *canamus*). However controversial the *Appendix Virgiliana* may be, one thing is certain: Virgil's poetic and emotional beginnings approach a frivolity of soul and sense that combines, in a fashion we can scarcely conceive, the faunic with the sentimental. We shall never know what event in his life raised the imitator of Catullus and Priapic poet to the vates of Orphism, to the laureled servant of the will of the State and prophetic annunciator of the turning-point in history. Was it resignation? Was it initiation? Was it both at once as well as an early, pre-Christian form of sanctification? It must be left in that twilight, which the poet himself desired and loved.

It is the strange twilight that gleams so often in Virgil, and that Victor Hugo, in a spirit of emulation and artistic fellowship, graciously acknowledges:

> ... dans Virgile parfois
> Le vers porte à sa cime une lueur étrange,

> [... sometimes in Virgil the verse at its summit bears a strange gleam,]

a reflection as it were of that numinous radiance which, full of future promise, shone in Troy's darkest night upon the head of Ascanius.

So through all the ages of Rome and the Romania,[3] through all those historical realms still touched by the Roman will to order, Virgil's silent flame shines as a guarantee and a promise. For fundamental to Virgil is the strength and the will to preserve the permanent through all change. Repetition as restoration, invention as rediscovery, renovation as confirmation and sublimation of what is already possessed—this was Virgil's most cherished concern.

[2] This use of the comparative that Virgil favored is probably also characteristic of the Virgilian ethos. Cf. *Aeneid*, VII, 44f.; XII, 429ff.

[3] For this term, see Curtius, *European Literature and the Latin Middle Ages*, trans. Willard R. Trask (New York, 1953), pp. 30ff., where it is defined as "the sum total of the countries in which Romance languages were spoken."—TR.

6

So Dido (IV, 327ff.) seeks for herself a childish copy of Aeneas:

> . . . si quis mihi parvulus aula
> Luderet Aeneas, qui te tamen ore referret.

[. . . if in my hall a little Aeneas were playing, whose face would recall yours.]

So for Virgil's herdsmen, heroes, and rulers, the law of life is identity (the *flumina nota* of the First Eclogue) and stability, or, lacking these (for exile as sociological necessity and constraint is the *fatum* of both Meliboeus and Aeneas), renewal and palingenesis, repristination and instauration in one. To take the lost and past and rebuild it out of new substance on foreign soil, this is the will and the way of Virgilian wisdom.

The individual character of Virgil's art, which it is so difficult for our vulgar aesthetics to grasp—the much discussed *imitatio*—perhaps also has its roots in this emotional disposition, which we are probably correct in perceiving as an essential trait of Virgil's personality: a need for security, born of elegiac sorrow and longing, that has been ennobled by piety and transmuted by lofty historical relations into constructive will. This personal quality is linked to one that lies beyond the personal: to the Roman function of continuity, and perhaps, indeed, to the fundamental law of life that applied throughout Antiquity; the law, according to which the sanction for all new creations was in the traditional works from which they derived and to which they had to refer: as the colony to the mother city, the statute to the founder, the song to the Muses, the copy to the original, and the work of art to the model.

We can have no idea what Virgil would have become had he not met Augustus, but he would certainly not have become the poet of the *Aeneid*. His personal contact with the Emperor made him into the poet of Rome:

> Scilicet et rerum facta est pulcherrima Roma.

> [Indeed Rome became the most beautiful city in the world.]

And yet we shall fail to understand Virgil if we see in him only or primarily the poet of the State. Underneath, at a deeper level, lives a contemplative, artistic person who is not moved by affairs of state: "non res Romanae perituraque regna." He is aware of his detachment from the sphere of mere politics and history which, being essentially impure and infelicitous, is subject to the vicissitudes and the inscrutable wrath of the Gods:

> Ferus omnia Juppiter Argos transtulit . . .
> Excessere omnes adytis arisque relictis
> Di quibus imperium hoc steterat. . . .

> [Savage Jupiter transferred all our possessions to Argos. . . . All the gods have left their sanctuaries and abandoned the altars, the gods on whom this empire had depended.]

The authentic ancient and Romanic philosophy of history as *vicissitudines* speaks in these lines. Dante and Vico hold it too. It contains an element of resignation, but only dialectically, as a moment of transition. Far from enjoining a negation of history, it leads rather to a cyclical conception of it. The prophecy of the Fourth Eclogue, the soteriological hope of both Virgil and Dante, the pious expectation of a *restitutio in integrum* ["restitution to wholeness"], of a return of the Golden Age, is possible and makes sense only if the *ruere in peius* ["collapse into the worse"] is also accepted as true. It goes without saying that to our historical realism, our poverty-stricken sense of historical reality, this dimension of experience is as lost as eschatology to our religion. But it is the only dimension capable of resolving the contradiction between Virgil's two statements about Rome: "peritura regna" and "imperium sine fine dedi" ["I have given (Rome) unlimited dominion"]. The ethos of the Roman Odes gives us a palpable sense of how completely different could be the moral and political experience awakened by the Augustan age in two of its representative poets. The comparison with Horace brings out Virgil's uniqueness all the more clearly.

Virgil's most secret longing is quite simply the Golden Age and its sensuous representation in rustic surroundings.[4] Its content is blessed idleness, conferred by divine favor. *Otium* is one of the key words of Virgil's poetry.

The God Augustus bestows this happiness:

> O Meliboee, deus nobis haec otia fecit.

> [Meliboeus, a god gives us this leisure.]

The God of the shepherds approves too:

> . . . amat bonus otia Daphnis.

> [. . . the good Daphnis loves leisure.]

It is the felicity of rural life:

> . . . secura quies et nescia fallere vita
> Dives opum variarum, et latis otia fundis.

> [. . . tranquil quiet and a life which knows not how to deceive, rich in various resources, and leisure amidst broad estates.]

And this image of earthly leisure also serves Virgil as the model for the bliss of Elysium. Of course we agree with Fénelon when he measures this description against the glories of the Christian Paradise.

"Ce poète," he writes, "ne promet point d'autre récompense dans l'autre vie à la vertu la plus pure et la plus héroique que le plaisir de jouer sur l'herbe, ou de combattre sur le sable, ou de danser, ou de chanter des vers, ou d'avoir des chevaux, ou de mener des chariots et d'avoir des armes.

---

[4] Virgil's primary aim is passive happiness. The burden of his life was to prove himself continually, through accomplishment, "labor improbus." Cf. Aeneas's words: "Disce, puer, virtutem ex me verumque laborem, Fortunam ex aliis" (XII, 435f.) [Learn, youth, virtue and true labor from me; good fortune from others].

. . . Voilà ce que l'antiquité proposoit de plus consolant au genre humain" ["This poet promises no other reward in the next life to the purest and most heroic virtue than the pleasure of playing on the grass, or fighting on the sand, or dancing, or singing verses, or having horses, or driving chariots and possessing arms. Such is the greatest consolation that antiquity proposed to the human race"].

Of course Dante was the first who was able to create out of the plenitude of the grace of Revelation the vision of the hereafter to which not even the most pious paganism could attain. But as grace is said not to supersede but to fulfill nature, so in the region of Virgil's soul to which *otium* is the password it is possible to discern a bit of eternal human nature, with its eligibility for grace. I am certain that much of the deathless charm that continues to attach new generations to Virgil comes from this region. For despite the wretched efficiency-ethic of our modern age, does there not live in all of us something of that elemental longing for a pastoral world, for the earthly paradise, for the divinely-blessed gardens of Eden and Elysium?

The bucolic idyll cannot be explained away as simply the wish-projection of Hellenistic urban culture. It is an innate archetypal image of our species that moves us with a melancholy joy, like a song we had long thought to be forgotten. It is the *dulce refrigerium* of Christian-Asiatic mythology, the refreshing coolness of brook and meadow, "muscosi fontes et somno mollior herba" ["mossy springs and grass softer than sleep"]. *Otium* is only the time-honored name for a type of idleness rooted in the social conditions of Antiquity, but belonging to the images of a golden life, and reminding us that we can fully realize our human destiny only where the compulsion of labor has been lifted from us. Our ethic of work lacks the balance of an ideal of leisure. It could, of course, be derived from Goethe's *Westöstlicher Divan* [*West-Eastern Divan*], were we ever to liberate ourselves from the pedagogical scheme that grants the German nation its greatest poet only on condition that he admonishes it to tireless effort.

Actually, the "cultural poet" Virgil is a singer who has the most original and immediate tones for all the fundamental moods of human nature. What has been said about *otium* is only one example. All the elements of man's nature, insofar as they coincide with his humanity, have been represented by Virgil in exemplary fashion. His rich, autocthonous, yet delicate soul created a canon of affects that was as authoritative as the one created in a later period by the cartoons of Raphael. He had the power to sound the natural notes of the soul. This naturalness is classical and ancient. But such is the emotional intensity of Virgil's language that it is understood by modern ages too. This combination of simple nature and feeling intensified by passion is the distinguishing mark of Virgil's finest verses. They carry their own conviction as surely as that "sunt lacrimae rerum," which eludes grammatical analysis; as that "per amica silentia lunae" or "nunc scio quid sit amor": each an example of the highest concentration, in which the conciseness of the Latin seems bathed in an aura of infinity. Virgil is not only the herald of the State, of the Penates, of *pietas*, of the meadows and fields. He has also been the poet of love for nearly two thousand years, and neither Laura nor Juliet has kindled the hearts of so many young men as Dido, "cette figure d'immortelle ardeur qui, de son bois de myrthes virgiliens, enchante à travers les âges l'élite des adolescents:

> Hic quos durus amor crudeli tabe peredit. . . ."

And Anatole France continues: "Heureux qui frissonne aux miracles de cette poésie! Il y a au monde un millier, peut-être, de vers comme ceux-là; s'ils perissaient, la terre en deviendrait moins belle."

> ["that figure of immortal ardor who, from her wood
> of Virgilian myrtles, enchants throughout the ages
> an élite among adolescents: Here, those whom
> harsh love has consumed with cruel wasting. . . .
> Happy are they who thrill to the miracles of this

11

poetry! There are perhaps a thousand lines like that in the world; if they should perish, the earth would become less fair"].

It cannot be denied, of course, that Dido is the very character who does not share in the author's inner sympathy. Like Virgil's other female figures she leads a shadowy and pallid existence, even though one decked out with the trappings of ideal dignity. She has not been nourished with the blood of a living love, and it may be surmised that Virgil's life was lacking in the flame from which Catullus' odes to Lesbia and Propertius' to Cynthia took their fire. Does not Suetonius relate: "He was barely touched by male desire, and he remained unmarried. Such purity lay over his mouth and heart that in Naples he was popularly known as Parthenias (the Virginal)?" Aeneas may be the son of Venus, but he inherited few of her gifts. Furthermore the Venus of Virgil is less Aphrodite than Artemis: the virgin huntress whenever she is not the strong-willed disposer. Creusa too appears shadowy, and is soon removed to the shades. She is only allowed to follow her husband at a distance: "pone subit coniunx." The poet indicates the nuptials of Dido and Aeneas only by their attendant cosmic meteorological phenomena; and when the forsaken woman reproaches him, the hero replies rather sheepishly. Only in her tragic fall does Dido rise to impassioned life. So she lives on in poetry and memory as a romantic heroine: "colui che s'ancise amorosa" (*Inferno*, v, 61).[5] The substance that Virgil had to deny her is compensated by the dignity of her function within his universal poem. Not the Aphrodisian female is the highest embodiment of womanhood for the "maidenly" poet, but the consecrated virgin: the Sybil, the Astraea, the Muse.

A breath of adolescent shyness and innocence plays round the figure of Virgil. This area of his sensibility, so palpably evident in all his works, is the source of his bucolic and heroic

---

[5] Cf. Augustine's tears over Dido (*Confessions*, I, 13).

young men. They constitute one of the most significant and personal elements in his poetry. Eduard Fraenkel writes:[6] "The Roman character is not only unyouthful, it is alien to youth, almost hostile to it," and he cites the pejorative meaning of the term *puerilis*. The conclusion of this learned specialist is incontrovertible, and it is especially gratifying as it sets off the originality of our poet all the more distinctly. Engraved in the heart of every reader of the *Aeneid* are the flower-like youths—"purpereus veluti flos"—Nisus and Euryalus, Lausus and Pallas, and, above all the rest, Ascanius. The very word *puer* acquires, in Virgil's usage, a tender, almost sacred tinge. Nisus addresses his companion as "venerande puer," and with the same solemnity ("iuvenis memorande") the poet raises his own voice to the honored memory of Lausus. In the "incipe, parve puer" of the Fourth Eclogue and the offering of lilies upon the early grave of Marcellus ("miserande puer") this sympathy of Virgil's extends to what is highest and holiest. Virgil's young male figures, the "warrior and history-making *pueri*," "one of the poet's most significant inventions," according to Wili, undoubtedly vibrate with the recollection of his own youth and that of Octavian. But beyond that they live by virtue of an inner affiliation with Virgil's cyclical view of the universe, and with his prophecy of a new golden age. They stand as the poetic guarantee and spiritual anticipation of Virgil's belief in the rejuvenation of the world. They cast upon the grave dignity of the *Aeneid* a luminous shimmer of youthful beauty that is still capable of mysteriously touching receptive young people today.

In the autobiography of a great English critic[7] anyone who has not felt it himself will find proof of how the first contact with Virgil can bind a young reader with a sudden and magical spell. The stimulus to the imagination provided by novel or idyll can explain this effect only in part. The Vir-

[6] *Die Stellung des Römertums in der humanistischen Bildung* (1926), p. 34.

[7] Edmund Gosse, *Father and Son* (1907), Chap. 6.

13

gilian magic, in the last and deepest analysis, emanates from the beauty of the sound and the vibrations of the rhythm. Here we touch upon a new aspect of the inexhaustible phenomenon of Virgil's uniqueness. The *Odyssey* can be enjoyed in translation; the *Aeneid* cannot; not even in the Romance tongues. Virgil is as essentially untranslatable as Dante (while Shakespeare would be an example of the contrary). In the two great Italic poets form and content are fused in a different and as it were more intimate manner than in Homer. Only this unsatisfactory way of putting it enables us at least to intimate a fact of experience which is no less self-evident for defying all analysis. The most that can still be said is that an adequate understanding of the Virgilian hexameter (like that of the Dantean terza rima) also comprises an aesthetic initiation—the sudden radiant "having" of "art." I say comprises, and am thereby arguing against a misleading dichotomy of form and content. The sense of satisfaction provided by "formal beauty" always yields much more than and, consequently, something essentially different from, "form." Without getting lost in subtleties one can still distinguish various grades within the possibilities of linguistic pleasure, and only poverty of language prevents us from doing more in this respect than feeling our way. That Virgil's beauty cannot be transferred is partly due to the properties of the Latin language; but only partly, for of Horace and Ovid less is lost in translation. It can most readily be explained by reference to our experience of great statuary. Sculpture defies reproduction in a very different sense from music or painting. Of all the plastic arts none fails so miserably in reproduction as the plaster cast beside the marble original. None affords so little room for the workings of caprice or chance, be it on the side of technical execution or of appreciative reception. Sculpture subdues the greatest fullness to the hardest matter, the greatest lifelikeness to the most rigid austerity. The paradoxical legend of Pygmalion could only be told about a sculptor.

People like to speak of Virgil's musical beauties, by which they usually mean verses like:

Saltantes satyros imitabitur Alphesiboeus

[Alphesiboeus will imitate the dancing satyrs]

or

Formosam resonare doces Amaryllida silvas.

[You teach the woods to ring with beautiful Amaryllis' name.]

Such lines have a sweetly seductive allure and draw the neophyte into the innermost recesses of the magical edifice. But the typical style of the poet's maturity is of another and a higher kind. It tends not toward ethereal undulations but toward the solidity of metal and marble. The soul of Virgil's poetry cannot be detached from its matrix, which is unalterable and unique; nor does it exist outside it. Strictly speaking, Virgil's mastery is coextensive with the Latin language, no further. Let those who will regard this as a defect; those who may as a good fortune.

The judgment of French Classicism on Virgil was that he had more "taste" than Homer. In our own terms this means that he is more of an artist. At the risk of contradicting current opinion, we would maintain that to be an artist and to be a poet are not necessarily the same thing. There are poets who are not artists. Art, in poetry, means the conscious and expert handling of language—the opposite of inspiration. Virgil spent seven years on the 2,000 lines of the *Georgics*. He estimated that he would need three more years to bring the *Aeneid* to perfection when death caught up with him. He had written both works on commission, well aware (as a letter to Augustus reveals) of the enormous difficulties involved, but trusting in effort and the knowledge of his craft. It remains a miracle that in spite of their origin these works did not end up as frigid virtuoso performances but full of vitality in their perfection.

Perfection—not force or immediacy or emotion—is the distinguishing mark of all classical works. The aesthetic appreciation of this quality is not popular today, but it is still worth contemplating. Admittedly there are dull spots even in Virgil, but then it was not granted him to give definitive shape to his work. Nevertheless, in the *Georgics* and the *Aeneid* he attains an ultimate in formal perfection, as can be seen most clearly by reference to the *Stanze* of Raphael. In both cases the loftiness of the style is distinguished by ideal naturalness and perfect serenity, and its specific character stands out all the more if, for comparison, we think of Michelangelo or Shakespeare with their qualities of abundance, spirit, force, urgency. We enjoy perfection for the feeling it gives of assured, knowing guidance, not for that of surprise.

Dante's famous utterance that he received "lo bello stile" from Virgil has puzzled many of the commentators because they were unable to find any external similarities in the style of the two poets. This, of course, is not the issue; rather, it is the deeper affinity in their artistic aims: the achievement of beauty and sublimity by means of the selection and arrangement of words. In this larger sense Virgil, supported by the example of the Alexandrian poets, created the model for all of Western artistic poetry. In this elevated sense he is an aesthete. For this reason he, more than any other poet, is a guide to aesthetic culture. This is how Dryden's laudatory characterization of the *Georgics*—"the best poem of the best poet"—is to be understood.

One of the most fruitful and fateful errors of Taine, and of all the historico-sociological conceptions of art that consciously or unconsciously derive from him, is to suppose that the great works are to be read as "signs" or "expressions" of their cultural milieu—or even (and this only compounds the error) to be appreciated as such. Virgil moreover would seem to confirm the rightness of this conception. But it is not enough to consider him merely as the representative of Augustan Rome. He is more than that, and his work cannot be measured by the standards that suffice for the *Ara Pacis Augustae*. He is also more than the representative of the eternity of Rome and the permanence of Latinity, however exalted and mighty he may be in this function. He must be apprehended beyond it in his absolute greatness and importance as an artist, in the sphere of the timeless, if our aim is purity and clarity of aesthetic judgment.

As a historical phenomenon Virgil is Roman and more than Roman at the same time. He is the spiritual genius of the West throughout the millennia. His mission in world history is evidenced in Dante, and perhaps after several further centuries he will demonstrate it again. At any rate, in the present turmoil and distress of our part of the globe, we cannot forbid our hope to scan the horizon for a future restorer of the Muses and the religion of the Occident.

> Si nunc se nobis ille aureus arbore ramus
> Ostendat nemore in tanto!

[If only that golden bough on the tree would show itself to us now in so great a grove!]

In Virgil's serene element the great spiritual and historical antitheses of our past seem to achieve an equilibrium. He contains the pure nectar of Antiquity, but he reaches beyond Antiquity as does only Plato besides him. There are Asiatic roots in the *Aeneid,* oriental prophecies in the Fourth Eclogue. Roman sculptural form is united in an unfathomable way with a prophetic, otherworldly radiance, a Sybilline piety that seems to stay upon revelation. Roman *virtus* and Greek love of beauty, mature craftsmanship and moral refinement are attested in the same material. Virgil's work is the triumph of Classicism and at the same time (consider the Tenth Eclogue) the primal fount of all Romanticism. All these forces, which would clash in isolation, attain in him a settled harmony and a rich symbolic fullness. The whole of human existence is mirrored in the wanderings of Aeneas: the weary way to a promised second homeland, far from the first.

1930

Rudolf Borchardt

on Virgil

++

IT IS A strange feeling for me to be speaking to British listeners about Virgil.[1] For my love for Virgil was brought about through a friend from Oxford, and that will soon be half a century ago. My friend had come to Germany to study Bible criticism at its source. When riding on the train, he would read Virgil in a Clarendon Press edition on rice paper. As an *ex libris* he used the beginning of one of Virgil's verses in which his name was concealed and his martial ideal was hinted at: *fit via vi*. Once, when we were traveling together, I asked whether I might borrow his Virgil. Although I was familiar with the *Aeneid* from my schooldays, it did not mean much to me. But now I discovered the *Eclogues* and soon hit upon a verse that filled me with a hitherto unknown joy:

> Mille meae Siculis errant in montibus agnae.

> [My thousand sheep are straying on the mountains of Sicily.]

These words cast a spell over me. At that time I had not yet been to Italy—but all of a sudden a southern landscape spread out before my eyes: mountains, flocks, and a view of the deep blue of the sea. Afterwards, when I visited my friend at Oxford, I bought myself the same edition. Another Oxford student, who was preparing for the Indian Civil Service, invited me to read the sixth book of the *Aeneid* with him. A third, who has since become a bishop, introduced me to The-

[1] BBC broadcast, October 1951.

18

ocritus. Later, the *Oxford Book of Latin Verse* became my companion. For many years England seemed to me a kind of modern Arcadia: a happy exception in the world of today; a land in which Humanism was a living heritage and not a specialty for philologists. In Germany I did not find anyone who read the ancient poets for pleasure—least of all Virgil.

What I have told you is more than a personal reminiscence. It is part of my theme. For I would speak of tradition. The little incident that I have related is an exemplary instance of the handing down of tradition. I received a book from the hand of an older friend. I read it because I wished to share in his world. Tradition only comes alive when it is transmitted through a person whom we wish to emulate.

What fell to my lot at that time through Oxford seemed to me to be a biographical coincidence. And yet it was more. For in the same year in which I discovered Virgil, a little book was published in Leipzig wherein German philology was measured by the standard of Oxford Humanism and found wanting. It was called *Das Gespräch über die Formen* [*The Discussion of Forms*] and its author was Rudolf Borchardt. Borchardt lived from 1877 to 1945. When he published the *Gespräch über die Formen* in 1905, he was still quite unknown. And if you were to ask a young German about Borchardt today, you would probably conclude that he has become unknown again. This is partly due to the fact that his name could not be mentioned during the Hitler regime. But there are other reasons too. Borchardt lived for decades in northern Italy, in a villa near Lucca. He kept aloof from Germany's public literary life, when he was not condemning it with the greatest severity. His books were hard to come by and are practically unobtainable today. What he had in view was the purification and restoration of German literature. He drew his criteria from Antiquity and from the German classics. But he included the Provençal troubadours and the Tuscan poets of the Trecento in the great tradition of European poetry. To integrate Borchardt's oeuvre and to explore his legacy will be an important task for German criticism.

His fledgling work, the *Gespräch über die Formen*, already contained vehement attacks upon the German intellectual Establishment. They are concerned, among other things, with the subject of my talk to you today. Borchardt takes exception to a German scholar, whose name he does not mention and whom I am unable to identify, who presumed "to insult the sacred shade of Virgil." "But," Borchardt continues, "who cares? Who reads Virgil in Germany?"

During his years in Tuscany, Borchardt became familiar with the rural Italy of gardeners and winegrowers. It was the Italy of the *Georgics*, the Italy of the odes in which Horace praises his Sabine farm. This is where Borchardt's magnificent essay on the *Villa* (1907) originated, which begins with the provocative statement: "The Italy of our forefathers has, as we know, ever since the railways opened it up to traffic, become one of the most unknown countries in Europe." This sentence is quite typical of Borchardt's style and attitude. When Borchardt has something to communicate, he first frightens the reader off with a brilliant paradox and then speaks as the possessor of some higher knowledge from which the masses are excluded. He lends his presentation the accents of an initiate into the mysteries. But that does not detract in any way from the importance of his little piece about the Villa. In describing a typical form of Italian life it broadens out into a characterization of Italianness as such; and even more, of Latinity. In this way it created a new basis for the appreciation of Latin poetry in Germany. This rediscovery of Latinity was not the result of scholarly research but of living contact with the Italian soil. It is true that Borchardt had acquired a comprehensive knowledge of philology at the universities of Berlin, Göttingen, and Bonn. But Antiquity was not alive in those places. The contact with Oxford was essential for enabling Borchardt to write the *Gespräch über die Formen*; the contact with Tuscany, to produce the essay on the Villa. I consider it a landmark in modern German intellectual history. Allow me to explain what I mean.

The great epoch of German literature, which is called Ger-

man Classicism and Romanticism, comprises the two generations from 1770 to 1830. Its seminal genius was Herder. Herder's theory of history taught that the achievements of the
great nations constituted a unified progression in which the
idea of humanity realized itself. Poetry, whether as folk song,
heroic epic, or psalm, was, according to him, the creative self-
expression of the various nations: "the mother tongue of the
human race." His ideal of humanity led Herder to a negative
evaluation of the Romans. He saw in them only the soldier
and the oppressor. "The spirit of national independence and
love of mankind was not their genius." Contemplating the
pompous architecture of the Romans, their gladiatorial
games, the "voluptuousness of their baths," "one would almost believe that some demon, inimical to the human race,
had founded Rome."

As for Roman poetry, it was "only an imported flower,"
not *Urpoesie, Naturpoesie*. When Herder wrote these words,
he had discovered Homer and Shakespeare. By comparison
with them Virgil seemed pallid. Herder's view of history descended to German scholarship; indeed, it became stronger
and coarser. Even Friedrich August Wolf, who revived classical studies in Germany, was averse to Virgil. But so was Nie-
buhr, the historian of Rome; so were Wilhelm von Humboldt
and the Romantics. That was how matters stood throughout
the entire nineteenth century and beyond. A change did not
take place until about 1925. At that time our philologists began to discover the meaning and value of the Roman world
for a humanistic education. Scholars like Eduard Fraenkel
(now at Oxford), Günther Jachmann, Kurt Latte, and Friedrich Klingner brought this change about. It is noteworthy that
Klingner began his career with a study of Boethius, who has
been called the last of the Romans and who forms a bridge
between the declining world of Antiquity and the Latin Middle Ages. He then went on to study the idea of Rome in its
historical transformations, and has contributed more than any
other scholar to the renewed appreciation of Virgil in Germany. The evidence for it is in the studies that he collected

in 1943 under the title of *Römische Geisteswelt* [*The Mind of Rome*].

This glance at the history of philology in Germany was necessary if only to show that the point of view current around 1930 was quite different from the one that prevailed in the first decade of the twentieth century, at the time, that is, when Borchardt was just starting out. But gratifying as this change in outlook was, it could not extend much beyond narrow professional circles. The lover of Virgil owes a debt of gratitude to Virgil studies. But they were quite obviously unable to exercise a decisive influence upon German education. For that, energies of a more elemental kind are needed. A poet can only be revived by a flow of energy from new poetry, or, alternatively, by creative criticism that has been nourished for its part by the experience of new poetry. Borchardt's early writings were creative criticism in this sense. For Borchardt's crucial experience had been the renewal of German poetry through the work of Stefan George and Hugo von Hofmannsthal.

It matters little that Borchardt's relation to George was problematical, while he rendered Hofmannsthal unqualified homage. Even where he criticizes George, he pays him the tribute of great reverence. He calls George's poem "Porta Nigra" "one of the most magnificent, most thoroughly realized creations of this great creator," and "one of the most extraordinary ventures in world literature." I stress this poem dedicated to the Roman gateway at Trier deliberately. At the end of the imperial age Trier was one of the four capital cities of the Imperium. Emperors had their residences there, Roman villas adorned the banks of the Moselle, Latin verse was composed there. George was a son of the little town of Bingen, where even today the Drusus Bridge still testifies to the presence of Rome. Romanic-German substance, as an ancestral heritage, became alive again in George's poetry. But the Viennese, Hofmannsthal, also bore the heritage of the Imperium and acknowledged it. Both poets felt that they were related to Rome by blood, that is, through the strength of their native soil, in the Rhineland as in the Danube basin. From these roots there sprang for both poets a love for the ancient Roman world, but also for the languages and literatures of the Romanic nations. In the work of both men the conflict not only between Greek and Roman but between Classical and German culture is resolved. The Roman continuity of the European form of mind was once more made a possession of consciousness. Borchardt's study of the Villa can be understood as a symptom of this process. But its radiations gradually penetrated the German intellectual atmosphere, so that twenty years after Borchardt's first works were written its validity was acknowledged even by academic scholarship. The reevaluation of the idea of Rome and of Virgil which philology undertook in the 1920s is related, consciously or not, to this process. It created a favorable atmosphere for the celebration of Virgil's two-thousandth anniversary in 1930.

That Rudolf Borchardt was invited to address the University of Kiel on that occasion represented, in effect, an encounter of the new scholarship and the new poetry. Borchardt did not conceal from his audience "the glances of frigid anticipation with which European humanists were peering, at the hour of the Virgil festival, across intellectual frontiers into the land of Herder and the Romantics." But at the same time he asserted Germany's right, on the basis of its history, to adjust the conflicting elements in the heritage of Antiquity; to resolve, that is, the antitheses between the Western European and the German reception of the Classics into a single all-encompassing vision, in which the German Hellenistic tradition could include Virgil "without abandoning Hellas; it satisfies its prescribed exploration of the changing without violating its obligation toward the permanent, its gratitude toward what is above the changing, and its duty toward that sacred element."

Borchardt pointed out that the Greek epic was a unique historical event, which had already concluded its life cycle by the sixth century and admitted of no renewal. But at the same time he rescued the *Aeneid* by demonstrating that it was something quite other than a Roman copy of a Greek original. It is as little an Homeric poem or even an epic "as Dante's *Commedia*, undertaken in the spirit of Virgil, is a comedy or Virgilian." Mankind does not have an unlimited capacity for creating new forms. That is why in crucial periods the new enters upon the scene in the guise of the old. As an end, "achieved by Antiquity in the last stage of its decline and with its last breath," but as an end that is simultaneously a beginning, "which, in a magical moment, relives the entire past even as the portals of the future burst open to it, full of the gold of eternity"—that is how Borchardt interprets Virgil's poem. The *Aeneid* is one long soulful retrospection. Epic narration and the sensuous immediacy peculiar to it underlie the *Aeneid* as already exhausted forms. They are transposed to the plane of historical contemplation. Virgil's poem is proof that "the tragic nature of human life as such, the terrible law of historical causality, has touched him and destroyed with its touch his pleasure in mortal things." With Virgil, Antiquity ends, "but it ends, as it does in Plato, by reaching out once more beyond itself." It discovers the primacy of the soul, thereby gaining access to the new era of Christianity. For Borchardt the *Aeneid* is "the Old Testament of the whole European West," just as Plato is the Old Testament of the Hellenic East. Both point forward to the New Testament, both are capable of assimilating it and adapting it to a new mode.

This conception of Borchardt's, which I have outlined here to you, is a brilliant, a magnificent construction. Borchardt's point of departure is German Classicism's idea of Hellas as established by Herder. Homer, Pindar, the Greek tragedians are its main pillars. Borchardt retains this image of Greece, but with marked accentuation of its archaic features (the end of Antiquity starts as early as Plato). To arrive at a positive evaluation of Virgil from this basis was not easy. Borchardt only succeeded thanks to a very personal philosophy of history. However it may be judged, it was an attempt to reintegrate Virgil into the German tradition.

It would be of little interest to review the German contributions to the Virgil celebration of 1930. They carry as much or as little weight as do the manifestations for the Dante celebration of 1921, or the Goethe celebration of 1932. Such celebrations do not prove that Dante, Virgil, or Goethe were a living possession of the educated classes in Germany between the two world wars. They prove the contrary. In 1830 Virgil was not celebrated because he was still read. Virgil is even today an unread poet in Germany; indeed, it must be said: today more than ever. The decline of classical studies which set in at the end of the nineteenth century has currently assumed, not only in Germany but also in the United States, the proportions of a natural catastrophe on the order of Noah's flood. Because of this the stability of the German educational tradition, which was never deeply rooted, is in jeopardy as well. The great Greek poets are as imperiled as the Latins. Books like *The Private Life of Helen of Troy* have more readers than Homer. The classic has been replaced by the best seller. In Germany the slogan "death of the classics" was proclaimed twenty years ago. Even Stefan George and Hofmannsthal, our last great poets, are already forgotten today, at least by those who in the daily press determine the rates on the literary stock exchange. Fortunately there are still a few people even in Germany who do not acknowledge the validity of these market quotations. Only a few—by a generous estimate, several thousand. But in the biology of tradition even infinitesimal minorities can have their mission. The small number of German readers of Virgil may rejoice in an auspicious omen, with which I should like to conclude these reflections. We still have among us a poet who is simultaneously a preserver of the great tradition of German culture and a master translator such as we have not had since August Wilhelm Schlegel. I refer to Rudolf Alexander Schröder, in youth the friend of Hofmannsthal and of Borchardt. He has presented us with new versions of Homer and Horace; of Virgil's *Eclogues* and *Georgics*. We may look forward to the work on which he has been engaged for decades: the German *Aeneid*.[2]

1951

---

[2] Published in 1953.

Goethe as Critic

✦✦

1

LITERARY criticism has no acknowledged place in German intellectual life. Germany has had no Sainte-Beuve and probably could not have had one. With us, literary culture is the affair of a few scattered individuals, not a need of the general reading public. We lack an established body of literary tradition. What is produced as literature is usually consumed as *Weltanschauung*. The leading German newspapers have had regular music and drama critics (music, theater, and film, as we know, constitute "culture" or "the arts"—they can be "pursued," like trades). But they have not had a literary critic. Books were casually assigned to journalists whose words carried no weight, could not carry any. It was no better with the leading periodicals. The brief flowering of the *Süddeutsche Monatshefte* with Josef Hofmiller as its critic was the exception that proved the rule. France had an Albert Thibaudet, England a review organ like the *Times Literary Supplement*. We have had nothing comparable to offer.

This was not always the case. It is a symptom of decay that deserves to be analyzed. Tacitus and Quintilian investigated the decay of Roman rhetoric. Adam Müller gave *Zwölf Reden über die Beredsamkeit und deren Verfall in Deutschland* [*Twelve Discourses on Eloquence and its Decay in Germany*] in Vienna in 1812. One could write a whole chapter on criticism and its decay in Germany. For between 1750 and 1830 German criticism did exist. This period parallels Goethe's lifespan. But it comprises at the same time the era of revolution from which the modern world emerged. In England it was the Industrial Revolution; in France the social; in

Germany the philosophical and scholarly, characterized by the names of Lessing and Herder, Winckelmann and Friedrich Schlegel, Kant, Fichte, and Hegel. Of these three revolutions the French was the easiest to recognize. The German, understandably, was at first noted only within Germany, and that through the Romantic movement. Friedrich Schlegel and Adam Müller viewed it as a parallel to the French Revolution. The Industrial Revolution in England was recognized as a crucial historical process only much later, and got its name then.

In speaking of a philosophical and scholarly revolution, the German Romantics adopted a political metaphor. But they designated thereby a real and significant process: a movement which embraced all spheres of intellectual life. It involved three overlapping generations. Philosophers and classicists, poets and historians—all worked together, not deliberately and yet as if they had been set a common task. But the mediating element, the all-pervasive aura was the spirit of criticism. Criticism here is to be taken in the broadest sense so as to encompass Kant's critique of reason as well as Lessing's *Laokoon*, Winckelmann's history of art as well as the Schlegels' lectures on literary history, Schleiermacher's *Reden über die Religion* [*Discourses on Religion*] as well as Adam Müller's *Vorlesungen über die deutsche Wissenschaft und Literatur* [*Lectures on German Scholarship and Literature*] (1805).

The essence of the whole movement was: the recovery and understanding of the entire European tradition. But such an understanding meant at the same time a reevaluation and a new awareness. It meant, if I may so put it, an integration. This was only possible from a new stage of consciousness: the overcoming of the Enlightenment by means of a critical philosophy. In the half-century that extends from Kant's *Critique of Pure Reason* to Hegel's death, this philosophy passed through all the stages of a dialectical evolution, a process which has its only analogy in the thought of the pre-Socratics. German philosophy split into opposing schools. But for criticism this only represented a gain. It could free itself from every scholastic point of view in order to conceive of the activity of philosophy itself as a pure function, as a higher potential of mind. This is the meaning of Novalis' saying, which Walter Pater liked to quote: "Philosophieren heisst vivifizieren" ["to philosophize means to vivify"]. This is also what Friedrich Schlegel means when he defines criticism as "understanding of the understanding."

Aristotle's theology conceived the divine world-spirit as the "thinking of thinking." German Idealism claimed this function for philosophy. Friedrich Schlegel's formula transfers it to criticism. The substance of the idea could also be formulated thus: Criticism is the literature of literature. Or more explicitly: Criticism is that form of literature whose subject matter is literature. T. S. Eliot once said that the novel is the form whereby literature "affects the greatest number." Criticism, we would add, is the form whereby it affects the smallest number. Hermetic poetry has its adepts and exegetes. Criticism seems to be reserved for the "happy few"—in Germany, at any rate.

2

In the great period of German criticism Goethe is both recipient and participant; he collaborates but he also resists. He accepted Lessing, Herder, and Winckelmann. On February 21, 1781, he wrote to Frau von Stein: "I had made a plan to visit Lessing not a quarter of an hour before the news of his death arrived. We lose much, very much in him. More than we realize." His relations with Herder, highly productive in spite of many strains, were described in *Dichtung und Wahrheit* [*Poetry and Truth*]. Goethe devoted one of his loveliest and least known works to the "magnificent" Winckelmann, a biography with a world-historical perspective. In this work he also has something to say about philosophy and its position in the German intellectual movement. Philosophers, he writes, have always drawn upon themselves the hatred of "worldly and practical men." Since philosophy by its very nature lays claim to all that is highest and most universal, "it must necessarily consider the things of the world as comprised within it and subordinate to it, and treat them accordingly." Goethe saw in this an "overweening pretension," just as Winckelmann had complained bitterly about the philosophy of his day and its extensive influence. "However," continues Goethe, "in considering the events of recent times, one observation, which can be borne out by experience, may not be out of place here: it is that no scholar has with impunity rejected, opposed, or despised the great philosophical movement that began with Kant—none, that is, except the true classical scholars, who seem favored above all other men by the uniqueness of their pursuit." Reverence is paid to philosophy, but the classical scholar is formally exempt from it. He is thus doubly favored. Goethe frees historical scholarship from the totalitarian demands of philosophy. The position which Ranke and Burckhardt will occupy is already indicated. This detachment toward philosophy points ahead to the nineteenth, the historical, century. At the same time it represents a boundary line that Goethe draws between himself and the younger critics. The course of this boundary cannot be traced here. With the border populations (the Schlegels and Adam Müller) there may be contact and even conflict. But from Goethe's "state of art" they are excluded.

We defined criticism as that species of literature whose subject matter is literature itself. This broad phrasing of the terms is particularly appropriate in view of a critical achievement as universal as Goethe's was. The judgment of new works is only one province in the domain of criticism. So far as I know there exists only a single comprehensive account of this domain—George Saintsbury's *History of Criticism*, now already half a century old. The author dismisses Goethe's reputation as a critic as a "stale superstition." And yet in 1858 Sainte-Beuve had paid homage to Goethe as the "greatest of all critics." The contradiction, as I see it, arises from the fact that Saintsbury knew little of Goethe and hence could not view him properly. For Goethe's critical position becomes clear only in the context of his total intellectual cosmos. His reviews of Grübel's *Gedichte in Nürnberger Mundart* [*Poems in the Dialect of Nuremberg*] or of Hagen's *Olfried und Lisena*, for example, may seem mere curiosities unless they are seen within the economy of Goethe's position as a systematizer and a shaper of taste. The critic Goethe is to be found least in his writings on literature. His reflections on poetry and on the function of the poet in society are scattered throughout *Wilhelm Meister, Tasso,* the *Noten zum Divan* [*Notes to the Divan*], and the *Maximen* [*Maxims*]. The conversations with Eckermann offer rich material. They are, of course, to a great extent conditioned by the fluctuating moods that affected Goethe during his entire life, for he was highly sensitive to the state of the sun and the barometer. They are conditioned too by the rather subservient character of the hearer. But they are nevertheless authoritative insofar as Goethe overlooked the transcriptions. Still more must be added to make up the corpus of Goethe's criticism: something from the early dramas, which mock the literary epidemics of the day in the manner of Aristophanes and Lucian; much from the poetry, from the notes to *Rameau's Nephew,* and from the inexhaustible profusion of the letters. Even the scientific writings are shot through with precious veins of critical ore. In the *Materialien zur Geschichte der Farbenlehre* [*Materials toward a History of the Theory of Colors*] there is a discussion of the notion of transmission which gives rise to a comparative characterization of the Bible, Plato, and Aristotle.

3

We may go even further. Goethe's literary theory becomes transparent only in the light of his theory of nature. As is well known, for Goethe, as for the Biblical account of creation, the primal polarity of light and darkness is a fundamental manifestation of nature (*Grundphänomen*). Goethe too considers light as a creation of God: "Light is one of the original, God-created forces and virtues, which strives to represent its image in matter." Matter may be either transparent, opaque (dark), or semi-transparent (turbid). "Now if the virtue of the light strives to pass through a turbid medium in such a manner that its original force, though constantly checked, yet persists in its efficacy, its image will appear as yellow or orange." This is one of the teachings of the *Farbenlehre*. Transposed into the language of poetry it becomes:

Als die Welt im tiefsten Grunde
Lag an Gottes ew'ger Brust,
Ordnet' er die erste Stunde
Mit erhabner Schöpfungslust,
Und er sprach das Wort: "Es werde!"
Da erklang ein schmerzlich Ach!
Als das All mit Machtgeberde
In die Wirklichkeiten brach.

Auf tat sich das Licht: so trennte
Scheu sich Finsternis von ihm,
Und sogleich die Elemente
Scheidend auseinander fliehn.
Rasch, in wilden wüsten Träumen
Jedes nach der Weite rang,
Starr, in ungemessnen Raümen,
Ohne Sehnsucht, ohne Klang.

Stumm war alles, still und öde
Einsam Gott zum erstenmal!
Da erschuf er Morgenröte,
Die erbarmte sich der Qual;
Sie entwickelte dem Trüben
Ein erklingend Farbenspiel,
Und nun konnte wieder lieben,
Was erst auseinanderfiel.

[When the world, in its profoundest depth, lay at God's eternal breast, He ordained the first hour

32

with a creator's sublime delight, and he uttered the words: "Let there be!" Then a painful sound of woe was heard as the All, with a powerful gesture, broke into reality.

Light arose; then, shyly, darkness separated from it, and at once the elements part and flee in all directions. Swiftly, in wild hectic dreams, each strove into the distance, rigid, in measureless spaces, without desire and without harmony.

Everything was dumb, silent, and waste, God lonely for the first time! Thereupon he created the dawn, which took pity on this torment, evolving for this turbid matter an harmonious play of colors; and now that which had previously fallen to pieces was able to love again.]

The dawn corresponds to yellow or yellowish red. "If, however, a dark substance so limits the turbid medium that the light's virtue cannot pass through but is turned back as a reflection from the turbid medium that has been illuminated, then its image is blue or bluish-red." Light: an image of God; colors: images of light—even when he enunciates the basic axioms of his theory of color Goethe thinks in metaphors. Serene and turbid, gloomy and dark, themselves then become metaphors for states of history and of the soul. "Man's states of gloom and illumination constitute his fate" (to Eckermann, 1828). Applied to history and literature: "We have as little to gain from the gloomy Old German period as we have got from Serbian songs and other such barbarian folk poetry. One reads it and becomes interested for a time, but only to lay it aside and then leave it behind. Man's passions and fortunes generally darken his condition enough so that he has no need to seek out the gloom of early barbarian eras. He requires clarity and serenity, and it is good for him to turn to those epochs of art and literature in which excellent men achieved such complete cultivation, that they themselves were content and hence capable of sharing the blessings of their culture with others." The relation of barbarism and culture corresponds to that of illumination and darkness. There occurs a necessary alternation, a pendulum movement, between the extremes of both contrasting pairs. Thus dark ages must recur periodically. If this is understood as a regular process, then a point has been reached from which one may contemplate a new period of barbarism—such as we are witnessing today—if not with complacency, at least without complaint. "The circle that the human race must run is sufficiently well-determined, and in spite of the great standstill caused by barbarism, it has already completed its course more than once. Even if we ascribe a spiral movement to it, it nevertheless returns again and again to that region through which it has already passed."

Predominance of light over darkness is the condition that suits Goethe best. He designates it with the word *heiter*. In the corrupted linguistic usage of the present this is taken to be a synonym for "joyous," but originally it was used only for a cloudless sky, by day or night, like the Latin *serenus*. While writing the fourth act of *Iphigenie auf Tauris*, Goethe notes at Schwalbenstein near Ilmenau: *sereno die, quieta mente.* In 1775 he chooses the "glorious morning star" as his escutcheon. In the summer of 1828 in Dornburg he often lies by the window before daybreak in order "to feast on the magnificence of the three planets now in conjunction and to refresh myself with the growing brightness of the dawn." Israel's passage through the desert is seen in an image of increasing gloom: "The serene evening sky glowing with endless stars, which God had shown to Abraham, no longer spreads its golden canopy over us. . . . All joyful phenomena have disappeared; only tongues of flame appear on all sides. The Lord, who had called to Moses from a burning bush, now passes before the host in a turbid scorching vapor, which by day seems a pillar of clouds, by night a fiery meteor."

In the starlit clearness of a night sky Goethe beholds an image for the most perfect relation of man and cosmos:

Hast du so dich abgefunden,
Werde Nacht und Äther klar,
Und der ew'gen Sterne Schar
Deute dir belebte Stunden,
Wo du hier mit Ungetrübten,
Treulich wirkend, gern verweilst,
Und auch treulich den geliebten
Ewigen entgegeneilst.

[When you have thus resigned yourself, may night
and ether grow clear, and the eternal host of stars
show you vivid hours; here, where among un-
troubled spirits, faithfully working, you delight to
abide, and, also faithfully, hasten toward the beloved eternal ones.]

In 1826, in a notice of a historical work by Schlosser, Goethe
commented: "The author belongs with those who strive to
emerge from the darkness into clarity, a race of which we also
profess ourselves." "Dark," "gloomy," "turbid" are expressions of rejection in Goethe's critical language. On the other
hand, the highest praise is intended when he writes of
Longus' pastoral novel: "There is the clearest day in it . . .
no trace of dull days, of fog, clouds, or moisture, but always
the bluest, purest sky." He prefers this work to the "good
Virgil"—an offense against the orthodox credo of Classicism.

4

The estimate of Longus should serve as a warning to
those who would seek to pin Goethe down to Greek classicism. A classicistic tendency is, in fact, active during his Italian period, although by no means exclusively (the Witches'
Kitchen scene of Faust was written in the garden of the Villa
Borghese); and it is also present during the period of
the friendship with Schiller. But in his later years Goethe
achieves a new relation to the ancient world. It is late Antiquity that becomes his preferred field. He imagines that he
had a previous existence during the reign of Hadrian (in a let-

ter to Boisserée, 1815).[1] The "classical" Walpurgis Night is an abridgment of the whole of Antiquity, in which the battlefields of Pydna and Pharsalus are as markedly accentuated as the earliest heroic age. Its mythological and philosophical trappings are derived chiefly from authors of late Antiquity; even Faust's descent to the Mothers employs material from Plutarch. Not merely a "classical" segment—no, Antiquity in all its phases and metamorphoses is affirmed; and without *paideia* or *furor pedagogicus*. It is a ghostly Antiquity, presented in the allusive and abstractive manner that characterizes the late work of great masters. "The treatment had to be directed away from the specific toward the generic," Goethe once remarked to Riemer, and the latter continues: "Goethe often related with reference to himself an anecdote about Titian: how in his old age the great colorist painted the same textiles that he had earlier known how to render so concretely only *in abstracto*, as it were; for example, velvet only as the idea of velvet."

Herman Hefele once characterized the poetry of the Classical Walpurgis Night in terms of "Baroque force and magnificence." He saw in the ocean episode, in the hymn to movement, "one of Bernini's decorative fountains cast into words." And he continues, "for it is characteristic of the German mind that its purest achievements of Classical art should be in Baroque forms." An ingenious formulation which, however, when stripped of its art-historical drapery, means nothing but that *Faust II* does not fit into the category of the Classical. The essence of Antiquity is viewed here from the perspective of a later age, one not tied to any historical epoch. The Rome of the civil wars is reflected in the epic of Nero's time. The Hellas of the heroic age stands beside that of the Crusader castles; Germanic tribes settle the Peloponnesus. Philemon and Baucis are transplanted from the sphere of

[1] Goethe alludes to verses of Hadrian in 1770, then in the *Römische Elegien* [*Roman Elegies*] (Book i, No. 15). In *Wilhelm Meisters Wanderjahre* [*Wilhelm Meister's Travels*] the blessed memory of "that noble imperial wanderer Hadrian" is invoked.

Ovid and Hellenism to the North Sea. Times and places become interlocked and transposed in an allegoric-symbolic simultaneity that is familiar to us from the mediaeval mystery plays, from Calderón and Hofmannsthal. This artistic manner, so far removed from anything Greek, could almost be regarded as a continuation of mediaeval and Renaissance impulses were it not for the caesura of a classicism (*Iphigenie, Tasso*) modeled on Racine. We are dealing not with continuity but with recurrence on a higher level—a "spiral tendency," to borrow a concept from Goethe's scientific work.

Such a transposition is in harmony with Goethe's mode of thought. The fundamental polarity of serenity and turbidity encompasses, as we saw, the spheres of nature and of mind. In the theory of complementary colors Goethe perceived "a great principle which pervades the whole sphere of nature," the principle of "necessary alternation." "Perhaps," he continued, "this principle is also the basis for the scenes of gaiety and serenity interspersed in Shakespeare's tragedies . . . but it does not appear to apply to the purer form of Greek tragedy." Here we have an instance where Classical, exemplary works seem to contravene a pervasive law. So, too, the study of nature can result in a relativization of Classical norms. Goethe's response at such an intellectual juncture is characteristic. He notes that everything is interrelated; a law from the theory of colors may lead to an examination of Greek tragedy. "Only one must beware of pushing such a law too far and trying to make it the basis for a great many other things; one is much safer in using it only as an *analogon,* as an example." For Goethe, then, the transposition of concepts of nature to concepts of the mind always signifies only an analogical relation. This applies eminently to the concepts of metamorphosis and organic growth. "The plant proceeds from node to node and terminates in the blossom and the seed." Goethe finds analogies for this in the formation of the caterpillar, of vertebrates, finally of "whole corporations" such as the beehive. "It is thus that a nation produces its heroes, who stand at the forefront as a source of protection and well-being, like demigods; and similarly the poetic powers of the French concentrate themselves in Voltaire." To the naturalist's eye great nations like the French appear like the corporate communities of bees. The hive brings forth a queen and sets it at its head. Similarly, Voltaire is France raised to a higher power. This is to be taken as a witty and playful aperçu. We should be mistaken if we tried to reduce Goethe's morphology of history to the structural patterns of nodes and vertebrae. It is instructive to see that for the phenomenon of Voltaire Goethe establishes another derivation, one that is independent of botany and osteology: "We may notice in families which have long survived that nature finally produces an individual who includes in himself the qualities of all his ancestors, an individual who is able to concentrate and bring to full expression all the gifts that have hitherto been present only in dispersed and incipient traits. It is the same with nations, whose various qualities may once, if fortune allows, find expression in an individual. Thus there arose in Louis XIV a French king in the highest sense, and thus in Voltaire the highest imaginable, the most appropriate embodiment for the French of a writer." Or yet a third variation of the same idea: "It was the metamorphosis of a century-old literary tradition that had been evolving since Louis XIV and finally reached its full flowering."

Nature and history are comprehended in the same glance. The critic Goethe is also an historian. He exhibits the productions of the mind against their historical background. Paris, "where an historical event has taken place on every street-corner," provides the conditions for the development of that splendid literature which unfolds from Molière to Diderot. Scott's novels "are founded upon the splendor of the three British kingdoms." Contrast this with the German writer! Germany's early history is too deeply buried in obscurity, its later history, "for want of a single ruling house," is devoid of national interest. Klopstock essayed the theme of Arminius, "but the subject is too remote, nobody has any connection with it." And Lessing! In his *Minna von Barnhelm* he had to make do with the clashes of Prussians and Saxons because he could not find anything better. He was born into a bad time and this forced him into polemical writing: in *Emilia Galotti* his "pique" was with the princes; in *Nathan der Weise* with the priests. Goethe himself had been lucky in his choice of Götz von Berlichingen. "In *Werther* and *Faust*, on the other hand, I had to delve into my own breast, for no traditional material was available." In *Wilhelm Meister* he had had to choose the most wretched stuff imaginable: "a troupe of strolling players and hard-up country squires." It is the man full of days who speaks thus (1826). "Had I known, however," he continues, "as clearly as I do now, how many excellent things have been in existence for hundreds and thousands of years, I should not have written a line but done something else."

5

This utterance may seem daunting, but it is quite revelatory. Not until his middle period did Goethe discover that he was "actually born to be a writer." But in 1791 he observes to Jacobi that he is becoming daily more attached to the natrual sciences and that "by and by they may come to occupy me exclusively." For a long time he believed himself destined to be an artist. It was—to use a significant formulation—a "wrong tendency." The story of such an error is *Wilhelm Meisters theatralische Sendung* [*Wilhelm Meister's Theatrical Mission*]. Goethe himself had long cherished the "illusion" that it might be possible to form a German theater and that he might contribute to it. "I wrote my *Iphigenie* and my *Tasso* in the childish hope that in this way it would work. But nothing moved, nothing stirred, and everything remained as it was." Designer, naturalist, reformer of the stage, servant of the state, writer—these and other possibilities were in him. Only in his old age was he able to review the limitations of each. He had become historical to himself; indeed, in his last years, as a solitary survivor, "mythical." Even a late production like the *Divan* grew strange to him after a decade: "it is like a snake's skin that has been sloughed off and left by the wayside" (1827), an image that Goethe had already applied to himself in his early Weimar period. The historicizing of his own life, in which foolish cavillers see an occasion for finding fault with *Dichtung und Wahrheit,* does not signify stiffness or rigidity, but rather a fulfillment of his entelechy. The stages of a life nearing completion become transparent and can be contemplated simultaneously as parts of a higher unity. That is why Goethe called the poem *Um Mitternacht* [*At Midnight*]—that pure triad—his "song of life," "one of my favorite productions." Only at this highest stage does Goethe feel that he knows "how many excellent things have been in existence for hundreds and thousands of years." The "excellent" as a category of evaluation befits the stage of life represented by extreme old age—for it implies permanence and consequently a sense of time that reckons in centuries and millennia. Youth thinks in years, age in lustra, decades:

> Lustrum ist ein fremdes Wort!
> Aber wenn wir sagen:
> Lustra haben wir am Ort
> Acht bis neun ertragen
> Und genossen und gelebt
> Und geliebt bisweilen,
> Wird, wer nach dem Gleichen strebt,
> Heute mit uns teilen. . . .

[Lustrum is a foreign word! But when we say, we have endured eight or nine lustra in this place, enjoyed ourselves, lived, and sometimes loved, then whoever has a similar aim will join with us today. . . .]

In 1825, the fiftieth anniversary of Goethe's career as an official was celebrated. In 1827, he is of the opinion, it would be worth the effort "to hold out for some fifty years more"; for he wants to live long enough to see the Panama Canal, the Suez Canal, the Rhine-Danube Canal. Canal-building figures as one of Faust's ameliorative activities. The palace in the last act is situated in a spacious ornamental garden, beside a "large rectilinear" canal, on which goods from the far corners of the world are shipped. Faust is a centenarian. The habit of thinking in centuries has been projected upon the stage of human existence. At this point we touch the sphere of the macrobiotic, by which Goethe's contemporaries were so magically attracted. Goethe himself liked to regale his visitors during his last years with the longevity of Ninon de Lenclos. He disapproves of Semmering, who let himself die at seventy-five. He ponders the "advantages and disadvantages" of the various ages of life and finds that he possesses advantages in his eightieth year that he would not exchange for his earlier ones. After the death of the Duke Karl August he is grieved that "there are no distinctions," that even such a man must pass away prematurely. "Only one paltry century longer and, highly placed as he was, how much he would have done to advance his era!"

To the lifespan of a hundred years demanded by Goethe must correspond a historical consciousness of thousands. When, in 1827, the supervisor of construction Coudray mentions that he wants to secure Wieland's tomb by means of an iron enclosure, Goethe remarks: "Living as I do in millennia, it always surprises me when I hear of statues and monuments. I can never think of a statue being erected to the memory of a worthy man without imagining it torn down and trampled to bits by future men-at-arms. Coudray's iron bars around Wieland's tomb I already see gleaming as horseshoes under the hooves of a future cavalry." If a man cannot take three thousand years into account, he remains "in darkness, inexperienced."

With the eye of a Lynceus watching the cargoes of distant lands, Goethe surveys the royal treasures of the millennia. With how much modesty! Contemplating Pompeian paintings he lapses into a meditative silence, which he then breaks with the words: "Yes, in every department of art the ancients are unattainable. You see, gentlemen, I think that I too have achieved something, but compared to one of the great Attic poets like Aeschylus and Sophocles I am nothing after all." Or: "In five centuries the Arabs had only seven poets whom they were willing to count, and among the rabble of those they rejected were several who were better than I." He calls Tieck a talent of high importance. "Only, if one wishes to raise him above himself and put him on a level with me, one is mistaken. I can state this quite frankly, for it is no concern of mine, I did not make myself. It is as though I were to compare myself to Shakespeare, who did not make himself either and who is nevertheless a being of a higher type whom I look up to and must revere." And a final instance: "On all that I have accomplished as a poet I do not pride myself in the least. Excellent poets have lived at the same time with me, even more excellent ones lived before me, and there will be others after me." Such and similar utterances show us how Goethe ranked himself from the standpoint of the millennia. They provide a gloss on his statement that he would not have written a line had he known clearly "how many excellent things have been in existence for hundreds and thousands of years." Finally, these words refer to a demand that may be made of any higher type of criticism, however generally it remains unsatisfied: the ranking of authors. But that also means—discriminating among minds.

6

The assimilation of Oriental poetry expanded the horizon of the critic Goethe. It was like Alexander's campaign: it placed Hellas and Asia in a new relation, one fraught with fertile tensions. In the *Noten und Abhandlungen zum Divan* [*Notes and Dissertations on the Divan*] the Europeans are called "Occidentals." Orient and Occident could no longer be separated. But the Orient must not be made to resemble the Occident. Sir William Jones loved and esteemed his Orient. Still, in order to "smuggle in" its productions among his countrymen, he compared them to those of the Greeks and Romans. He was obliged to do so by the prejudice of

English "critics of Antiquity" (Goethe also refers to them as "Classicists"), who refused to acknowledge anything as valid "except what had been bequeathed to us by Rome and Athens." Goethe's discovery of Arabic and Persian poetry made a breach in his classicism, but it confirmed and reenforced a layer of his culture that extended all the way back to his youth and even to his childhood: that of the Bible. The Old Testament was for Goethe the archetypal image of tradition. It contained doctrine, poetry, and the oldest records of mankind. In Goethe's youth there could be found "among the Protestants of Germany" readers of the holy scriptures who knew all the principal sections by heart, held them ready for application, and were "living concordances." Such people were called "Bibelfest" ["firm in the Bible"], and an epithet of this sort "conferred an exquisite dignity and an unambiguous commendation." Goethe was reminded of this when in his studies of Oriental poetry he met with believers who were "firm in the Koran," and to whom was accorded the honorary title of *Hafiz*. Asked why he bears the title, Mohammed Shamsuddin replies:

> Weil in glücklichem Gedächtnis
> Des Korans geweiht Vermächtnis
> Unverändert ich verwahre
> Und damit so fromm gebahre,
> Dass gemeinen Tages Schlechtnis
> Weder mich noch die berühret,
> Die Propheten-Wort und-Samen
> Schätzen, wie es sich gebühret—
> Darum gab man mir den Namen.

[Because in my happy memory I preserve intact the Koran's sacred legacy, comporting myself so piously therewith that the common day's evil can touch neither me nor those who esteem, as is fitting, the word and seed of the Prophet; and that is why the name was given to me.]

And the Occidental poet can chime in:

> Und so gleich ich dir vollkommen,
> Der ich unsrer heil'gen Bücher
> Herrlich Bild an mich genommen,
> Wie auf jenes Tuch der Tücher
> Sich des Herren Bildnis drückte,
> Mich in stiller Brust erquickte,
> Trotz Verneinung, Hindrung, Raubens,
> Mit dem heitern Bild des Glaubens.

[And so I resemble you completely, I who have received the splendid image of our Holy Books as that handkerchief of handkerchiefs received the likeness of Our Lord, and despite negation, obstacle, violation, have refreshed my tranquil heart with the serene image of faith.]

Hafiz and Goethe meet in the sign of the holy scriptures, and absorption in Eastern poetry coincides with a renewed study of the Bible. "For just as all our wanderings in the Orient were occasioned by the holy scriptures, so do we return to them over and over again as to the most invigorating of sources whose waters, though turbid here and there and hidden beneath the ground, always spring forth again fresh and pure." Goethe's penetration of the world of Islam was not a mode of exoticism but a reversion to the pure patriarchal air of the East. Through the accounts of travelers like Marco Polo, Pietro della Valle, and Chardin, his outlook was then extended to more recent centuries and, spatially, to China, which already had superb novels at a time "when our ancestors were still living in the woods."

No concept from Goethe's view of history has become so well known as his idea of world literature. One of its roots is the assimilation of the Orient and its integration into the tradition of mankind. Another is the theory of cultural stages, of which Goethe distinguished four: the idyllic, the social or civic, the more general, and the universal. The last "is the reunion of all the educated circles which formerly had barely been in touch, the recognition of a *single* purpose, the conviction of how necessary it is to keep up with conditions in the world as they are happening at the moment. All foreign literatures align themselves with the national literature, and we are not left behind in the course of world events." The course of world events, the increased "facility of communication," was an aspect of his time that Goethe welcomed. He praises the express mails, this innovation of the German transportation system; he has himself informed of the opening of steamship travel on the Rhine and of Degenhardt's flying machine. The canals of the Parsees, "from whose circulation sprang the fertility of the land," point ahead to the construction of Faust's canal. He hopes for German unity, that is, for the merger of Prussia with the South German customs-union, as well as for uniform currency, weights, and measures—but not, be it noted, for political confederation: "suppose that for several centuries we had had only the two capitals in Germany, Vienna and Berlin, or even only one—I would like to see what would have happened to German culture in that case." German unity he expected "from our good highways and future railroads." All this is implicit in the notion of world literature. He explains to two Polish visitors, to whom he serves "a magnificent turkey with truffles," that for the blind masses national differences grow into insurmountable barriers. It follows that the more educated have the same duty to improve the intercourse of nations as they have to make it easier to travel by ship or to build roads over the mountains. The general wealth and welfare of mankind is increased by free trade in ideas and sentiments as it is by farm and manufactured products. The term world literature does not seem to have occurred during the conversation, but its concept is developed—as a complement to the ideal of free trade. Just as the abolition of tariffs is not expected, in Goethe's view, to bring about political unification, so Goethe does not contrapose world literature to the national literatures. At times he will emphasize the universal more strongly, at others he pays more attention to the national. World literature, like all of Goethe's concepts, is not a limiting definition but the focus of many relations, a center of diverging perspectives. It is a proposal to be fulfilled. During the period of the *Divan* it acted as a corrective to classical prejudices. But when that period has receded, the pendulum swings back to Hellenism again: "National literature does not mean much any more, it is time for the epoch of world literature, and everyone must assist in bringing this epoch about as quickly as possible. But for all our appreciation of foreign literatures, we must not fix on one in particular and regard that as the model. We must not think it is the Chinese, or the Serbian, or Calderón, or the Nibelungen; but rather, when a model is needed, we must always return to the ancient Greeks, in whose works the beauty of man is always represented. Everything else we must consider historically, appropriating what is good in it as far as possible to our own use."

As far as possible! Goethe's wide-ranging mode of thought is the opposite of systematic: when he establishes a position its negation is implied. "Germany," he says after a visit by a young poet, "occupies such a high place in all subjects that we can hardly take everything in, and now they expect us to be Greeks and Romans and English and French besides! Yes, and on top of that they have the folly to point to the Orient too, so that a young person cannot help becoming completely confused." *They* have the folly . . . in which Goethe had no share at all? But even six years later: "It is vain to imagine that one can rise to the demands of all literary phenomena; it cannot be done; one gropes about in all centuries, in all corners of the world and is still not at home everywhere, but has only blunted one's sensibility and lost one's time and effort. I do the same; I regret it, but too late. One reads through folios and quartos and is no whit the wiser for it than if one read every day in one's Bible. One only learns that the world is stupid, and proof of that can be had right here in the next street."

Folios and quartos: we can verify it by Goethe's use of the Weimar library, which is attested in documents. The compilations show that Goethe read on the average at least one moderate-sized quarto a day. The index of works borrowed reveals the breadth of his interests. Goethe possesses something of that polyhistorism which we also find in Herder and Jean Paul. This too is a source of his conception of world literature. But with Goethe polyhistory is placed at the service of a superior mode of observation—that of comparison. It embraces his theory of nature and his theory of history. Applied to literature it results in the idea of comparative literary history, and this, in turn, is of use to criticism. So, for example, Goethe elucidates the mannerism of Jean Paul, which he had condemned in his classical period, by relating it to similar features in Oriental poetry, thus gaining a new appreciation of it. By virtue of the comparative method polyhistory is raised to the level of genuine historical contemplation. This leads to a further connection. Both as natural scientist and as historian Goethe takes the history of these disciplines into account. The *Noten und Abhandlungen zum Divan* as well as the *Geschichte der Farbenlehre* [*History of the Theory of Colors*] present history of science and history of scholarship interspersed with his own reflections. Literary history is thereby assigned an area in which, to be sure, it hardly ever sets foot. With us it all too often restricts itself to the history of poetry, though the question of how literature is to be reasonably marked off from poetry may well be left in suspense.

What is the nature of poetry? What is its place in the system of "objective spirit?" Its function in the human community? These are questions that have been raised since Homer and answered in varying ways. The complex of these problems may be defined as theory of poetry. It is high time it were investigated historically. Such an investigation would benefit literary history as well as criticism. But it would also offer much that is essential to our understanding—which is by no means complete—of Goethe. This understanding is obstructed by conventional notions. When Goethe's theory of poetry is discussed, it is usual to mention that he regarded his works as fragments of a great confession, but that he also referred to them as occasional poems. What does that designation really mean, anyway?

The case of the occasional poem is as follows: in late Antiquity, rhetoric was almost entirely confined to its use on private and public occasions, in so-called occasional orations. There was a need for eulogies and ceremonial addresses, for speeches of invitation, welcome, farewell, for wedding, birthday, funeral, consolatory orations, and the like.[2] During the Middle Ages, the Renaissance, and the following centuries, all these genres were transferred from prose to poetry, which was considered a part of rhetoric. "Casual" oratory has its counterpart in "casual" poetry. Occasional poems for festive circumstances were commissioned. Many were in circulation in Goethe's youth. The boy looked at them with envy as he believed he could do such things "just as well and, indeed, better." An opportunity soon presented itself in the tender idyll of first love that revolves around the Gretchen from the town of Offenbach. Goethe places it charmingly before our eyes in *Dichtung und Wahrheit*. Epithalamia and other carmina were composed. These are occasional poems in the authentic and original sense of the word. Free lyrical creation, on the other hand, was subject to entirely different laws. After recounting his studies of Spinoza in Frankfurt, Goethe adds: "I had arrived at the point where I regarded my innate poetic talent as wholly nature, the more so as I had been induced to consider external nature as its subject. The exercise of this poetic gift could be aroused and directed by an occasion, but it was most happy and abundant when it burst forth spontaneously and, indeed, against my will." This spontaneous, natural kind of writing is characterized here as the opposite of the composing of ceremonial verses. But in *Dichtung und Wahrheit* there is already a shift of usage. In an appreciation

[2] Cf. the chapter *Rhetoric* in my book, *Europäische Literatur und lateinisches Mittelalter* (2nd ed., Bern, 1954); *European Literature and the Latin Middle Ages*, trans. Willard R. Trask (New York, 1953).

of Johann Christian Günther the occasional poem is described as "the first and most authentic of all the poetic kinds." In the 1820s the term has the approximate meaning of objective poetry. Concerning his works Goethe declares that they were all "inspired by a more or less important occasion, in the direct contemplation of some object." Even more explicitly to Eckermann: "The world is so vast and rich and life so variegated that there will never be a lack of occasions for poetry. But they must all be occasional poems, that is, reality must supply the motive and the material. . . . Poems made up out of thin air I do not value at all." Subjectivity is "the endemic illness of the age." As long as a poet "expresses only his few subjective emotions he is not yet worthy of the name; but as soon as he has learned how to assimilate the world and express it he is a poet." Occasional poetry is thus the opposite of the expression of personal circumstances. It is poetry that has an objective content.

This clarification seemed necessary because the phrase about Goethe as an occasional poet has become a meaningless convention. Nor is there much to be gained from the outworn formula of "Erlebnis und Dichtung," poetry and lived experience. Goethe found entirely different formulas for his activity as a poet. Examined closely, they arrange themselves as a series of stages. We shall attempt to indicate it.

In the first stage poetry manifests itself as a phenomenology of human life. It perceives and gives shape to the perplexities of the heart, the entanglements of life in society. This means that it paves the way for wisdom and healing. The poet, says Wilhelm Meister, "sees the chaos of the passions, sees families and empires moving without a purpose, he sees the insoluble enigmas of misunderstandings which for want of a one-syllable word to unravel them cause untold fatal complications. . . . Inborn in the ground of his heart, the fair flower of wisdom blossoms forth, and when others dream awake and are frightened out of their wits by monstrous imaginings, he lives the dream of life as one awake, and the rarest occurrences are to him as past and future. And so the poet is at once teacher, prophet, and friend to gods and men."

The alleged egoist Goethe (Schiller regarded him as such in 1788–1789) can pronounce, as "friend to man," the moving words:

> Warum sucht ich den Weg so sehnsuchtsvoll,
> Wenn ich ihn nicht den Brüdern zeigen soll?

> [Why did I seek the way so fervently, if not to show it to my brothers?]

He seeks the way, sees his life as an "erring labyrinthine course," but at the same time as a pyramid which it is his task to construct. He climbs it step by step:

> Weltverwirrung zu betrachten,
> Herzensirrung zu beachten,
> Dazu ward der Freund berufen,
> Schaute von den vielen Stufen
> Unsres Pyramidenlebens
> Viel umher, und nicht vergebens. . . .

> [To observe the confusions of the world, to heed the errors of the heart, this was the friend's vocation; from the many steps of our pyramidal life he looked about him, and not in vain. . . .]

The final stage of this phenomenological development is found in the stanza:

> Des Menschen Leben scheint ein herrlich Los

> [Man's life appears to be a glorious lot]

with the key verses:

> Keins wird vom andern wünschenswert ergänzt,
> Von aussen düsterts, wenn es innen glänzt.

> [Neither is the other's desirable complement, the exterior is dark, when we are bright within.]

Here, however, the "reconciliation" is left to music.

Poetry as representation and clarification of a "confused aspiration" within the framework of a phenomenology of human existence—this is a constant of Goethe's poetics. In the traditional schematism of poetic theory there was no place for this conception. But it is a key to large areas of Goethe's creation. It can unfold in the lyric, in the drama, in the masque, in the novel. It cuts across all genres, binding them into an organic whole which is discernible under the most varied shapes. Before Goethe it did not exist, after him no longer. It is Goethe's contribution to the theory of poetry, and it is tied to his monad.

But Goethe the historian and lover of literature must have encountered the older poetic theory along the way. A scholastic tradition, bequeathed by Antiquity to Islam as well as to the West and persisting through the Middle Ages and the Renaissance up until the eighteenth century, connected poetry and rhetoric as the "arts of beautiful discourse." On his peregrinations through the world's literature Goethe censured this "general rubric." It degraded poetry in his view by placing it on a level with, or even subordinating it to, rhetoric. In an account of European literature, this "protest" of Goethe's would have to be judged historically significant. It grew out of his investigations of Oriental poetry. There, moreover, he came in contact with the pure form of a genre which, with the ripe wisdom that enabled him to survey millennia, he made his own: the encomiastic, as he calls it, now himself borrowing a term from the art of Greek rhetoric. *Enkomion* means praise. Encomiastic poetry is first and foremost praise of the ruler. We find it at Hellenistic and Occidental courts, but it is nowhere so richly developed as in the Orient. The Persian Anwari is "a liberal encomiast and thinks that there is no finer profession than to gladden the hearts of his contemporaries with praise. He adorns princes, viziers, aristocratic and beautiful women, poets and musicians with his commendations, and he knows how to apply to each some graceful ornament drawn from the vast treasure-house of the world." Praise is the office of the court poet. Praise—but now the word becomes the cipher with which Goethe indicates what to him is the quintessence of all poetry. Even more! The word "praise" is filled, in the usage of the late Goethe, with a solemn content—it becomes an abbreviation for a transfigured view of the world. It gets detached from saying and is transferred to being. On a clear, starry night Goethe beholds the infinite,

> Wenn sie sich einander loben,
> Jene Feuer in dem Blauen.

[When they praise each other, those fires in the blue.]

History becomes a Te Deum: "Mankind's song of praise, which the Godhead loves to hear, is never silent, and we ourselves feel a divine happiness when we perceive the harmonious effusions distributed throughout all times and regions, sometimes in single voices, single choirs, sometimes as a fugue, sometimes in a magnificent full chorus." A paean ascending through all the spheres to the empyrean—this is now discovered to be the essence of poetry. "In this respect so much is to be noted: that the vocation of the genuine poet is to receive the splendor of the world, and for that reason he will always be more inclined to praise than to blame. It follows that he will seek the worthiest subject, and after he has tried them all, will in the end prefer to apply his talent to the praise and glorification of God."

Poetry as praise and hymn to God—*carmen Deo nostro*—would be a further aspect of Goethe's theory of poetry. Praise of God, to be sure, of a believer who was not an orthodox one. But had his esteemed Persian poets been orthodox? Was there a place for poetry in the legalistic religion of Islam? Its founder was himself to protest against being placed on a level with the poets of the pagan era. But in its later development, by the side of law and dogma there arose a mysticism that could contravene the orthodox practice, especially when it availed itself of erotic symbolism. Among the great Persian poets were men like Hafiz, whose poems admitted both secular and religious interpretations. The Orient, then, seemed to hold the possibility of a poetic faith, at once secular and supernal, which had been denied to the West; and therewith also a "new" splendor of poetry. A splendor "in which pure humanity, noble manners, serenity and joy have taken refuge so as to console us for caste warfare, fantastic religious monstrosities and abstruse mysticism, and to convince us that in it finally is preserved the salvation of mankind." In its "splendor" poetry includes the salvation of mankind. Salvation, however, is a concept drawn from the sphere of religion. Then this sphere, too, is approached by a determination of poetry which consciously stresses its detachment from the perversions of faith. The religion of the Prophet left the poet his rights after all. It harbored both spiritual types, although distinguishing the one as the complement of the other. "If we wish to indicate more nearly the difference between the poet and the prophet, we would say: both are seized and inspired by a God; the poet, however, squanders on pleasure the gift he has been endowed with in order to produce pleasure and to attain honor by his productions, or at any rate a comfortable life. He neglects all other purposes, tries to be varied, and to show that he is boundless in conception as in representation. The prophet, on the other hand, has only one end in view; to attain it he avails himself of the simplest means."

New perspectives open here. Poetry as the fruit and means of pleasure. Our pedagogues are of course fond of repeating the maxim, pleasure makes a man vulgar. But Goethe has something quite different to tell us on this subject. He presents an ethic of pleasure, both personal and, at a higher stage, vicarious:

> Was ihr sonst für euch genossen,
> Lässt in andern sich geniessen.
> Niemand wird uns dann beschreien,
> Dass wirs uns alleine gönnen;
> Nun in allen Lebensreihen
> Müsset ihr geniessen können.

> Und mit diesem Lied und Wendung
> Sind wir wieder bei Hafisen;
> Denn es ziemt, des Tags Vollendung
> Mit Geniessern zu geniessen.

[What you used to enjoy for yourselves, let it now be enjoyed by others. Then no one will upbraid us with keeping it for ourselves. Now in every stage of life you must be able to enjoy yourselves. And with this turn in our song we are back to Hafiz again: for it is fitting to enjoy the day's completion with men who understand pleasure.]

The poetry of pleasure of Anacreon, of Hafiz, of Goethe: steps in the pyramidal life of world literature.

The poet as a consumer and producer of pleasure is a prodigal. This idea serves as a bridge between the *Divan* and *Faust*. In the masquerade at the imperial palace the herald announces different kinds of poets, "nature poets, courtly and chivalric minstrels, tender as well as enthusiasts." In the throng of competitors of all sorts, no one allows anyone else to recite. The satirist sneaks past with a few words. The night and graveyard poets beg to be excused, "because they are in the midst of a conversation with a freshly-risen vampire, from which a new poetic genre might evolve." They are dispensed with and Greek mythology is summoned, which, "even under a modern mask, loses nothing of its character or charm." A chariot, guided by a beautiful boy, appears in the procession of figures. In reply to the herald's question he gives his name:

> Bin die Verschwendung, bin die Poesie;
> Bin der Poet, der sich vollendet,
> Wenn er sein eigen Gut verschwendet.

[I am prodigality, I am poetry; I am the poet who fulfills himself when he wastes his own substance.]

If in Plato Eros is the son of poverty and wealth, so the boy-charioteer has been given wealth (Plutus) for a father, "a king rich and mild." Plutus brings treasure to the imperial palace. When the chests are unloaded, he turns to the boy-charioteer:

> Nun bist du los der allzu lästigen Schwere
> Bist frei und frank, nun frisch zu deiner Sphäre!
> Hier ist sie nicht! Verworren, scheckig, wild
> Umdrängt uns hier ein fratzenhaft Gebild.
> Nur wo du klar ins holde Klare schaust,
> Dir angehörst und dir allein vertraust,
> Dorthin, wo Schönes, Gutes nur gefällt,
> Zur Einsamkeit!—da schaffe deine Welt.

[Now you are quit of the all too tedious burden, are frank and free—now rush up to your sphere. It is not here below! Confused, checkered, hectic, a distorted apparition besets us here. Only where you gaze clearly upon sweet clarity, possess yourself and trust in yourself, there where only the good and the beautiful please—in solitude! there create your world.]

The counterpart of the boy-charioteer is Euphorion. Both figures signalize the same archetypal image, that of poetry in its "splendor," as manifested in a soaring, youthful genius. Both are boys, both are initially safe under the tutelage of a mild father, who afterwards releases them. It would be an error to interpret the father in accordance with an overly rigid psycho-symbolic scheme. So much is certain, however: the embodiment of genius in a boy—this final incarnation of Goethe's conception of poetry—should be seen simultaneously with the image of a generative potency whose sphere surpasses that of the son. The sphere of poetry is a delimited and purified region of the universe: "Only where you gaze clearly upon sweet clarity"—this one line contains, in utmost concentration, the essence of Goethe's doctrine of poetry and of life: the clear gaze into clarity, the clarity within responding to the clarity without. Light of day, "aus Morgenduft gewebt und

Sonnenklarheit," "woven of morning fragrance and clear sunlight"; light of the eternal stars when night and ether grow clear: twin manifestations of that "serene" world to which Goethe, avid of light, knows he belongs. The Middle Ages were acquainted with a metaphysics of light. In Goethe we find a poetics of light in which the divine and the human, Occident and Orient, past and present, are enfolded.

Lass den Anfang mit dem Ende sich in eins zusammenziehn—

> [Let the beginning and the end be drawn together
> into one—]

This verse expresses what is most peculiar to the Goethean sense of life and evokes in his reader the memory of many utterances that point toward the same thing. We shall cite only one more, as it affords a last look at the workings of metamorphosis in Goethe's art: "certain great motifs, legends, ancient historical traditions impressed themselves so deeply upon my mind that I kept them alive and active within me for forty to fifty years. It seemed to me the most beautiful possession that I could often see these precious images anew in my imagination, since, despite constant transformations, they remained unchanged as they matured toward a purer form, a more distinct representation." For half a century Goethe carries within himself images imparted to him by tradition and which chose him as the vehicle in which to take shape. This revelation is significant. It reveals the interaction of the conscious and the unconscious in Goethe's creative work, while the "great motifs, legends, ancient historical traditions" may be considered a hardly mistakable anticipation of the archetypal images in the sense of C. G. Jung. They rise again and again upon the stream in which legend and history mingle. Goethe gives us a view of his poetry here which entirely excludes its interpretation by way of "Erlebnis." He links his creation to the golden chain of the tradition of mankind. Those images are the cargo of the transpersonal and transhistorical. They occupy the first order in the hierarchical world which Goethe denominates "objective." It is a concept which prevails—although much attenuated in the degree of its content—as a characteristic of his evaluative criticism. The norms and fundamental principles of that criticism shall not be discussed here. Let it suffice, if we have clarified our comprehension of Goethe in a few particulars.

1948

Goethe as Administrator

++

JOHANN GEORG ZIMMERMANN (1728–1795) of Brugg in the Aargau, who through his writings on moral philosophy (*Von der Einsamkeit, Vom Nationalstolz*) [*On Solitude, On National Pride*] and his skill as a physician became a European celebrity—he attended Frederick the Great in his last illness —also crossed Goethe's path on a number of occasions. In May, 1775, he showed the poet several silhouettes, among them that of Frau von Stein. Goethe wrote under it: "It would be a fine spectacle to see how the world is mirrored in this soul. She sees the world as it is and yet through the medium of love." In September of the same year Zimmermann resided as a guest at the home of Goethe's parents, which earned him a character sketch in *Dichtung und Wahrheit*. He also inquired at the time about *Faust*, the publication of which was believed to be near. He actually got to see it, but in a strange shape: "Goethe apporta un sac rempli de petits chiffons de papier. Il le vida sur la table et dit: voilà mon Faust!" ["Goethe brought out a sack filled with little scraps of paper. He emptied it on the table and said: there is my Faust!"] This was reported—"une anecdote que je tiens du célèbre Zimmermann"—by August Wilhelm Schlegel on 31 December 1832 in a letter to Abraham Hayward (1801– 1884), who translated *Faust* in 1833, but was to achieve permanent fame through his treatise *The Art of Dining* (1858). That the incident should still seem worthy of note after more than fifty years indicates that both the witness and the later reporter found something remarkable in it. It is unusual for poets to preserve their drafts in a sack.

This sack, however, was probably not made of canvas but of paper. In southern Germany the word "sack" is used for

58

"pouch." Even today in business large manila envelopes are called pouches. These were demonstrably used by Goethe throughout his life for the ordering of papers. He writes to Schiller on 10 January 1798: "Meanwhile in these colorless and joyless days I took up my 'Theory of Colors' again and, the better to review what I have done so far, put my papers in order. For I have kept records from the beginning and in this way preserved both my errors as well as my proper procedures, but especially all experiments, experiences, and ideas; now I have separated all these volumina, have had paper sacks made, indexed them according to a certain schema, and stuck everything into them." These sacks are also occasionally called capsules. "Looking through the capsules. Older and more recent manuscripts" (Diary of 5 March 1818). Kräuter reports in a letter to the Countess von Hopfgarten: "You will never find single sheets lying around in his presence; if they do not fit in anywhere, he will paste up a capsule out of a sheet of paper, write a heading on it, and not until then do they become (illegible)."[1]

Besides sacks and capsules Goethe also used "Tecturen"; these are probably folders. I give a few examples from the Diaries: "Arrangement of the expeditions[2] up to the present in Tecturen" (25 May 1816). "Distributed collectanea among the various Tecturen" (1 July 1816). "Made ready several Tecturen toward the Dutch masters" (13 Oct. 1818). "All papers in Tecturen" (3 Sept. 1819). "Principal occupation, to determine the next rubrics for Art and Antiquity and to arrange the Tecturen" (1 Nov. 1823). "Laid out Tecturen for 1826" (14 Jan. 1826). "Schema of the Wanderjahre [*Wilhelm Meister's Travels*]. Likewise Tecturen toward the chapters" (23 Jan. 1826). "Headed the different Tecturen and noted their contents" (23 July 1828). "Continued to clear up and complete the botanical Tecturen" (30 August

---

[1] Kräuter's letter (of 26 Jan. 1821) was published by Arthur Pollmer in the second *Jahrbuch der Sammlung Kippenberg* and thereafter reprinted in the *Inselschiff*, volume four, number two, Easter 1923.

[2] This legal term is explained on p. 63 below.—TR.

1828). "Attended to the most necessary matters. Arranged provisional Tecturen for the year" (1 Jan. 1830). "Began filing the documents relative to the affairs of her ladyship the archduchess, which had been lying in Tecturen up to now" (4 Jan. 1830).

Collecting and ordering his collections was a fundamental trait of Goethe's nature. Its first attestation is the *Ephemerides*, an anthology of extracts from his reading which Goethe started in January 1770 in Frankfurt and then continued in Strasbourg. But through his study of law, his practice as a lawyer, and, finally, his public offices, one of which, the "supervision of the immediate institutes for science and art," he exercised until his death, he was compelled to handle documents daily for sixty years. A new publication of the Weimar State Archives (*Goethes amtliche Schriften* [*Goethe's Official Writings*], ed. W. Flach, vol. 1, 1950) grants us an insight for the first time into this side of Goethe's life. It presents the records of the Privy Council from 1776 to 1786. About seven hundred and fifty sessions of this body fall within this decade. Thousands of documents record the proceedings, in every existing style and form; as for instance: rescripts, votes, protocols, postscripts, memoranda, elaborations, writs of chancery, drafts for copyists, orders, decrees. The whole thing a source of cultural history of great charm. We get glimpses of the quarrel between the masons' and the roofers' guild, the purveying of cloth for court livery, the filling of the chairs at the University of Jena, the encroachments of Prussian recruiting officers, the borrowing of capital from the Canton of Berne, the purchase of a library, a campaign against a plague of sparrows, measures to control student societies. The head of the mounted escort, Linder, has called the Jewish merchants in the market at Erfurt louts; the Jews have retorted and been arrested. How shall the matter be resolved? Goethe declares: "For returning the abuse the Jews are sufficiently punished by their arrest, which cannot be revoked, and *meo voto* the fine should be restored to them; Linder, however, should be placed under arrest for the same length of time as the Jews and, as *autor rixae*, be made to pay the expenses incurred, which ought likewise to be restored to the Jews." On another occasion Goethe proposes that the student Nolten, who had been expelled from the university, should be sent off to the Prussian military in exchange for a local boy:—"it would be a useful way of getting rid of a troublemaker." Or, the musketeer Schmidt has put a girl "in the family way"; alimony is to be deducted from his wages. Goethe is instrumental in having the proposal rejected. The procurement of suede trousers for the corps of Hussars is regulated by a draft in Goethe's own hand. When the wigmaker Besser in Eisenach wishes to take on two apprentices a rescript from the Duke is required. Likewise when a student addicted to drink is punished with eight days in jail. The attempt to prevent the import of pure coffee, which was under consideration "on account of the excessive coffee-drinking in our territories," is abandoned, because Chur-Saxony refuses its assistance. So one scene follows another. From sheaves of documents situations, men, destinies emerge—and all of them engaged Goethe's mind and Goethe's heart. In the Privy Council the young jurist could apply his training to the daily tasks of government administration and acquire a technique for the handling of business which would become a permanent part of his personality. In 1785, when Serene Highness proposes a simplification of the chancery style, Goethe casts a highly characteristic vote: "As I do not know the occasion for the change in the form of our chancellery expeditions, I cannot give a precise opinion about it. In general I hold such a change to be rather harmful than beneficial in that such seemingly arbitrary forms are bound up with all sorts of associations which will henceforth be broken and which will nevertheless have to seek some other shape. No saving of time is accomplished, as the votes submitted show. A chancellery does not deal in material things and anyone who has only forms to observe and to work with must have a bit of pedantry in him. Eliminate the pedantry from garrison duty and what is left of it? Indeed, were the By the Grace of God preserved only as an exercise for government clerks in Gothic script and chancery style, it would have a purpose, and a sovereign owes something to propriety. He so often decides the lives of men that he ought not to deprive them through over-hasty edicts of their belief in the sedateness of the deliberations. Order cannot subsist without duly-proportioned speed. Haste is as much an enemy of order as delay." It is necessary to know that the "Von Gottes Gnaden Carl August" ["By the Grace of God Carl August"] at the head of an engrossed re-script represented a masterpiece of calligraphy that required years of practice. The large V in vigorous Gothic emerges at left from the labyrinthine tangle of a flourish[3] whose curvature passes from comfortably-nourished down strokes to prettily curled hair strokes and whose outline resembles a bunch of grapes six lines high made up of volutes and figure eights. At the end of the line to the right the t in August releases the same flourish with mirrorlike symmetry. Both figures are connected and surmounted, however, by a web of broadly sweeping lines in which the chancery pen *con bravura* shouts coloratura arias. Final transformation of mediaeval initial-illumination. The "sedateness" of sovereign deliberations emerges visibly in the script. And how uncommonly indicative the vote in which Goethe defends this graphically figured "By the Grace of God"; his aversion to change, his esteem for seemingly arbitrary forms but to which vital associations still cling; the *festina lente* of "duly proportioned speed"! The consiliarius Goethe is at home with the formulas and flourishes of the curial style. It is as though a family heritage were alive in him. Had not Goethe's father, the imperial councillor, been an administrator restricted by circumstances to household affairs? The maternal grandfather Textor, however, had occupied the office of chief city magistrate for nearly a quarter of a century and numbered among his ancestors a director of a chancellery, a syndic. Goethe has described the old man for us as he sorts flower bulbs and grafts roses: "all

[3] See the facsimile at the end of Goethe's *Amtsschriften* [Official Papers].

this gardening he performed just as regularly and precisely as his official business: for before coming down he had always put the register of his applicants in order for the following day and read the documents."

During his early years in Weimar Goethe still possessed a quick sense of the gulf between life and paper: "I live with these people, speak with them, and listen to what they tell me. How different what is happening looks on the spot from when it has run for a while through the filtering mechanism of the expeditions" (to Frau von Stein 4 March 1779). Such reflections no longer occur later on. After only six years—in the suffrage of 1785—the sedate formalism emerges which will mark Goethe's character to the end of his life. The management of administrative affairs furnishes him with the model and the technique for organizing his personal existence. We breathe something of the atmosphere of Goethe's life when we observe him in the planning and keeping of the most diverse kinds of records.

The transaction of business through administrative channels is a procedure that falls into several phases. Goethe begins with a "schema." This is followed by a "draft," which is then "supplemented." Then the final "redaction" is "engrossed." The execution of a written decree is called "expedition." An inventory is kept of incoming and outgoing papers. All of life's happenings are caught in a broad network of "rubrics." If it is examined more closely, the numerous annotations contained in the Diaries come alive: "Prepared rubrics for varia and outlined schemata" (15 Aug. 1821). —"Schema on Trier" (23 Jan. 1822). "Edited essay on Trier" (24 Jan. 1822). —"A number of drafts of letters, fair copies, and the like. Filed and arranged them differently. Drew up a schema for the agenda. Traveled to Belvedere with Ottilie" (5 June 1828). —"Supplemented the remaining letters and prepared the expedition." —"Fascicles newly laid out for incoming and outgoing letters" (30 Dec. 1816). All of this does not proceed without some circumstance. In December 1809 Wilhelm Grimm sojourns in Weimar and confers with Goethe about literature. Jacob had asked to have manuscripts of the Minnesingers sent to him from the Weimar library. And now, Wilhelm's report to his brother for 25 December 1809: "I went to see Goethe, who finally gave me a definite answer regarding the Weimar manuscripts. It is oriented, like much else about his person, toward formal, ceremonious behavior. You are to write to him in your own character and as a librarian and to request formally the communication to you of the two manuscripts, furthermore to refer to the other gentlemen who are also in charge (i.e., you needn't mention them by name), then he would bring the matter up and the manuscripts should be sent to you by post." Transmission took place on 19 January 1810. For the old Goethe, to handle everything as administrative business has become routine. There are Diary entries like: "expeditions, inventories, functions, projects"; "recapitulated and annotated the expedienda"; "adjusted and sealed the expeditions." "Adjusted and bound the documents concerning Renner for tomorrow's expedition" (29 Oct. 1816). "Dictated all sorts of things. Prepared them to be sent off by the next post" (11 Aug. 1826). "Moved forward everything at a standstill. The next expeditions partly drafted, partly engrossed" (10 June 1827). Remarks and annotations in the files are called *notata*. "Redaction and transcription of the previous notata" (Frankfurt, 6 September 1814). "Notata and allegata from Lucretius" (22 Feb. 1821). "Adjusted and compiled separate notata" (9 May 1821). "Made a fair copy of the notata" (5 August 1822). "Transcribed from the slate the previous notamina" (19 June 1822).

The beginning of the year demands order in the documents. "With John attended to the current registers and documents; bound and paged" (7 Jan. 1823). "Went through the most urgent letters and exhibenda" (5 Jan. 1825). "Carried on the most urgent affairs. Wrote down the agenda. Bound and paged documents, noting whatever was necessary" (1 Jan. 1827). Documents that have been sorted are "reposed" (filed away). A laconic entry states: "Reposed a number of things" (25 July 1819). "Set things in order. Reposed original letters of Schiller and myself for 1797, '98, '99. They were under 1800, among the papers to be fair-copied" (26 June 1824). "Arranged a repository of current affairs" (17 Nov. 1816). "The repositorium in the parlor was installed" (2 June 1825). "Took in hand the cabinet with all private papers and documents." "I made a provisional index of the contents of the rear cabinet. Numbering the drawers. Reposed the Oppenheim cathedral in the carton on top of the collection of engravings. Schlesinger of Berlin announces a copy of the paper for conversation and art. Read through the last letters from England again and considered what should be done about them. Letter from Director of Salt-Works Glenck taken up again" (23 May 1828).

How old-fashioned and amusing is the effect produced by the prickly Latin words of Goethe's administrative language. Agenda and exhibenda, registranda and proponenda, Tecturen and Reposituren march past, so that it is a joy to behold. My greatest pleasure, however, is in the loculamenta. This word is a specimen of rare magnificence. I can verify its use only once. In Seneca and Pliny it means a bookshelf, in Goethe the compartments of a filing cabinet. But in a letter to Zelter for 5 October 1831 this technical term from registration is raised to the dignity of a metaphor designating the highest regions of the mind. Goethe has "perused" Alexander von Humboldt's *Fragmens de Géologie* and credits the author with a talent for "persuasion." "Few people are capable of being convinced, yet most will allow themselves to be persuaded, and thus the treatises that are presented to us here are real discourses, delivered with great facility, so that in the end we are ready to imagine that we can grasp the impossible. That the Himalayas have risen 2500 meters out of the ground and still jut into the sky as rigidly and proudly as if nothing had happened remains outside the limits of my comprehension in those dark regions where transubstantiation dwells, and my cerebral system would have to be completely reorganized—which, after all, would be a pity—if it had to find room for such wonders. Now there are minds, certainly, which have compartments for such articles of faith along with otherwise quite reasonable loculamenta; I do not understand it, though I hear of such things every day. But does everything have to be understood? I repeat: our conqueror of the world is perhaps the greatest rhetorician."

The loculamenta of Goethe's mind are reflected in the division of his documents into rubrics ("Documents divided into rubrics and filed"). In the Diaries we find rubrics such as: Publica — Privata — Domestica — Religiosa — Oeconomica — Politica — Botanica — Physica — Optica — Chromatica — Osteologica — Graeca et Latina — Orientalia — Sinica — Poetica et Rhetorica — Grammatica — Theatralia — Francofurtensia — Coloniensia — Vinariensia — Gallica — Romana — Novissima — Varia.

Poems that have been disposed provisionally Goethe calls paralipomena. On 2 and 3 May 1822 the Diary reports the sorting and rearranging of the paralipomena. What this means becomes clear from the "Repertorium über die Goethesche Repositur" ["Repertory of Goethe's Repository"] compiled by Kräuter. There we find on page 18 (*Tagebücher* VIII, 371f.):

> Paralipomena. Three capsules 4° obliq.
>
> a. Occasionis. With explanatory notices on their origin.
> b. Lyric poems.
>   Politica.
>   God and the Universe.
>   On Faust.
>   Erotica.
>   Priapeia.
>   Juvenilia.
>   Ex tempore stanzas on Schiller's *Glocke*.
>   Prometheus (twice).
>   Nausikaa. Beginning.
> c. Invectives.
>   Moralia.
>   General.

To keep records of everything—that had become a necessity for Goethe since the end of the century. It shows conspicuously in the letters which he addressed to Schiller from his third journey to Switzerland: "From my own experience I have learned the true state of an attentive traveler and perceived where the error in travel descriptions often lies. No matter what position we may take on our travels we see things from one side only and jump to a conclusion; on the other hand we do see the thing vividly from this side and the conclusion is in a certain sense correct. For that reason I have made files for myself and have had all sorts of published papers such as I just happen to come across—newspapers, weeklies, extracts of sermons, regulations, theater programs, price lists—entered in them; I also file what I see and observe as well as my conclusion of the moment: afterwards I speak about these things in company and advance my opinion, as I then readily perceive how far I am well informed and how far my conclusion coincides with that of well-informed people. I then file the new information and instruction with the other documents, and so materials are obtained which ought to remain sufficiently interesting to me in future as a history of outer and inner events. If, with the knowledge I already have and my practised mind, I continue to take pleasure in this occupation for a while, I can accumulate a great deal" (22 Aug. 1797). Later: "Now in a few days we are to go to the Lake of Lucerne. As we shall be so near, I must contemplate again the great natural scenery which surrounds it; for the rubric of these enormous cliffs must not be missing from my chapters on travel. I have already gathered a couple of stout fascicles of documents in which everything that I have discovered or that has otherwise presented itself to me is to be found noted down or filed, up to now the most variegated stuff in the world . . ." (25 Sept. 1797). The cliffs have become a rubric to be filled in. Nature is entered among the documents.

But poetry too is brought into proximity with administrative affairs. An entry in the Diary notes: "Redaction of the poems, of the museum records" (15 Feb. 1815). Of a purely business nature are annotations like the following: "Acta concerning the commission of Duke Orlow Denisow, to provide him with a tutor, 1813"; "acta concerning the field kitchen, 1814"; "establishment and condition of the art institute *in forma patenti*" (20 Sept. 1816); "completed the engrossment of the vote on the Isis"; "directive to Inspector of Road Works Götze at Jena; commission to invigilate the garden property to be sold at auction" (8 Oct. 1816).

On 14 June 1828 Carl August died on the journey home from Berlin at Graditz in the vicinity of Torgau. Goethe had often submitted official reports to him ("Relation ad Serenissimum"). Now in the form of a report he takes cognizance of his death: "Prepared various expeditions. The chancellor informed me of insertions in the necrology. At noon Dr. Eckermann. My son dined out. Displayed older discovered drawings. Toward evening Prof. Riemer. Before that Major v. Germar, presenting the circumstances of the departure of our most gracious sovereign in an essay which I read over" (4 July 1828). The sculptor David d'Angers' wish to portray Goethe is not immediately granted but taken under advisement as it were for determination. "Sculptor David of Paris was announced, bringing with him letters of recommendation, a number of notebooks and sketchpads, also proposed to execute a bust of me, which was taken *ad referendum*" (23 Aug. 1829). Goethe has long since ceased merely to administer affairs of state. He administers his own existence. And when he lacks the energy to do more, he finds contentment in the well-regulated course of self-administration: "Rose early. Soon lay down again. Awaited the arrival of Privy Councillor Vogel. Once more futile attempt to get up. Meanwhile I continued to work. Wrote, dictated, had fair copies made, so that by evening everything had been satisfactorily accomplished" (22 June 1830).

In the aforementioned letter of 1821 Kräuter graphically depicts the old Goethe's customary procedures as a bureaucrat: "While I happen to be on the subject of these laudable habits of Goethe's, I must add that he is at pains to impart elegance, neatness, and an agreeable appearance to even the most trivial business, and as he does not receive the assistance he expects from those around him, despite their good will, he performs a great deal with his own hands just to see it carried out in his fashion. Thus in letters, whether addressed to a person of high or low estate, I must always try to leave a broad, pleasing margin on all sides, and I earn praise every time I succeed in dividing a letter so that all sides are filled out equally. Everything turns under his hands into a picture. He alone knows how to fold a letter so daintily with the creaser; the inkwell must never be too full, he dips the pen in carefully, not a drop must be allowed to spill; to sand what has been written is strictly forbidden, he would rather stand a while with it next to the stove. With similar elegance he seals all letters, and in order that the folded leaf may fit the envelope precisely, the bookbinder must cut the paper with great accuracy. He keeps a supply of small sheets a square inch in size for the purpose of placing one upon the spot where the seal is to be impressed; by this he wishes to prevent the sealing wax from also sticking to the written page in case the envelope should be somewhat too narrow. And all this is done with so much dexterity, calm, and decorousness that I must admire him even here. As he is in the habit of saying or muttering single words to himself, I usually hear on such occasions his 'Gently now—easy does it,' etc." The Diary entries confirm the care Goethe had for "elegance and neatness." On 30 September 1829: "The Orientalist who was here this morning showing a Chinese manuscript. He pretended to have made out the title, 'History of Famous Generals.' I reproached him for displaying it rolled in paper instead of keeping it safe in a cardboard cover." On 23 March 1830: "I tried to maintain order so far as my circumstances allowed. I used a thicker blotting-pad while sealing a letter, for it often happens that fine volumes of a book are spoiled by careless hot sealing or that a dedication copy is ruined. The same thing happens with the main portions of a letter, where the very word that is most important has already been destroyed in advance. People's careless haste is just too great." We are reminded of the "duly-proportioned speed" which had been recommended in 1785.

But now the process of sealing also becomes a means of eliminating the undesirable. On 29 April 1830 Goethe announces to Zelter: "After swift, strict resolution have abolished all reading of newspapers." This agrees with Soret's report of 6 March 1830: "Goethe va ainsi par lubies. Après avoir lu par plusieurs mois de suite le Globe et le Tems avec la plus grande assiduité, il les a quittés tous deux à la fois depuis environ 15 jours et il accumule les numéros sans les ouvrir; il va même jusqu'à les cacheter pour bien montrer qu'il ne les lit pas . . ." ["Goethe proceeds in this way by caprice. Having for several months in succession read *Le Globe* and *Le Tems* with the greatest assiduity, he abandoned both of them at the same time about 15 days ago and accumulates the numbers without opening them; he even goes so far as to hide them in order to show that he really does not read them . . ."]. Goethe himself to Chancellor von Müller on 24 April 1830: "One must be constantly changing, renewing, rejuvenating oneself so as not to become boring. Only just now some super-Hegel from Berlin[4] sent me his philosophical books; it is like a rattlesnake, you want to flee the damned stuff and look into it anyway. The fellow goes to work with a vengeance, bores mightily into problems which I knew as much about 80 years ago as I do today and about which none of us knows or understands anything. I have now sealed these books up so as not to be tempted to read them again." One asks oneself whether it would not have been easier to destroy the offending newspapers; to donate the books to the Weimar library. Every system of registration implies accumulation and for that reason also requires a method of elimination. Mere "reposition" is not enough. What has become superfluous must be disposed of. And we do in fact find allusions to it in the Diary. Since we still do not

[4] According to Biedermann perhaps H.F.W. Hinrichs.

possess a lexicon of Goethe's vocabulary, I dare not decide, of course, which procedure is meant by the word "dispose" in the following entries: the destruction of documents or the dispatch of business: "Preparations for spending the day in the lower garden. Disposed of several things. Pondered request of Dr. Meyers and his son" (5 May 1830). "Supervisory matters. Thought over the business in hand, also disposed of it. Selected some poetic material for Wendt; to be given to Prof. Riemer. Assigned Kirchner a comparison of the area at Pompeii with a section of Vienna. Disposed of other things" (6 May 1830).

The abolition of newspaper reading by way of a "strict resolution" is a sovereign act that Goethe executes upon himself, in the same way as Carl August condescended to "resolve" himself regarding the conduct of his subjects' lives by issuing a rescript to his "steadfast, worthy and most learned councillors, his dear devoted and loyal ones." Goethe felt constrained to such severe measures against himself because with advancing age he suffered from indecision. The family doctor, Vogel, relates on this subject: "For Goethe, who, apart from his early youth, tended at all times to be deliberate and circumstantial, it became uncommonly difficult in his later years to make decisions. He himself was of the opinion that this peculiar trait, which he actually spoke of as a weakness, derived from the fact that he had never in his life been compelled to act quickly, and he would occasionally praise the profession of a general practitioner on this ground, among others, that it was not permitted the doctor to delay his decisions. On the other hand he could not easily have been surpassed in the perseverance and even audacity with which decisions were carried out once they had been made; at such times, as a man of affairs, he was fond of citing the papal commissarial formula, *non obstantibus quibuscunque,* and in the given case of acting accordingly. If quick decisions were unavoidable, indeed, if the instances demanding them piled up, he would readily become sullen. This was particularly the case when after the decease of his only son he had again to take over the administration of his extensive private affairs, to which he had long grown unaccustomed."

"Faust" too had to pass through the "filtering mechanism of the expeditions." In Frankfurt in 1775 it consisted of scraps of paper which were preserved in a "sack." On 5 May 1798 the announcement is sent to Schiller: "I have carried on my Faust by a good bit. The old, highly confused manuscript which was still in reserve has been transcribed and the parts have been placed one after the other in separate quires according to the numbers of a detailed schema." On 21 July the Diary announces: "Conclusion of the main business"; on 22 July: "The main business accomplished. Final engrossment. Everything fair-copied filed away." In August, finally, the manuscript is sealed and the friends are notified of the event (to Graf Reinhold, 7 September 1831; to Sulpiz Boisserée, 8 September 1831; to Wilhelm v. Humboldt, 1 December 1831). The circle has been run and has closed itself, as we would like to say, to use one of Goethe's favorite formulations.

1951

Fundamental Features
of Goethe's World

++

IN HIS ESSAY on granite (1784) Goethe mentions that this rock was forced to "endure some moments of humiliation" when an Italian naturalist advanced the opinion that it had been artificially produced from a fluid mass by the Egyptians. "But this opinion was soon dispelled, and the dignity of the rock was definitively confirmed by the excellent observations of many travellers." In his *Farbenlehre* Goethe says of red: "This color, on account of its high dignity, we have sometimes called purple. . . ." From the "complete determination of the limbs" he derives the "dignity of the most perfect animals." The principal purpose of all sculpture for him is "to represent the dignity of man within the confines of the human form." Latin and Greek are the languages "in which the worth and dignity of the ancient world have been most purely transmitted." But Goethe can also speak of the "natural dignity of the kingdom of Bohemia," "whose nearly square space, enclosed by mountains, does not branch off on any side. . . . A continent in the midst of the continent."

By juxtaposing these sentences one gains a deeper insight into Goethe's intellectual world than is to be obtained from many a scholarly dissertation. Rock, color, animal, man, history, the formation of the earth—everything is apprehended by the same luminous eye; the highest of its kind, in every area, can be designated by the same word. No one did this before Goethe, no one after him. Goethe's gaze comprehends the totality of nature and of spirit; and when he puts his vision into words, he diffuses a stately radiance over the objects of

73

his regard. By being mirrored in Goethe's mind the world participates in an act of transfiguration. It is purified and elevated. To my knowledge, we have no description of Goethe's language. And yet someone with the proper sense for it could build up Goethe's world for us from his language as ancient sarcophagi have been restored splinter by splinter.

WHILE reading about the "dignity" of granite we were already struck by the peculiar sound of the word. To be sure, this sound was still isolated and uncertain. But with each succeeding example a new sound was added harmonically to the original. The result was a full rich chord. But a chord contains a key, and this is also a key to the spirit.

By established rules we may pass from one key to another; from examples of dignity to the concept of the most dignified men.

In his son's album Goethe wrote:

Halte das Bild der Würdigen fest! Wie leuchtende Sterne
Teilte sie aus die Natur durch den unendlichen Raum.

[Hold fast the image of dignified men! Like luminous stars nature distributed them throughout infinite space.]

If we try to find sounds which will yield a consonance with this distich, we hit upon "the only fine aperçu that still permits us to take pleasure in history: that the authentic men of all ages herald one another's coming, point toward one another, pave the way for one another." As in infinite space so the dignified men are distributed throughout the duration of time. If we examine older states of mankind, "there come to meet us everywhere out of the dark past capable and excellent men, brave, fair, good, and of splendid stature. Mankind's song of praise, which the Godhead loves to hear, is never silent, and we ourselves feel a divine happiness when we perceive the harmonious effusions distributed throughout all times and regions, sometimes in single voices, single choirs, sometimes as a fugue, sometimes in a magnificent full chorus." This is Goethe's philosophy of history. History is not sanctioned as a whole as it is in Ranke. It exists for the sake of the individual.[1] "The slender thread that moves through the sometimes very extensive fabric of knowledge and science, even in the darkest and most confused ages, is drawn by individuals. These, of the best sort, are born in one century as in another, and always maintain the same attitude toward every century in which they occur. That is, they stand in opposition to the crowd, indeed, in conflict with it."

Necessary and constant opposition between the individuals "of the finest kind"—the Aristoi, to use the Greek term—and the spirit of the age ("toward every century"), the "crowd," on the other: an axiom of Goethe's theory of history. The experience of the French Revolution was to confirm it, but did not engender it. Goethe's aversion to the crowd was innate. In 1775 he writes to Lavater: "Yesterday, amidst the tumult of the ceremonies in preparation for the fair I was reminded of Ariosto's saying about the vulgar: deserving of death even before birth." Later, after the death of this friend of his youth, Goethe concluded: "Lavater, as an eminent man interested in general affairs, felt the effect of adverse conditions. He wanted to influence the masses, and so the grimace of the masses rose up dreadfully against him."[2] The masses as a distinct phenomenon were not discovered and analyzed by sociology until around 1900. But Goethe, whom some today would like to stamp a democrat, lays down the maxim: "Nothing is more repugnant than the majority: for it consists of a few energetic leaders, of rogues who accommodate themselves, weaklings who assimilate themselves, and the masses that trundle behind, without having the slightest notion of

[1] "L'histoire du monde est celle de quelques hommes qui ont eu la foi en eux." So Vivekananda according to R. Rolland, *La Vie de Vivekananda.*

[2] Allusion to Lavater's writings against the French Revolution and to his death (he was assassinated by a French soldier).—Translator's note in French edition.

what they want." Goethe's conception of the state and the people was patriarchal and had its basis in the estates of the realm. We cannot revive it, but neither should it be obscured. We also find it in the Chinese sages.

FOR us today it is more important to understand how Goethe's aristocratic individualism affected the conduct of his life. "My chief wish has always been to live with the good men of my time," he writes as a youth (to Gerstenberg, 1773). He calls himself a man "whose supreme happiness is to live with the best men of his time" (to Auguste von Stolberg, 1775). In 1805 the highest value seems to him "to unite one's life with kindred spirits by concerning oneself seriously with what they are doing and accomplishing." In the *Annalen* he notes for 1813: "Here now is the place to state briefly how I sought to deserve the happiness of living as the contemporary of the most eminent men."

Even in so late a poem as *Einlass* [*Admittance*] (1820) the same thought is expressed:

> Mit den Trefflichsten zusammen
> Wirkt ich, bis ich mir erlangt,
> Dass mein Nam in Liebesflammen
> Von den schönsten Herzen prangt.

[I worked in concert with the most excellent until I obtained that my name in flames of love shines in the most beautiful hearts.]

We are not to see in this stanza, as Burdach would have had it, a profession of love for mankind. Nor is it a matter of Humanism to which, as we know, "nothing human" is alien. Goethe draws the circle far more narrowly. He seeks a connection only with the "most excellent"; to anticipate the feelings only of "noble souls" is for him the most desirable of callings.

It is a moral and social ideal of a character peculiar to Goethe himself, firmly adopted in youth, maintained throughout an entire lifetime, and corroborated in poetic utterances that have remained in our memory and accompanied us all our life. The ideal of "uniting one's life with kindred spirits" operates as a need for friendship: enthusiastic and all-embracing in youth, resolutely choosing and loyally preserving in maturity. The cult of friendship (Fritz Jacobi, Lavater), but also the painful experience of its dissolution by death (Schiller) or estrangement (Herder), is part of the substance of Goethe's life. The connection with the "dignified men" of Antiquity, who pointed toward those of the present, heralded them, and paved the way for them, is an additional element. It represents a friendship that transcends, as it were, separation by space and time; it is the piety toward the "fathers"; it is the connection with the chorus of the spirits of Antiquity:

> Doch rufen von drüben
> Die Stimmen der Geister,
> Die Stimmen der Meister:
> Versäumt nicht, zu üben
> Die Kräfte des Guten!

[Yet from the beyond call the voices of the spirits,
the voices of the masters: do not neglect to exercise
the forces of good!]

Goethe had passed his middle sixties when, in growing isolation, he lamented the fathers and friends who had been reft from him:

> An dem öden Strand des Lebens
> Wo sich Dün auf Düne häuft,
> Wo der Sturm im Finstern träuft,
> Setze dir ein Ziel des Strebens.

> Unter schon verloschnen Siegeln
> Tausend Väter hingestreckt,
> Ach! von neuen, frischen Hügeln
> Freund an Freunden überdeckt.

[On the barren shore of life, where dune is piled
upon dune, where the storm rages in darkness, set a
goal to your striving. Beneath seals already effaced,
a thousand fathers lie buried, and alas, new fresh
mounds cover friend after friend.]

But there remains the legacy of faithful work with "the un-
troubled ones." This is a concept from the *Farbenlehre*.
It refers to spirits in whom light has triumphed over darkness
and serene clarity over confusion. And there remains the
loyal hope in a reunion:

> Hast du so dich abgefunden,
> Werde Nacht und Äther klar,
> Und der ewgen Sterne Schar
> Deute dir belebte Stunden,
> Wo du hier mit Ungetrübten,
> Treulich wirkend, gern verweilst
> Und auch treulich den geliebten
> Ewigen entgegeneilst.

[When you have thus resigned yourself, may night
and ether grow clear, and the eternal host of stars
show you vivid hours; here, where among untrou-
bled spirits, faithfully working, you delight to
abide, and, also faithfully, hasten toward the beloved eternal ones.]

The uniting of his life with a realm of spirits outside of time
is a trait that emerges more and more strongly in Goethe's old
age. Speaking to himself he says:

> Du hast getollt zu deiner Zeit mit wilden
> Dämonisch genialen jungen Scharen,
> Dann sachte schlossest du von Jahr zu Jahren
> Dich näher an die Weisen, Göttlich-Milden.

[You reveled in your day with wild demonic youths
of genius; then gradually, year by year, you asso-

ciated yourself more closely with the sages, the divinely-mild.]

And even more decisively:

> Teilnehmend führen gute Geister,
> Gelinde leitend höchste Meister
> Zu dem, der alles schafft und schuf.

[Sympathetically, good spirits lead us, gently the highest masters guide us to Him who creates and created all things.]

Across vast distances of space and time the German poet knows that his place is in this realm of the masters. In every age, in every historical epoch they work in silence, removed from the crowd but bound in companionship to one another. Consequently, one of Goethe's highest maxims reads:

> Du prüfst das allgemeine Walten,
> Es wird nach seiner Weise schalten,
> Geselle dich zur kleinsten Schar.

[You consider the world in general, it will direct things in its own way, associate yourself with the smallest number.]

The concept of the smallest number must not be equated with the concept of the elite in modern sociology and theories of history. An elite is a leading minority, whether it operates as "creative" or "dominant" (Toynbee). Its function is to influence the social body either through inspiration or through decisive action. This is precisely the influence that Goethe did not want. The world in general will and may "direct things in its own way." One should leave it to its devices.[3]

[3] "What is truly reasonable and adequate is really the inheritance of a few individuals who carry on their work in silence" (to Zelter, 4 March 1829). "As the world does these days, one must constantly say to oneself and repeat again and again: that there have been and

Truth is for the few. It is that which binds them to one another beyond all the ages. It resembles a golden chain wound through the millennia. The noble souls hand it on to one another. Now it is our turn to seize it:

> Das Wahre war schon längst gefunden,
> Hat edle Geisterschaft verbunden;
> Das alte Wahre, fass es an!

[The truth has long since been discovered, it has united companies of noble spirits; the age-old truth —lay hold of it!]

Scarcely any idea contradicts modern opinion so fundamentally as that the truth was already discovered thousands of years ago. Since Goethe's death dozens, nay, hundreds of new philosophical and poetic revelations have been bestowed on us. In the light of this Goethean principle, how are they to be judged? This question, which could undoubtedly be answered, shall only be glanced at here. The more important matter is to understand the meaning of Goethe's theory of truth. He did not develop it anywhere explicitly; we shall see why not. But he gives us a number of hints. "The main thing," he says to Eckermann (16 December 1828) is to have a soul that loves truth and is receptive to it wherever it may be found. Moreover, the world is now so old and so many important men have lived and thought for thousands of years that there is little new to be discovered or said."

In saying this he was thinking of his theory of colors, which he found prefigured in Plato and Leonardo. But the Eternism of truth (if I may be allowed this abbreviation) is as valid in art as in science. It is not a form of archaism: "The old is not classical because it is old, but because it is strong, fresh,

---

will be capable men, and to such must be granted a good word, expressed in writing and left behind on paper. That is the community of saints that we profess. With my lips I am but seldom able to utter something true and fundamental; people usually hear something other than what I say, and I suppose that it is just as well" (to Zelter, 18 June 1831).

cheerful, and healthy" (to Eckermann, 2 April 1829). But what is valid for art and science must hold even more strongly for the knowledge of divine matters. In this sense the belief in an eternal revelation may be ascribed to Goethe. Were I asked to indicate its contents, I should choose the following text: "Man must be capable of elevating himself to the highest form of reason if he wishes to come in contact with the Divine, which manifests itself in physical as in moral archetypes (*Urphänomene*), concealing itself behind them even as they emanate from it. The Divine, however, is active in living matter, not in dead; it is in the changing and developing, not in what has changed and congealed. That is also why reason, as it tends toward the Divine, deals only with what is vital and developing; but the understanding deals with what has already developed and congealed in order to make use of it" (to Eckermann, 13 February 1829).

I refrain from commenting on this text. Only one maxim, which elucidates it, may be added: "Light and spirit, the former in the physical realm, the latter in the moral, are the highest conceivable indivisible energies." Form as well as content of this utterance deserve attention. It is not an aphorism or a fragment of thought; nor is it a philosophical reflection or scientific thesis. It is a wisdom-saying which recalls those of the pre-Socratics. A prospect is opened upon two of the archetypal phenomena in which, as we heard, the Divine reveals itself. Such sentences are beyond philosophy. The specifically Goethean element is the linking of the physical with the moral, the simultaneous contemplation of God and the world, to use another of Goethe's formulas that stem from Antiquity. What Goethe intuits as the highest truth he does not fit into a system. He "stablishes" it, to use one of his favorite words. He sets it before us in a concise, visionary utterance.

GOETHE's theory of truth has been alluded to. But every theory of truth must likewise contain a theory of error. Where do the errors of mankind come from? Once more it is

Goethe's theory of light and color that gives us the answer. What is light? "One of the original God-created powers and virtues, which strives to represent its image in matter." And what are colors? "Colors are the actions of light, its actions and sufferings." The sufferings of light consist in its becoming troubled or dark. In the physical sphere this is a necessity, but it remains a form of suffering nonetheless. In the moral sphere we find the same phenomenon. Here too it is necessary; here too it remains a form of suffering. But it takes place in the realm of spirit, where freedom and necessity meet. And how is it to be confronted? By handing down the truth.

"If only men did not turn the right upside down, once it has been found, and darken it, I should be content; for mankind has a need for something positive which should be handed down to it from generation to generation, and it would be a very good thing if the positive were also the right and the true" (to Eckermann, 1 February 1827). Goethe's theory of tradition, so far as I can see, has never been properly appreciated. Amid the confusions of the present it might well be the most important part of his message. Goethe calls "tradition" "those revered values by which the remote is bound, the torn made whole." Within the tradition he distinguishes three main "masses": the Bible, Plato, and Aristotle.

Imperilment, destruction, denial of tradition are events to which the history of our civilization testifies again and again. Goethe encountered them in the barbarism of the early Middle Ages, in the iconoclastic riots, in the literary "sansculottism" which he saw follow on the heels of the political sansculottism of the French. Finally, in what he called the "graphoclastic rage," and described as follows: "Nothing that has been said heretofore is to be held valid, everything that once was wise is to be regarded as foolish, that which was salutary as harmful, that which for a long time proved beneficial as by now actually a hindrance." This is, were I to apply the expression of a contemporary philosopher, "the intellectual situation of the age," of our age. It is the confusion of the epoch that begins with Rousseau and continues up until the present.

The remedy could only lie in a resumption of tradition. In Goethe's youth the original geniuses had declared war on a tradition that had become ossified. Tradition and originality seemed mutually exclusive. But there is a balance between them. Goethe suggests it in a little-known passage, when he says the happiest man would be one "who has the persistence, will, and self-abnegation to acquaint himself thoroughly with the tradition while retaining enough strength and courage to develop his original nature independently and to treat the divers assimilated elements in his own way." Originality on the firm basis of tradition: it is attested in Dante, in Shakespeare, in Racine, in Goethe himself. In our own day in Hofmannsthal. It ripens like a fruit for the poet and for the sage. And only for them.

THE MAN who is attached to tradition and defends it is always unpopular. I need only to mention the grotesque misjudgments of Hofmannsthal that have been current for the last twenty years. But the "supremely reasonable thinker" will not allow himself "to be misled by one or two decades" (Goethe, 1827). Goethe's sense of time soared over lustra, decades, centuries, millennia. He anticipated a relation to time which in our own day has been grounded philosophically by Toynbee. That is why he thought it imperative that the past "should be preserved from complete extinction, especially in modern times, when one day paints over the next, carelessly covering splendor with triviality, as though that were the way it had to be." His opinion of the claims of the moment was very low. He was independent of time, and as unwilling to acknowledge the dictatorship of the Zeitgeist—which people were trying to interpret even in his day—as we are willing to have it dictated to us by the literary men of our own. The follies of the day, he maintained, should be "opposed by vast masses of universal history."

These were not the convictions to win him favor. He was aware of it, but to the loyal Eckermann he had to say so explicitly: "My dear child, I am going to confide something to you that will help you in many present difficulties and that will stand you in good stead for the rest of your life. My things cannot become popular; anyone who supposes they can and works to make them so is in error. They are not written for the masses, but only for individuals who have similar desires and aims and who are tending in a similar direction" (11 October 1828).

Max Scheler, in his *Ethics*, endeavored to set up an ontological scale of "personal embodiments of value" or "models"; the sole philosopher, to my knowledge, to make such an attempt, which is a pity. For it would be illuminating and salutary for the self-comprehension of our civilization to know the nature of the saint, the sage, the poet, the thinker, the hero, and the order of value to which he is to be assigned. But even if we had such a scheme of values, it would be difficult to fit Goethe into it. He is a poet of the highest rank, but he lacks Dante's perfection, Shakespeare's vital fullness. He is a thinker and a sage, but he is not a philosopher. I shall not pursue these indications. Let it remain undecided whether this *via negationis*, through comparison with other great minds, could lead us to a clearer comprehension of Goethe's essence. At all events I find in him one essential trait not borne by any of the geniuses of our culture: his resistance to the general public; his need to exist only for a few or even to go in quest of secrecy. I have cited his admonitory words to Eckermann regarding popularity. Another saying from his later life is even more significant: "In the aesthetic and moral field too it is becoming the fashion to contend and work against me. I know pretty well where it comes from and where it is going, its why and wherefore, but I do not explain myself further in the matter. The friends I lived with will know how to uphold me and my memory." This note is struck again and again: "Even to this day I live in a world about which I can communicate something only to a few" (1817). —"Everything I really know I have learned from myself." —"Stones are mute teachers, they render the observer silent, and the best lesson to be learned from them is not to communicate."

We shall not have a correct view of Goethe until we recognize the mystery that invests his person like an aura.

THERE is a cosmopolitan Goethe who studies the plans for the Panama Canal and has himself informed of the method of electing a president in the United States or the supplying of drinking-water to Constantinople. The "facilities of communication" that Europe enjoyed around 1820 seem to him a physical symbol for the rise of a world literature. He studies world history and can bestow praise upon Schlosser's *Universalhistorischer Übersicht* [*Survey of Universal History*] because he himself "has devoted his entire life to such reflections." The hemispheres of nature and history conjoin in his *globus intellectualis*.

> Ich bin Weltbewohner,
> Bin Weimaraner,

[I am a citizen of the world, a citizen of Weimar]

he could say of himself. The house on the Frauenplan in Weimar is arranged with such a twofold existence in view. In front are the reception rooms in which Goethe exercises his representative functions: "In black clothing decorated with a silver star, he strode in with his erect carriage, bidding a friendly welcome to the visitors who bowed low before him" (Biedermann IV, 33). But his study and bedroom are located toward the back, separated from the rest of the house. There he stands at his desk in his long, open dressing gown. Once a young friend of the household ventures in, because upstairs the guests are waiting for tea. "What does the young miss want," he grumbles. . . . "Do you imagine, little girl, that I run to everyone who waits? What would become of that there?" and so saying he pointed to the open sheets of paper. "When I am dead there won't be anyone to do it. Go upstairs and tell that to the company! . . . An old man who wants to go on working cannot suit his mood to please everyone; if he does, he will not please posterity at all." That is the solitary Goethe, turned toward his inner world.

For the public, Goethe conducts his official duties, for the court he composes ceremonial pieces, for the German stage his dramas. His novels, his autobiographical works, his writings on art and literature are directed toward the outer circle. But the *Geheimnisse* [*The Mysteries*], *Pandora*, the *Divan*, the *Maximen und Reflexionen* belong to an inner circle whose center eludes our view:

> Niemand soll und wird es schauen,
> Was einander wir vertraut:
> Denn auf Schweigen und Vertrauen
> Ist der Tempel aufgebaut.

> [No one must or will see what we have confided to each other: for on silence and mutual confidence is the temple built.]

The lines are from 1816. They are presumably the most solemn indication of the arcane discipline that fences off Goethe's innermost region. For parallels to it in cultural history, we are led back to the ancient mysteries.[4] Goethe shares with them even the moment of horror that may not be revealed. It is hinted at in the quatrain *Genius, die Büste der Natur enthüllend* [*A Genius, unveiling the bust of nature*]:

> Bleibe das Geheimnis teuer!
> Lass den Augen nicht gelüsten!
> Sphinx-Natur, ein Ungeheur,
> Schreckt sie dich mit hundert Brüsten.[5]

---

[4] Goethe applies to *Faust II* the motto: *Eleusis servat quod ostendat revisentibus* (to Iken, 27 September 1827).

[5] A representation of the Near Eastern mother goddess, the so-called Artemis Ephesia, is intended. In H. Thiersch's *Artemis Ephesia* (1935), her iconography can be followed up into the eighteenth century. Rauch too, if I remember correctly, created a statuette of "Nature" after this type.

[Let the secret remain precious to you! Let your
eyes not covet it! Nature the Sphinx, a monster,
affrights you with her hundreds of breasts.]

IF THE consecration of the initiate into the Eleusinian
mysteries presents one analogy to Goethe's esotericism, another may be found in the figure of the magician Merlin, with
whom Goethe was familiar from Ariosto. He is evoked as
early as the *Cophtisches Lied* [*Coptic Song*] (1788):

> Merlin der Alte, im leuchtenden Grabe,
> Wie ich als Jüngling gesehen ihn habe. . . .

[Merlin the Old, in his shining tomb, as I saw him
when I was a boy. . . .]

Thirty years later, to Chancellor von Müller: "Let me hasten,
children, let me hasten alone to my rocks; for after such discourse it befits the old Merlin to renew his friendship with the
primal elements" (29 April 1818). In this conversation in
Dornburg, Goethe had shown himself unusually communica-
tive. To the thinker who casts his eye over thousands of years,
he had said, certain general formulas are revealed which have
moved men from the very beginning with magic force. They
are the mysterious parting-gift that a higher power grants to
our life.[6] Of course they may often be obscured and mixed
with impurities. But their original significance emerges again
and again, "and from such formulas the attentive observer
constructs for himself an alphabet of the universal spirit." It
might be tempting to supplement these indications (to "supply" them, as Goethe liked to say) and associate them with
other of Goethe's statements. But how easily might we go
astray in the attempt! How little we know of Goethe's most
secret thoughts! Let us be content if we understand that "after
such discourse" Goethe hid behind the mask of Merlin in
order to "renew his friendship with the primal elements."
Chancellor Müller concludes his report with the words: "For

[6] In other words, what I have called "eternal revelation."

a long time we followed him cheerfully with our gaze as he solemnly descended into the valley, wrapped in his long gray overcoat, stopping now and then at this or that rock, or again at certain plants, and tapping the former with his mineralogical hammer. From the mountains longer shadows were already falling, into which he disappeared from our view like a ghost."

As late as 1830 Goethe remarks in a letter to Zelter that they stood at opposite ends of the social world. Zelter had been swallowed up in the whirligig of the populous imperial city of Berlin; "while I, lonely, like Merlin from his shining tomb, let my own echo be heard tranquilly and occasionally near by, and probably also afar." We see how a symbolic figure accompanies Goethe's thought for more than five decades because he perceives in it an aspect of himself. Merlin is the profoundly significant antitype to Faust. Faust is the man who is always active and avid, whom nothing can satisfy. He will never say to the moment:

> Verweile doch, du bist so schön.

> [Stay yet awhile, you are so fair.]

Goethe's late wisdom is the opposite pole to Faust's striving:

> Geniesse mässig Füll und Segen;
> Vernunft sei überall zugegen,
> Wo Leben sich des Lebens freut.
> Dann ist Vergangenheit beständig,
> Das Künftige voraus lebendig,
> Der Augenblick ist Ewigkeit.

[Enjoy abundance and blessing in moderation; let reason be at all times present where life delights in life. Then the past is enduring, the future alive in advance, the moment is eternity.]

TODAY, people are asking whether Goethe's view of the world can still be our own. They point out that we are living through a crisis in the very foundations of our culture. Consequently,

Goethe is out of date, for reasons that philosophy believes it can specify. I doubt whether philosophy is competent to do so. For philosophy thereby enters areas that are alien to it: history and art. When I examine what modern philosophers say about history, I find in every case that they "construct" (according to the exigencies of their philosophy, of course, and upon an insufficient basis of fact). Their constructions are founded upon borrowings made from outmoded presentations of history. That is why I am not convinced when philosophers call Goethe in question on the grounds of a "diagnosis of the age." Plato, Aristotle, Descartes, Leibniz, Kant made no such diagnoses. Their philosophies were developed out of the subject, not out of the situation. Today, the latter practice seems to be necessary. That would imply a change in the structure of philosophy. At present, however, philosophy resembles a war of all against all. It seems doubtful whether out of this anarchy of first principles a new culture can be evolved.

But of course everyone, philosopher or no, has a perfect right to reject Goethe on some grounds or other. I believe that I have made it abundantly clear that Goethe never pretended to be a teacher for everyone. He wanted to have an effect on a few friends, on kindred souls and spirits. There has never been a unanimous image of Goethe and there cannot be one today. But it may indeed be asked, what the present image of Goethe can be to his friends, as compared with that of previous anniversaries.

ON THIS a few more indications. It is a notable fact that since Goethe our world has brought forth no more classics. Poets like Hugo and Whitman do not fill out the dimensions. The great problematical writers like Dostoevski and Nietzsche do not do so for other reasons. Whether a classic is still possible in a declining civilization is questionable. All our experience speaks against it. In that case Goethe would be the last classic of Europe as Virgil was the last classic of Rome. A classic can never be replaced except by a new classic, who will then be of an entirely different type. We shall not live to see it. The last classic at any given time need not be greater than his predecessors. Shakespeare was not greater than Dante. The great classics can be separated by large expanses of time —between Virgil and Dante there are thirteen hundred years. So long did it take the peoples of northern Europe not only to assimilate the two Mediterranean traditions—the pagan-antique and the Christian—but to be able to express what they had absorbed in their own language. The bond between Virgil and Dante, however, was their share in this historical substance. In the fullness and depth of this substance Shakespeare and Goethe also have their roots.

Dante, Shakespeare, Goethe: these three move close together today. Each of them—and each in his own way—can be viewed as a self-concentration of the western mind in one person. This totalization of tradition in an original creation is successful for the last time in Goethe. But Europe's intellectual foundations were even then being shaken by the first earthquakes. Cracks were beginning to appear in the mass of tradition. Goethe created a universal, positive oeuvre in an era of incipient disintegration. That is why this oeuvre sometimes shows rifts, sometimes too a certain pallor. This may also account for much that is problematical in Goethe's relation to his profession as a writer, a theme which would have to be pursued on a separate occasion. Finally, it may account for his sensitivity toward every sort of opaqueness and obscurity—which, to be sure, he was able to transform by taking the perplexities of the human condition as the subject of his poetry. He felt all these resistances—and not least, "the resistance of the dull world." That at any rate is one of the motives which, as the years advanced, drove him more and more to seek the tiny "company of saints," even if he did not withdraw from external representation. Goethe's esotericism may perhaps be understood as a reaction to the age of the masses, which was then beginning.

But if Goethe is the final self-concentration of the western mind in a great individual, it means that he is something more and something other than a German poet. He is solidary with the spiritual heritage of Europe. He stands in the line of Homer, Sophocles, Plato, Aristotle, Virgil, Dante, and Shakespeare. The consciousness of his place in this series is very much alive in him. His piety toward the "fathers," his alliance with the "dignified men" of old and with the chorus of the spirits of the past, his conviction that there is a realm of the "Masters," with whom he feels he belongs—this most characteristic and remarkable trait of his form of mind acquires its deeper sense only now. This consciousness of solidarity through the millennia Shakespeare could not have had, Dante only within the Latin tradition. To Goethe it was given as a legitimation and corroboration of his mission. It is a sign, so to speak, from the "alphabet of the universal spirit." It is the seal of succession. Was Goethe the last in this line? For those who venerate him as a master that would only increase his importance.

Goethe described himself on occasion as an "epigone poet." "We epigone poets must revere the legacy of our ancestors—Homer, Hesiod, *et al.*—as the authentic canonical books; we bow before these men whom the Holy Spirit has inspired and dare not ask, whence or whither" (to Creuzer, 1817). This attitude can today be the one that a "small number" adopts toward Goethe.

1949

Friedrich Schlegel
and France

✦✦✦

WE HAVE serious amends to make to Friedrich Schlegel, for no great author of our golden age has been so misunderstood, indeed so malevolently maligned as he, not only in his own lifetime, but also, curiously, for long afterwards, in fact even to the present day. It is distressing and almost incomprehensible how tenaciously prejudices and misjudgments continue to flourish in the scholarship of our German universities. And at bottom Friedrich Schlegel has always been judged from the musty atmosphere of the study. The famous Leipzig philologist Gottfried Herrmann set the tone as early as 1796, when he designated the young Friedrich Schlegel as *homo omnium pessimus*,[1] i.e., as an out-and-out scoundrel, in a Latin letter to his friend Volkmann. What was it that so incensed the German professors against Friedrich Schlegel? Why did they treat him as a naughty student who does nothing but make trouble?[2]

If one examines the reproaches directed at Friedrich Schlegel in the usual literary histories,[3] one ends up with a

[1] Heinrich Finke, *Über Friedrich und Dorothea Schlegel* (Cologne, 1918), p. 8.

[2] Schlegel's biographer Muncker is able to report that Friedrich Schlegel was "awarded the doctor's degree without taking the oral examination" in Jena in 1800 (*Allgemeine deutsche Biographie* 33, 737). Is this meant to cast suspicion on Schlegel? What do the Jena University documents say?

[3] Let us gratefully mention the name of Josef Körner, who for decades has been furthering the study of Schlegel through most valuable articles. Cf. most recently his *Marginalien* (Frankfurt, 1950).

strange collection. First of all, he is reproached because he was lazy; second, because he was impudent, for he defended laziness in writing and had written in praise of idleness. To this must be added the fact that he found Schiller's poem *Die Glocke* ludicrous and, what is more, said so in print. Furthermore, Friedrich Schlegel was immoral. The combination of idleness and insolence alone would have been proof sufficient of this. Now, however, the same author had also presumed to write a novel which extolled the joys of love. For this the custodians of German literature took him severely to task. But there is still worse to come. Friedrich Schlegel was quite simply an epicure. He liked to eat and drink and in so doing acquired a comfortable corpulence. This fact, too, is exploited to his disadvantage. Others are permitted to get fat without their continuing to be harassed for it even after death. It is well known that in some cultures a certain embonpoint is considered to be a sign of holiness. Even St. Thomas was said to have been corpulent. That Friedrich Schlegel, however, had a tendency towards portliness is generally labeled "turning to fat," and the unfavorable overtones of this term are supposed to indicate that it was not just a matter of a physical process, but of a mental one as well. Strangest of all, many critics associate with this reproach the other one, that Friedrich Schlegel, together with his wife, was converted to Catholicism at the age of thirty-four. The same people for whom Schlegel is too immoral and insolent are not pleased when he becomes respectable and pious.

On the whole, the judgment on Friedrich Schlegel has until now been shaped by that moral indignation which was produced in supervisors' conferences of the old style. But a total presentation and a new evaluation are still lacking. I am convinced that they will produce a fundamental change in his image and bring to the fore much that has hitherto been overlooked.

This is also true of his significance for Romance studies. Until now only his relation to the Romance Middle Ages has been taken into account, while the interest that he showed from the very beginning in contemporary manifestations of the French mind has been overlooked. In the romantic years of his youth he already quotes Diderot and reviews Condorcet's philosophy of history. And this involvement in the living France remained with him throughout his life and led to the formulation of some highly interesting problems. It is precisely in this ability to take up both the Middle Ages and the modern era, and to work on both, the oldest and the most topical at the same time, that I see his special place and importance. There is hardly an area in the Romania with which Friedrich Schlegel did not at some time concern himself. Without documenting this in detail, I would nonetheless like to point out that he was the first to recognize the significance of Provençal language and literature, and that he thought about doing extensive research in this field. That was in the year 1803, that is to say, thirteen years before the first text-edition of the songs of the troubadours by the Frenchman Raynouard, and more than twenty years before Friedrich Diez's epoch-making books about the life and art of the troubadours.

In the years 1803 and 1804 Schlegel had gone to Paris for his studies, and there, in this short period, the notorious idler had not only learned Persian and Sanskrit, but had also found time to edit a periodical and to publish articles in it about the Provençal manuscripts in the Paris libraries.

Paris was at that time a common center of attraction for German intellectuals. We find there Wilhelm and Alexander von Humboldt, Heinrich von Kleist, Achim von Arnim, and many other high-sounding names. But so far as I can see, Friedrich Schlegel is—next to W. von Humboldt—the only one for whom this personal, living contact with France became the object of conscious reflection. The periodical *Europa*, which he edited from Paris, opened with a report about his journey. Here we find highly interesting reflections on the national character of France and Germany and on the historical destiny of the two countries. During this trip Schlegel also came in contact with the Rhine, and at the sight of the regal stream wrote down a few phrases which can again seem peculiarly apt to us today: "Here would be the place," he writes, "where a world could come together and from here it could be surveyed and ruled, if a constricting barrier did not surround the so-called capital, but if, instead of the unnatural natural boundary and the pitifully rent unity of states and nations, a chain of fortresses, cities, and villages the length of the magnificent stream formed a new whole and a larger city, as it were, as the venerated center of a happy part of the world." Schlegel crossed the Rhine and continued his journey to Paris.

His mental attitude toward Paris and France was at that time quite ambiguous. He came from the Germany of Kant and Fichte, which was also the Germany of Goethe and Novalis. As an idealist philosopher and as a Romantic he could justifiably feel that he was in possession of an intellectual standpoint against which the France of the time had nothing significant to set. To be sure, he found much that attracted him, much that was charming and challenging. He gratefully made use of the scholarly and artistic treasures of the capital, he took delight in the bright lights of the metropolis and in the various amenities of life.[4] "The menagerie here is also very nice," he wrote to his brother; "the elephant in particular imbued me with much respect and sympathy. Besides myself, he is unquestionably the one who feels least at home here." Friedrich Schlegel certainly did not feel at home. Here on foreign soil he became intensely aware of his Germanness and of the intellectual stamp he had received from his fatherland. He felt, as he wrote, that he was "an idealist and poet in partibus infidelium." No doubt every young German who comes to Paris for the first time, if it is not merely for a hurried tour but to study and live there, has experienced this condition of homelessness and intellectual foreignness. And what makes Friedrich Schlegel's sojourn in Paris so fruit-

[4] Cf. his letter to Caroline Paulus (*Briefe von Dorothea und Friedr. Schlegel an die Familie Paulus*, ed. Rudolf Unger [1913], p. 27).

ful is precisely this necessity he felt from the very beginning for formulating and clarifying his inner relationship to France as a whole. We shall see that this process continued and expressed itself productively in his works throughout his life.

One of the first intellectual discoveries Friedrich Schlegel made in Paris was his observation that French literature looks quite different when seen from the perspective of Paris than it does from Germany.[5] What the Germans primarily esteem it for are "the products of *esprit*, in which the native cheerfulness of the French character shows itself in its finest flowering as the culture of wit." Was he referring to popular products of satire and comedy that are forgotten today? We do not know. But the following observation is interesting: "these works of wit so peculiar to the French are the ones least regarded and valued by the French themselves." What strikes Schlegel is the importance of French tragedy and its immense influence, "which one can only learn to appreciate fully in Paris." For it was at just that time that the great actor Talma was reviving the tragic heroes of the French stage.

As far as contemporary French philosophy is concerned, Schlegel mentions Materialism as a youthfully vigorous error, and also Ideology, that is to say, the late form of French Enlightenment philosophy, characteristic of the turn of the nineteenth century. He grants them validity at their own level, but from the standpoint of German Idealism this level quite rightly seems primitive to him. The Ideologists take consciousness "at a disproportionately lower power" than do the Idealists.

The conclusion Friedrich Schlegel draws from these observations is that there is a need for a revision of the German judgment of French literature and of France in general. Expressed in his language, this means that the Germans ought "to put themselves on a philosophical footing with this nation" instead of "a polemical one." France's literature and philosophy especially are "a phenomenon to be grasped and

---

[5] *Re* the following: *A. W. und Fr. Schlegel, in Auswahl herausgegeben von Oskar Walzel* ("Kürschners Deutsche Nationalliteratur," 143), pp. 311ff.

explained in its total environment and living influence." He sees his task as consisting "in an apology, i.e., a clarification . . . to be directed against the altogether too great disdain for French literature prevalent in Germany, and one not coupled with the requisite knowledge of the subject." This continues to be the typical insight with which every real attempt at mediation between France and Germany has begun.

At that time there were two great historical and intellectual phenomena of French culture which a German thinker was bound to encounter and with which he had to come to terms. These were the Classicism of the seventeenth century and the Enlightenment philosophy of the eighteenth century. The German mind had wrestled with these two manifestations, but whereas many of the best Germans remained at the stage of one-sided criticism or sterile negation, Friedrich Schlegel alone was able, in the course of his development, to go beyond mere contrast, beyond the mere contradiction between the German and French cultural ideals, and to rise to a higher level of insight. But this was possible only because through his residence in France he had experienced the conflict of vital principles and intellectual worlds in his own person, so to speak, or better still, in his own soul. The experience he had of France in 1803, divided and contradictory as it still was, was nonetheless the necessary presupposition for his later thinking and writing.

In those years he already draws from his problematical situation the one positive and productive conclusion with which every more searching study of France by a German begins: it is to communicate and convey French cultural values to the German public. To this task the periodical I have already mentioned, and whose very title *Europa* reveals such a significant meaning, is essentially dedicated. For in this— that in Paris and through France a leading German intellectual should be stirred to reflections about the concept of Europe, a concept to which Novalis had not long before given such profound meaning—we may indeed see an historical necessity. "The true Europe has yet to come into being,"

Friedrich Schlegel writes. Even today we have not yet advanced beyond this point.

When one leafs through the two volumes of this short-lived periodical, one finds categories such as: *German Foreigners in Paris—The Paris Art Exhibition—News from Paris—The Latest Works of the Parisian Philologists—The State of Music in Paris—Discussion Concerning the Most Recent Novels by Frenchwomen*—finally also: *Good Advice for Travelers.* The contemporary character of the periodical, its effort at lively and many-sided reportage and communication, is clearly expressed in such titles. But we also find in it articles and reports of an altogether different sort, for example, the attempt at a verse translation of Racine, with a very interesting preface—both by Friedrich Schlegel himself (cf. *Aus Schleiermachers Leben* 3, 369). This was in the year 1803, and in this context one must now recall that Racine, the peak and flower of French Classicism, was the subject of ever-renewed debate from Lessing to Victor Hugo. Racine's dramatic work is, so to speak, the geometrical locus for the philosophical and critical endeavors to determine what poetry is or ought to be. And closely related to this vast problem of evaluation, which is not yet settled today, is a second problem, namely, the dispute between Classicism and Romanticism. The situation is complicated even further by the fact that both of these concepts, already so ambiguous in themselves, have been used in such different contexts in France and in Germany. In the *Europa* of 1803 Racine is still hedged about with many reservations and a clear critical estimate is still avoided. Nevertheless, his significance is established. The counterblast came in 1807, in an article by August Wilhelm Schlegel. He measured Racine by Euripides, and was therefore bound to remain stuck in biased negation. However, August Wilhelm, probably under the influence of Mme. de Staël, had thereby given support to the development of French Romanticism and its dramatic forms. I introduce this only as an example of how diversely entangled and intertwined were the paths of poetry and criticism in both of these countries at that time. This was not to be the last word on Racine.

At the end of April 1804 Friedrich Schlegel left Paris, and did so in the company of three young men from Cologne with whom he had become acquainted and whom he had taken into his house. They were the two Boisserée brothers and Johann Baptist Bertram. The Boisserées had invited Friedrich Schlegel to come to Cologne, and in so doing initiated a significant change in his life. Friedrich and Dorothea Schlegel's Cologne period lasted from 1804 to the end of April 1808. Here they took the decisive step of changing confession: a step which should not be regarded as a disavowal but rather as a further stage, philosophically and psychologically quite comprehensible, in Friedrich Schlegel's development. Here Friedrich Schlegel worked on the abundant and varied scholarly material that he had gathered in Paris. Here he also delved deeply into the spirit of German architecture and painting of the past, and nothing is more certain than that his residence in Cologne, however frequently disturbed by external cares and disappointments, was of decisive significance in the formation of the philosophical outlook of his maturity. In later years he was appointed councillor to the Austrian legation to the Federal Council of all the German states in Frankfurt and from here, together with his brother, he once again visited Cologne[6] and greeted old friends. A draught of "excellent *Ahrbleichert*" at Christian Bertram's seems to have been, according to Friedrich's letters, a high point of the visit.

A fresh impetus to the development of Schlegel's relation to French literature was provided from without by the lectures which Adam Müller delivered in Dresden in 1805, *Vorlesungen über die deutsche Wissenschaft und Literatur*. Adam Müller too is one of the great unrecognized men of the German intellectual heritage. For almost a hundred years his writings were well-nigh forgotten, and people only began to

[6] Beginning of June, 1818.

99

take up and analyze his works again right after the First World War. That effort has fallen into oblivion again today. The lectures of 1805 are a classic in the fullest sense of the word and in many respects. Josef Nadler could quite rightly designate their author as the first modern literary historian. His views and insights have a fullness and depth that have not yet come near to being exhausted. For our context these lectures are significant because in them Friedrich Schlegel's critical writings are seen for the first time as a historical fact and are integrated into the total corpus of German criticism. Lessing and Friedrich Schlegel are for Adam Müller the twin lodestars of German criticism. And he is correct in saying of both of them that they found themselves "in unyielding opposition to the principles of French poetics and rhetoric." In Friedrich Schlegel's critical feat Müller sees nothing less than a revolution that constitutes a fruitful, significant stage of development.

But at the same time he calls Schlegel's view of literature an unhistorical one. He objects to the fact that only the Greeks and the Minnesingers, Shakespeare and the great Spaniards are to be considered the representatives of true poetry. In Schlegel's position he sees a romantic bias which is at bottom no less inadequate than the French theory of literature attacked by Schlegel. He does not regard mere polemical contradiction as a definitive critical achievement. He demands a higher criticism, the "truly German conciliatory criticism," as he says, "which is not only able to contend, but to mediate in the midst of the contest itself." Mediation was indeed for him one of the fundamental determinants of the German mind, and this mediation was also supposed to prove its validity in assessing the claims of rival historical constructions and aesthetic systems. It is characteristic that in this connection he turns back to Racine. Polemic—that was one of the young Friedrich Schlegel's favorite words. Adam Müller opposed an irenic attitude to this polemical temper. Although Adam Müller admits that he "would gladly give up French literature with all its dependencies" for that other realm of poetry that Romantic criticism had staked out, he nonetheless demands the same historical right for the century of Louis XIV as for that of Pericles. And thus is evident once more the central significance that the task of understanding France has had for the development of the German self-consciousness.

The opposition to Friedrich Schlegel in which Müller finds himself on this particular point is the more interesting as the points of view of these men were otherwise extremely close. The same forces are operative in both. Both had conquered the ferment of the *Zeitgeist* through conversion to the Roman Catholic Church. Both had later been actively engaged in the restoration of an organic-conservative political theory—from Vienna and in association with Metternich. But this agreement only developed slowly. In the year 1808 Friedrich Schlegel published in the *Heidelberger Jahrbücher* a review of Adam Müller's *Vorlesungen* that was appreciative, but at the same time skeptical. The problem of "France" is touched upon again in this article, too. To Friedrich Schlegel France seems exceptionally suited to be and to become "the focal point for a European exchange of thought," by virtue of its geographical location and political conditions. He expects that French literature will assume this role as soon as it regains any degree of vitality and a new epoch can begin. His statements betray both sympathy and familiarity with the latest French intellectual movements, which in the following years and decades were to lead to a new flourishing of French literature, to French Romanticism. Through his brother and through Mme. de Staël, with whom he himself had also had a close personal association, Friedrich Schlegel was informed of the intellectual change that was in the making. And we have the first evidence of his interest in budding French Romanticism in his review of 1808. He takes issue with the "wrathful zeal of the old guardians of the literary Zion" who seek "to preserve the pure restrictions of the classical century." He himself was at that time no more able to evaluate this classical century without prejudice—in spite of all his good intentions—than when he was editor of *Europa*. Several years would still have to pass before he reached the standpoint that Adam Müller had marked out for him. The change is complete in the lectures on the *Geschichte der alten und neuen Literatur*, which Schlegel gave in Vienna in the winter of 1812.

These lectures were a great social event, whose atmosphere is brought home to us by the descriptions in the diary of the young Eichendorff. They were given "in the ballroom of the Roman emperor," probably the Redoutensaal in the Hofburg. Schlegel was dressed in black, reading from behind a small table placed on a rostrum; a resplendent audience, in the front a coterie of ladies, the Princess Liechtenstein with her princesses; in all thirty-nine princes. The hall was heated with aromatic wood; downstairs there was a great crowd of coaches, as for a ball—this is the outward image of these affairs. As far as *Geistesgeschichte* is concerned, according to Nadler they are "the last, the most mature and the greatest utterance of Romanticism." A survey of the entire course of world literature from the Greeks to the present, this was what Schlegel presented to his audience.

Now for the first time the course of more recent French literature is given a clear evaluation within this large frame. A significant shift in historical emphasis becomes discernible. The French Middle Ages, yes, even the sixteenth century, are now resolutely judged from the standpoint of a refined classical taste, Richelieu's founding of the Academy is approved as necessary and beneficial, and Racine is heaped with the highest praise. He is said to have achieved a harmonic perfection in the art of language and of versification such as Milton did not possess in English or even Virgil in Latin. To be sure, one might have wished that a somewhat greater freedom for other poetic forms and subjects had subsisted alongside this high artistic style, but such remarks now seem to be made for the sake of completeness and polish. What is essential is the recognition of French tragedy as the most splendid achievement of the nation, as an entirely national form of art, one which in its own way is utterly perfect and particular, and which certainly could not serve as a norm or rule for any other nation. The only negative judgment in this section is directed at Boileau (II, 154), but rightly so.

Certainly the development of Friedrich Schlegel's Catholic view of the world and of history is involved in his new assessment of French Classicism. But quite apart from this, his judgment broadened and deepened; indeed, he can even praise one of Voltaire's tragedies as being the work of a true poet and entirely worthy of his two predecessors. If, then, these lectures solve one of the chief problems in the German view of France, namely, the appreciation of French Classicism, they also address themselves to another, no less significant phenomenon of French intellectual history, namely, the philosophy of the French Enlightenment.

But now the Catholic thinker of 1812 adopts an entirely different position from the idealist critic of 1803, the student of Kant and Fichte, the friend of Schleiermacher. Now the materialism and rationalism of the French Enlightenment are no longer viewed with the benevolent and somewhat disdainful tolerance of a transcendental philosopher, but rather they are firmly rejected as an "obscuring of all higher truth." To be sure, Schlegel's standpoint is even now that of philosophy, but, naturally, of a philosophy "that has no aspiration and no purpose other than to understand religion" (II, 221).

It is, however, highly significant that it was precisely from France itself that this new Christian philosophy had received fresh energies. In the Revolution's cult of reason the French Enlightenment had not only reached its apex, but also its dissolution. A rebirth of religious feeling and of Catholic life and faith had taken place in France itself and was the signature of the age. For this very reason, however, a new factor was bound to emerge in the dialectic of Friedrich Schlegel's personal and intellectual relations with France. The Catholic Schlegel could and of necessity did affirm the young Catholic France. In this development too we may today very clearly perceive the anticipation of the typical process by which the

German mind has sought to come to terms with France. Since that time France has remained the intellectual leader among the Catholic nations, and in this capacity has retained a lasting significance for the life of Catholic Germany.

From this new standpoint Friedrich Schlegel was able to welcome the works of Chateaubriand, even though they evidenced more of the outward splendor of religion than of its inner spirit (II, 218). With warm sympathy, even though not without carefully considered criticism, he speaks of two men whom he calls "the two greatest French thinkers of our time," Saint-Martin and Bonald (II, 230ff.). What attracted him to Saint-Martin was the mystic-theosophical mode of thought which, of course, became an important factor in the life and thought of Schlegel's later years. Bonald he valued as the theoretician of the restoration of the monarchy.[7]

But the lectures of 1812 do not yet represent the last and highest stage that Friedrich Schlegel reached in his efforts to understand the French mind. We have followed the stations along this road. They describe a line of ever deeper, ever more universal appreciation, for which a sense of history alone did not suffice, for which, rather, an understanding of art and a receptive sympathy were indispensable concomitants. But the further development of French literature led Friedrich Schlegel to make one last statement and afforded him one supreme conciliatory and enthusiastic prospect which had the effect of a musical resolution of all dissonances.

Late in life Friedrich Schlegel was still able to witness the first flowering of French Romanticism and to profess his sincere sympathy with it. The occasion for this was the publication in 1820 of Lamartine's first volume of poetry, which proclaimed the resurrection of the poetic spirit in France.

This work, to which Schlegel dedicated a notable review, must have struck him with the force of a revelation, for it resulted in nothing less than a complete revision of his views on literature as a whole.

[7] The principal works of J. de Maistre had not yet been published.

Ever since Herder, poetry in Germany was considered to be the natural language of the nations. From here came the contrast of natural poetry and art poetry. It was this contrast that had made the evaluation of French literature so difficult for the Germans. To be sure, Schlegel had overcome this inhibition, he had evaluated French Classicism and its rhetorical style in an authoritative and exemplary fashion. But he still felt acutely the antithesis between the German and the French conceptions of poetry and saw in it one of the most clear-cut antitheses "in the entire field of cultural criticism." Among the Germans he found a deep awareness of imagination and a feeling that floated off into the infinite; among the French a representation of passion as defined by social convention. Hence a polarity that apparently would permit of no middle ground. But now the new spiritual note of Lamartine's *Méditations* led him to observe that there really was a deeper mediating element in which the antithesis was resolved and which constituted the common source of both forms. He calls it enthusiasm, or even animation. "For it is precisely this deep, fervent animation from which all life springs, even that of the imagination, just as every flight of the spirit is carried upward on its own wings."[8]

And with deep emotion, with an almost youthfully-rhapsodic tone, Schlegel sings the praises of the "new poet," thanks to whom "the great wall that separates the French and the German language disappears. . . . One can hear kindred notes in the echo of the inmost feelings of the soul, and one thinks he hears his own language, because it is the only one, the everlasting one that is the basis of all the fragmented national languages and that gives inner life."

We have outlined in brief the inner development of Friedrich Schlegel's relation to the French mind. Attraction and repulsion, in other words a "polemical relation," is the *initial* form of his personal association with French culture. But this polemic contained the seed of an unending, fruitful dialectic

[8] Fr. v. Schlegel, *Sämtliche Werke* (2nd ed., 1846), Vol. 8, pp. 186ff.

which continued throughout his life. The "transmission" of French cultural values to intellectual Germany is the *second* part of this process. As yet the conflict between the sense of life and philosophical contemplation has not been settled, but the need to convey a more authentic knowledge of France to the German intellectual through publicistic activity has already made itself felt. This knowledge, derived from vital personal contact, was even then powerful enough to advance from the German-French dialectic to a "new conception of Europe" and to give a historical estimate of France's contribution to the European intellectual tradition. Finally, in the *last* stage, the rich yield of historical reflection is melted down again into a direct relation to life. A great new poet has arisen in France, and to the aging visionary and thinker he represents the guarantee of a never-imagined understanding in the realm of true eternal poetry. It is a most notable occurrence that Friedrich Schlegel, once a youthful fighter in the vanguard of German Romantic spirituality, finds in the firstborn of the French Romantic Age the solution and reconciliation of his lifelong controversy with France.

Friedrich Schlegel's endeavor to understand the French mind is unique among his German contemporaries. It can be said that this struggle for France occupied him during an entire lifetime, and that in the process he anticipated the most important theoretical stages that all Germans who were concerned with understanding France had to pass through again.

1932

Stefan George in Conversation

+++

BERLIN, winter of 1906 to 1907. . . . The artist couple Reinhold and Sabine Lepsius[1] had invited me to spend the evening: I was to meet Stefan George. The Lepsiuses lived in the old Westend, in the Kastanien-Allee. It was a scholarly residential quarter from the 1890s. Simmel, Wilamowitz, Roethe dwelt nearby. Plain brick houses. But when you had crossed the Lepsiuses' threshold, you were in a different atmosphere. The large living-room had a tapestry after a "cartoon" by Lestikow: horse-chestnut leaves, green shading to brown, on a brown background. A low, deep sofa, covered in yellow silk. There sometimes the beautiful Frau Siemon sat, the former wife of Otto Eckmann, the artist who had designed the "stylized" 7 on Scherl's magazine *Die Woche* (in those days everything had to be stylized). She was one of the daughters of General von Kretschmann, whose letters on the Franco-Prussian War (1903) had created a stir. Many years later I was to see Otto Braun, the son of Frau Siemon's sister Lily, sitting on this sofa. He was wearing the uniform of a cuirassier and was impatient to return to the front, where he became a victim of the spring offensive of 1918. Does anyone still remember his astonishing notebooks (*Aus dem Leben eines Frühvollendeten* [*From the Life of One Who Died Young*] 1919)? With the letters of the young von der Marwitz they are among the finest legacies of the youth cut down by the First World War. At the Lepsiuses' you could

[1] Cf. Sabine Lepsius, *Stefan George. Geschichte einer Freundschaft* (Berlin, 1935).

107

frequently also meet the philosopher Georg Simmel, who was considered "corrosive" and whose courses were attended by the best students in Berlin—at his lectures you saw the same faces as in Wölfflin's seminar. He was usually accompanied by Gertrud Kantorowicz, as sublime for her intelligence as for her goodness,[2] and as much an admirer of George as of Simmel. The salon of the Simmels (Margarete Susman might have described it) had an entirely different character. Philosophy was discussed there. Groethuysen was *facile princeps*. But there, too, the arts were held in honor. Simmel collected Chinese vases and old lace. Also, he was one of the first to take sides publicly for George.

But on that evening at the Lepsiuses' George and Gundolf were the only guests. The poet was cheerful and completely natural—not at all as the Berlin legend of the time pictured him. After supper the company gathered around the fireplace in the large living-room. Reinhold had been to Spain and had brought back some incense for Sabine, a grain of which she allowed to smolder on her cigarette. George sipped a glass of cognac. Then Gundolf read the introduction to his selection of letters of the Romantics (*Romantikerbriefe*, published by Diederichs in 1907). George requited his pupil's presentation with the simple comment: "Die junge Leit wolle heit alleweil so gescheit sein." [Hessian dialect for: "The young folks to-day want to be so clever all the time."] No one had anything to add. It is important to know that George spoke the dialect of Rhine-Hesse, as Goethe did the neighboring dialect of Frankfurt. Only he was fond of interspersing French words like *dangerös, tutelage,* and similar borrowings.[3]

At this point something must be said about George's relation to France. We have his own testimony in the poem *Franken* (published in 1907). The poet looks back on his twentieth year. He thought he would suffocate in Germany at that time:

[2] Cf. Ludwig Curtius, *In memoriam Theresienstadt* (Merkur, 1948).
[3] *Tutelage* from *tutelle*, guardianship.

Hier die gemiednen gaue wo der ekel
Mir schwoll vor allem was man pries und übte.

[Here, the shunned provinces where disgust swelled
in me at everything that was prized and practiced.]

The contrast:

Da lud von Westen märchenruf . . . so klang
Das lob des ahnen seiner ewig jungen
Grossmutigen erde deren ruhm ihn glühen
Und not auch fern ihn weinen liess; der mutter
Der fremden unerkannten und verjagten. . . .
Ein rauschen bot dem erben gruss als lockend
In freundlichkeit und fülle sich die ebnen
Der Maas und Marne unterm frühlicht dehnten.

[Then from the West came a legendary call . . . the
sound of his forebear's praise for his eternally
young, magnanimous land, whose glory made him
glow and whose distress, though far, still moved his
tears; mother of strangers, of the unrecognized and
the exiled. . . . A murmur of waters greeted the heir
as, beckoning with friendliness and fertility, the
meadows of the Meuse and Marne stretched out in
the early light.]

George's ancestor (the grandfather) felt, then, that he was
French. France was "his land." He glowed with ardor
at France's glory and shed tears, "though far," at its distress.
That "distress" is the terrible year of 1870–1871. The ancestor shared it, but from afar, that is, from the Rhine. He had
implanted in his grandson the idea: magnanimous France
is a mother and a refuge for the stranger, the unrecognized,
the exile. When Stefan George went to Paris in 1889, he was
a stranger and unknown, but at the same time he thought of
himself as an heir returning to the mother country.

Was the grandfather really French then? The Georges
come from Lorraine, or to be precise, from the German-

speaking village of Rupeldingen (Roupeldange) near Bolchen (Boulay). Friedrich Wolters writes on this question: "When Napoleon, at the turn of the 18th and 19th centuries, severed the last national ties between Germany and upper Lorraine—its grandees had, up to the Peace of Lunéville (1801), retained their seat and their vote in the German imperial and provincial assemblies—; when German rule was entirely extinguished in this region for the first time in seven decades, Johann Baptist George left the land of his fathers and migrated to Büdesheim, near Bingen on the Rhine. There he bought land and, being without issue, sent for the sons of his brother in Rupeldingen: his future heir Stefan George the first, later a well-known deputy in the Hessian Landtag and the poet's godfather; and Anton George, the poet's grandfather. Both gave up their French nationality and became Hessian citizens. Thus, although the poet's forebears had lived for a while under French rule, they were as little of French origin as other Germans living in Lorraine or on the left bank of the Rhine during the Napoleonic era. Their mother tongue was German, and they struck deeper into German territory when their homeland, Lorraine, fell entirely to France. The grandfather, who served as a French rifleman under Charles X and was in Paris during the July Revolution of 1830, did not learn French until his apprenticeship and military service. Like the males, all the female members of the family are descended from strongly Catholic, moderately wealthy landowners, and according to family recollections all the maternal ancestors from Lorraine bore German names. The stories of George's Celtic or Walloon descent, of the drop of foreign blood in his veins, are pure fabrications."

The historian Wolters has committed a blunder here. The duchy of Lorraine, as is well known, was already annexed to France in 1776. Thus the poet's great-grandfather, Johann George (1772–1853), had been born a French citizen and did not have to wait for the Peace of Lunéville to become aware of it. Was it the sentiment of German nationalism that induced him to emigrate? A sentiment that did not even exist at the time? Has the historian made a second blunder here and attributed his own sentiment of 1929 to the farmer Johann George, whom we meet again in 1804 as a landowner and community tax-gatherer at Büdesheim?[4] The reason for this transplantation was assuredly not "to strike deeper into German territory," but rather to better his lot. What was the situation on the Rhine? Jourdain's victory at Fleurus (July 26, 1794) had opened up the Rhineland to the armies of the Revolution. Between August and October, Trier, Coblenz, Bonn, Cologne, and Düsseldorf were occupied by the French. "The humiliation of having to submit to a foreign power was scarcely felt in these territories, where enemy armies had so often held sway for the last two hundred years," wrote the Cologne historian Joseph Hansen in 1922.[5] No doubt the populace grumbled at the requisitions, but the French army was a liberator of the Rhineland in the sense that it put an end to the outmoded division of the country into petty states. From 1798 on the French government had begun to extend the modern, centralized administration of the Republic to the Rhineland. The German language was excluded from official transactions. In 1800 a prefect was installed at the head of each of the four *départements réunis*. "On account of its simplicity, speed, and efficiency this administration soon found favor with the population" (Hansen). Total constitutional annexation took place on September 23, 1802. "The sale of secularized Church property, which had begun in May, 1803, produced a great shift in the ownership of land in the country. The feudal obligations which still encumbered real property were suppressed in 1804 without compensation to the nobility; the peasants became

---

[4] A. Ph. Brück, *Die Familie George in Bingen und Büdesheim* (Katholischer Kirchenkalender der Pfarreien Bingen und Bingen-Büdesheim, 17. Jahrgang, 1933).

[5] *Geschichte des Rheinlandes, herausgegeben von der Gesellschaft für rheinische Geschichtskunde*, i, 252.

free landowners. . . . The Napoleonic system of protective tariffs produced an increase in trade and industry. . . . The middle class, as the most active commercial element, began to rise in the towns and in the country. . . . When Napoleon made a journey through the Rhineland in September, 1804, the new emperor was received everywhere with acclaim." And it is precisely on September 22, 1804 (1. Vendemiaire of the year XIII) that the name of Johann George appears for the first time on the official register at Büdesheim. The husbandman has become a landed proprietor and fiscal employee. The most likely assumption is that he was one of the many German Alsatians and Lorrainers who, by virtue of their knowledge of the German language, could be utilized on the left bank of the Rhine—as was the case with the commissary Rethel in Aachen, the father of the great painter.[6]

Johann George then sends for the sons of his brother Jakob, who had remained in Rupeldingen. In 1818 Stephan George I (1806–1888) comes to Büdesheim, where from 1829 to 1836 he is municipal tax-collector; he is followed in 1833 by Anton George (1808–1881), who had previously served as a French soldier; a cooper by trade, he was also for a time director of the Bingen savings bank. Of his marriage to Anna Müller of Büdesheim was born Stephan George II, the poet's father (1841–1907). He kept an inn at Büdesheim, and settled in Bingen in 1873 as a commission agent in wine. The inn "zur Traube" in Büdesheim is the poet's birthplace.

If his Lorraine ancestors spoke only German, their descendants nevertheless did learn French, whether as tax collectors in Rhine-Hesse or under Charles X in Paris. In Büdesheim George showed me the house of an uncle who had translated Fénelon's *Télémaque*. French was also spoken in the poet's home, and he himself was called Etienne. Were further testimony needed, it could be supplied by the

[6] Cf. the essay by Leo Just in the *Elsass-Lothringer Jahrbuch*, VII (1928).—In the public record office at Darmstadt (*Fonds Départe-ment Mont-Tonnerre*) more details might perhaps be found.

memoirs of the journalist Maurice Muret (born in 1870). He studied Old French under Adolf Tobler in Berlin in the winter of 1889–1890 and relates: "Je lisais un jour, avant l'arrivée du professeur, une gazette française, quand je vis s'asseoir à mon côté un jeune homme . . . qui, se penchant vers moi, me dit gentiment: 'Je suis de la même race que vous.' . . . Et tout de suite, il me conta qu'il était poète, qu'il était d'une famille d'origine française fixée sur les bords du Rhin, à Bingen, qu'il avait gardé l'amour de son pays d'origine, qu'il venait de passer plusieurs mois à Paris, qu'il avait lié amitié sur les bords de la Seine avec un aîné, poète génial, qui s'appelait Stéphane Mallarmé. . . ."[7] ["One day, before the arrival of the professor, I was reading a French newspaper when I saw a young man sit down next to me . . . who, leaning toward me, said to me nicely: 'I am of the same race as you.' . . . And immediately he told me that he was a poet, that he came from a family of French origin settled along the Rhine, at Bingen, that he had preserved the love of his country of origin, that he had just spent several months in Paris, that he had formed a friendship on the banks of the Seine with an elder, a poet of genius named Stéphane Mallarmé. . ."]. At the time of the poet's birth in 1868, his family had already been assimilated to French culture for two generations. He himself cultivated this acquired and inherited portion, considering it beneficial till well into the 1890s. In Paris, Albert Saint-Paul had introduced him to Mallarmé's circle.[8] The dedication to *Algabal* reads: "To Albert Saint-Paul the poet and friend of many an experience and many an artistic pleasure Paris 1892." The poem *Franken* contains tributes to Villiers, Verlaine, and Mallarmé as well as an allusion, in the last stanza, to the funeral of Leconte de Lisle (1894):

[7] *Journal des Débats, édition hebdomadaire*, for January 12, 1934. Muret received two letters from George, one from Bingen in 1890, signed Etienne, and one from Munich in 1894, signed Stefan.

[8] Saint-Paul gave an account of it in the *Neue Zürcher Zeitung* for July 12, 1928.

Mag traum und ferne uns als speise stärken—
Luft die wir atmen bringt nur der Lebendige,
So dank ich freunde euch die dort noch singen
Un väter die ich seit zur gruft geleitet. . . .
Wie oft noch spät da ich schon grund gewonnen
In trüber heimat streitend und des sieges
Noch ungewiss, lieh neue Kraft dies flüstern:
RETURNENT FRANC EN FRANCE DULCE
TERRE!

[Dream and distance may nourish and strengthen
us—but air to breathe only the living can bring;
therefore I thank you friends who still sing there,
and fathers whom I've since escorted to the tomb.
. . . How often, late, when I had already gained
ground, still struggling in the dreary homeland, and
still uncertain of victory, did this murmur renew my
strength: RETURNENT FRANC EN FRANCE
DULCE TERRE!]

In *Der siebente Ring* [*The Seventh Ring*] George for the first
time drew political conclusions from his relationship to
France. The Lorrainese origin of his stock is now referred to
Lotharingia, the intermediate kingdom of the Franks; the rebirth of this kingdom is prophesied; with that the demarca-
tion from both France and imperial Germany is completed.
I have shown this elsewhere.[9] George was in Paris for the last
time in 1908. Gide's *Journal* for April 7 records: "Déjeuné
hier chez Albert Mockel avec Stefan George, Albert Saint-
Paul et un assez agréable jeune homme qu'on appelait Olivier
(je n'ai pas pu comprendre si c'était seulement son prénom).
Admirable tête de Stefan George que depuis longtemps je
souhaitais connaître et dont j'admire l'oeuvre, chaque fois que
je parviens à la comprendre. Teint blanc bleuâtre, peau mate

[9] *Europäische Literatur und lateinisches Mittelalter* (2nd ed.,
Bern 1954), p. 20; *European Literature and the Latin Middle Ages,*
trans. Willard R. Trask (New York, 1953), p. 10.

et plus tirée que ridée, belle accusation de l'ossature. Impeccablement rasé; abondante et solide crinière, plus noire encore que grise et rejetée d'un coup en arrière. Mains de convalescent, très fines, exsangues, très expressives. Il parle peu, mais d'une voix profonde et qui force l'attention. Grande veste-redingote de clergyman avec deux agrafes dans le haut, qui s'ouvre sur une cravate-écharpe de velours noir, passée pardessus le col, et débordant. La simple glissière d'or d'un cordon qui retient montre ou monocle met un éclat discret dans tout ce noir. Chaussures (à elastiques, je pense!) d'une seule pièce de cuir, bridant un peu le pied, et qui m'ont déplu. ... Il s'exprime dans notre langue sans faute aucune, encore qu'un peu craintivement, semble-t-il, et fait preuve d'une connaissance et compréhension surprenantes de nos auteurs, poètes en particulier: tout ceci sans fatuité mais avec une conscience évidente de son évidente supériorité" ["Lunched yesterday at Albert Mockel's with Stefan George, Albert Saint-Paul, and a rather pleasant young man whom they called Oliver (I never could make out whether it was merely his first name). Wonderful head of Stefan George, whom I have long wanted to know and whose work I admire each time I manage to understand it. Bluish-white complexion, skin dull and more drawn than wrinkled, sharply-defined bone structure; impeccably shaved; full, heavy hair, still more black than gray and all brushed back. Hands of a convalescent, very delicate, bloodless, very expressive. He speaks little, but in a deep voice that forces attention. A sort of clergyman's Prince Albert with two clasps toward the top, which opens for a necktie-scarf of black velvet, above and overflowing the collar. The simple gold slide on a ribbon leading to a watch or monocle gives a discreet accent to all this black. Shoes (elastic-sided, I fancy!) of a single piece of leather tightly gripping the foot, which I didn't like. ... He expresses himself in our language without a single mistake, though yet a bit cautiously, it seems, and shows a surprising knowledge and understanding of our authors, particularly our poets; and all this without self-satisfaction, but with an evident awareness of his evident superiority"].[10] Since those last years before the First World War, George's turning away from France became more and more marked. The place of Lotharingia was taken by Germania.

What else was talked about at the Lepsiuses' on that evening I can no longer recall. In the company of George and Gundolf I set out for home. We had to walk to Spandau (the underground did not yet go as far as the Reichskanzlerplatz) and catch the metropolitan railway there. I sat next to George, who was leaning his head on his hand and his hand on his walking-stick, motionless and silent. How was I to find something to say? And yet I knew: if you do not say it now—the opportunity will never come again. But shyness and admiration kept my mouth shut. I had, as Aeschylus says, "an ox on my tongue." At the last second, at the Bahnhof Zoo, I stammered something. "Why didn't you say so right away?" was the friendly reply. I was to inquire of Gundolf when I might call on George in Bingen.

In the years that followed I was often in Bingen. Often, too, I was with the poet in Heidelberg or in Darmstadt. Once I happened to meet him in the station restaurant at Geissen; once he looked me up in Mürren in the Bernese Oberland and took me along to Isenfluh, where he was spending the month of August. In *Der siebente Ring* is a poem that contains images of the Alpine landscape of Switzerland. The poet, who was a wanderer, climbs the heights "beyond the last stone pines."

George was reputed to be severe, unapproachable, solemn. But in his earlier years at least, he could also be easygoing. At a friend's house on the Karlsplatz in Heidelberg he read with amusement a book by Abel Hermant that had been placed by his bedside. He would also go with Gundolf and me to the Café Wagner, which was on the main street, and enjoy a glass of beer. But he was the son of a Rhenish vintner, and wine was his drink, wherein he showed himself a connois-

[10] Trans. Justin O'Brien.

seur, as in tobacco, as in everything. In Bingen he poured me
wine from his father's cellar, with which some pastry was
served ("Hier habe Sie etwas zum Knabbere" [dialect for
"Here is something to nibble on"]).

The little house in Bingen was situated in a modest lane,
"Hintere Grube," not far from the banks of the Nahe and the
Drusus Bridge. You entered through a small walled-in front
garden planted with oleander bushes. George's room was on
the ground floor, to the left of the entrance. It had a window
facing the garden. Books on a set of low shelves, among them
back numbers of the *Mercure de France* and the *Ermitage*.
On the wall, a painting by Toorop; in full view, the
large photograph of Maximin (three-quarter length), a detail
of which serves as the frontispiece for the commemorative
volume *Maximin* (1906). A desk, turned toward the window;
a green wooden bench propped against the row of book-
shelves; sofa, table, and chairs along the back wall. It was at
once exhilarating and depressing to stand in this narrow cell
face to face with "the most important man in Germany today." That was what Gundolf had called him in the first *Jahrbuch für die geistige Bewegung*,[11] [*Annual for the Intellectual
Movement*], which elicited an indignant reaction from the
Berliner Tageblatt (March 16, 1910).

Bingen, "where Rhine and Nahe wed," had been rightly
praised to me by Gundolf as an "heroic landscape." George
loved to wander through it. In May the oak groves and the
vines smelled sweet:

> Schon lockt nicht mehr das wunder der lagunen
> Das allumworbene trümmergrosse Rom
> Wie herber eichen duft und rebenblüten
> Wie sie die Deines volkes hort behüten
> Wie Deine wogen—lebengrüner Strom!

[No longer does the miracle of the lagoons attract,
nor Rome, by all sought after, great with ruins—so
much as harsh scent of oaks and vine-flowers, as

---

[11] A review edited by George's disciples.

117

they which guard your people's treasure, as do your
waves, O stream green with life!]

One would climb up to the Chapel of Saint Roch, with its
memories of Goethe, or downstream by way of Bingerbrück
as far as the "Schweizerhaus." A signpost there indicated:
"Eighty leagues to Bonn." That to me was like a mysterious
summons which I did not know how to interpret. It was soon
to become a reality.

I had grown up along the Upper Rhine. At eighteen, two
friends of mine from Strasbourg and I had made a journey on
the Rhine that was only cut short by lack of funds. When we at
last reached Bingen, having come down the Nahe Valley, and
boarded the white steamer, I discovered a new landscape: the
beauty of the Middle Rhine. Our final destination was Cologne. At that time *Maria in Capitol* was still standing. This
church, where I was later to accompany Scheler to high mass,
affected me more strongly than anything else. How much was
contained in those words: Maria—Capitol! Christianity and
the Roman World; tangibly revealed, historically confirmed;
fused and preserved in one edifice; present. This had been an
initiation, a prelude to that impression of the Rhine I was
later to receive thanks to George.

Subsequently, when George permitted me to visit him in
Bingen, I used to put up at a hotel on the Rhine. The proprietor would say to me the next day: "Mr hawwe Sie mit un-
serm Herr Schorch spaziere gehe sehn" [dialect for: "We saw
you out walking with our Herr George"]. The citizens of
Bingen had heard of George. They regarded him as a curiosity, but one they could be proud of all the same. He was the
son of respectable people.

I was very young and foolish (the terms were synonymous
in those days) at the time I was introduced to George. And
he was still practically unknown. A "Circle" did not exist as
yet. This did not change till 1910, when the *Jahrbücher für*

die geistige Bewegung began to appear. A Youth Movement did not exist as yet either. Or, at any rate, none that had become visible. The *Jugendbewegung* was not consolidated till 1913 at the meeting on the Hoher Meissner. George was astonished and incredulous when I told him in 1914 that he was the hero of these young people. They took *Der Stern des Bundes* [*The Star of the Covenant*] to the war with them. The George-"Movement" was still esoteric even then, and confined to the smallest circles. They thought of themselves as the bearers of a light hidden from the common multitude. As late as 1918, on the occasion of his fiftieth birthday—the 12th of July—the *Berliner Tageblatt* carried an article disapproving of George by an author who is still being read today. The other important newspapers were silent.

It was only around 1920 that George's fame began to make him notorious even to the middle class. Gundolf's books contributed a great deal to this change, more than the officious biography by Wolters (1929), in which Gundolf discovered "fifty-six gross inaccuracies" (from a conversation). Even before the appearance of this book the time had become ripe for George to receive the Frankfurt Goethe Prize. It was conferred upon him—*in absentia*. That was characteristic of George. He let things happen, but he would not comment. All the possibilities of interpretation remained open.

The Germany of 1950 knows George little—as little as it does Hofmannsthal. It seems as though George had receded into a great distance—a blessed distance! At the same time the ranks of his companions are growing thin. With Karl Wolfskehl (1869–1948) died the last of those who had been close to him from the earliest years. In faraway New Zealand he found his grave. There, in 1944, he completed his poetic testament, the poem *An die Deutschen*[12] [*To the Germans*]. Neither the sufferings of exile nor the recovery of the ancient faith of his fathers could alienate the poet from the Master:

[12] Published in 1947 by the Origo-Verlag, Zurich.

Und ich folge, und ich weine,
Weine, weil das Herz verwaist,
Weil ein Tausendjahr vereist.
Aber ob zum Morgenscheine
Wieder lenkt umwölktes Wort,
Wo ich mich Altvätern eine
Harrnd, dass Haggadol erscheine,
Ob der Ruf mich fernhin reisst:
Kür verheisst und Sende weist.
Weit aus heilig weissem Feuer
Reckt die Hand und heisst der Meister:
Überdaure! bleib am Steuer. . . .

[And I follow, and I weep, weep because my heart is orphaned, because a millennium has turned to ice. But whether in the light of morning a cloud-wrapt word again shall guide me, when I am united with my forefathers, waiting that Haggadol appear; whether the call transport me far: promising election and showing me my mission; forth from holy white fire the Master stretches his hand and bids: Outlast! stay at the helm. . . .]

Another of George's contemporaries was the Dutch poet Albert Verwey (1865–1937). His association with George began in 1895 and continued till 1910, although it was fraught with tensions from the very beginning. These led, in 1914, to open conflict, because Wolfskehl had proclaimed in the *Frankfurter Zeitung* that the "war we had not wanted and which had been forced upon us" had been willed by God and prophesied by George. A reconciliation, which proved specious however, took place in 1919. Then their ways parted.[13]

[13] Verwey's book, *Mein Verhältnis zu Stefan George* (Strasbourg, Heitz & Co., 1936), contains much valuable information about George that is unobtainable elsewhere. Reminiscences from the 1880s were presented by Ida Dehmel in the *Berliner Tageblatt* for July 1 and 2, 1935. A selection from the literary remains of Maximilian Kronberger ("Maximin") was published in Zurich (Adolf Bürdeke, n.d.) during the Second World War. Besides poems it contains a journal the

Wolfskehl and Verwey were joined, among the older contemporaries, by Henry v. Heiseler (1875–1928) and Ludwig Derleth. They too were poets, had something of their own to say, and refused to follow George in his later development. Hence the rebuke *An Henry* [*To Henry*] in *Der siebente Ring*:

> Das Leben zog um dich den schönen zaun.
> So braucht dir nicht vor schlucht und flut zu graun.
> Für viele zier gibst du dich keinem ganz
> Und fliehst mit letztem streit den letzten kranz.

[Life drew a beautiful fence about you. So you were spared the fear of precipice and torrent. Ornament to many, you give yourself wholly to none, and fleeing the ultimate battle flee the ultimate crown.]

Even Wolfskehl had to hear it said of him:

> Dein leben ehrend muss ich es vermeiden.

[Though I respect your life, I must avoid it.]

At the age of twenty George had begun to gather friends among poets and artists. On reaching the Dantean middle of life he began to cast them off. In the preface to the third volume of selections from the *Blätter für die Kunst*[14] [*Leaves for Art*] (1909), the warning was sounded: "Let it not be forgotten by those who have strayed from this Circle, provided that they have not yet been able to consent to the complete debasement of their Muse (Hofmannsthal as librettist!), that

---

purpose of which is "to develop the character of Stefan George through his relations with me." It covers the years 1902–1904. The postscript states: "Max Kronberger left for Vienna on March 24 to see some relatives and visited George, who was also stopping there, on the 30th. On April 10 he returned home, very ill with spinal meningitis. On April 15, the day after his sixteenth birthday, destiny set a term to his earthly career."

[14] The review edited by George and his Circle (1892–1919).

they wait in vain for the plaudits of the crowd. May this serve as an admonition to those who have abandoned the temple and are already in the outer courts, indeed, in the streets, to return to the sanctuary." George no longer needed friends; he needed disciples. In 1899, through Wolfskehl, he had made the acquaintance of Friedrich Gundolf, who was nineteen years old at the time. The epigram, not published till 1907 in *Der siebente Ring*, dates from that period:

> Warum so viel in fernen menschen forschen und in sagen lesen
> Wenn selber du ein wort erfinden kannst dass einst es heisse:
> Auf kurzem Pfad bin ich dir dies und du mir so gewesen!
> Ist das nicht licht und lösung uber allem fleisse?

> [Why inquire so much into distant men and read in legends, when you yourself can invent a word such that some day it may be said: For a brief stretch I was this to you and you were so to me! Is this not a light and a solution exceeding all industry?]

At that time poetry ranked much higher than discursive and scholarly modes of thought. But the Maximin experience transcended poetry. It was felt as an epiphany of the divine. The innermost substance of George's poetry became cultic. This caused a change in the poet's attitude toward the age. Prophet of a new gospel, he set himself against the epoch as its judge and proscriber. That was to many people the surprising new turn in *Der siebente Ring*. George demanded adherence of his disciples. A manifesto from the pen of Gundolf on *Gefolgschaft und Jüngertum* [*Adherence and Discipleship*] appeared in 1909. It was the first proclamation of the change in regime. The second, more intense than the first, was issued by Friedrich Wolters (1876–1930): *Herrschaft und Dienst* [*Authority and Service*] (1910). Wolters was four years older than Gundolf but did not find his way into the Circle till 1908. Gundolf was gentler, warmer, simpler, gayer. None of George's disciples did so much for the dissemination of the new outlook. The study of "distant men" now bore fruit: *Shakespeare und der deutsche Geist* [*Shakespeare and the German Mind*], a work of both youthful effervescence and masterly organization, appeared in 1911, the first of an impressive series. The bond between Gundolf and George seemed unbreakable. And yet it too was to be broken. Gundolf's *Gedichte*, which were published in 1930, one year before his death, and bore the dedication *To my Wife*, indicate the tragic extent of the rupture:

> Meine Jugend war gelenkt
> Dumpf, dann willig von dem Meister,
> Bis ein Stärkerer mich entschränkt:
> Wahrer schreit ich, als Verwaister,
> Ohne Stab, Geleis und Strang
> Wissend nur noch Gott und Liebe
> Durch das schütternde Geschiebe
> Den vom Tod gewiesnen Gang.

[My youth was guided, first listless, then willing, by the Master, till a stronger hand unbound me. I march truer as an orphan, without staff, track, or cord, now knowing only God and Love, through the shattered rubble, along the path marked out by death.]

A third and a fourth generation of disciples arrived on the scene after Gundolf. They have handed down the image of George in his later years (Robert Boehringer, *Ewiger Augenblick* [*Eternal Moment*], Basel, 1945). "Scholarship" too has got hold of George. For a reevaluation, which would have to be quite sweeping, the time has not yet come. This is not the place to discuss it. My contribution to the great subject consists only in a few sparse diary entries concerning two visits to Bingen (1911, 1912) and two to Heidelberg (1917, 1919). I kept no notes of the many other encounters. As a young man one believes in an eternal noon, an eternal present.

I must state in advance that I came as a confirmed and devoted admirer. But two—very different—things made me uneasy. I could respect the cult of Maximin, but not share it. I loved Greek culture with a passion, but I belonged to the Christian world. George was to me the greatest living poet. But I also admired several living French writers and was planning to write about them. I hoped for George's indulgence on both points. I did not obtain it. In a message dictated to Gundolf he sought to dissuade me from my Frenchmen. "What does one of these little Frenchies know about poetry?" the note said. In the margin, in George's own hand, was written: "affectionately all the same, St. G."

IN GEORGE'S immediate entourage there were many Jews (cf. Werner Kraft, "George und das Judentum," in the *Neue Schweizer Rundschau*, February 1950). George spoke to me about it on 16 April, 1911: "Jews are the best conductors. They are skillful in spreading and transforming values. Of course they do not feel things as elementally as we do. They are altogether a different kind of people. I never allow them to be in the majority, either in the society or in the *Jahrbuch*. . . . I sometimes have a nostalgia for France. This Péguy, whom you praise so much, I want to read him and then give you my opinion. I shall visit you in Strasbourg. . . . The Rococo period: a poison in the body of mankind; it has been cured now. But the nineteenth century is utterly corrupt, must be radically rejected. The idea of progress through science is madness. All great ages have known that knowledge is only for the few and can only be communicated by degrees. . . . Yes, I was in Paris in 1889, before that in England. I stayed a whole summer in Paris, also traveled to Spain at the time. I knew Mallarmé, Verlaine, Moréas, Mockel, Gide . . . and many others. Albert Saint-Paul gave me a perfect introduction to both language and literature. Germany was unbearable at the time; think of

Nietzsche! I would have thrown a bomb if they had tried to keep me here; or I should have been destroyed, like Nietzsche. My father was glad to be rid of me, for he suspected the danger. In Paris I found human beings, people whom I could live with and like. My real truth they did not understand, of course. Some people think my first books are purely artistic and contain nothing of the will to a new humanity. All wrong! *Algabal* is a revolutionary book. Listen to this sentence from Plato: 'The orders of the Muses change only with those of the State.' *Algabal* and *Der siebente Ring*— it is the same substance, only spread over a narrower plane. Before *Algabal* I wrote a five-act drama. All these things were already in it. I realized, however, that drama was not the right way.—All partial emancipations, partial reforms ('rights of women,' 'child-rearing,' 'labor problem') are folly. Children must be kept in tutelage. The maternal instinct speaks in Sabine. I can only tell her the truth in jest. *Taceat mulier in ecclesia!*—Simmel tried to sound me out, so did Dilthey. But I could not tell them more than they were permitted to know." George makes me a present of a wonderful photograph of himself (profile, with open collar), which had been taken in Lechter's studio in 1899; also an issue of the *Ermitage* with excerpts from *Pilgerfahrten* [*Pilgrimages*] in the translation of Albert Saint-Paul. He shows me an issue of *Floréal* (1892 or 1893), containing an original French poem by him. "I have made five or six poems in French and then translated them into German. There was a moment when I was undecided whether I wished to become a French or a German poet."

The next morning an excursion to the Burg Klopp in splendid spring weather. "All my close friends have sat on these benches.—To the 'religious wave' of the present I attach no importance at all. People want to have everything too cheaply. The distress will have to get much worse. Were one to say to them now: Yes, you shall have a religion, but first thousands will have to be killed—they would say, they can still get along without it.—I can get every single point of my program endorsed, but never all of them at once.—All poets have wanted to raise the level of mankind. Nietzsche has some fine things to say about this. His tragedy was, he was born too early. He had tremendous intentions. Immediately the *Birth of Tragedy*! Can one measure what that means: to present an image of Greece not derived from an accumulation of details but from a vision, modeled upon a living presence (Wagner)? Even if it might have been an error!—There are two paths, paganism and the morality of purity. But you see, even though I am a pagan, I do have these purifications.—'Das Ewig-Weibliche zieht uns hinan' ['The Eternal-Feminine draws us upward']:—perhaps that ought to be interpreted mystically. Everywhere else Goethe represented the other type of attitude toward women: the pagan attitude.—The Ancient Mysteries are the eternal type of higher knowledge. Catholicism has preserved something of it and might renew itself from there.—Theory is alien to my nature. You young fellows have forced me into it.[15] Only what is humanly vital interests me. Only knowledge transmitted through a human medium is valuable and fertile.— There is such a thing as magic!—if you call it hypnotism, people will believe in it.—The Nordic, Germanic genius has no generative principle. I consciously contrast it with my own genius, which is southern and pagan.—You must not view me too theoretically." We descend toward Schloss Rheinstein. At the tilting-ground he repeats a phrase from Jean Paul to himself: "And they were astonished at the heaviness of their bodies and the sound of their steps."

Bingen, May 3, 1912. "Sometimes I must pour water on all of you and sometimes oil. . . . The imminent danger for the world is Hinduism. Lechter's book on India! There you find a vague religious backwash made up of Christian and Hindu ingredients!—For my followers a rallying-point is now needed. In Franconia? It is something to consider."

[15] An allusion to the *Jahrbücher*, which I, of course, had nothing to do with. On the contrary, I had always thought them a stumbling-block.

Heidelberg, April 1917. "If they ask us to eat bread that has a strong admixture of tree-bark, we can still put up with it. But there are situations where a man has got to say: here I would sooner die; for example, if we are expected to eat rats and mice. . . . The French have only *littérature*, not poetry. They are two-faced: *politesse* on the one side, brutality on the other. Because they are brutal as beasts they have to have a cultivated exterior.—The ideal of an enlightened humanity has failed utterly, so has Anglo-American Christianity. Possible and justifiable would only be a renewal of the early, heroic Christianity.—Wilde and D'Annunzio: great artists." He gives me to understand that his existence constitutes a legitimate ground, *the* legitimate ground for a German victory. "But we shall have to wait and see where the Good Lord draws the line."—"Relations between men ought not to be based solely on personal feelings but on something objective as well."

Heidelberg, 1919. "All this Catholicizing today. But people always want to skim the cream off the top. One must understand how laws come about. In his primitive state man is pure nature. But in the long run life cannot be preserved that way. To save it the great intelligences come and give laws. All these laws contain restrictions, inconveniences, ablutions. But one has to accept all that and assent to it along with the rest. The important thing is: that there be laws, whether they suit the particular little individual or not. Religion can also be regarded as a subdivision of the law. A direct access to God doesn't exist. God-seekers do not exist. These are perverted modern Protestant ideas. What comes of pursuing them to their ultimate consequences is shown by Frau Simmel's book:[16] complete despair. This book is so instructive because Frau Simmel is one of the most serious people I have ever come across. With her one can forget gender and simply speak of a human being." But isn't there communication with God through prayer? "But only for him who already *has* God.

[16] Marie Luise Enckendorff (Gertrud Simmel), *Über das Religiöse* (1919) (cf. *Hochland* [1919], pp. 139ff.).

Genuine Catholicism is something venerable, pure, and right. I lived in it myself up to my eighteenth year. Then the transformation took place within me. But you are not yet mature enough for me to tell you about it.—People obey the laws made by the state because if they didn't they would be put in jail. But other laws they do not wish to obey. As for me, I would rather obey a power that ordered me to go to mass every day than one that ordered me to pick up a rifle. Those who are faithful to the Church must keep her commandments. Those who are faithful to me, must do as I teach. Truth is different in every eon."—But must there not be an Ultimate above the changing eons? George, flaring up all of a sudden: "Yes, there is. But that is none of your business. Not even I may concern myself with that."

The conversation turns to the present. "Many things are possible. But there are things that are *not* possible: that Bingen should become French. . . . You ask about the promise for Germany expressed in my poem *Krieg* [*War*]? Mark my words: everything that is written in the sacred texts has always come to pass and always will come to pass. It is always thus with the sacred texts. We shall first have to go through total disintegration. But then things will improve. That is a consolation I can give everyone. Whether we shall live to see it is uncertain, naturally. But the spiritual solutions have all already been found. Events always lag cumbrously behind. The only cause for worry now is whether one will be able to save one's own person and those on whom the future depends. Situations may arise where it is impossible to submit. Then one must say: it's been nice; and let oneself be shot." Taking my leave at the door of his house: "I have spoken a bit harshly to you at times, but that cannot hurt. Anyhow, you haven't been eaten; and, actually, everyone gets a piece of my mind."

1950

To the Memory of

Hofmannsthal

✦✦✦

A. HOFMANNSTHAL'S GERMAN MISSION

*Quand une révolution inouïe ébranle les
colonnes du monde, comment s'occuper
d'autre chose?*   Rivarol

IN A "best-seller" for the 1929 season the contrast between
the German youth of today and the youth of the turn of the
century is exemplified in the fact that the latter read Hofmannsthal, the former no longer read him, no longer wish to
read him. The youth of 1905 wanted to be aesthetic, that of
1925 political. In the earlier period, "aestheticism" constituted an offense in the eyes of the old; today it is condemned
in the forum of the young. These resistances have a sociological interest, but no other. It is the interest most general in
form but poorest in substance that can accrue to a subject.

If one of the functions of art is to create beauty, then every
refinement, every new foundation of the sense of beauty—but
also every invention of a new beauty—signifies an enhancement of being, a gain in value. Aestheticism—only for the
sake of convenience do I choose this appellation that serves
the categorizing needs of literary historians—aestheticism
was both: a renewal of the sense of beauty and a new beauty.
It was a new form of beauty in the sense that the Renaissance,
Classicism, Romanticism, and the Decadence were new forms
of beauty, or were so at least in part. For that reason from an
intellectual (not pedagogical) standpoint, to say that one "rejects" aestheticism is meaningless. It was necessary during a

129

period in which German literature, under the pretext of naturalism, satisfied a craving for the ugly that is deeply ingrained in certain strata of our sensibility (we find it in the painting of the fifteenth century, but also in Expressionism). The cultivation of beauty was so essential at the time that even Stefan George, in the *Blätter für die Kunst*, called for it "to the exclusion of everything social and political." Should it have become quite superfluous today? Not because it was necessary, not because it was revitalizing, does aestheticism deserve to be saved. It was beautiful, it was fruitful, it augmented the expressive possibilities of art and the dynamic tensions of life. This must be said in Germany today when Germany commemorates Hofmannsthal.

But this is only a provisional explanation, intended to clear away one of the gravest of the misunderstandings that encumber the figure of Hofmannsthal and prevent him from being recognized in his true character. The second misunderstanding consists in the opinion that Hofmannsthal was a "mere" aesthete, an opinion that would still be erroneous even if the word "aesthete" were given a positive value. What is "mere" aesthete supposed to mean? The artist creates life through forms, and that alone is enough to connect him with the fundamental elements of life, that is, with a potency more actual and more enduring than markets or machines. The artist whom the sense of beauty inspires to create always creates more than "mere beauty." One of the earliest poems of the "beauty-mad" Hofmannsthal ends with the line:

Nur dass er dienen durfte freute ihn.

[That he might serve was joy enough for him.]

This line of verse contains the germ of the thousands of lyricisms that shot up out of the ground twenty years later when goodness was discovered and exploited by literature under Slavic influence just as depravity had been at an earlier period under the influence of the French.

The reaction against the aestheticism of the nineties (in England too the nineties are in bad repute today) forgets that

none of the great writers whose youth unfolded at that time—
and could unfold in no other atmosphere but that of aestheticism—remained a "mere" aesthete. Not George, not D'Annunzio, not Hofmannsthal. Nor does it apply to the earlier
poets of the love of beauty: Poe, Rossetti, Baudelaire, Wilde.
All of them, by many and diverse routes, advanced from
aesthetic beauty to a sphere of mysticism that in Hofmannsthal became symbolically visible through his approach
to Calderón. The sole exception is Théophile Gautier, and
Gautier has been dead as a poet for a long time.

No, Hofmannsthal was really not a "mere" aesthete. Nor
was he a "mere" poet. Oh, this dreadful, unthinking "mere,"
which in the language of German public opinion shuts everyone into his compartment, then locks all the drawers and
labels them!

"The process of which I speak," declared Hofmannsthal
in concluding a lecture at the University of Munich on January 10, 1927, "is nothing less than a conservative revolution
of a magnitude unknown to European history. Its aim is form,
a new German reality in which the entire nation can participate." Are these the words of a poet? Is this the language of
a man of letters? Is it not rather the voice, so seldom heard
in Germany, of an intellectual authority, of an authority
charged with the administration of our poetry, our language,
our literature, of the possessions and energies not only of our
culture but of our people and our state?

Such authority can manifest itself in various forms of personal effectiveness: in the form of the writer, the scholar, the
philosopher, the politician. But it reaches beyond them all
and cannot be subsumed under any functional concept of the
division of labor. The personal type to which this authority
belongs can only be described by examples. One would probably have to go back as far as Adam Müller, and Germany
has forgotten him.

Hofmannsthal was this type of intellectual and moral authority. We did not know it and to a large extent still do not
know it. That is why it is necessary to refute the misconcep-

tion that sees in the poet who has been torn from us only the poet.

Authority should not be confused with either leadership or power. The essence of authority consists in the fact that it operates without conscious exercise and without challenge. It springs up mysteriously and is then simply there as by a natural process of development. Leadership is striven for and striven against. Will and resistance are of its essence. The leader acts, authority rules. It rules in the sense of "le roi règne, il ne gouverne pas." The monarchy is the archetype of all genuine authority.

To exercise this intellectual and moral authority in Germany is nearly impossible in view of the fractiousness of our intellectual and moral world, this veritable *bellum omnium contra omnes*. That is the fateful and tragic fact that Hofmannsthal perceived and expounded in his Munich lecture on *Das Schrifttum als geistiger Raum der Nation* [*Literature as the Spiritual Space of the Nation*]. One of the functions of authority is representation. But Germany does not wish to be represented intellectually. And the duties of this representative authority are rendered even more difficult when it is aware of its affinity with the whole of our national life and the whole of our national history; when it confronts the inveterate tendencies of the German—his tendency to flee from the world, from reality, from society, and to seek refuge in the solitude of his inner self, in circle or sect, in originality at all costs, in utopian demands for dictatorship, in the absolute as freedom from ties, obligations, and responsibilities *per se*.

To bind, to connect, to conserve—this was one of the functions that Hofmannsthal had assumed on behalf of the nation. It was in the consciousness of this task that he presented us with the *Deutsches Lesebuch* [*A Book of German Readings*] and that other anthology *Von Wert und Ehre Deutscher Sprache* [*Value and Dignity of the German Language*]. This great cosmopolitan of the spirit had roots in the deepest strata of our national psyche and national mind. To protect these roots, to cultivate these energies, to bring these treasures to light was for him the constraint of a great love. I see him striding through the tangled forests of our heritage with the gaze and concentration of a treasure seeker, a dowser, a stargazer; with the pensive and visionary glance of one acquainted with all growing things; of one intimately allied with all the substances of nature because they course through his own bloodstream. This is how he ranges through our history, through the nation and the nations, through the populous precincts of past and future life. From this fostering love grew that ethic which we agree with him in calling conservative.

To understand this ethic seems to me the most important thing to be done now for Hofmannsthal's memory.

Criticism has long been in the habit of classifying Hofmannsthal as a Romantic or neo-Romantic. This seems to me to be a negligent use of language. In a quite provisional and hazy sense the term may stand. But nothing precise or definite is conveyed by it. Either Romanticism is conceived as an idle contrast to Classicism, a contrast which is no more substantial for being identified with that between infinity and form or some other such formulation that breaks down upon the slightest contact with a concrete person or situation. Or else it denotes a world of experience and art that manifested itself in Europe between 1750 and 1850, without being in any way coextensive with the total content of that period.

Hofmannsthal is a Romantic neither in the abstract nor in the historical conception of the term. It is true that he loves Romanticism (though also Classicism, the Renaissance, the Alexandrians!)—but he carefully and deliberately dissociates himself from it. He is a representative of the Restoration, and that means of a way of thinking that integrates romantic elements and in so doing "sublates" them in a more comprehensive synthesis. The conservative revolution he speaks of is "an inner countermovement to that spiritual upheaval of the sixteenth century which in its two aspects we are accustomed to call Renaissance and Reformation." It is "a process of a magnitude unknown to European history."

I designate this conservative-revolutionary thinking the

Restoration principle, after the first historical form in which it appeared between 1790 and 1830.

The founders of this disposition of mind and will are Rivarol, Burke, Joseph de Maistre, and Karl Ludwig von Haller. They were assuredly not Romantics. But Joseph Nadler also makes the following judgment concerning related phenomena within Germany: "Restoration and Romanticism happen to coincide, but they are essentially distinct and opposite cultural processes." The Restoration as a movement that embraced all of Western Europe, as nourishment for conservative thought, as cultural and political ideology, must be separated from the phenomenon of Romanticism. Today, moreover, in France with Maurras, in England with T. S. Eliot, it is polemically hostile to Romanticism. Whoever wishes to dismiss it anyhow as Romanticism does so because it runs counter to his instincts and interests. But "Romanticism" in that sense is only a patronizing and polite way of expressing political disagreement. Nothing intellectually tangible is intended by it.

In Germany these things are far less clearly seen than in the more western nations. The reason for this is that the conservative classes in the country have no leaders of sufficient intellectual stature to impress themselves upon the entire spectrum of the political intelligence. Conservatism of the Prussian type can never be valid for all of Germany, let alone for all of Europe. But the energies which could bring about a spiritual and political revolution of a conservative type are still alive in such regions of German nationality as Franconia, Bavaria, and Austria. Out of the cultural consciousness of Old Austria Hofmannsthal developed his ideas.

If we return to the point of departure for these reflections, we are faced with the paradox that politically-minded youth are turning away from one of the most cultivated and significant authors of their nation, from one of the most qualified and esteemed custodians of their tradition, because they see in him an aesthete remote from life; and do so at the very moment when this profound and aristocratic spirit turns his attention to the realm of politics, when he appeals for a "new German reality in which the entire nation can participate."

But his summons will not fade without an echo. "For ascending from synthesis to synthesis, charged with a genuinely religious sense of responsibility, neglecting nothing, taking no shortcuts, omitting nothing—an effort so strenuous, provided that the genius of the nation does not let it down, must attain to this supreme height: that spirit shall be made life and life spirit; in other words: that politics shall be conceived spiritually and spirit politically for the establishment of a true nation."

B. Hofmannsthal and the Romance World

As yet the pain of our loss is too keen for the hour of quiet reflection to have arrived. For the present—and how long will it continue to be so!—our spirit is wholly concerned with groping forward in every direction of Hofmannsthal's work; of measuring the wide twilit vault of his creation; of exploring its hidden treasures and unplumbed depths. We cannot yet pace off his greatness and our loss. I do not know who these readers and experts are that even now presume to calculate to the last penny the sum of this existence and define its limits. For myself, I am still lost in boundless immensities, and no sooner do I think I have perceived some detail, grasped some particular, than it changes before my eyes, alters its luster and shape, and, eluding the theoretical understanding, merges once more with the vision of the whole. "No one escapes the great ceremony; the king and father, however, is placed in the center."

Monarchy was the innermost form of Hofmannsthal's relation to the world. His literary work was only one of the modes in which this relation manifested itself. Monarchy is the knowledge that one has been placed at the center of a vast realm, laden with every dignity and responsibility, always having to embrace the whole: the scale of all degrees from beggar to prince; the meaning of all destinies; the order of the great ceremony. The personae of beggar and king return in both the *Grosses Welttheater* and the *Kleines Welttheater* [*Great* and *Little Theater of the World*]. All of Hofmannsthal's works, from the earliest poems to the late play *Der Turm* (*The Tower*), aspire to the ideal form of the *theatrum mundi*, a universal allegorical and symbolic poem which should raise all the perplexities of existence to the order of the great fundamental laws so that the eternal may shine through temporality. Here allegory is not an attenuation of vitality nor the mask mere appearance. The reverse is the case: only when we have perceived the deceptive character of our existence do we gain insight into its deeper truth and meaning. Only rarely and in a few passages would the poet reveal this meaning to us. It is the point where the boundary ceases that divides theater from destiny; the here from the beyond:

> Hier und Dort sind gleich,
> So völlig wie zwei Pfirsichblüten sind;

> [Here and yonder are alike, as fully as are two peach blossoms;]

boundary between life and death: "The wonderful words, deeper than everything, of Jalal-Ud-Din Rumi: He who understands the power of the round dance does not fear death. For he knows that love kills." These are the moments in Hofmannsthal's work when his characters are overcome by a kind of vertigo and imagine that they are falling.

Our literature contains too much world-sentiment and not enough world; too much world-view and not enough worldliness. In Goethe there was the possibility of combining both and establishing the precise relations between them. It was necessary for him to introduce his Faust at the Imperial Court. For Goethe still had ties with the Empire, and the jubilant splendor of an imperial coronation had shed its radiance upon his childhood. But he was too late to feel the heartbeat of the Empire. Weimar was too far from Vienna, and Rome too much the guarantee of a freedom achieved at long last—

as well as too much of a cultural center—to be significant to him as a metropolis.

The cosmopolitan horizon of the old Hapsburg Empire was Hofmannsthal's birthright. Venice and Madrid belonged to it no less than

> das Wien des Canaletto,
> Wien von siebzehnhundertsechzig.

[the Vienna of Canaletto, Vienna of seventeen hundred and sixty.]

Hofmannsthal's Austria had preserved the spiritual dimensions of the old universal monarchy and the cultural heritage of its aristocratic classes. Here West and East did meet, here the cargoes of all the great European nations mingled. Wonderful, rare mixtures! Byzantium lives on in Hofmannsthal (*Der Kaiser und die Hexe*) [*The Emperor and The Witch*] as it does in his beloved Venice. And what alchemical transformations did Venice undergo in turn—from Saint-Réal through Otway through Balzac (of whose imagination Pierre and Jaffier were the lifelong companions)—to be caught at last, as the true *Gerettetes Venedig* [*Venice Preserved*], in the magic mirror of Hofmannsthal's poetry and incorporated into Germany's intellectual inheritance.

We Germans approach the Romance world as indigents; he, the Austrian, treated it as a possessor. He had no need to conquer what was his by right. He set foot upon ancestral domains as one who recognizes them as his patrimony.

Struggle and longing, study and conquest—these modes typify the German attitude toward Romanity. Dürer and Winckelmann, Goethe and George conform to this law. Not Hofmannsthal. He was the heir who could afford to be prodigal; he was the rich man:

> Dieser ist der Letzte von den Reichen,
> Von den Mächtigen der Letzte, hilflos.

[This one is the last of the rich, of the powerful the last one, helpless.]

Early in life he had recognized his destined affinities, had made himself the contemporary of the centuries of aristocracy and royalty. In the winter of 1891, while still a pupil at the Gymnasium, he writes: "I have read MM. de la Rochefoucauld, de la Bruyère, de Saint-Simon, de Montaigne, de Montesquieu, de Buffon and also the Messrs. Chamfort, Courier, Chateaubriand, Voltaire, La Mettrie, Louvet, Jean-Jacques, Diderot, Prévost, Gresset, Mably, and (*hélas*) Volney." Was it some vital inner prompting, was it deliberate, that in this enumeration the boy already distinguishes the nobles from the roture? He took up the classics of the French (and English) monarchies as representatives of an aristocratic sense of life, not as detached intellectual figures in the cultural landscape. An aristocraticism of blood and instinct attracted him to the times of Philip Chandos, of Marshal de Bassompierre. And in this there is further confirmation of the fact that he did not regard the Romance world as a foil, much less as a contrast, to the Germanic world,[1] but rather as the inherited land of the soul and of the gestures. "The Germans especially," writes Hofmannsthal in 1901, "ought always to remind themselves that they are neither the spirit of classical Antiquity nor of humanity *kat' exochen*, but a nation like any other."

These words occur in the introduction to the *Study of the Development of the Poet Victor Hugo by Hugo von Hofmannsthal, Doctor Philosophiae, submitted to the Faculty of Philosophy of the University of Vienna for the purpose of obtaining the venia legendi in the field of Romance Philology*. In the end, the defense of the dissertation was not carried out.[2] But it is worth bearing in mind that a sovereign genius, at once poet and scholar, critic and connoisseur, was im-

[1] This is also the reason why it does not provoke in him any kind of Classicism, Humanism, or Paganism but merges with the Austro-Spanish Baroque.

[2] More details in H. A. Fiechtner, *Hugo von Hofmannsthal. Die Gestalt des Dichters im Spiegel seiner Freunde* (Vienna, 1949), p. 298.

pelled, at a turning point in his youth, to choose the Romance world as the object of his studies.

What attracted Hofmannsthal to Victor Hugo? He was the model of a brilliant poetic career, actively involved with the life of the nation as a whole and at the same time having all the resources of a strict linguistic and formal tradition at his disposal. Hugo was the patriarch of words: "And it becomes evident that this incomparable poetic *oeuvre* was erected on the immense foundation of the entire national stock of words, and that there is scarcely a word in the French vocabulary that has not been summoned to participate in a more exalted and splendid existence."

The nation as represented by its literature—this, in Hofmannsthal's eyes, constituted France's exemplary importance. It was a phenomenon that never ceased to engage him. In the preface to the *Deutsches Lesebuch* he still speaks of it, and in his Munich discourse on *Das Schrifttum als geistiger Raum der Nation* he formulates a problem and a program for Germany that is incomprehensible without this background of France.

Victor Hugo was the quintessence of a grandiose eloquence, hence of something enormous (to use one of Hofmannsthal's favorite and characteristic words) to which only a kind of poverty-stricken subjectivity would refuse admiration. How could he not be receptive to it, the artist and lover of language, and especially of that French language about which no one has said such fine things as he in *Französische Redensarten* [*French Expressions*]? But in the same language that allowed a Victor Hugo to invest the emptiest, most general notions with purple pomp, books had been written, as it turned out, in which the mystery of life itself could be felt like the heartbeat of a bird in the palm of one's hand. In these books the most ephemeral events of daily life, the most sublime and the most common experiences, were amalgamated with the eternal forms of destiny, with the timeless concatenations of tragedy. In these books there was more tangible reality than in any others. They were the books of Balzac and Flaubert.

For Hofmannsthal's view of Flaubert one must read his preface to Alfred Gold's translation of the *Education Sentimentale*—one of those scattered, inaccessibly concealed, forgotten and precious utterances of Hofmannsthal's that a collected edition of his works must restore to us, as the Chassidim collect the scattered sparks of the Most High Glory.

It will also have to reprint the great essay on Balzac that Hofmannsthal composed for the Insel edition of the *Human Comedy*. In 1923 he wrote to me: "Your friendly interest reconciles me to this piece of which I have always retained an unpleasant memory, so much so that I never wanted to include it in a collection of my prose writings. I have now read it over for the first time in many years and found that it really does contain much that is right; in the essentials indeed, as a poet, I could not be mistaken."

Hofmannsthal had never read anything about Balzac besides Léon Gozlan's collection of anecdotes which, as a boy of fifteen, he had discovered among the books of his Italian grandmother. But his creative instinct reverted to Balzac two more times, in the introduction to Ernst Hardt's German version of *La Fille aux yeux d'or* and in the dialogue *Über Charaktere im Roman und im Drama* [*On Characters in the Novel and in the Drama*] which he has Balzac conduct with Baron Hammer-Purgstall—in Vienna: such was Hofmannsthal's need to draw the genius he admired into his own orbit. He was fond of combining distinct intellectual and spiritual realms and of having the one within the other, of rediscovering the *Thousand and One Nights* in the story of the girl with the golden eyes or of having Leonardo's tiny drawings from the Windsor Codex projected on a screen: "words cannot convey this intuition, one of the strongest of my life with respect to the fundamental secret of the plastic arts, on becoming aware that all these figures (horses, fishes, gnomes, machines, tools) consisted of nothing but spheres."[3] And from this impression other associations led to Delacroix's theoretical notes and to Balzac's *Chef-d'oeuvre inconnu.*

Venice—how often did it grant Hofmannsthal intuitions of the fundamental secrets of art and life. This city, where Greece and the Orient have compounded a strange, legendary marvel out of Italian substance; which the Spaniard hoped to gain by conspiracy; which after a thousand years of peerless statecraft fell prey to the Corsican until the Restoration annexed it to the Hapsburg monarchy—this city, fraught with the weariness of quite forgotten peoples, incorporating into the cathedral of its soul, as into the encrusted walls of San Marco, all the tribute of East and West;—this city seems to me to be the only symbol for Hofmannsthal's relation to Romanity and for all that in him for which this vital association itself was, in turn, only a symbol.

When the Emperor Francis I restored the horses of San Marco to the city of Venice, which had brought them back from Byzantium during the Fourth Crusade only to lose them, after nearly six centuries, to the French general, a legend was devised by an unknown to celebrate the joyous occasion:

> *Tropaeum Venetum an. 1204*
> *Spolium Gallicum an. 1797*
> *Munus Austriacum an. 1815*

From the language and soul of the Romance world Hofmannsthal gathered the most priceless treasure for his crown jewels. We preserve it as his legacy, as *munus Austriacum.*

1929

[3] From the letter cited above.

George, Hofmannsthal,
and Calderón

AFTER an early meeting in Vienna in 1890, the paths of Hofmannsthal and George did not cross again. Their destinies obeyed different laws. They sought and found fulfillment in worlds between which there was no longer any connection. And yet there was much that the youth of George and Hofmannsthal had in common. I wish to draw attention to only one significant element in it: the assimilation of the linguistic and literary spirit of the Romance world.

France, Italy, Spain—varied as are the national characters, the intellectual visages, the cultural forms of these three countries, they still present themselves to the eye of the German people as one great common entity, in which it sees a threefold development of Romance culture. That which we term Romania is, in spite of its inner diversity and division, held together by the close and firm bond of linguistic affinity. This linguistic and intellectual Romania borders on German territory in the West and in the South: an orientation to the West and an orientation to the South can be distinguished in the German relation to Romania. At the same time, however, one can observe that the German intellectual spirit, whenever it has been made productive through contact with the Romance element, reaches out both to France and to Italy and finally also to the Iberian southwest. So it was in the Middle Ages, with Goethe, with Romanticism. And the process repeated itself about the year 1890, when Stefan George and Hugo von Hofmannsthal began their careers.

Affinity attracted the young George to France. When he first went to Paris as a young man of twenty, he set foot upon French soil conscious of being an heir. And at the same time he was happily surprised to find there the enlivening effect of an artistic atmosphere in which he could breathe. What the contact with Mallarmé and Verlaine, the participation in the literary movement of the eighties and the close association with its spiritual substance meant to him is certified so often in his work that I do not wish to dwell on it. It should be enough to recall a few sentences from the *Blätter für die Kunst*, in which George declares how little the German atmosphere, a compound of decadence and naturalism, suited him and how necessary the finding of a way to the West, a way out to the West, became for him. He outlines the historical situation in these words: "a totally distorted Romanticism and a sickly epigonism revolved unrhythmically about our youth: and when in the streets and in the public squares gross natures presented to us as real the upside-down world which the barbarous error of their eyes conveyed to their uneducated souls: then sadness gripped us, and some lost courage. But for others a dawn rose through their tears . . . *poets were still singing in Gaul.* And such among us as felt strong enough to do so, took up the staff of pious pilgrimages."

From the French literature of those days George received the experience of a completely rarefied art that made no compromises with life, a stately and mysterious music of the soul. It contained much twilight, much loneliness, much vision. But in the measure that George's genius grew more robust, he was driven to seek a more intense existence. The weary enchantment of symbolism started to pale; it was supplanted by the lure of the Romance South. "To seek completeness in the South," that after all had been, as the *Blätter für die Kunst* were now saying, "eternal law in the Holy Roman Empire of the German Nation." And there too one could read the moral lesson: "There is little left for the German to learn from the

Nordic spirit that he does not already possess, and without the distortions. But from the Romance spirit he can learn clarity, breadth, luminosity." These words and this situation of George's life indicate the turning of the axis from West to South, from France to Italy. But while still in France, George had already turned toward Spain late in the summer of 1889. "There he was overcome," as his biographer says, "by that rare feeling of reunion with a homeland that had long since disappeared: the remembrance of a dominion that had died away long before grew with every step that he took into the unknown country, and in the 'island garden' at Aranjuez it distilled into that clear-cut recognition that later took poetic form in the *Pilgerfahrten* [*Pilgrimages*] and *Hängenden Gärten* [*The Book of the Hanging Gardens*]." What George received from Spain seems to have been "intense images of a regal solitude and an unapproachable majesty"—in other words, a new and stronger resonance for the figure of Algabal as it was then taking shape in his mind.

Thus the young George gained essential elements of experience and art from France and Spain. He must also have felt the need to master the Romance languages technically. To know that he had attended lectures on Romance philology at the University of Berlin is after all not entirely without significance. To be sure, the fact that George created his own language, composed of Latin and Spanish elements, is of much greater importance. In this *Lingua Romana,* as he called it, George wrote poems which only the complete edition of his works has made accessible to us. Thus in George's encounter with the languages of the Romance world an intellectual will to power already asserts itself, compelling him to reshape, nearly to the point of violation, what he had laid hold of by elective affinity.

A basic trait of George's intellectual nature was to shape and control all that was foreign according to his own law. He handled all the elements of culture like a dictator. Hofmannsthal's intellectual attitude was completely different. His cultural development was one long process of assimilation. He

144

yielded to what enchanted him. But, while appearing to lose himself, he nevertheless found again in whatever was most alien only the provinces of his own ancestral realm. This inner realm of the soul was to the young Hofmannsthal like a broad landscape seen in a dream. But in the process of inner maturation, which the last phase of his creativity documents so wonderfully, this dream world revealed itself to him as a reflection of Austria's destiny. "Ancient European soil," so he wrote at that time, "has been given to us as our heritage, we stand upon it as the successors to two Roman empires, this is our charge, we must bear it, whether we wish to do so or not: the soil of our homeland is sacred and heavy with destiny." For 2000 years the border march of the *Imperium Romanum*, for 1100 years that of the mediaeval empire, bearer of the universal monarchy of the Hapsburgs—this to Hofmannsthal was the meaning of Austria's historical heritage. It embraced the faded glory of the *Sacra Caesarea Maiestas*, but also a people and a soil stamped by its venerable and responsible character. George's intellectual dominion was derived from self-constituted power. He was founder and lawmaker by his own decree. The authority of Hofmannsthal, however, if we may use a political metaphor, rested on legal succession and tradition. We can see this salient contrast in every intellectual manifestation in the lives of the two poets. We see it too in their relation to the Romance world.

The assimilation of this world had been one of the most significant experiences in Hofmannsthal's education as well. During his sixteenth and seventeenth years he absorbs the intellectual stimulants of Parisian literary fashion. From 1890 on, what is "modern" is one of his points of departure. The first of the critical essays which he wrote while still a student at the *Gymnasium* and which he signed with the pseudonym Loris is dedicated to Paul Bourget's work on *The Psychology of Modern Love*. There follow studies on Maurice Barrès and his *Culte du moi* [*Cult of the Ego*], on the confessions of Amiel and Marie Bashkirtseff. The name Stendhal appears. As Loris defines it: "Two things seem to be modern:

the analysis of life and the flight from life. . . . One practices the anatomy of one's own psychological life, or one dreams. . . . Modern are old furniture and young neuroses." But these Parisian actualities soon disappear, never to recur. Their place is taken by the influence exerted by the great French poets and prose writers from Molière and Racine to Balzac, Flaubert, and Victor Hugo. If I select these five authors in particular, it is because each of them was of creative significance for Hofmannsthal and had a decisive effect on his intellectual development. In 1901 Hofmannsthal intended to submit a study of Victor Hugo to the University of Vienna in order to qualify as a lecturer in Romance Philology. As it turned out, this plan was not realized, but it does indicate—as do Hofmannsthal's critical essays—an interest in the Romance intellectual world that was much ampler, much freer, much more receptive than that of George, for whom the work of a Victor Hugo was unacceptable. As unacceptable as that of Balzac or Flaubert. Hofmannsthal admired the French novel of the nineteenth century as he did the French Classicism of the seventeenth for their incomparably rich and vivid presentation of the world and their knowledge of it. He was of course aware that this French view of the world was restricted to the entanglements of the human comedy. It remained tied to the social sphere, but this circle it filled completely, traversing all the inextricably intermingled strata, from the commonplace to the tragic. Hofmannsthal's outlook was universal, as only Goethe's before him. Cosmopolitan in every sense of the word, from the religious to the gentlemanly, he might have said of himself, like the great Leibniz: "je ne méprise presque rien."

George on the other hand was a great despiser. What he could not absorb, he denied, when he did not condemn it. He disapproved of Hofmannsthal's cosmopolitanism as irresponsible indolence. It was his titanic ambition to oppose an esoteric counterworld to that of ordinary reality. The novel, the theater, the opera, ultimately music in general—for him all this did not exist. A magnificent intolerance was intrinsic to his cast of mind. He created for himself his own language, his own circle—finally, out of the Maximin experience, his own cult. Whereas Hofmannsthal always felt the urge to unite with everything, George was driven by his daemon towards separation, exclusion, and the breach with his contemporaries. Thus in his late period George also broke off all ties to the Romance world, with a single exception: the poetic association with Dante. Despite the intervening centuries a secret affinity bound him to the Florentine. Like Dante, he thought of himself as the judge and censor of the age.

IT IS characteristic that Dante's name is seldom mentioned by Hofmannsthal, and then only in the early period. If Goethe chose Rome, Nietzsche the cliffs of the Ligurian coast, George Florence—then Hofmannsthal's Italian home was Venice. Hofmannsthal's "Venetian Cycle" begins with the *Tod des Tizian* [*Death of Titian*] (1892). Then follow *Der Abenteurer und die Sängerin* [*The Adventurer and the Singer*] (1899), *Das gerettete Venedig* [*Venice Preserved*] (1905), *Christinas Heimreise* [*Christina's Journey Home*] (1910), *Der Brief des letzten Contarin* [*The Letter of the Last Contarin*] (1929), *Andreas oder die Vereinigten* [*Andreas, or the United*] (1932). These works would require separate treatment. In Venice Hofmannsthal found the rarest mixture of historical elements—a breath of Byzantium, a glimmer of the Orient, a legacy of Austria: all blended into an indefinable enchantment from which many of his most exquisite works are drawn. And when I say enchantment, I use the word in the precise sense that Hofmannsthal himself gives it. "Where is your self to be found?" he once asks. And he replies: "Always in the deepest enchantment that you have suffered." Magic, enchantment: in Hofmannsthal's mouth these are not the devalued clichés of our everyday language. If Hofmannsthal speaks of magic, we must recognize in it a primary mode of experience and one which figures again for us today as a constant and significant factor in human life. We know today that the primitive's magical picture of the world possesses an inner regularity and order which is in no wise inferior to the scientific concept of causality. This magic universe is not a curiosity from the lumber-room of ethnology, but a possibility which can be realized over and over again on high and even the highest levels of intellectuality. Nothing is more natural than that this possibility should manifest itself precisely in the creative power of the poet. We think of the magic idealism of Novalis, of the esoteric fragments of the lucid Goethe, or even of the vision of man and the world which constitutes the key to Balzac's *Human Comedy*.

In ordinary thinking we trace every effect back to one or several specific causes, and we base our conception of cause and effect on the image of a sphere which is set in motion by a push. Thus man is moved by "motives," or he is determined by natural laws of nationality, heredity, social structure. In the magical view of the world, on the other hand, everything depends on everything else: every partial event is in reciprocal relation with the whole of the world. And to this world belong the most distant suns and stars. Astrology also presupposes such a mode of thought. It is the ancient conception of man as the microcosm that corresponds to the macrocosm of the universe. Whenever the poet or artist contemplates the world in magical correspondences, man is always seen as the bearer of cosmic ties. Magical poetry, like all magical thinking, always endeavors to reestablish these correspondences, which reach beyond man and the earth. Man is now no longer the center of creation. He stands somewhere on this scale which at either extreme points to infinity. By placing himself at the center of things he becomes guilty of a naïve presumption. This is affirmed in Hofmannsthal's aphorism: "Anthropocentrism, too, is a kind of chauvinism."

From its earliest beginnings Hofmannsthal's work as an artist circles about the relationship between the self and the universe. Just as in his dramatic poems the beggar stands beside the emperor, the madman beside the poet, the adventurer beside the maiden—so his spiritual person could only find its resonance in the All. We may interpret what the emperor of Byzantium says to his crown in an early play of Hofmannsthal's as a declaration of the poet himself:

> Und er schliesst das Weltall ein:
> Diese ganze Welt voll Hoheit
> Und Verzweiflung, voll von Gräbern
> Und von Ackern, Bergen, Meeren,
> Alles schliesst er ein. . . .

> [And it contains the universe:
> This whole world that's full of doubt
> And majesty, is full of graves,
> Full of ploughland, mountains, seas,
> For all things it contains. . . .]
>
> [Michael Hamburger]

This conception of the world expressed by the emperor is also only a symbol of a more elevated and still more comprehensive vision of the world, which we can observe developing from synthesis to synthesis in Hofmannsthal's work. But we must be sure to remind ourselves that any philosophical problems that might arise from such a view of the world are not present as such for the poet. Ever since Plato a perpetual conflict has existed between the poets and the philosophers. But the poet is superior in that for him problems are not solved through concepts but through form. The work of thought is never-ending, but the creation of the poet is the perfected form. The poet expresses the inexpressible in the language of symbols. From his hand we receive an ordered structure of the world, purged of all philosophical loose ends. "We can love only form, and he who pretends that he is in love with ideas, always loves them only as form. Form settles the problem, it answers the unanswerable."

THE form of a work of literature that aspires to represent human existence in its relations with the entire cosmos can only be the drama. But not, to be sure, the classicistic tragedy of the French or the Germans. This classical form of drama, born of the Renaissance and Humanism, is anthropocentric.

It separates man from the cosmos and the forces of religion, and imprisons him in the noble solitude of the realm of ethics. The tragic characters of Racine and Goethe are confronted with moral decisions. The reality with which they are involved is the play of human spiritual energies. The greatness and the limitation of classical tragedy is its being enclosed within the psychological sphere. The circle of its strict laws can never be broken. The tragic hero can only dash himself to pieces against them. He cannot reconcile himself with fate. But this form of tragedy is an artificial plant on the soil of the European tradition. It grew out of the misunderstood doctrines of the Humanists. Its impossible ambition was to span the millennia that lie between Pericles and Louis XIV: Goethe himself had had to shatter this form when he created his universal poem *Faust*.

Hofmannsthal too had to find a connection with the almost buried, or rather forgotten, form of the mediaeval mystery plays, the morality plays, the religious and secular drama which the Baroque theater had inherited from the declining Middle Ages and which by way of the folk drama of Bavaria and Austria extends into the present. He was able to infuse new life into these rigidified forms. In 1911 he successfully made his first great renovation, the *Spiel vom Sterben des reichen Mannes* [*Play of the Death of the Rich Man*] that bears the title *Jedermann* [*Everyman*] and harks back to an English work of the fifteenth century. In the earlier play, too, God, the angels, and the devil appear. Allegorical figures such as Death and Faith take part. And the character about whom the entire play revolves is not a hero with a name, but the nameless Everyman: man, entangled in terrestrial matters and now placed before the judgment seat of God. This religious play was presented in Salzburg, in the Cathedral Square. "The fifteen-foot figures of saints, between which the actors made their entrances and exits, seemed perfectly natural; perfectly natural the droning of the great bells at the end of the play, the procession of the six angels into the twilit portal. . . . As natural as the symbolism, the tragedy, the gaiety, the music. The whole thing seemed natural to the peasants, too, who came streaming in first from the periphery of the city, then from the nearest villages, then from farther and farther away. They said: 'The theater is playing again. That is good.' " Hofmannsthal's creative instinct always tended toward theater. Toward theater, not toward drama, if I may be allowed to indicate in so abbreviated a formula an essential difference between two forms that are easily confused. Theater is a primary phenomenon of mankind. It grows out of ritual ceremonies and has a background in magic and religion. Mime, ceremony, dance, music are fused in it. Gesture, indeed the language of movement altogether, is as essential to it as words. Only in the late stages of enlightenment, when a civilization is aging, does this original unity disintegrate. Mime degenerates into farce, the element of religion detaches itself, to end as drama of ideas, as psychology, as rhetoric. What began as a ceremonial representation of life turns into a petrified literary form. But all great epochs bring drama and theater together again. The great writer of plays is always an actor at the same time—like Shakespeare and Molière—or at least active for a troupe—like Calderón and Goldoni. "His inspiration is never merely rhetorical or merely psychological, but always mimic." To reunite poetry and theater was Hofmannsthal's high aspiration. Consequently, as in Salzburg, the people was once more drawn into the delights of play-acting. But this attempt, which Hofmannsthal had ventured for the first time with *Everyman*, carried immense significance: for it meant nothing less than the bridging of a gulf which had grown ever deeper in the last centuries of the development of European culture: the gulf between the enlightened educated world and the original play-instinct, between modern intellectual problems and timeless symbolism.

WITH *Everyman* Hofmannsthal had renewed a timeless Middle Ages and entered upon the path of metaphysical drama. In pursuing it, he was bound to encounter Calderón. From this encounter originated *Das Grosse Salzburger Welttheater*

[*The Great Salzburg Theater of the World*] in 1921. This encounter was a fulfillment. But it had long since been prepared for, had already been anticipated in dreams and presentiments. The great images of the Spanish Golden Age must have been close to the Austrian from the start. Like Grillparzer, he felt that Spain "in a certain sense was part of Austrian history." If even today the Spanish Riding School in the Vienna Hofburg attracts the foreign visitor, it is nevertheless but one last tiny remnant of a world-historical community of culture which, without touching Paris, bound together Madrid and Vienna in imperial splendor. We forget too easily that from the time of Charles V until late in the seventeenth century this cross-connection determined the style of European culture: in state and clerical matters as well as in art, fashion, and mode of life. France itself was culturally dependent on Madrid even into the period of Louis XIV, and Versailles is an Escorial translated into French. Only after the Treaty of the Pyrenees in 1659 does the dominant role in Europe pass to France. But then, to be sure, it makes its way so forcibly by every means of politics and culture that to this day it has almost extinguished the older Spanish-Austrian hegemony in our picture of history. Our usual historical view shows us the splendor of the Italian Renaissance, the power of faith of the German Reformation, the universal power of the French mind, to which the great Frederick still paid homage—it shows us these stages of our humanity up to the threshold of the nineteenth century. Both French and North-German Protestant historiography shaped this conception. But things looked different from Vienna. In the dynastic tradition, in the popular piety molded by the Reformation, and in the Baroque attitude toward art, traces of the old bond with Spain lived on. The Austrian poet did not need Romantic telemagic to conjure up an airy vision of Spain; Spain was close to him through living historical connections.

These were organic ties of a more than personal nature. They constitute, as it were, the rootstock from which Hofmannsthal's relation to Calderón could spring. They created the propitious atmosphere. But for that relation to become a decisive encounter, a genuine fulfillment, a secret affinity of the soul was necessary, whereby the one could recognize his own self in that of the other. This secret and complex process had already begun in Hofmannsthal's youth. We can follow it step by step and rung by rung. It is the guiding thread which leads us through the intricate mazes of Hofmannsthal's existence as a poet. It is a spiritual event which penetrated in its progress all the strata of Hofmannsthal's world; a key which opens hidden regions to us. We may see the first station along this road in the free adaptation[1] of Calderón's *La vida es sueño* [*Life is a Dream*] (1902). The motifs of this drama subsequently continued to accompany Hofmannsthal's imagination and were finally reshaped and reborn in the tragedy *Der Turm* [*The Tower*] (1925). Hofmannsthal revived an entirely different side of Calderón's work in the *Grosses Welttheater*, as previously mentioned. But that is still not all. After the war Hofmannsthal published a free translation of *Dame Kobold* [*The Elfin Lady*], one of Calderón's elegant comedies of intrigue. This is the first and only volume of an announced series of *Dramen des Calderon, teils in getreuer, teils in freier Übersetzung* [partly in literal, partly in free translation]. A redaction of Calderón's Phocas drama which was among Hofmannsthal's literary remains was probably also intended for this series. From these remains sketches for two dramas, representing different versions of the Semiramis legend, were published in 1933; dramas that had been inspired, but no more than inspired, by Calderón's *La hija del aire* [*Daughter of the Air*]. For in these as yet hardly known, hardly interpreted fragments the most wondrous metamorphosis of source-material into something brilliantly new and personal takes place. This enumeration alone reveals how many and how diverse were the ways by which Hofmannsthal approached Calderón. His Calderón creations sometimes remind one of the changes of a kaleidoscope,

---

[1] Published in 1918 in the *Rodauner Nachträge* as "a paraphrase after Calderón."

whose iridescent colors never cease to amaze. But each of them corresponds to an inner change in Hofmannsthal: to a change in emotional content as well as in poetic form. In the corpus of works that we can designate as Hofmannsthal's Calderón-Cycle, we find in the first place all the transitional stages from translation to free adaptation right up to re-creation. With this we touch upon the most fundamental quality of Hofmannsthal's literary work, which I should like to describe as *integrative imagination*. For Hofmannsthal, as for his brother in magic, Novalis, it was a fundamental insight that all intellectual substance which has been given form can become matter for new creation. For on the infinite ladder of the All everything is at once form and matter. "It is not enough for the intellectual products of an epoch, except for the most outstanding, simply to exist; something must then be done with them." The higher always comes about through integration. "Everything higher requires synthesis. The superior man is the union of several men, the superior work of poetry demands several poets in one in order to be brought forth." Such and similar statements have their roots in a view of the nature of the intellect which is close to that of Romanticism and Goethe. The laws of intellectual creation are seen in the image of chemical and biological processes.

In this alchemy of the intellect, inherited cultural possessions and artistic forms are melted down, transmuted, and summoned to a new and higher life. Thus Hofmannsthal's imagination takes possession of the mediaeval Dance of Death, or (as in his *Ariadne*) a comedy of Molière, or, finally, the drama of Calderón. These substances are dissected, dissolved, volatilized; what is unsuitable is separated out, and, at last, the regenerated form issues from the integrative imagination. This is, viewed from within and according to its truth, the creative process that the incomprehension of the critics and the public used to dismiss contemptuously as the reworking of older materials.

But the question we must now ask ourselves is this—what element of Calderón's world could so affect, attract, and bind Hofmannsthal's emotions? The dream experience runs through the poetry of Hofmannsthal's youth like an eternal melody.

> Dein Antlitz war mit Träumen ganz beladen . . .

[Your face was wholly laden with dreams . . .]

> Den Traum vom Leben niegeahnter Wesen . . .

[The dream of the existence of never-suspected beings . . .]

> Und drei sind eins: ein Mensch, ein Ding, ein
> Traum . . .

[And three are one: a man, a thing, a dream . . .]

Lines like these appear again and again. They express a dreamlike apprehension of all of life's possibilities:

> O wüsst ich mehr von diesem Abenteuer,
> Denn irgendwie bin ich darin verwebt
> Und weiss nicht, wo sich Traum und Leben spalten.

[Oh, that I knew much more of these adventures,
For in some way I'm interwoven with them
And do not know where life and dream divide.]
>   [Michael Hamburger]

This psychological disposition enabled Hofmannsthal to find the way to Calderón's *La vida es sueño*. With it was interwoven, I believe, the motif of the prince imprisoned in the tower: an image with which Hofmannsthal, as we may guess from many indications, identified himself. To be sure, these are but two tender buds which only unfolded much later. We know from Hofmannsthal's letters that Calderón's drama about the dream of life and his own adaptation of this drama "in the last analysis became completely intelligible only through the experience of the war" (to Hermann Bahr, 1918). This was also the case with the second Calderón drama that occupied him: the Semiramis tragedy. It, too, was "only comprehended in its total symbolism and taken up anew because of the war."

One of Hofmannsthal's favorite sayings, which he found in Lichtenberg, runs: "The whole man must move at once." He found that it expressed a law of his own nature. Always involved with the whole, always striving toward the whole, he was forced to suffer every transformation of his nature in such a way that it affected the whole of his artistic capacity. This applies, therefore, also to the embryonic works within him that were struggling to be born; and to those, as well, which he received from foreign sources. The change wrought in him by the war has nothing to do with what is generally understood as the "experience of war." Rather it was the experience of a tremendous shock: a world was coming apart at the seams. It was the world of the nineteenth century that had been unmasked as a world of "materialism, of the dominion of money over the mind, of the dangerous abasement of man, whom a constant fear of death in a thousand disguises had condemned to impotent slavery." It was the threat of chaos and disintegration. And to all this was now added the new distress of the war. "A thousandfold acceptance and anticipation of death. . . . The most bitter suppression of egotism, even of the desire for self-preservation." Suffering was experienced "as a divine principle." Elemental forces awakened: "the people, the sacred and fertile depths, they for whom life was an eternal war. Once again the superpersonal was the real." Everything else that Hofmannsthal wrote and thought from 1917 until his death in 1929 is irradiated by this immense experience of divine suffering, and simultaneously of mysterious regeneration through the divine elemental powers. From a despair which threatened his very life he was delivered because he suffered it to the end and in so doing conquered all mortal fear. As a consequence he became estranged from all the events that were taking place upon the foreground of the times. "With other earthly fears," he wrote at that period, "we cast from us all fear of time: more and more the present becomes a veil to us, the sense of a higher present becomes distinct."

Now Hofmannsthal lives and contemplates *sub specie aeterni*. He dwells in timelessness. He recognizes transience and change as delusory appearance. He turns to the eternally-same, to the abiding root of things. He has the mystic's experience of the simultaneity of all things: "The lands and the peoples of the earth, the teeming masses and the immobile solitudes, the secrets of time and space, everything stands, ordered as for processions, in an immense expectation." "Everything is, as though it had always been there, and everything else is there, too, everything is there at the same time." This transcendental view of the world and of history can only be obscured by attending to the moment, by gazing fixedly at the present. "One has to transcend the feeling of the present, as when in listening to music one transcends the perception of the timbres of the instruments." "In order to see at all, one has to get the sand out of one's eyes which the present constantly throws into them." In his youth Hofmannsthal's emotional state was a dreamlike indulgence in the infinity of the world. But as early as the first draft of *Semiramis*, which was written before the war, there is the unsettling realization "that the infinity of life is not to be exhausted in enjoyment, as actuality, but only symbolically and through suffering." This is the prelude to the spiritual transformation that Hofmannsthal experienced during the years of war and revolution.

IF WE look back at the road we have traversed, we shall now also understand that search for a timeless Middle Ages which was announced in *Jedermann* and which finally grew to perfection in the wonderful recasting of Calderón's dramas. From the earliest periods of its history, Spain has always gone its own way. It never shared the common destinies of Europe —except for a brief moment: during the era of Philip II; but at that time it ruled these destinies instead of enduring them. The great historical memories of Spain: the Gothic kings, the sway of the Moors, the Reconquista, then the founding of an overseas empire, finally the colorful decline and fall—all this is joined together in a national history which shows different destinies and different accents from those of the rest of Europe. Spain takes little or no part in the great movements with which the modern era begins: the Reformation, the Renaissance, Humanism and the classical attitude toward art. It has different obligations and a different ambition. Out of Castile and Aragon it forges the unified dynastic state; it breaks the last remnants of Moorish domination and in the latter half of the sixteenth century still has to carry on tenacious struggles with the Moriscos. It discovers and conquers the new world, it engenders in asceticism and mysticism the prototypes of Catholic orthodoxy, which then radiate out to all of Europe —and it creates a grandiose literature that springs from its native soil and its own genius in simply inexhaustible abundance. The art of this Spanish Golden Age is little concerned with the classical models of Antiquity or with Aristotle's alleged system of rules. It has no intercourse at all with the spirit of rationalism in France. In aesthetics as in philosophical outlook, it draws upon the boundless wealth of a tradition that never broke with the Middle Ages. Monarchy and the Catholic faith are the pillars that support this world. It is permeated by the powers of magic and miracle. Whereas the heroes of the French stage fight out psychological conflicts, Calderón's spiritual plays revolve around the mystery of the Holy Sacrament. European Classicism finds edification in a stoic Roman world and erects an image of Antiquity that stands in immediate and unreconciled juxtaposition with the Christian state religions. In Calderón's world Rome and Greece are never models for ethical or human attitudes: they are always a mere decorative background, in quite the same sense as Semiramis's Babylon, Phocas's Byzantium, Sigismund's Poland. To the Spaniard's eye, world history is a single vast picture-book in which all the pages are equally important: an "Archive of the Ages," in which the nations of all periods and places have recorded their memoirs: the

Goths as well as the Arabs, the Dutch as well as the Peruvians. The Atridae are no more eminent, no more interesting than the kings of Nineveh or the "Landgraves of Asia." History is a great procession of marvelous figures. The demigods of Greek mythology stand beside the crowned martyrs of Christianity. They all form part of the great chronicle of the miraculous. They are all actors on the great stage of the world. The world as a stage on which divine powers direct the destinies—this ancient idea, which can be traced back to Plato: in Calderón's dramatic survey of the world it has been realized as never before or since. And, in addition, all these human destinies are now interwoven with the orbits of the stars, with the poisons and the healing powers of Nature, with the movement of the eleven celestial spheres. Magic and cosmic forces rule in this world; diabolical witchcraft flares up—and yet in the last analysis everything is governed by ordinance of divine grace and wisdom.

That is Calderón's world. And we now understand why this world could be a guidepost for Hofmannsthal, pointing to that timeless Middle Ages, that metaphysical drama, that he sought. The term Middle Ages is not to be understood literally here. It does not denote a unique period of history, but a spiritual realm in which the Catholic-Christian view of the world prevails. In this sense the Middle Ages is the creation of Christian philosophy, not, to be sure, of scholasticism, but of the Church fathers. From them comes Christian history's image of the world, which takes shape in accordance with the cardinal facts of the Creation, the Fall, the Redemption, and the Last Judgment. This image was decomposed by the new paganism of the Renaissance, by the systems of Rationalism, by the mechanistic view of nature, and by the spirit of the Enlightenment. But these forces could not be operative in Calderón's Spain. There, the mediaeval Christian image of the world still held undisputed sway in an era which, from the European perspective, is called Baroque and which is separated by scarcely three generations from the year in which Goethe was born. It is this image of the world, however, that supports the magnificent structure of ideas that is Calderón's metaphysical theater.

This theater is just as remote from that of Shakespeare as from that of French and German Classicism. It cannot be measured by any of these standards. In spite of profound differences in structure, the English, French, and German theaters are connected with each other by a common conception of man. The human being is the pivot of this theater. He rises to his greatest majesty in the person of the tragic hero. This hero bears individual traits. He is a "character," a unique person. And his character is his destiny—indeed, character is the only form in which destiny becomes at all comprehensible and effective. The more exclusively the dramatic action is determined by the characters of the heroes, the higher we tend to value it. Neoclassical aesthetics demands the greatest degree of inwardness. The spokesmen for this aesthetics have always reproached Calderón with not knowing how to depict characters. This reproach misses the essence of the Calderonian drama. Naturally, Calderón shows familiarity with psychological conflicts too. But with him they never become the pivotal points of the drama, because his drama is not centered in man; on the contrary, man always acts as defined by cosmic and religious ties. It is the movement of the constellations and, on a higher plane, the mysterious reciprocity between divine mercy and human freedom that determine his destiny. Calderón's stage, at least in his *autos sacramentales*, is theocentric. Allegorical figures: the world, wisdom, death, vanity, idolatry, light, the four elements . . . and many others, appear as intermediaries between God and Mankind. Accordingly, Calderón's people are not characters independent in themselves, but types. Such types are the wise man, the soldier, the droll servant, the king, the beggar, the peasant . . . and many others. Under ever-new names they come together for the intricate play of the most diverse and colorful plot. The essential element of this theater is rapid flow of action combined with surprising changes of situation. It satisfies the people's delight in spectacle no less than the thinker's need for profundity. These dramatic situations are not resolved psychologically; they exist for their own sake, they symbolize the infinite nature of cosmic relations. They are alive with symbolic significance.

FROM here another road leads to Hofmannsthal. In his aphorisms we find the remark: "Situations are symbolic; it is the weakness of men today that they treat things analytically and hence dissolve their magic." And also this statement: "Allegory is a great vehicle that ought not to be disdained. What friends really mean to each other is more likely to be made clear through an exchange of magic rings or a magic horn than through psychology." *Symbolism of situation* as a dramatic moment—this term of Hofmannsthal's, which we have made use of, is certainly the most accurate statement that the critical mind has ever made about Calderón's dramas. With this we touch upon a new connection between the two poets, one of the most remarkable. It is not only that Hofmannsthal became better acquainted with himself in the mirror of Calderón: one may also maintain the opposite, that through Hofmannsthal Calderón again became comprehensible to us. But how are we to understand the idea of "symbolism of situation"? I would like to demonstrate it by an example. In Calderón's theater we again and again encounter the figure of the royal personage who has grown up and been kept in solitude, either in the wilderness, in a grotto, or in a dungeon, far from the world. Such figures are Prince Sigismund in *La vida es sueño*, the sons of the king in the Phocas drama, Semiramis herself, but also mythological figures like Narcissus and heroic ones like Achilles. All these figures are then torn from their dream existence, their cave, their prison by a reversal of fortune. At the moment of their awakening to the world their souls are subject to the most awful tensions. This "awakening to the world," as I term it, is one of the typical situations of Calderón's theater. How rich is the symbolism of this situation! It is already hinted at in Plato's allegory of the cave, and to conceive of the body as the prison of the

161

mind is likewise a Platonic myth. But this cave-existence, this prison-tower represents at the same time the preexistence of souls before birth, which is exhibited in Calderón's *Gran Teatro del Mundo* as in Hofmannsthal's *Grosses Welttheater*. And, finally, Prince Sigismund's awakening to the world, his liberation from the tower, his failure in this trial, is only the allegorical vesture for the destiny of the human soul through preexistence, birth, the Fall, and redemption. Calderón himself hinted at this allegory by writing a sequel to *La vida es sueño*, a sacramental play with the same title that transposes the action of the first drama to the theological plane.

But Hofmannsthal carried these possibilities further. In his tragedy *Der Turm*, Sigismund is Prince of Poland, but he is at the same time "the man who enters an existing order of life from the complete innocence of the state of nature and endowed with a rich inheritance of eternal powers" (Grete Schaeder). Beyond that he is the suffering righteous man, drawn "on the model of Christ's suffering" (Nadler). In this sense Hofmannsthal's tragedy is also a passion play. Here too suffering is revealed as "a divine principle." And from this we understand Hofmannsthal's statement, that the Calderón material only became completely intelligible to him through the events of the war. Allusions to the outcome of the World War, to the collapse of Austria, and to revolution are also woven in other ways into the Tower drama. It is no longer the tragedy of a prince, but of an entire state of the world. The same Calderón material which had originally affected the young Hofmannsthal only as a melancholy fantasy about the dream of life is transformed, extended, and ultimately intensified into the tragedy of social revolution.

THE exact counterpart of this palingenesis we now find in the Semiramis dramas. The ancient historians impressed Semiramis on the memory of the millennia as the founder of the Assyrian Empire, the constructor of Babylon, and the creator of one of the seven wonders of the world: the hanging gardens. She was said to have been the daughter of a fish-goddess, nursed by doves after she had been exposed, found by shepherds. As the consort of the governor of Syria she undertakes a sudden offensive which alters the fortunes of the land. King Ninos snatches her away from her husband and makes her his queen. She bears him a son: Ninyas. Ninos dies. Semiramis now rules for forty-two years and conquers one country after the other. Finally she resigns the throne to Ninyas and dies. For Antiquity Semiramis is a superhuman woman, as titanic in her greed for power as in her voluptuousness, which assured her a place in Dante's *Inferno*. Calderón omitted the latter trait. He emphasizes her pride and her craving for power. He loves such heroic women, as is also shown by his *Zenobia*. The second quality that may have attracted Calderón to this material was its aura of the miraculous and the astonishing. By this I mean the essence of all that the Romans called *prodigium* and the Middle Ages *mirabilia*. The feeding by the doves fits in here, but so does the miraculous construction of the hanging gardens, and so does an anecdotal element (which was still used by Hofmannsthal): the impending danger of war is announced to the queen while her hair is being done and she rushes from her dressing table into battle. Finally Calderón, like many others, made this material more significant through the rule of fate, which man struggles against in vain. For decades Hofmannsthal was occupied with this material. In 1905 he plans a Semiramis tragedy. In 1908 the project for a Semiramis opera arises. "The Calderón play," so he writes to Richard Strauss at the time, "will be only the point of departure for me, not the model. I did not know how to deal with Semiramis' reign and the entire proceedings of state; actually, the whole thing must first be dissolved into my own dreams and then recrystallized from these into a drama." The Semiramis of this draft has been approximated to the Mother- and Astarte-deities of the Near East. She is uncertain whether she is a goddess or a woman. She must demand of the man who embraces her that he be more than a human being. "A god, an all-encompasser, ought to have embraced her." She receives the prophecy that she will kill her husband, behead her lover, fight battles, burn cities. In the course of the action Semiramis' faith in her own divinity was to have crumbled and finally collapsed completely. "The holy river, dammed up by the dead, rises over its banks; Semiramis senses in horror that she can become ill and die." And now the realization dawns upon her that only suffering exhausts the meaning of life: "that he alone lives who has learned to possess death." Not until she has become aware of death is she able to feel love; only now does she live. So death is here, too, as in all of Hofmannsthal's work, the "interpreter of life" (Nadler); it is "revelation and completion."

That is the *Semiramis* of 1908. But after ten years, four of them war years, how great is the change! The new version now bears the title *Die beiden Götter* [*The Two Gods*]. Ninyas takes his place beside Semiramis as the polar complement. Semiramis now represents sovereign authority, lack of spirituality, duress, the existing order. Ninyas, however, represents spirit and love. Two cosmic principles thus confront one another, two "gods": Power and Love; and that means at the same time: West and East. Semiramis is heroic, actually virile. Heroism wants to give permanence to the deed and the person. Ninyas, however, embodies the Tao, the "cosmos, which is indestructible even when imprisoned." He does not want heroism, but rather the eternal revolution of the cosmic forces. Ninyas is incapable of action "because he has recognized the world for what it is." But Semiramis is always afraid of being absorbed by Ninyas: "of being annulled: just because he does not act." Semiramis keeps Ninyas imprisoned. But the prisoner has an effect on the people. He escapes with the aid of the people. Semiramis has him banished again and herself pretends to be Ninyas. (In Calderón she is able to do this since her face exactly resembles that of Ninyas.) As Ninyas she rules and dictates (this scene too has its prototype in Calderón): "introduction of laws, stabilization of currency, violent founding of cities, introduction of weights and measures, regulation of trade" (whereas Ninyas had ordered abolition of money, barter, abandonment of cities, partition of land). Semiramis has Ninyas killed, but as he dies she humbles herself before him. "She makes him divine as Adonis-Marduk, as both hero and god, whose servant she now is."

In the *Semiramis* of 1908, Hofmannsthal had excluded everything connected with government and political action because he did not know how to deal with it. In 1918, however, the entire subject has been turned toward politics. The theme develops into a meditation on two forms of sovereignty: sovereignty through force and sovereignty through service. The heroic ideal of European culture is measured against the powerless Tao of the East; the money economy of the commercial nations against the barter economy of a timeless peasantry. The latter motif is elucidated for us by one of Hofmannsthal's reflections in his *Buch der Freunde* [*Book of Friends*]: "To circumvent the money system is perhaps the meaning of the moral and even religious revolution we seem to be in the midst of." All these motifs display the clearest references to the present. At the same time the adherence to Calderón is much closer than in 1908. But everything that is to be taken literally in Calderón (e.g., the dictation-scene) is elevated to the symbolic level. The imprisoned and sacrificed Ninyas is a second Sigismund. Had Hofmannsthal been able to finish his *Semiramis,* it would have stood beside *Der Turm* as another example of an allegorical *theatrum mundi* of the historical, political, social world. But the Semiramis plans are pushed aside by *Die Frau ohne Schatten* [*The Woman without a Shadow*], on which Hofmannsthal worked between 1911 and 1919. It has been observed that he had "taken during those war years the world of the Orient as a poetic subject as Goethe had done a hundred years before in his *Westöstlicher Divan.*"

What Hafiz meant to Goethe, the tales from the *Thousand and One Nights* meant to Hofmannsthal from the time of his youth. The Orient, or rather, the East—oscillating between Syria and China—is also the sustaining spiritual element in

Semiramis. Hofmannsthal gave Semiramis two handmaidens named "Europa" and "Asia"—a motif he could have found in Balzac's *Splendeurs et misères des Courtisanes.* But Oriental spices and fragrances are also palpably evident everywhere in Calderón's work. They had flowed to him from Spain's Islamic culture. They bring his language, as Goethe had also felt, into an approximation of the ingeniously contrived speech of Oriental poetry. But underneath this filigree work subsists, as it were, the *Christian* Orient: the poetic revival of that Christian segment of the world upon which Egypt, Syria, Asia Minor, and Byzantium had impressed an indelible seal of the spirit—and had done so at the very time of the fathers of the Church, of whom so many were "Oriental fathers." That was long before the primacy of Rome and long before the emergence of Islam. In Hofmannsthal's *Semiramis* there is, however, no Christian element. The religious poles of this work are the orgiastic cult of Syria on the one hand and the mysticism of Lao-Tse on the other. Perhaps that is the reason why *Semiramis* remained a fragment.

CALDERÓN was free to function and create in a world whose monarchical and Catholic structure was still firm; indeed, it seemed unshakable. The incipient decline of the state and the nation was concealed by dynastic and ecclesiastic pageantry. Hofmannsthal's historical situation is exactly the reverse. He found he had been born into a world disintegrated by materialism and relativism. As a grown man he had to live through its dissolution to the catastrophic end. It was his task —an almost superhuman task—to descend once more to the "abiding root of things": to extract restorative values out of the buried treasures of tradition; and finally to erect the images of a regenerated world. It was his profoundest intuition "that life only becomes livable through valid ties." To cleanse and glorify these bonds again—this was his task, his painful and arduous mission on earth: bond between man and woman in marriage; bond between people and ruler in the state; bond between man and God in time and eternity. On this road the wisdom of Asia could be a station and a symbol —but not a home and a solution. These could be found only in the revelation that had gone forth to West and East alike: in Christianity. To this end Hofmannsthal was directed by the tradition of his nation and his soil, by his Neoplatonic mentality, by a secret call that he had to follow. And he followed it. The works of the last seven years of his life are Christian not only because of their symbolism, but because of the conversion of his heart, because of a great and silent *sursum corda.*

If my view is correct, this turn toward Christianity is the most fundamental reason why *Semiramis* remained incomplete. And at the same time we now comprehend the encounter between Hofmannsthal and Calderón in its most profound and conclusive aspect, the one which surpasses all the others. There are only two poets of the Christian world: Dante and Calderón. They alone have mirrored the entire Christian world with its hierarchical gradations of classes and spheres. Also, they alone wrote for the entire Christian world. Nevertheless, within this common province they represent the most extreme antitheses. Dante forged in language of metallic strength a mathematical and strictly circumscribed work which grew to perfect form and which carries the stamp of his person from the first to the hundredth canto. Calderón's work is as limitless as the web of an immense tapestry that has neither beginning nor end, and which the eye, proceeding from figure to figure, from ornament to ornament, has to take in piece by piece. The person of the poet is nowhere to be seen. What we see is only the immense spectacle of the theater of the world. Dante is the methodical calculator and the implacable judge. He possesses the ordering will and the realism of eternal Rome, from which he traced his descent. His solitary work remains a standard outside of and above time. Calderón writes for the people and the Church, for kings and lords, for soldiers and scholars. In the magic mirror of his two hundred plays he catches all the variegated activity of the world and interweaves it with the symbols of the superterrestrial. If Hofmannsthal wished to connect his Christian theater with a great tradition, it could only be with that of Calderón.

From the Middle Ages and the Baroque Hofmannsthal took, not historical local color, but that timeless European mythology which he has made visible to us: "There is a certain timeless European mythology: names, concepts, figures with which is connected a higher meaning, personified forces of the moral or mythical order. This mythological firmament spans all of the older Europe."

When, in 1846, the young Burckhardt predicted "universal barbarism" and "social revolution," he concluded: "We might all perish; I, however, want at least to select the field of interest for which I am to perish, namely the civilization of Old Europe" (to Hermann Schauenberg, 5 March 1846). Hofmannsthal was the last poet of Old Europe.

1934

Hermann Hesse

++

NOVEMBER 1918. . . . Leaden despair weighs upon men. For the old generation, Germany is shattered, because to them Germany means the empire of the Hohenzollern. There are dignitaries of the fallen regime who do not wish to survive the entry of the occupying forces. But the younger generation do not mourn the passing of this unreal world. To them Germany was, in George's words, "the land still imbued with great promise." Through the collapse of the regime all the progressive forces had been set free. In the German universities great teachers were functioning at the height of their powers: Ernst Troeltsch in Berlin, Max Weber in Munich, Max Scheler in Cologne, Wilhelm Worringer in Bonn, Alfred Weber and Friedrich Gundolf in Heidelberg. A springtime of the mind, lavish in its wealth, had begun to blossom. Students, still wearing their field-gray uniforms, crowded into the lecture halls, the most open-minded student generation since the summer of 1914. In many of them the spirit and the traditions of the *Freideutsche Jugend* were still alive. Their sacred texts were the parables of Chuang-Tsu, Plato, Hölderlin, Nietzsche, and George. Their attitude was a wonderful cosmopolitan openness, an awakening to a new day.

It was this generation that Hermann Hesse addressed in the periodical that he edited in collaboration with Richard Woltereck, *Vivos voco*. It bore witness to a new spirit, a spirit striving to overcome the evil forces of national hatred. In 1920, I had the opportunity to report on "a voice from the youth of America" in its pages. Hesse's literary work had made no impression upon the young. That was to change as by magic with the appearance of *Demian* in 1922. This work

169

spoke directly to the students in field-gray. Here were the sufferings of school; the perplexities of sex; the experience of myths and mysteries; the War, felt as a premonition, endured, paid for in death. The dying Demian to his wounded friend: "Little Sinclair, pay attention! I shall have to go away. Perhaps you will need me again some time. . . . If you call me then, I shall not come again so rudely, riding on a horse or on the train. You must listen to what is inside yourself, then you will see that I am within you." A message as simple as it is profound. Nothing else in Hesse's work attains the level of this utterance. You say something like that only once.

In the same year, 1922, I was surprised by a letter from T. S. Eliot. His friend Hermann Hesse had brought me to his attention. Whether I would like to contribute to *The Criterion*? The first number (October 1922) contained Eliot's *The Waste Land*—and an essay by Hermann Hesse on "New German Poetry." In the notes to *The Waste Land* we read that several lines were inspired by Hesse's *Blick ins Chaos* [*A Look into Chaos*]. A single crossing of the paths. But how many paths and encounters there were in the spiritually relaxed Europe of the time! Rilke translated poems by Valéry, who showed them to me in manuscript. At Scheler's I saw the first issue of Ortega's *Revista de Occidente*. Valery Larbaud introduced Joyce in France. Sylvia Beach's bookstore, "Shakespeare and Company," was an international meetingplace as was that of her friend Adrienne Monnier diagonally opposite. From 1922 on the "Décades" at Pontigny were taking place again. The Pen-Club was founded. . . . A Europe of the mind—above politics, in spite of all politics —was very much alive. This Europe lived not only in books and periodicals but also in personal relations. One visited the venerable Ivanov in Rome. In Heidelberg, one saw Thomas Mann and André Gide during the same week. "European Conversations" (*Europäische Gesprache*, the title of a Hamburg periodical) were conducted in those days. . . .

Hermann Hesse no longer took part in them. It was not his way. He was the hermit of Montagnola: gardener, dreamer, painter and writer—"the literary man Hermann Hesse" (as he styles himself in *Kurgast* [*A Guest at the Spa*]); an idler, a timewaster, an easygoing, work-shy man, to say nothing of his other vices" (*Nürnberger Reise*) [*The Journey to Nuremberg*]. Meanwhile he turned fifty (July 2, 1927). For this date an official biography appeared from the pen of Hugo Ball (1886–1927), that profound and solitary spirit, who had found his way back from Dadaism to *Das Byzantinische Christentum* (1923) and the Roman Catholic Church. His *Kritik der deutschen Intelligenz* (1919) was an apocalyptic cry of alarm which has not even now reached its destination. Ball's biography may be called official because it is illustrated "with fourteen photographs from the family collection," and is based on a great deal of information furnished by the poet himself. The account of Hesse's home and family, of his Germano-Russian and his Swabian grandfather (two splendid characters), of the Hindu-Pietistic atmosphere of the Basel mission, is vivid cultural history. At thirteen, the gifted boy broke out of this protected world. It is the decisive break, which the poet himself, in a later retrospect (*Kurzgefasster Lebenslauf* [*Life Story Briefly Told*], *Neue Rundschau* [1925]) merely notes, without explaining it. "When I was thirteen, and that conflict had just begun, my behavior at home and at school left so much to be desired that I was exiled to the Latin school of another town. One year later I became a pupil in a theological seminary, learned to write the Hebrew alphabet, and was well on the way to grasping what a *dagesh forte implicitum* is, when inner storms suddenly broke over me, leading to my flight from the monastery school, my confinement in the 'dungeon,' and my expulsion from the seminary. For a while I made an effort to continue my studies at a Gymnasium, but the outcome, confinement and dismissal, was the same there too. After that I was a shopkeeper's apprentice for three days, ran away again, and to my parents' great consternation disappeared for several days and nights. I was my father's assistant for half a year, then, for a year and a half, a locksmith in a machine shop and clock-tower manufactory.

171

In short, for more than four years everything they tried to do with me went awry—no school would keep me, and I couldn't stand any apprenticeship for long. All attempts to make a useful person out of me ended in failure, sometimes in ignominy and scandal, at other times in escape and expulsion. And yet people were ready to grant that I had ability and even a certain amount of sincere good will!"

Conflict with the school is a normal experience and since 1900 had become a popular subject for literature. *Flachsmann als Erzieher* [*Flachsmann as Educator*] by Otto Ernst (1901) and Wedekind's *Frühlings Erwachen* [*Spring's Awakening*] ran to full houses. Emil Strauss (*Freund Hein*, 1902), Hermann Hesse (*Unterm Rad* [*Beneath the Wheel*], 1905), Heinrich Mann (*Professor Unrat*, 1906), Robert Musil (*Die Verwirrungen des Zöglings Törless* [*Young Törless*], 1906) were the classics of the *Schülerroman*, the novel of student life. Even *Buddenbrooks* concluded with the catastrophe of little Hanno's schooldays. Thomas Mann himself got no further than the "Einjährig-Freiwilliger-Examen" (high-school-leaving examination),[1] with which one could bid school farewell at the end of the sixth year. But the rare combination of talent, determined application, and luck led him rapidly to success, esteem, prestige. "Gustave Aschenbach, or von Aschenbach, as his name has been officially known since his fiftieth birthday"—thus begins *Der Tod in Venedig* [*Death in Venice*] (1913). This Aschenbach, "the author of the lucid and powerful prose epic on the life of Frederick the Great of Prussia," at the age of forty already had "to cope daily with post that bore the stamps of every country in the world." The school authorities have included selections from his writings "in their prescribed textbooks." Early in life he had chosen Munich for his place of residence, "and lived there amid such civic honor as the intellect may in rare instances be privileged to enjoy." When Thomas Mann was fifty years old

---

[1] Literally, examination for one-year volunteers. It enabled the holder of the certificate to reduce his military service to one year.— TR.

in 1925, there was a banquet in the Munich Town Hall and many other corroborations of civic honor. Thomas Mann knew the value of representation as well as Senator Buddenbrook.

Hermann Hesse's fiftieth birthday passed without ceremony. He would not have had it any other way. As a "reply to the greetings" he published, in 1928, the angry volume *Krisis*, forty-five poems only fifteen of which were later included in the collected edition (*Gedichte* [Zurich, 1942]). These verses give utterance "to one of those stages of life where reason becomes weary of itself, abdicates its authority, and leaves the field free to nature, chaos, and the animal instincts." Animal instincts, in this context, mean the shimmy, whisky, cognac, bars, and hangovers. *Armer Teufel am Morgen nach dem Maskenball* [*Poor devil the morning after the costume ball*] ends:

> Ach wäre dieser Sonntag schon vorbei
> Und ich und du und dieses ganze Leben.
> Ich höre auf, ich muss mich übergeben.

> [If only this Sunday were over at last, and you and me and this whole dreary life. I've got to stop, I'm going to be sick.]

But that is still too tame. Everything must come out, though it were in the diction of a schoolboy:

> Das Leben ist darum so beschissen,
> Weil wir doch alle sterben müssen.

> [The reason why life is so shitty is that we all must die.]

Even in the charming *Nürnberger Reise* we hear of the "peculiar sadness and, pardon the expression, shittiness of life." In such moods Hesse crossed the threshold of his sixth decade, "more concerned with the fear of aging and dying than with the pleasure of celebrating" (*Krisis*, postscript). *Krisis* is the birthday child's sullen requital: a document of emo-

tional stresses but a gesture of provocation as well. The revolt
of the thirteen-year-old has turned into a defiance of social
conventions. It makes the aging man into an "unsociable hermit . . . , who is deeply pained when he has to obtain a certificate of residence from the local authorities or even to fill out
a census slip" (*Kurgast,* 1928).

Hugo Ball informs us that in Switzerland, in 1916, Hesse
suffered an acute nervous crisis. Psychoanalytic treatment,
administered by a student of C. G. Jung, provided relief. Between May 1916 and November 1917 there were more than
seventy sessions. The fruit of this period was *Demian*: release
of new creative power and depth perception. Psychoanalysis,
as we have seen, was unable to resolve the tensions in Hesse's
nature, or even to prevent their recurrence. But neurotic conflicts are not operable injuries or unmitigated disasters. They
are part of the very substance of life and therefore part of the
material and the problems to be shaped by life. That this is
true was demonstrated in Hesse's finest book, *Narziss und
Goldmund* [*Narcissus and Goldmund*] (1930). We know that
Hesse's early novel *Unterm Rad* depicts his escape from the
monastery school at Maulbronn. After a quarter of a century
the poet returned to this theme, but transposed now to a timeless Middle Ages, and purged of all the passions of youthful
revolt. Goldmund, a student at the monastery, admires his
teacher, the ascetic young monk Narcissus, with a shy and
worshipful love. He wants to devote his entire life to the
Order. But Narcissus explains to him that that is not his destiny. "You are an artist, I am a thinker. You sleep at the
mother's breast, I watch in the desert. For me the sun shines,
for you the moon and the stars. Your dreams are of girls,
mine of boys." Narcissus awakens Goldmund to a knowledge
of his own nature. Instead of study, monastic discipline, and
virtue, powerful instincts take possession of Narcissus: sex,
love of women, longing for independence, travel. He roams
through woods, mountains, towns, cities; women's favors accompany him on his journey. He knows how to fend off
treacherous companions with a knife. He sees whole terri-

174

tories laid waste by plague; orgies of brutality and lust at the edge of the grave. He becomes a woodcarver and is about to be inducted with honor into the guild. But restlessness drives him to seek new adventures. He is on the point of losing his shirt and his head when Narcissus, the powerful abbot, intercedes for his release and brings him back to the monastery. The whole thing is a wonderfully colored picture out of the German Middle Ages, in which romanticism and realism are blended. Fruity, fragrant, round, self-contained, neither didactic nor problematical; a variegated tapestry of the everlasting powers of life, steeped in magical essences that recall Arnim, Tieck, Novalis—but as a result of a secret affinity of blood, not of literary borrowings or an overlay of antiquarianism. No single work of Hesse's has a greater claim to a place in the heritage of German literature. It is a completely German book, unaffected by the lure of the Orient to which the poet was succumbing even then.

Hesse's maternal grandfather, Dr. Hermann Gundert, was one of the first pioneers of the German evangelical mission in India. Upon his return he worked for thirty more years on a dictionary of one of the Indian dialects, on behalf of the Basel mission. He had married in India; Hesse's mother was born there. All the thoughts of his parents and of their friends from the mission revolve around the fabulous land. So it is not surprising that in 1911 Hesse embarks on a journey to India. He has personal reasons for going, were it only the need to see India with other eyes than those of his parents. His book *Aus Indien* [*Out of India*] appears in 1913. Around the same time Waldemar Bonsels (*Indienfahrt* [*Voyage to India*], 1916) and Graf Keyserling (*Reisetagebuch eines Philosophen* [*Travel Diary of a Philosopher*], 1919) had visited India. Thus, with his book on India, as with his school novel and psychoanalysis, Hesse had unwittingly and unintentionally set foot on a terrain that was soon to become a playground of intellectual fashion (Rabindranath Tagore's *Gitanjali* had appeared as early as 1914). Hesse's encounter with India proved a disappointment. He thought that he would

175

find there the innocent and simple children of paradise. "But," the travel book concludes, "we ourselves are different. We are strangers here and have no rights of citizenship. We lost our paradise long ago and the new one that we wish to have and build is not to be found on the equator or beside warm Eastern seas. It lies within us and in our own Northern future."

The next book about India, *Siddhartha* (1922), is merely a transposition of Hesse's revolt against his pietistic home to an Indian setting. Siddhartha, the devout son of a Brahmin, can find peace neither in the teachings of his ancestors nor in asceticism nor in sensual pleasure. Nor can he accept Buddha's doctrine: "No, a seeker after truth cannot accept any doctrine, not if he truly wishes to find. One who has found, however—he can approve of every doctrine." In the end the seeker finds peace by listening to the great stream, "surrendering himself to its streaming, at one with Oneness." A rather more novelistic than philosophical solution to the problems posed. A stage, of which there are many in Hesse's work, destined to be superseded by more impressive elaborations. *Die Morgenlandfahrt* [*Journey to the East*] (1932) is pretty much along the same lines. The East here is "not only a country and a geographical location but rather the homeland of the soul's youth, the everywhere and nowhere," "the union of all the ages." The travelers to the East are an Order;[2] all disclosures regarding the secrets of the Order are forbidden. The journey takes place for the most part in Europe (a proceeding justified by the indication "everywhere and nowhere"). The narrative is confused, with no attempt at construction. "How to make the story of our Journey to the East tellable? I don't know." A significant admission. In this instance Hesse availed himself of the literary puzzle in the manner of E. T. A. Hoffmann in order to legitimate the irreality of his account. The narrative ends in Basel, where it turns out that Leo, "the perfect servant," is at the same time the head

[2] Cf. *Demian*, p. 143: "the first fulfillment of my life and my admission to the Order."

of the Order. The "servant" might easily be a preliminary version of Joseph Knecht of *Das Glasperlenspiel* [*The Glass Bead Game*], whose name means squire or servant. Hesse likes name symbolism, and he also likes to play hide-and-seek with names. One of the officials in *Das Glasperlenspiel* is called Dubois—like Hesse's grandmother. Her first husband, Isenberg, lent his name to Knecht's friend Ferromonte. Thomas Mann appears in the book as Meister Thomas von der Trave, Jacob Burckhardt as Pater Jacobus. Knecht's friend Designori ("of the nobles") is of patrician stock; his name is the antithesis of "Knecht." Such playing with names may be regarded as a system of correspondences invented by the writer for his personal use. It enables him to establish cross-connections between widely separated periods in his life and work. Its function is similar to the interweaving of themes that is so typical of Hesse's literary technique. In *Rosshalde* (1914), little Pierre wants to know what carnations are called in the language of the bees and what the robin redbreasts say to each other. On his wanderings through the woods Goldmund would have liked to become a woodpecker, perhaps for a day, perhaps for a month. "He would have spoken woodpecker language and extracted good things from the bark of trees." Among the travelers to the East is one who hopes to learn the language of the birds with the aid of Solomon's key. And now the same thought without the dress of fiction: "To feel life throbbing in me . . . to have a soul so nimble that by the play of hundreds of fancies it can slip into hundreds of forms, into children and animals, and especially into birds, that is what I want and need in order to live" (*Wanderung* [*Tramping*], 1920). To understand the language of the birds—eternal motif of fairy tale, of legend (cf. Wagner's Siegfried), of dream; the longing to be in harmony with all living creatures, not merely with the birds. One of Goldmund's wishes is never to find his way out of the forest, never to see people again, never to love another woman—to become an animal, "a bear or a stag." In the tale *Der Wolf* [*The Wolf*], the hero is the wounded animal: driven off and sad, on the heights of the snow-covered montains, the wolf feels the approach of death and sees the red moon rise. The singer Muoth (*Gertrud*, 1910) "had been emaciated by solitude like a wolf." The motif is transformed and developed fully in the novel *Der Steppenwolf* (1927).

Fish too are fraught with symbolism for Hesse. Fishing in the Nagold, depicted by the painter Veraguth in *Rosshalde*; Goldmund at the fish market: there is always a mysterious correspondence to life. Fish and moisture—these are related like bird and air, wolf and wood. The fish-motif participates in the water symbolism, and water, as we know, signifies the unconscious in the language of dreams. Water is allurement and peril at the same time. The book that made Hesse famous, *Peter Camenzind* (1904), begins and ends by the Lake of Lucerne. The lake plays a prominent role in *Rosshalde*. Joseph Knecht will meet his death in an Alpine lake. Peter Camenzind's best friend drowns while bathing "in a ridiculously small South German stream." The monastery school pupil Hans Giebenrath (*Unterm Rad*) finds his death in the waves. Death by water—one of Hesse's basic themes.

Giebenrath and Heilner: a friendship that is tragically severed. Siddhartha and Govinda: a friendship that dissolves because the worthy Govinda runs out of breath. In *Demian* friendship ceases to be conflict, parallelism, or interrelation and becomes psychagogy. This pattern is repeated on a higher plane in *Narziss und Goldmund*. Here friendship mirrors the polarity of mind and life. The poet has embodied two dominant traits of his own character in the two figures. We are close to Novalis' theory of the "truly synthetic person": "Each person, though divided into several, is also capable of being one. The genuine analysis of the person as such brings forth persons. . . ."

THESE would be some examples of Hesse's themes, suggestions toward an analysis that could be carried much further. Thematic and technical analysis—that rarely practiced art—

is the only adequate method for interpreting an author. As such, it is the preparatory course for all criticism that wishes to rise above verbiage, circumlocution, and inconsequentiality. Years ago I tried to explore Proust and Joyce by this method. The incentive was especially strong because both authors were using new techniques to render new aspects of life. They were artists in a sense of the word that can hardly be applied to Hesse. The epic writer makes a new aspect of the world visible. He constructs an objective reality. The opening sentence of *Ulysses* places us *in medias res*. Not personal experience but a series of images and characters detached from the writer is communicated. With Hesse this occurs only in *Narziss und Goldmund*. All the rest of his works are autobiographical ectoplasms, transposed life histories. The writer remains trapped in his own subjective sphere. He cannot contrive to set down an objective world and gain a footing in it. The conventions of art are as repugnant to him as those of society. In constantly renewed departures and variations he makes the reader privy to a development that begins in failure to master the tasks of life (*Peter Camenzind, Unterm Rad*, the novel of marriage *Rosshalde*), and then registers the attempts at a cure (psychoanalysis, India-cycle). Sometimes he will deviate into lyrical prose jottings (*Wanderung*), sometimes into diary-like reportage (*Kurgast, Nürnberger Reise*), occasionally into "magic theater" (*Steppenwolf*). Epic presentation is not one of his native gifts. It can happen that the form will grow brittle in his hand (as in the passage cited above from *Die Morgenlandfahrt*). He has a "mistrust of literature in general." "I can only consider the endeavors of contemporary German writers (my own included, naturally) to produce really articulated forms, genuine works of art, as somehow always inadequate and epigone." Literature having lost its certainty, he can grant it value only "insofar as it confessedly expresses its own poverty and the poverty of its age with the greatest possible candor" (all in *Nürnberger Reise*). The dichotomy in this evaluation is reflected by the slack diction,

179

with its conversational jargon ("somehow"), self-conscious doublets ("real forms," "genuine works"), and turgidity ("confessedly," "with the greatest possible candor"). These sentences have no rhythm, no tautness, and are therefore not compelling. The writer not only mistrusts literature; he has no responsible commitment to the exigencies of his craft, to syntax and style. But is it his craft? In *Gertrud* and in *Das Glasperlenspiel* he is a musician, in *Rosshalde* a painter, in *Narziss und Goldmund* a woodcarver. In *Nürnberger Reise* he toys with the idea "that perhaps I might still manage to run away from literature and take up painting for a living, a craft I find more attractive." Is it unfair to lend weight to these utterances? Are they merely the result of passing moods? But the author did think them worth communicating, and they illuminate the problems of his art. They explain too why we were able to say something about Hesse's themes but very little about his technique. It is variable, often groping; now clumsy, now sedulous. The watercolors that Hesse added to a few of his books are done with a coloring box. His handling of language, too, gives the effect of careful daubing, now childlike, now amateurish. There is never any sparkle to this prose. But once in a while—as in Demian's farewell—a note is sounded that touches the heart with its magic.

The copious stream of Hesse's lyric poetry is also for long stretches nothing but diligent rhyming. I choose a poem from *Das Glasperlenspiel*:

> Die ewig Unentwegten und Naiven
> Ertragen freilich unsre Zweifel nicht.
> Flach sei die Welt, erklären sie uns schlicht,
> Und Faselei die Sage von den Tiefen.
>
> Denn sollt' es wirklich andre Dimensionen
> Als die zwei guten, altvertrauten geben,
> Wie könnte da ein Mensch noch sicher wohnen,
> Wie könnte da ein Mensch noch sorglos leben?
>
> Um also einen Frieden zu erreichen,
> So lasst uns eine Dimension denn streichen!

Denn sind die Unentwegten wirklich ehrlich,
Und ist das Tiefensehen so gefährlich,
Dann ist die dritte Dimension entbehrlich.

[The eternal die-hards and the naïve cannot, to be
sure, bear our doubts. The world is flat, they declare
simply, and the legend of depth mere drivel. For if
dimensions other than the two good old familiar
ones really did exist, how could a man still
live without anxiety? So in order to reach a peaceful settlement, let us strike one of the dimensions.
For if the die-hards are really sincere, and the view
of depth is so dangerous, then the third dimension
is dispensable.]

This poem looks like a sonnet and was perhaps on the way
to becoming one. For this purpose, unfortunately, a line is
missing. The rhyme scheme of the first quatrain is abandoned
in the second. The rhymes are more miss than hit. "Die-hard"
is the worst sort of newspaper jargon. The whole thing
is versified prose with intrusive padding. For that matter, the
weakness of Hesse's style generally has always been that he
cannot leave anything out. In a preface to a collection of
poems, *Die Harfe. Vierundzwanzig Gedichte* [*The Harp.
Twenty-four Poems*], published in 1917, Alfred Kerr wrote:
"Poets fill ten printed volumes. But a few islands finally
project above the flood of time. Not to burden the world, I
present the islands immediately." A few islands project above
the flood of Hesse's lyric poetry too. They could fill one of
those thin "Insel" volumes and in such a selection become a
German possession.

THIS essay does not aim at a comprehensive evaluation of
Hesse's work. That would be impossible in any case, if for no
other reason than that many—and important—books are in-
accessible. I have traced only a few of the main lines that con-
duce to an understanding of *Das Glasperlenspiel* (1943). The
appearance of this work, impressive in content and scope, of

the poet's old age, came as a happy surprise. When a writer in the seventh decade of life sums up his existence in a broadly-conceived work, it is noteworthy. But when it is a poet who has accompanied us from the days of our youth, whom we encountered in a new shape after the First World War, and who now speaks again across the abyss of calamitous years, we are moved and grateful. Something takes place in us that transcends everything literary: an exchange of greetings by the survivors of a catastrope; the rediscovery of a familiar voice. Memories of long decades are stirred and give the work a resonance which vibrates with many destinies. The generations that awakened to maturity in the first decade of the twentieth century found their intellectual orientation in the writers born before and after 1870: George (1868), Hofmannsthal (1874), Rilke (1875), Thomas Mann (1875), Rudolf Borchardt (1877) in Germany; Romain Rolland (1866), André Gide (1869), Paul Claudel (1870) in France. Proust and Valéry (both born in 1871) did not achieve prominence till after 1918. Ten proud names radiating from one decade. Lives that intersected, attracting one another, repelling one another. And yet, from the perspective of the present, belonging to the same world. In the eighties a new generation emerges: the "moderns" of 1920: Joyce (1882), Ortega (1883), Eliot (1888). Between the first and the second row stands Hermann Hesse. He stands by himself, in scarcely more than fleeting touch with any of those named. We have referred to the slight contact with Eliot. Romain Rolland is mentioned once in a dedication; the *Nürnberger Reise* records a visit with Thomas Mann. But Hesse was never affected by the works of his great coevals. He shunned the living Europe of the twentieth century. France had nothing to give him. "Paris was ghastly," opines Peter Camenzind. "Nothing but art, politics, literature, and sluttishness, nothing but artists, literary men, politicians, and low women" (tautology as a stylistic device). The *Nürnberger Reise* informs us that the poet has "hitherto succeeded" in avoiding Berlin. Merely the journey to Nuremberg was a hazard. "It was beautiful and mysterious, but to me, as a south German, depressing and frightening as well. I thought to myself, if I should travel on, there would be more and more pines, and then more snow, and then perhaps Leipzig or Berlin and pretty soon Spitzbergen and the North Pole. Good Lord, what if I had gone so far as to accept the invitation to Dresden! It was unthinkable." "Except for my native town in the Black Forest, I have felt really at home only in the region around Locarno."

Fortunately, between the Black Forest and Locarno there is a place called Switzerland—one of those friendly gifts of a durable kind that history has conferred upon our small, tormented portion of the globe. A country and a people secure in themselves; small enough to be protected from the troubles of their neighbors; large and varied enough to be a mirror of Europe. Years ago the Basel philosopher Karl Joël gave a lively description of the "Switzerizing" of Europe in the eighteenth century. Pestalozzi and Rousseau became the educators of the continent. Haller and Gessner transformed the view of nature, Bodmer and Breitinger prepared the ground for the revolt against French Classicism. Voltaire lives near the Swiss border; Gibbon completes his history, conceived in Rome, at Lausanne. Goethe pledges fellowship with Lavater. In the nineteenth and twentieth centuries Switzerland becomes an asylum for those politically persecuted or disaffected in their own countries. Hesse, who had many ties with Basel, adopted Switzerland as his homeland. Transposed into the utopian "Castalia," it becomes the setting of *Das Glasperlenspiel*.

The work has been called a novel of education. That is one of its many aspects, but it does not touch the core of the book. We can approach it more closely by asking ourselves why Hesse picks up the theme of education again, and why he presents Joseph Knecht first as a student, then as a teacher, and finally as "magister ludi," the master of the game. *Unterm Rad* depicts the boy's failure in school. In *Das Glasperlenspiel* the delinquent pupil catches up on his schooling, as it were, and becomes a teacher himself (at a monastery school, like Narcissus). Thus a theme from Hesse's early period is taken up again in his latest, changed in value from negative to positive, and "reconciled on a higher level." Not just this theme alone. All the poet's themes (among which we found conflicts but also attempts at a cure) are taken up again and treated contrapuntally in this work. The *Versuch einer Lebensbeschreibung des Joseph Knecht* [*Essay at a Description of the Life of Joseph Knecht*] is the last and now definitively realized transposition and sublimation of all those personal histories in which Hesse depicted himself as Camenzind, as Giebenrath, as Sinclair, as Siddhartha, as Goldmund. All those personal histories crystallized around conflicts: conflict with the home and its pietistic atmosphere; with the school; with the middle-class world; with society in general. Finally, too, the conflict with the chosen profession —that of literature. As late as 1927 the poet notes: "As for myself, I am certain that no respectable, hard-working person would ever shake my hand again if he knew how little I value my time, how I waste my days and weeks and even months, with what childish games I fritter away my life." A fifty year-old writer who cannot stop playing games and admits it with a bad conscience. But is the play-instinct something to be ashamed of? Undetected and unanalyzed residue of a bourgeois prejudice! Play and the capacity for play is one of the most important functions of man's relation to the world. A learned historian of culture has meticulously examined American Indian games in order to confront *homo sapiens* with *homo ludens*. Animals and men play, and so do the Gods, in India as in Hellas. Plato views man as an articulated puppet fashioned by the Gods perhaps for the sole purpose of being their plaything. What conclusion shall we draw? The play-instinct is to be affirmed. A negative converted into a positive. To play one's own game with the deep seriousness of a child at play. The highest achievement would be—to invent a game of one's own. This the poet has succeeded in doing. He is the inventor of the glass bead game. He has learned to master it:

the game of life, the game of the beads. Thus he has become in two senses of the word *magister ludi* (in Latin *ludus* means both "game" and "school"). The glass bead game is the symbol for the successful completion of the school of life. The discovery of this motif determined the conception: at once inspiration and stroke of luck; the seed from which the golden blossom sprouted.

Motif and theme are two different things, and critics would do well to distinguish between them. The motif is what sets the fable (the "mythos" in Aristotle's *Poetics*) in motion and holds it together. Motif belongs to the objective side. Theme comprises everything that concerns the person's primary orientation toward the world. The thematics of a poet is the scale or register of his typical reactions to certain situations in which life places him. Theme belongs to the subjective side. It is a psychological constant. Motif is given by inspiration, discovered, invented—all of which amounts to the same thing. He who has nothing but themes cannot attain to epic or drama. Or, for that matter, to the great lyric. Here we touch upon a law of aesthetics the best formulation of which I find in T. S. Eliot: "The only way of expressing emotion in the form of art is by finding an 'objective correlative'; in other words, a set of objects, a situation, a chain of events which shall be the formula of that particular emotion; such that when the external facts, which must terminate in sensory experience, are given, the emotion is immediately evoked." By means of the motif, the "objective correlative," the insufficiencies of personal experience are overcome. The motif is an organic, autonomous structure, like a plant. It unfolds, forms nodes, branches out, puts forth leaves, buds, fruit. Once the bead game was in existence, a whole world had to be built up around it. That could only be an imaginary world, i.e., a Utopia, or a Uchronia (Renouvier's concept). But this world had to be transferred to an era which was not too distant in time from our own. For elements of our own culture must still survive in Castalia. Hence a—somewhat labored—introduction is necessary to serve as a bridge between the twenty-second and twentieth century. This allows for a critique of our age, but, what is more important, it demonstrates that the glass bead game has precursors in every epoch of the European mind. This means, however, the integration of western tradition into Hesse's spiritual universe.

And the Orient? Like all the main themes of the poet it is crystallized on to the new structure. The work is dedicated to the "Travelers to the East." The psychic techniques of Yoga are practiced in Castalia. India reappears in *Indischer Lebenslauf* [*The Indian Life*]. Nevertheless, the role of guide has passed to China. Castalia has a "Chinese House of Studies," it even has, as in a rococo park, a Chinese hermitage called the "Bamboo-grove." There one finds goldfish ponds, yarrow stalks for consulting the oracle, brushes and water-color bowls: pretty chinoiserie. But when the hermit is invited to Waldzell, there arrives in his stead only a daintily-colored Chinese letter containing the irrefutable assertion: "Movement leads to obstacles." Seneca, Thomas a Kempis, Pascal had stated something similar, if with less preciosity. Thus *Das Glasperlenspiel* also concludes and crowns the poet's Oriental cycle. And yet the world of the East is not the essential core of the book but rather the decorative background. Its effect is "antiquarian," as Demian says of Dr. Pistorius's Abraxas-mythology.

Das Glasperlenspiel is a western book. An ancestry is established for the bead game originating with Pythagoras and Gnosticism and continuing through Scholasticism and Humanism to the philosophy of Cusanus, the universal mathematics of Leibniz, and even to the intuitions of Novalis. Two names, however, with which only the fewest readers might be expected to be familiar, are mentioned with especial piety: Johann Albrecht Bengel (1687–1752) and Friedrich Christoph Oetinger (1702–1782), great Swabian theologians, in whom a strict belief in the Bible was united with apocalyptic doctrines, theosophy, chemistry, and Cabbala. They are intermediaries between Böhme, Swedenborg, and Schelling. Oetinger was pastor at Hirsau, near Calw, where Hesse was born. The prominence given these names implies the resolution of the conflict with the Swabian Pietism of his home and, by the same token, a rapprochement with Christianity. This rapprochement is further evidenced by Knecht's intimacy with Pater Jacobus and the Order of St. Benedict.

Castalia, too, is an Order. So Hesse's oldest theme is drawn into the organization of the work: the theme of the monastery. It is most remarkable how this theme too is transformed by a newly-won freedom. As he has invented his own game, so the poet has invented his own order. Psychologically this means: he has become his own master. By his own full power he can impose the authority with which he will comply. What had, as a neurotic conflict, been a stumbling block becomes, through "anagogy," a building block. The revolt against all external authority is now recognized as the passionate search for an authority derived from his own inner law. Joseph Knecht passes through all the degrees of the Order, submitting voluntarily to its regulations. After long service, long mastership, he "awakens" (we recall that Goldmund was "awakened" by Narcissus). Knecht's inner law compels him to quit the Order. His departure takes place in the prescribed ceremonial forms. To be sure, the administration of the Order cannot approve of this step. As he is about to leave, Knecht says to himself: "If only he had been able to explain and prove to the others what seemed so clear to him: that the 'arbitrariness' of his present action was in reality service and obedience; that it was not freedom he was going toward but new, unknown, and uncanny obligations; and that he was going not as a fugitive but as one who is summoned, not willfully but obediently, not as master but as sacrifice." So, after five decades, the boy's flight from the monastery school is repeated, only with its signs reversed from negative to positive; recast and purged of all slag it has come to be understood in its deeper significance: as a level of transcendence. In this work of the poet's old age, all the previous stages of his life have become transparent to him. It was conceived on the level of "illumination."

Where is the awakened teacher of the Order summoned by his inner law? To the "world outside," the ordinary human world beyond Castalia's serene precincts. The "unknown obligation" toward which he is moving is—death. But this departure for the unknown, no longer of a wandering scholar but of a man who is "summoned," is the heroic setting-out of the Nordic man whom Oriental absorption does not restrain. Final confirmation of the return to the West; Protestant nonconformism; Düreresque knight-errantry.

One last point! We found that in Hesse psychoanalysis and Oriental wisdom were attempts at healing neurotic conflicts. In addition, a theme to which we have barely alluded, although it runs through all the books from *Peter Camenzind* on—the escape into alcoholic intoxication. *Das Glasperlenspiel* is the result and testimony of a self-cure, the only cure that is dignified and genuine because it proceeds from the very core of the person. Psychoanalysis, Yoga, Chinese wisdom, were only expedients. He who has been "awakened" no longer needs them. The conflicts are resolved in a blessed new period of creativity. It is brought on by the discovery of the bead game. This functions as the center around which the person and the productivity of the poet are reorganized. The resolution of discords is the great new experience. That is why music is so important in the work. It is a symbol of euphony and concord, of rhythmically articulated spiritualization—harmony with the All.

A more precise analysis, a more searching appreciation of the rich late work I must leave to others.

1947

New Encounter with Balzac

✦✦✦

THIS year, 1950, completes the first century since the death of Balzac. My thoughts wander back a generation. In the summer of 1918, having returned home wounded, I gave a course on Balzac. Five years later my book on the great author was published. It was what was known in Germany at the time as an "interpretation." My intention was to explore Balzac's work in all its greatness and depth. I thought that up until then Balzac had been unfairly treated and imperfectly appreciated by literary history.

It was Balzac's misfortune to have displeased not only a Sainte-Beuve but also the so-called *critique universitaire,* that is, the professors who write histories of literature. According to them, he had spoiled his novels with pretentious didacticism. His psychology was inadequate. He lacked emotional refinement. He knew no moderation and had no taste. He was totally devoid of any feeling for nature. He was a robust and vulgar genius. Worst of all, he had no style. All this added up to an impressive number of gross defects. But after they had been duly noted, one could afford to be lenient and acknowledge a few merits as well.

I found the injustice and incomprehension of these judgments exasperating. I was imbued with the sense of Balzac's unique greatness. His work seemed to me a world whose structure must be investigated. Here was a mystery to be unraveled. I thought I should discover it in a visionary experience that could be traced to Balzac's childhood. He had been vouchsafed an illumination that transported him to the spheres of the angels. He saw "the celestial powers ascending and descending, handing one another the pails of gold." The presentiment of a continuity pervading all things flashed through his mind. He felt within himself a nameless power that could find no outlet. We know that there are two philosophical novels by Balzac—*Louis Lambert* and *La Peau de Chagrin*—whose heroes, while living in a shabby Parisian garret, compose a treatise on the will, a *Théorie de la Volonté*. The critics like to count this among the abstruse chimeras which, they say, disfigure Balzac's work. And yet it must have been a very personal and central concern with Balzac. For Louis Lambert and Raphael de Valentin bear autobiographical traits. What they term will is assuredly not the faculty of willing but an all-pervasive *fluidum*, an essence, which can be condensed but also dissipated. It is the life force. Balzac did not write the Theory of the Will, but its formulas are, after all, the mere skeleton of a total vision of man and the world that could only be unfolded through artistic creation. Today, we would not speak of will but of libido in Jung's sense. A system of psychic energy can be derived from the *Comédie Humaine*; indeed, the entire work may be seen as a grandiose representation of the transformations and symbols of the libido. The talisman that Raphael de Valentin acquires from a mysterious antiquary, that piece of shagreen leather endowed with magical powers which fulfills its possessor's boldest wishes—but only at the expense of his vital energy—this talisman was a poetic symbol for the libido—a fairy-tale symbol. And just as the theory of the libido led Jung to the deciphering of alchemy, so too an alchemical novel found a place in the *Comédie Humaine*: *La Recherche de l'Absolu*. The theory of energy proved to me to be the magic word that one had to know in order to understand the whole and the true Balzac. Now his work revealed a surprising unity which I had previously only dimly suspected but never grasped. It was a discovery that excited and elated me. I am as convinced of its truth today as I was then, and I may say that it has received recognition.[1] But my scholarly research has since been directed toward very different fields. I have remained an admirer and a reader of Balzac, but not a Balzac scholar. So that if I am asked to say someting about Balzac today, I find myself in a peculiar position. A new encounter with Balzac means to me virtually a new encounter with myself.

My first contacts with French literature had been tentative and contradictory. While still in the last year at the Gymnasium, I had been lucky enough to see the great Coquelin in the role of Cyrano de Bergerac. At that time Rostand's play seemed to me to be one of the summits of poetry. The effervescent lines sparkled like firecrackers and by their reflection I saw spread out before me an enchanted landscape named France. Later, as a young student in Berlin, I heard Yvette Guilbert sing French folk songs. For me it was the captivating voice of *La France*, a summons that penetrated to my innermost being.

But then, when I began to study French literature, I became confused. On my first vacation I took along a volume of Corneille, and Flaubert's *Madame Bovary*. Corneille I found merely dull, but the novel, which had been recommended to us in the course, revolted me. What? This collection of disgusting, stupid, sordid human beings was supposed to be interesting? Suicide by arsenic was the end of the matter? What kind of a country, what kind of a people was it where such a thing could be produced? Not so much as a

[1] In his scholarly book on Balzac, *La Pensée politique et social de Balzac* (Paris, 1947), Bernard Guyon does me the honor (on page x) of counting me along with Paul Bourget among those who have taken Balzac's thought seriously but grasped it too systematically, "faute de s'être soumis à la réalitié de la vie." But in 1920 it was not possible to conduct biographical research on Balzac in Germany, and there was no access to the Balzac archives of the Lovenjoul Collection at Chantilly. Nevertheless, Guyon says further on (p. 110, n.1): "cet admirable ouvrage est, de très loin, la meilleure de toutes les études d'ensemble sur Balzac."

spark of grandeur, love, beauty, strength? And I was expected to admire it? At nineteen, I could not do so.

But a year later I became acquainted with the work of Balzac, and then everything changed. I was passionately carried away. I felt I was in the grip of a powerful magic. Countless readers on every level have had the same experience. Balzac's world casts its spell over everyone.

When I speak of magic and enchantment, I have something very specific in mind. Even at the outset of Balzac's literary career a critic observed that the word *fascination* occurred frequently in his work and that it was admirably suited to describe the effect that this author had on the reader. Fascination, in its original sense, is the power possessed by certain people of subduing animals with their eyes. It is a sort of magnetism that emanates from a person: an inexplicable but most real phenomenon. And how is this effect to be understood? Balzac himself was magnetically attracted by the promises of life. He was filled with an insatiable desire for beauty, pleasure, power, knowledge, wealth, fame, love, passion. "Je veux vivre avec excès," says one of his typical characters. To all of them he imparted this boundless craving for life. "All of them," writes Baudelaire, "are endowed with the ardent vitality that animated the man himself."

Balzac's life and creation always proceed at the highest temperatures, and he transmits his own fervor to the receptive reader. Our sense of life is heightened, our existence is intensified when we see the world through Balzac's eyes. This is the source of the fascination that emanates from him.

Balzac's limitless craving encompasses the realm of the mind as well as that of the senses and the soul. He reaches for the fruits of the tree of knowledge and of the tree of experience. He wants the whole, the unconditional—*La Recherche de l'Absolu*. When I look for something comparable, all I can find is Faust's striving. Not that I would maintain that Balzac was dependent on Goethe. It is only a matter of elucidating through comparisons a basic element in Balzac's intellectual makeup. In the gallery of archetypal figures created by the European mind, we find the hero, the saint, and the sage. We find the sensualist, seeking the absolute in sexual love: that is Don Juan. But Faust wants more: he lusts after magic, after Helen, after power over time and space, "insatiable at every moment." Let us not forget that Faust belongs to the sect of the alchemists. This infinity of desire is a psychological configuration known only to modern Europe: not to classical Antiquity nor to the Orient, despite the splendors of the *Thousand and One Nights*. It is in this world of the Faustian soul that Balzac must be viewed—this great modern genius to whom Europe's classical tradition meant nothing.

The Faustian element in Balzac, the insatiable and infinite desire for all of life's fulfillments, is only another aspect of what I have called energy, will, libido. It is the mainspring of his artistic activity, the motor of his imagination. He projects it upon all of reality. With Balzac desire becomes a creative principle.

French literature of the nineteenth century depicts life in predominantly dark colors. Since Chateaubriand's *René*, literature has preferred to deal with the conflicts of the individual, the shipwreck of ideals, the disillusionment of the heart, the quarrel with society. Baudelaire ushers us into a garden whose flowers have sprung from evil. For Flaubert life seems to consist of banality, stupidity, and despair. As a counterbalance to this world, artificial paradises had to be created. One becomes intoxicated on the products of dissolution and sees oneself reflected in the images of Roman decadence. Poetry becomes hieroglyph or hallucination. The repulsive, the disgusting, the Satanic become sources of pleasure. Man is degraded, the hierarchy of values shattered. Of course there is the robust, sane and sound Victor Hugo. He is a Niagara of alexandrines. Such a spectacle of nature can elicit amazement, but those imposing verbal cascades are composed of platitudes. The grandiose torrent of words sweeps by. It rushes past reality, it carries no intellectual substance. Victor Hugo's profundity is a sham.

Balzac is the only great Frenchman of the last century who affirms the world: this modern world in its immeasurable abundance, its prose and its poetry, its reality and its spirituality. Balzac loves his century. The enormous edifice of the *Human Comedy* was to have been capped by a "Philosophical and Political Dialogue on the Perfections of the Nineteenth Century," which was to have been preceded by a "Monograph on Virtue." We cannot have any idea of the content of these books. It was not permitted Balzac to complete his gigantic task. Destiny granted him only a brief span of fifty-one years. If we consider that he wrote his first fully valid work, *Les Chouans*, at the age of thirty, it leaves barely twenty years for the labor of a lifetime.

Balzac developed slowly and matured late. He loses ten years in professional and literary experiments that are a series of failures. But when he has found himself, his production bursts forth with unparalleled power and abundance. And in this fever of creation its inner meaning becomes clear to him. In the summer of 1833 he is suddenly struck with the idea of consolidating all his novels into a vast, coherent system, into a cosmos. He receives this idea in a state of illumination accompanied by a high degree of exaltation. It overwhelms him so completely that he dashes across half of Paris to see his sister and inform her that he is quite simply on the verge of becoming a genius. What went on in Balzac at that moment? A psychological breakthrough has taken place, an illumination that is integration at the same time. This means that an insight that had long been present as a vague intuition now enters the consciousness with precise outlines. Balzac feels that all the works he has already produced have an organic connection and that they are thus parts of a comprehensive whole. And this whole exhibits a purposeful order. It was a spiritual event which has its analogy in physical nature: a process of crystallization, a rapid conversion of the fluidum into a regular structure. Balzac preserved the insight of that day in the phrase: "Il ne suffit pas d'être un homme; il faut être un système." To be a system means: to apprehend one's own creation as a purposefully ordered continuity. To put it another way: it is not enough to produce works; one must reach the point where one perceives the organic relation between them. One must arrive at a theoretical understanding of one's own production, must come to know oneself from one's own works. Intellectual creation has a natural and an ideal side. It manifests itself in a plantlike, unconscious way. The creative person feels an urge to express something. Proust has described this magnificently in the scene where, as a boy, he is so thrilled during a carriage ride by the shift in perspective of the towers of Martinville that he jots a few notes down on paper. He has had an artistic intuition and has given it shape. The experience will recur. But years and decades will have to pass, in which he loses faith in his ability to become a writer, before a moment of insight reveals to him the ideal structure that will then be called *À la recherche du temps perdu*.

I have said that Balzac's experience in the summer of 1833 was accompanied by a state of exaltation. He realized that he was a genius. What does that mean? An integrative experience such as his releases the awareness of a hitherto unknown energy and power. The creative person feels that he is being raised to a higher potency. He can organize, plan, control. In the same year, 1833, he writes to his beloved: "I wish to dominate the intellectual world of Europe; two more years of patience and labor, and I shall walk on the heads of all those who would tie my hands and clog my flight." And in 1844: "Four men (in the nineteenth century) will have had immense lives: Napoleon, Cuvier, O'Connell, and I wish to be the fourth. The first lived the life of Europe; he inoculated armies upon himself! The second embraced the globe. The third incorporated a people. I shall have carried an entire society in my head!"

Balzac does not compare himself with, say, the great reputations of contemporary literature. No doubt he did not recognize any standard that he and they might have in common. The names he mentions seem disparate: the emperor elevated by legend to mythical grandeur; the great naturalist, founder of comparative anatomy and paleontology; finally, the emancipator of Ireland. What they have in common, in Balzac's view, is the range, the total character of their effective energy. They master a whole: whole armies, a whole people, the whole globe. They are individuals who bear an entirety within themselves. And this is precisely what Balzac can quite rightly attribute to himself. What a tremendous feeling of power was alive in him! One is reminded of the late Nietzsche. But Balzac's self-confidence is free from hubris.

In order to organize his work into a totality, Balzac invented the device of having his characters reappear in different books. He begins to use this device in 1834. He then arranged the novels in various groups; in 1842 he at last chose the collective title of *Comédie Humaine* and discussed his intentions in an introduction. A new and final plan for a system was drawn up in 1845. According to this design the *Comédie Humaine* was to consist of 137 works, of which 87 had been completed, 50 more sketched out or planned. In the few years still remaining to him Balzac wrote yet another half-dozen novels.

After Balzac had conceived and designed his creation as a system of novels, he proceeded to fit his earlier works into this system as well. The critics have found fault with him for this, maintaining that the systematization was an afterthought and artificial, and that it simulated a unity which did not exist. Marcel Proust, one of the greatest modern admirers of Balzac, has refuted these reproaches. According to him, the unity of Balzac's work is all the more convincing and genuine for having dawned upon its creator only after the event. Precisely because Balzac was not aware of it at first, it is a vital, not a logical unity. The separate parts tended of their own accord to form a whole. Even in the unfinished state in which we possess it Balzac's cycle of novels gives a total picture of humanity. I look in vain in the history of European literature for something to compare with it. Balzac's uniqueness stands out all the more clearly when we compare him with his imitators.

The best known is Zola. He undertook to become the Balzac of the Second Empire. His cycle of novels, *Les Rougon-Macquart*, was intended to portray the natural and social history of a family. As in Balzac, an attempt is made at a total representation of an epoch and, as in Balzac, the characters recur. But Zola believed that he had one advantage over Balzac, namely, access to modern natural science, i.e., to the physiology and genetic theory of 1870. It was an undertaking of great naïveté. Of Zola's pretentious edifice only fragments are left today. It was a monument of mindlessness.

In the twentieth century too there have been numerous attempts to create a human comedy of our age in the form of a series of novels in many volumes. They are equipped with all the current psychological and sociological innovations. Only one thing is missing: the impalpable essence of life. They are necropolises, inhabited by shadows whose names one can scarcely remember, let alone their destinies. They will have been long forgotten when Balzac's work is still alive.

All the imitators of Balzac have copied only the external features of his work. Its inner impulse they have not understood. They have taken Balzac to be a realist, and our unthinking literary histories in part still disseminate this belief today. From them we learn that literature consists of so-called currents that succeed one another. In the nineteenth century we have first Romanticism, then Realism. The latter continues in intensified form as Naturalism and is then replaced by Symbolism, which unfortunately cannot be satisfactorily defined. Such is the conventional scheme. It is grotesque. But it is explained by the fact that we divide world literature according to languages, nations, and centuries, and parcel it out in small pieces. Thus all perspective is lost. The reproduction of daily reality is not an artistic conquest of the nineteenth century. It can be found in Hellenistic poetry, in the novel of the Roman imperial age, in the Icelandic sagas of the twelfth century, but also in Chaucer, in Rabelais, in Cervantes, in Fielding. Realism in the plastic arts begins as early as the cave paintings of the Neolithic period. There are realistic tend-

197

encies in all ages and zones. There are dozens, if not hundreds, of realisms of different kinds, different styles, different techniques. Literary scholarship—like art history—will gradually learn to distinguish them.

The effort toward the faithful rendering of nature can correspond to the most diverse of motives. The realism of the Neolithic cave paintings is magical: it is intended to guarantee success in hunting. Late Gothic art or Spanish art of the seventeenth century displays the figures of saints with horrible traces of physical degradation—but only in order to make sanctity comprehensible in human terms to the beholder or the worshipper. That would be a sacral realism. There is satirical realism: sturdy in Hogarth, caustic in George Grosz. There are many other kinds besides. If we turn back now to the literature of the nineteenth century we shall observe similar distinctions. There is the comic realism of an Henri Monnier, that forgotten contemporary of Balzac, whom André Gide restored to honor a few years ago. Monnier was a petty official who sketched odd types from the bureaucracies of the July monarchy, and who created the type of the French philistine under the name of Joseph Prudhomme. Prudhomme is an ancestor of the apothecary Homais, who introduces a comic note into the gloomy atmosphere of Madame Bovary. But Flaubert's realism has complex psychological roots. It is the reaction of a disillusioned romantic who had sought refuge in extravagant dreams and fantasy worlds. He takes his revenge, as it were, in an emotional negation of all of life's values. "L'éternelle misère de tout"—that is the sum he draws from human existence. That is his perspective. He believes it to be an objective statement—as though there were an objective truth about life. Flaubert wants us to see it through his eyes. His realism is a nihilism. In this world there is nothing constructive, no elevating purpose, no faith and no hope. The hallucinations of Flaubert's St. Anthony culminate in the self-annihilating wish to dissolve into matter: "descendre jusqu'au fond de la matière—être la matière!" It is the cruel logic of psychopathy that leads to this outcry

In Flaubert there is a conflict between the desires and the realities of life that ends in an irreconcilable dichotomy. In Balzac it is the reverse: a boundless imagination of desire that succeeds in penetrating all of reality and assimilating it.

Flaubert finds life senseless and compiles a catalogue of human stupidity. He gathers incriminating evidence against man and the world. *Bouvard et Pécuchet* is a heap of such material which never received a definitive artistic form. Balzac has a burning interest in life and conveys his ardor to us as Flaubert conveys his disgust. Flaubert turns his back on reality. About the France of his period we learn little from the books of this realist, and nothing favorable. How very different with Balzac! He once summed up his aim as an artist in the phrase, he wanted to express his century—"exprimer mon siècle." And how graphically his epoch stands before us.

We know the role that money played in Balzac's life. Even at the peak of success he was often scarcely able to evade his creditors. He earned a great deal, but he spent even more. He was a collector of art; he loved luxury. He knew the part money plays in life from intimate personal experience. And he was the first to depict it. His work tells us what income people had. The miser is an ancient figure of comedy. But Balzac's Grandet is the first whose fortune we can see being made and whose profits we can audit. Financial operations on the largest and the smallest scale occupy a place in Balzac that seemed previously to have been reserved for grand passions. The sordid usurer is a member of the cast of the *Human Comedy* no less than the important banker who influences international politics. In Balzac's time industry was still in its infancy, as was modern transportation. No machines, no technology existed as yet. Balzac himself had been a printer. He can describe the business of printing and the manufacture of paper from firsthand observation. In another novel we follow the rise of a perfume manufacturer; we witness his bankruptcy, but also his rehabilitation on the Paris stock exchange. He dies a martyr to commercial honesty, assured of the palms of heaven. "This is the death of the just," says the priest at his deathbed. So the career of a Parisian merchant becomes a modern drama, ready to vie with the martyr tragedies of the seventeenth century.

But in Balzac one can also study the judicial system, the methods of the police, the psychology of the criminal, the election of a deputy. Ministers and tribunes of the people betray state secrets to us. Prostitution is analyzed as well as administrative affairs. We enter the salons of the aristocracy but also the student's garret, the artist's studio, the editor's office. Balzac presents a sociology of Paris. We come to know every aspect of public life. But Balzac also shows us the mysteries of Paris. One of his novels bears the characteristic title, *L'Envers de l'Histoire contemporaine*. We are introduced to a small group of people, sorely tried by fate, who have banded together to practice active Christian charity. Their breviary is the *Imitatio Christi*. It is a genuine touch of Balzac that we should also be precisely informed of their bank account. Mystery in all its forms possessed a magical attraction for Balzac. The *Human Comedy* is full of people who carry a secret around with them. There are artists ignorant of their parentage but whose destiny is guided by an unknown hand. There is the galley slave, Vautrin, who turns up under the most varied names and disguises and in the most diverse milieux to play the role of Providence in the lives of young men. Balzac shows us secret societies in the heart of modern Paris but also secret dramas like the story of the girl with the golden eyes, about which Hofmannsthal has said: "This is the magnificent and unforgettable tale in which sensuality grows out of mystery, the Orient uncloses its heavy-lidded eyes amidst the insomnias of Paris, adventure is entwined with reality, the flower of the soul blossoms on the brink of ecstasy and death, and the present is illumined by such a torch that it lies before us like the great ages of ancient dreams. . . . The story of Henry de Marsay and the girl with the golden eyes. The story whose beginning is a description of Paris, an immense portrait in words, a vast pile, a tower built of pale light and deepest darkness; and whose ending is an Oriental poem in which the stupefaction of the most profound lust mingles with the odor of blood and an indefinable something soars beyond sense into the unnameable; whose beginning might have been from the hand of Dante, whose end from the *Thousand and One Nights*, and which, as a whole, could be by none other than the man who wrote it." And Hofmannsthal concludes: "I do not know what cravings of the imagination could possess a reader which the books of this man might not satisfy."

If Hofmannsthal cites Dante and the *Thousand and One Nights* for comparison, he also invokes Shakespeare in order to suggest the poetic wealth of Balzac's imagination.

The fact is that Balzac cannot be fitted into any of the literary movements and revolutions of the nineteenth century. He never drew up a program, never wanted to found a school. The inner law of his work and of his person is self-development, realization of the vision that he carried within him. Nothing is further from his intentions than the break with the past proclaimed by Romanticism. The roots of Balzac's spiritual world are embedded in the venerable traditions of the French mind. Rabelais is for him one of the greatest of geniuses, Racine perfection itself, the *Fables* of La Fontaine sacred relics of mankind. But he reveres with the same enthusiasm a Montesquieu, a Diderot, a Buffon. He regards himself as an heir, never as a rebel. He cherishes a boundless admiration for France's classical centuries, but also for the France of the cathedrals, of the mediaeval builders' corporations, of the Gothic.

The *Comédie Humaine* is not merely a portrait of the present, like Zola's cycle of novels. Balzac's work has an historical dimension as well. Balzac was born on the threshold of the nineteenth century, in the midst of the tremendous historical drama that France enacted before the world between 1789 and 1815. Some of his most gripping works present scenes from the Revolution and the Napoleonic era. But in the *Comédie Humaine* we also find novels set in the seventeenth, sixteenth, and fifteenth centuries. Only one story, *Les*

Proscrits, goes back even further, to the early years of the fourteenth century. It shows us Dante as an exile in Paris and describes a lecture at the Sorbonne by the celebrated Scholastic philosopher Siger de Brabant. We know that this willful thinker, who was condemned as a teacher of heresy even in his own lifetime, receives a tribute in Dante's *Paradiso* that puzzles the interpreters to this day. What was it about this material that attracted Balzac? And why did he classify this novel among his *Études philosophiques*, which loom over the massif of the *Études de Moeurs* like the interpretation over the realm of facts? There is a precinct in the *Comédie Humaine* that has never become popular, but has always had a particular attraction for certain minds, even as Balzac himself set the greatest store by it. These are the novels in which he represents the mystical and magical thinking of an original religious revelation, for which his authorities are Jacob Böhme, Swedenborg, and Saint-Martin. On his own authority he assigned Siger de Brabant a place in this Mystery-Christianity. This, I believe, is the meaning of the story, or at least one of its meanings.

For of course it means much more. After all, in Balzac everything is related to everything else. It is not by chance that in 1831, on the threshold of his career, Balzac invokes Dante, the creator of the mediaeval synthesis, and a master of Christian philosophy. They are images that rise before him because they symbolize his own vocation. The poet who summons past and present to the bar of his justice and the intrepid spirit who proclaims Eternal Christianity as a thinker are symbols, interpreters; they are powerful patrons. Balzac was profoundly shaken by the Revolution of 1830. Apocalyptic visions tormented him. From the same period dates the wonderful legend *Jésus-Christ en Flandre*, which culminates in the vision of a rejuvenated Church and ends with the words: "To believe is to live! I have just seen the funeral of a monarchy; the Church must be defended!" The historical frame of the legend refers back to the fifteenth century. It is the century in which the *Imitatio Christi* was composed. Here, as in the Dante novella, Balzac is seeking a connection with the Catholic Middle Ages.

Balzac's interpretation of Catholicism contains gnostic and heterodox elements that are fed, in part, by murky sources. He personally tended toward an esoteric form of Christianity not recognized by the Church and for which he cites dubious witnesses. But even where, venturing on the track of Swedenborg and Saint-Martin, he loses himself in fantasy and ecstasy, a genuine mystical longing is unmistakable. He has been touched by the spiritual powers of Christianity. He confessed the conviction, moreover, that active *caritas* was the remedy for the ills of the time. And he powerfully exemplified this belief in novels like *Le Curé de Village* and *Le Médecin de Campagne*. His apostolic priest figures have become models for the social Catholicism of the nineteenth and twentieth centuries. All of Balzac's work places itself at the service of a political, social, and religious reform of France.

The Great Revolution split France intellectually and spiritually into two camps that have been contending with each other for a hundred and fifty years. The history of this century and a half is a *Kulturkampf*, indeed, a war of religion, the outcome of which is still undecided today. For the France of the belief in reason and progress, which was in opposition under Napoleon III and acceded to power with the Third Republic, Balzac's Catholic and Royalist position was a kind of incomprehensible obscurantism. Taine, who was the first critic to recognize Balzac's greatness, nevertheless spoke of his politics as a mere novel. Flaubert notes with dismay that Balzac was Catholic and legitimist. His laconic final judgment runs: "un immense bonhomme, mais de second ordre." What would Flaubert and Taine say if they could look around them at current French literature? If they were compelled to acknowledge as an intellectual force the contentious Catholicism of a Léon Bloy, a Bernanos, a Claudel?

If we ask ourselves which side of the *Kulturkampf* of nineteenth-century France Balzac was on, no doubt seems possible: he belongs in the camp of the Counterrevolution. It was only logical, therefore, that Paul Bourget, the representative of the conservative Catholic novel, should profess around 1900 that for him the social doctrine of the *Human Comedy* constituted one of its principal elements, indeed, its crowning glory. At that time France was shaken by the fevers of the Dreyfus Affair. When Balzac's native city of Tours wanted to celebrate the one hundredth birthday of its famous son, a credit of 1000 francs was applied for; it was refused by an overwhelming majority of the municipal council on the grounds that Balzac's work was "notoriously clerical and reactionary." But Balzac had also portrayed heroic rebels. He had described the corruption of the ruling classes. That explains why leading Marxists like Friedrich Engels, for example, have claimed him for Socialism. In 1947, a French scholar who had spent twenty years investigating Balzac's political and social ideas published his results in a volume of 800 pages—to which we might add that he only traces Balzac's development up to 1834. The conclusion is that in Balzac's work everything can be found: revolt and royalism, liberal and reactionary tendencies, Anarchism, and Fascism. The latter point the author, Bernard Guyon, dares only to hint at. Resorting to shamefaced periphrases he writes: "il nous semble que la pensée qui l'anime se rapproche . . . de certaines idéologies modernes dont l'extraordinaire force d'expansion et puissance de succès s'est surabondamment manifestée à nos yeux au cours des dernières années" ["it seems to us that the political thought that animates his work is close to certain modern ideologies whose extraordinary power of expansion and potentiality for success have been made more than abundantly clear to us in the course of the last few years"]. The underlying cause is supposed to be a tragic inner conflict that rent Balzac's soul. This hypothesis contradicts, to my way of feeling, everything we know about Balzac. He was a great affirmer. He lived in the euphoria of creation. In his titanic consciousness as a creator he compared himself to Napoleon. Power, fame, dominion, authority, legitimacy—these to him were forms of human greatness.

To these he gave admiration. His political convictions are not to be measured by the yardstick of strict adherence to party dogmas. Balzac was carried away by greatness in all its forms. For he was akin to it himself.

Greatness—no other word will serve in determining Balzac's rank. If we survey the broad landscape of European literature, we shall find only a few figures to whom we attribute unqualified greatness: Homer, Dante, Shakespeare. The nearer a poet is to us in time the more the judgments on him diverge. Goethe is a case in point. T. S. Eliot thinks the question of whether Wordsworth or Goethe is the greater poet cannot be decided. That is remarkable. But no more remarkable than that in Germany too there is no unanimity of judgment concerning Goethe's greatness. The consensus about Homer, Dante, and Shakespeare also did not crystallize until the nineteenth century. Which French author might we associate with them? Racine, perhaps? We have but to try this mental experiment to see that it will not work. We may see in Racine a miracle of artistic perfection. But he is not of the race of great men. Since the Renaissance the French mind has been dominated by the ideal of formal artistic perfection. This formal perfection can only be realized, however, within moderate dimensions. Taste becomes, in aesthetic matters, the final arbiter. The first critic who undertook to grasp French literature as an autonomous historical structure was Voltaire. He constructed a Temple of Taste. A century later Sainte-Beuve decided that the time had come to confer the rights of citizenship in this sanctuary on Shakespeare and Goethe: "il s'agit de reconstruire le Temple du Goût." But the traditional measurements and proportions of the groundplan condemned the undertaking to a compromise. Shakespeare was only just allowed in; he was a classic without knowing it. But to admit Dante as well—that Sainte-Beuve could not make up his mind to do. After all, Sainte-Beuve was likewise incapable of appreciating greatness among his contemporaries. His mistaken judgments on Baudelaire and Balzac are monstrous. Not until the end of the nineteenth century did disturbing rifts become evident in the *Temple du Goût*. It had been reared on a classicizing Parnassus, and this Mount of the Muses was convulsed by an earthquake whose tremors followed in ever more rapid succession. There were volcanic eruptions. The name of the first was Arthur Rimbaud. With him a new era begins. After the War of 1914, Rimbaud was elevated to the throne by the Surrealists. But Claudel also descends from him. One of his earliest dramas, *Tête d'Or*, from around 1890, shows the revolutionary effect of Rimbaud. The play catches something of the primitive violence of the most ancient Greek tragedy. Beyond Racine, Euripides, and Sophocles, Claudel found the way back to Aeschylus. Once more greatness is seen, once more greatness is striven for—at the expense of smoothness, of tasteful proportion, of polish. In Claudel's generation, there would be further indications that France had rediscovered the sense of greatness. Think of Péguy, in whom the France of the cathedrals lives again. But to me another witness, much less heard today, is also important: André Suarès, who died in 1948. What does he say about Racine? "To love Racine more than any other poet is a matter of taste; but to compare him with Shakespeare can no longer be taken seriously. I prefer Racine a hundred times to Victor Hugo, but a hundred Racines do not, in my view, make a quarter of a Shakespeare. What does it matter to me if some schoolmaster concedes the title of classic to the one and denies it to the other? . . . Goethe restores my confidence: he is vigorous enough to be classical when he wishes and romantic when it is necessary. . . . The divine Racine, they are always talking about the divine Racine. If Racine is a god, Olympus is a salon. . . . We overrate Racine, and we deprive the soul of France of an infinite portion of its greatness when we see all of it in Racine. Racine is indisputably narrower and smaller than France. The genius of France is no more comprised in Racine than the entire monarchy in Louis XIV. Measured against Saint Louis and the cathedrals, the Great Century, its great poet, and its great king reach no higher than the portal." The same Suarès wrote in 1917 about Goethe under the title of *Goethe le Grand*: "Il faut n'avoir aucun respect de la grandeur spirituelle, aucun amour de la poésie, aucun sens de la valeur humaine, pour disputer son rang à Goethe. Il n'est pas seulement le plus haut et le plus vaste des Allemands: il compte entre les dix ou onze plus grandes têtes du genre humain" ["One must be devoid of any respect for spiritual greatness, any love of poetry, any sense of human value to contest Goethe's rank. He is not only the highest and most vast of Germans; he is among the ten or eleven greatest minds of the human race"].

Ten or eleven. Suarès would also have numbered Pascal among them, but no other Frenchman.

I believe that Balzac too can expect to take his place in this illustrious company.

One of the most remarkable occurrences in the history of the French mind is the break which it effected in the sixteenth century with the Middle Ages, and that means with its great Gothic past. This break is located between Rabelais and Ronsard. If anything is evident, it is that Rabelais stems from Gothic France. The Renaissance elements in him, which are usually emphasized, are all on the surface. The rupture with the Gothic world involved a loss of substance of immeasurable extent. It is the price which France paid for its Classicism: for refinement, elegance, rationality, style, form. When once these qualities have been inbred, they shape the instincts. One seeks to reproduce them and, wherever possible, even to improve upon them—irrespective of all disjunctions in style. Thus sublime essences are engendered like the poetry of a Valéry. But the substance of Gothic France lived on underground. The historical eruptions of the Great Revolution, Napoleon, and the July Revolution loosened the soil. I can do no more than allude here to this transformed substance that emerges once again to the light simultaneously in Michelet, in Auguste Comte, in Balzac—and finally in Rodin. Is there any more impressive testimony to Balzac's greatness than Rodin's marble, from which the visionary Balzac gazes out at us? Than Balzac, as Rilke says, "in the ecstasy of vision, foaming with creation; in his superabundant fertility, founder of generations, lavisher of destinies?" Balzac's creative power can rival that of the greatest. Is he also equal to them as an artist? It is obvious that Balzac cannot be measured by the artistic ideal of Flaubert and his school. This is the ideal of *l'art pour l'art*. For Flaubert the value of a work depends upon the quality of the style, the immaculate purity of the language, the rhythm of the sentences and the music of the prose. His ideal was to take the matter of reality and shape it into imperishable linguistic substance. He called this process: "faire du réel écrit." Flaubert's language is artistic prose in the sense in which one speaks of the artistic prose of the Greeks and Romans. For Flaubert this was an inner necessity that has psychological reasons. At the same time, however, it was a martyrdom to which every page of his correspondence testifies. An author like Balzac, in whom a world of characters is struggling to be born, cannot and must not write that way. The factitious link that Flaubert established between artistry and the novel and that degenerated with the Goncourts into a mannered *écriture artiste* was a dead end.

Today we are revising the evaluations of the nineteenth century in every field. More than a century seems to separate 1900 and 1950. At the Paris World's Fair in 1900 an exhibition of modern French paintings was presented. But it lacked Monet, Degas, Puvis de Chavannes, Renoir, Cézanne. Instead, paintings by artists whose very names have been forgotten today were admired. With literature it is not very different. Around 1900, it was obligatory to admire Sully Prudhomme. In 1901 he was awarded the first Nobel prize for literature. Who knows anything about him today? Who still admires the sonnets of Hérédia? Who still considers Marcel Prévost and Paul Adam important novelists? And what of the great names in French criticism of the period—Faguet, Lemaître, Brunetière, Lanson?

Balzac, too, must be viewed differently in 1950 than in 1900 or even in 1920. It is a long time since Zola has been set beside him. Do people still put him on a level with Stendhal and Flaubert? I do not believe that they will long continue to do so. I believe I sense a shift in critical emphasis. In the field of literary criticism I find no problem so interesting as that of the order of rank and its changes. It is a very delicate task, which requires us not only to consult our own personal sense of values but to keep an eye out for signs of the weather. If I look at Balzac from this perspective, I notice that he has continually increased in stature over the last three decades. Time has brought out new aspects in him. We must bear in mind that since 1919 the entire situation of the French novel has been altered by the appearance of Proust. The advent of a new artist of genius also throws the art of the past into a new light. This is a regularly established process. Literary criticism does not take it sufficiently into account. But in 1936 a critic like Thibaudet had already drawn a portrait of Balzac that was seen through Proust. He found in Monsieur de Charlus a heightened Vautrin, and he calls Proust "le plus balzacien des écrivains français après Balzac," as Saint-Simon had been "le plus balzacien des écrivains avant Balzac." Proust is the most comprehensive and subtle intelligence ever to manifest itself in the medium of the French novel; an intelligence that was simultaneously intuition in Bergson's sense. For that reason it is doubly significant that Proust's art should have an affinity with Balzac and not with Stendhal or Flaubert. It was Paul Morand who remarked that only through Proust was one of Balzac's greatest novels, *Les Illusions Perdues*, discovered for the present day. And whoever reads Morand's wonderful novella, *Parfaite de Saligny*, will realize that this modern Frenchman follows in the line of Balzac's great tragic novellas—I am thinking of *El Verdugo* or *La Fille aux yeux d'or*. Moreover, in both Proust and Morand, elements recur which the democratic nineteenth and the socialistic twentieth centuries have charged to the great Balzac as improprieties: his need for luxury and his so-called snobbishness. Both are expressions of an aesthetic sense for which Baudelaire found the poetic formula: *Luxe, calme et volupté.*

It is remarkable that it has always been the poets who have understood Balzac most profoundly: Baudelaire, Browning, Hofmannsthal. Among contemporaries: Gottfried Benn. This influence of Balzac, in range and in depth, would also pose a problem for criticism, were criticism willing to recognize it. These poets respond to Balzac as to a related element. From this phenomenon we may gather that an inexhaustible poetic substance inheres in Balzac. But it tells us something else besides. These poets are completely distinct from one another. But in each of them we find the utmost refinement of soul and intellect. This means that Balzac receives the tribute of the European elite. Yet the same Balzac also speaks to the mass of readers. Stendhal wrote for "the happy few." In order to appreciate Flaubert, one must be initiated into the subtleties of artistic form. Balzac writes neither for intellectuals nor for aesthetes. Nevertheless, they too render him admiration. He is perhaps the only writer of the nineteenth century who bridges the gap between the elite and the masses. This too is a seal of greatness. Balzac as a Frenchman contains all mankind. That is why he could become the property of all mankind.

Balzac's greatness was still in dispute at the end of the nineteenth century and beyond. But today, a century after his death, it is emerging ever more forcefully. And it will grow, from century to century.

1950

Emerson

✦✦

RALPH WALDO EMERSON (1803–1882) was introduced in Germany by Herman Grimm in 1857. Nietzsche admired him. To the Germany of the present he has become a stranger. I consider him one of the most valuable legacies of the century after the death of Goethe. Emerson's *Essays* (only this book is to be discussed here) appeared between 1841 and 1844. What occupied the educated European at that time? The decade between 1835 and 1845 brought him in the way of literary novelties—we restrict ourselves to a few characteristic titles—the following:

1835: David Friedrich Strauss, *Leben Jesu.*
1835: Büchner, *Dantons Tod.*
1835: Gautier, *Mademoiselle de Maupin.*
1836: Musset, *Confession d'un enfant du siècle.*
1838: Dickens, *The Pickwick Papers.*
1839: Stendhal, *La Chartreuse de Parme.*
1840: Proudhon, *Qu'est-ce que la propriété?*
1841: Hebbel, *Judith.*
1841: Carlyle, *Heroes and Hero-Worship.*
1841: Balzac, *La Comédie Humaine.*
1842: Comte, *Cours de philosophie positive*
        (conclusion).
1842: Tennyson, *Poems.*
1843: Mill, *System of Logic.*
1843: Ruskin, *Modern Painters.*
1844: Heine, *Neue Gedichte.*
1844: Stifter, *Studien.*
1845: Stirner, *Der Einzige und sein Eigentum.*

Romanticism is singing its last songs; historical criticism, Positivism, anarchism are beginning their offensives: an artist's poem of sensual beauty is heard from afar; English idealism takes the form of social prophecy; the modern novel is created in England and France. Locked into themselves, out of touch with one another, melancholy German brooders rhyme and reflect, while the idea of a universal literary culture arrived at by Goethe and the Romantics lies forgotten.

Alien from all this and remote, like the "beautiful children of God," as Goethe would say, Emerson's *Essays* see the light in this decade preceding the Revolutions of 1848. If we try to find a respect in which they are connected with another intellectual production of the period, almost nothing valid presents itself (the comparison with Carlyle's ethical prophecy remains misleading, no matter how often it is undertaken)— unless it be in a region which, so far as I know, hardly anyone has investigated up until now.

A mysterious analogy links Emerson and Balzac.

In an earlier work[1] I sought to demonstrate that the nature, world, and work of Balzac can only be comprehended with reference to a mode of spiritual vision that may be designated the "Theory of the Unity of the All." It seems to have its origin in magical thinking. It apprehends reality as an infinitely diverse All, which is an animated unity, a single, active, coherence of life. In a wide variety of manifestations, yet always identical with itself, such a vision appears throughout the entire course of man's intellectual history. Its beginnings are enigmatic, its first sound an obscure murmur. From time to time it recedes, is apparently abandoned, and then reappears: changed into a conceptual form but unchanged in substance. It is a spiritual constant of human history. It must be embedded in the nature of man, in the nature of the universe. It can assume a philosophical shape, but it is not philosophy. It operates in myth and mystery worship, but it is not religion. It speaks in art and poetry and is nevertheless not a figment of the imagination. It turns up in the theories of physics,

[1] *Balzac* (2nd ed., Berne, 1951), Chapter 2.

of chemistry, of biology, and yet it is not a science. Perhaps it is all these things as well, but its origin is deeper and more unified. It outlasts all philosophies, all religions, all systems. It is eternal and indestructible. It is omnipresent and will not be refuted. It is dispersed throughout the world like a seed which can sprout everywhere and always.

Wherever this Theory of the Unity of the All makes itself known, it always avails itself of the same language. It has its own vocabulary of concepts and signs, which is self-consistent and always recurs. Since it conceives of the All as One, of appearances as forms of a unified power, it is a kind of Monism, Phenomenalism, Dynamism. But as the unity is divided into energy and appearance, inner and outer, cause and effect, this monism simultaneously becomes a dualism. In its dynamic aspect, the All-Unity-Theory is a system of energy. In this way it arrives at the concepts of polarization, antagonism, and compensation. When it advances from the scission of the one to the mystery of the three, it can turn into number mysticism and number symbolism. But infinity resides in number. The one is the beginning of an infinite series. An infinite series of degrees, following upon one another according to the law of continuity—this becomes another aspect of the totality that is a unity. The All is a single movement of infinite ascent.

This movement is life. The Theory of the Unity of the All is vitalism. It leaves the antithesis of materialism and spiritualism below and magically conveys matter to spirit. It brings all things together into one great harmony.

The Theory of the Unity of the All originates in Asia. It runs through the thought of Antiquity. It can be found in Neoplatonism, in Hermeticism, and in the Cabbala. It erupts enthusiastically in the intellectual ferment of the Renaissance and enters into intimate association with the newly burgeoning natural sciences and with Humanism. Traces of it are detectible in the seventeenth century in Leibniz and heterodox mysticism, in the eighteenth century in the natural philosophers, the social reformers, and the preachers of esoteric doctrines. In innumerable tortuous ways that have not been explored as yet, it penetrates the intellectual syncretism of the nineteenth century. One of its principal intermediaries is Swedenborg. But we are not concerned here with demonstrating its affiliation in the history of ideas. For it is in the nature of the mode of spiritual vision we are discussing that it is not propagated like other historical tendencies. Its manifestation in history does not resemble a stream, a single current that grows wider from source to mouth, but rather it is like a light that gleams now brighter, now more dimly, that disappears and reemerges, and yet always seems to cast the same radiance. It is a flame kindled in the soul itself, and that burns inside it like an eternal lamp. It is as if it did not require to be supplied with fuel from the resources of a particular historical era. This doctrine of the unity of the All is not transmitted by precept and cannot be adopted in part. It is given to the mind wholly or not at all. The mind that possesses it recognizes it in all its historical incarnations and welcomes it in the confidence of a secret affinity. The mind that does not will pass it by and fail to see it even where it is most strongly evident. It has its own laws not only of structure but even of perceptibility. The formula for this order is *similia similibus*.

It has its own symbolism too. And it is by this symbolism that it is recognizable to the seeker. Its foremost symbol is the sphere or the circle: closed infinity, totality as unity, beginning without end, end without beginning. If being is spherical, thought must be cyclical.[2]

And now let us turn back. The characterization of the All-Unity-Idea that I have tried to give here is the result of my deep absorption in the spiritual world of Balzac. But Balzac is mentioned here only as the representative of a certain type of mind, as an individual case from which a set of general laws may be inferred. Although Balzac was determined in many ways by the intellectual tendencies of his age and of the

[2] What I in 1924 called the "Theory of the Unity of the All" was presented from the point of view of the history of ideas in 1936 by Arthur O. Lovejoy, *The Great Chain of Being* (Harvard University Press).

age preceding, he cannot be grasped through mere enumeration of these tendencies. Between them and the core of his individuality lies an intermediate, and, as it were, supra-individual sphere; and this constitutes an independent mode of spiritual vision that is as removed from the course and development of the history of ideas as it is from the unique and particular personality of Balzac. This holds true more or less for all great figures in the history of ideas, but it is precisely this more or less that counts. Balzac belongs to a group for whom the *a priori* of the spiritual form is of far greater determining significance than the *a priori* of historical tradition. And this is the reason why all attempts to understand him and his work by pure genetic derivation must fail.

Now when I speak of an affinity between Emerson and Balzac it should be clear from what has been said that the reference is to the *a priori* of the spiritual form. Both Emerson and Balzac are typical representatives of the mode of vision that I have designated the Theory of the Unity of the All. In principle, therefore, the affinity between them is no different and no closer than their affinity with other minds that inhabit the same sphere. Balzac knew nothing of Emerson, and Emerson, at least in the thirties of the last century when he was writing his essays, could scarcely have known about his great French contemporary. And yet we are justified in speaking of a spiritual affinity, since it is possible to be related without being acquainted, and since the relationship of two things or two people who do not know of one another emerges in the process of their being perceived by the mind of the observer, whereupon they take their place in their full individual historical significance. It is not a matter here of a game involving subjective caprice or delight in random combinations, but of an authentic mode of perception that confers upon its object an increased measure of objective content.

Emerson's intellectual world can be more easily understood if one is familiar with Balzac's, and then one also understands something that had previously only been an inkling: the fact, namely, that for all their differences in environment and personal orientation, both of these minds produce a similar specific effect upon the reader, an effect difficult to describe but all the more clearly felt as tonic. It is that in Balzac which has been called his "magic," his "ardeur vitale" (Baudelaire), his impression of power; that in Emerson which we experience as his stimulating influence—and which provides the occasion for these reflections.

The Theory of the Unity of the All manifests itself throughout the entire construction of Emerson's intellectual creation by signs such as stonemasons use; and it may suffice us to pause for a moment in our wanderings before one or another of these ciphers. Here we find symbolic circles and spheres ("Circles" is the title of one of the Essays); we find a game of mystic numbers; we meet with allusions to the most ancient esoteric wisdom and to modern occult sciences; we encounter (also as in Balzac) reinterpretations on the spiritual level of concepts drawn from the natural sciences (compensation) and from the formulas of logic (*causa-effectus*). All these things (and how many others that will strike the attentive observer) are exponents of a mystical theory of knowledge, of a lore founded upon intellectual intuition, a secret royal road of the spirit. Emerson himself once stated it: "the heart which abandons itself to the Supreme Mind finds itself related to all its works, and will travel a royal road to particular knowledges and powers. In ascending to this primary and aboriginal sentiment, we have come from our remote station on the circumference instantaneously to the centre of the world, where, as in the closet of God, we see causes, and anticipate the universe, which is but a slow effect."[3]

[3] Balzac has the equation: God-cause, nature-effect. "And nature is captivating . . . ; but isn't the cause, in the eyes of certain privileged souls . . . superior to nature? The cause—that is God. In this sphere of causes live the Newtons, the Laplaces, the Keplers, . . . the true poets . . . and the sublime ecstatics. Every human sentiment contains analogies with this situation, in which the spirit abandons the effect for the sake of the cause." Emerson's "anticipation of the universe" squares precisely with Balzac's declarations concerning the "divinatory" character of his work.

The presence of being in the act of intuition, the visionary apprehension of the primordial reality—that is the source of Emerson's wisdom as of Balzac's fiction. Concerning this second sight of the artist Balzac says that it "leads him into the center of life," that it "transports him into the middle of the radiant sphere in which his thoughts can conjure up the entire world." And in another passage: "Il se passe chez les poètes ou chez les écrivains réellement philosophes un phénomène moral inexplicable, inoui, dont la science peut difficilement rendre compte. C'est une sorte de seconde vue qui leur permet de deviner la vérité dans toutes les situations possibles; ou, mieux encore, je ne sais quelle puissance qui les transporte là où ils doivent, où ils veulent être. Ils inventent le vrai, par analogie, ou voient l'objet à decrire, soit que l'objet vienne à eux, soit qu'ils aillent eux-mêmes vers l'objet" ["Among poets and genuinely philosophical writers an inexplicable and extraordinary spiritual phenomenon takes place which science cannot easily account for. It is a kind of second sight which permits them to divine the truth in all possible situations; or, better still, a certain inexplicable power which transports them to where they must be or where they wish to be. They invent the truth by analogy or they see the object to be described, be it that the object comes to them or that they go toward the object themselves"].

Such utterances give us a concrete idea of the basic mental phenomenon common to both Emerson and Balzac: the direct perception of being through spiritual vision. But an essential difference must be noted at once. For the poet reality unfolds as the colorfully interwoven realm of life; for the sage, as the intricately ordered realm of the mind. To the one it is revealed as the cosmos of persons, to the other as the cosmos of ideas. The one represents it in a system of novels, the other in a symphony of thought. What flashed before Balzac's inner eye in moments of inspiration was a concrete human destiny or a drama of passion, a demonic countenance or the scene of a crime. It is quite different with Emerson. What discloses itself to him in "divine moments" is the supercelestial seat of the ideas, the blissful glance at eternal beauty, the transfigured landscape of the soul. Emerson's writings are nothing other than the message of what he saw in that country. Life receives its sanction for him through the illumination provided by these blessed moments. He writes: "There is a difference between one and another hour of life in their authority and subsequent effect. Our faith comes in moments; our vice is habitual. Yet there is a depth in those brief moments which constrains us to ascribe more reality to them than to all other experiences." It is not a matter of sentimental moods here, of effusiveness and dreaming. In such divine moments we become aware of the truths in accordance with which our lives ought to be framed. Essential truth is given to us only at such moments. The distinguishing mark of this truth, which is unmistakable, is that it exists outside of all time and above all transience. Such moments assure us that not even time and transience have power over the deepest essence of our soul. We feel we are in the presence of pure being, of the eternal. All the disharmonies of life are resolved in one pure chord. "It is the highest power of divine moments that they abolish our contritions also. I accuse myself of sloth and unprofitableness day by day; but when these waves of God flow into me, I no longer reckon lost time. . . . For these moments confer a sort of omnipresence and omnipotence which asks nothing of duration, but sees that the energy of the mind is commensurate with the work to be done, without time."

Emerson's wisdom teaches us to derive the guiding principles for our view of the world and our conduct of life from the content of these eternal moments. Life as a whole presents us with a multitude of warring impulses, contrasting moods, irreconcilable points of view. Every instinct, as Nietzsche says, has its perspective; every state of emotion and every region of the mind has a philosophical scheme that corresponds to it. Every side of our nature can form the basis for a view of life, which can then subject everything to its angle of vision. Out of all these possibilities we half-consciously, half-unconsciously, choose one, which then becomes the prevailing habit of our mind and feelings. The position of common sense is probably the most widespread (and the most barren) of these attitudes of consciousness among which—within a certain amplitude of oscillation—we are able to choose. He who chooses this position confines himself to the world of the senses and considers it alone as real. But for Emerson this sensible world is a system of symbols in which a multiple meaning resides. He divides men into three classes according to the depth of the meaning to which they attain: "One class live to the utility of the symbol; esteeming health and wealth a final good. Another class live above this mark to the beauty of the symbol; as the poet and artist, and the naturalist, and man of science. A third class live above the beauty of the symbol to the beauty of the thing signified: these are wise men. The first class have common sense; the second, taste; and the third, spiritual perception."

Emerson's message is only accessible to those who are capable of "spiritual perception." But isn't the germ of this capacity in every one of us? And isn't it true that we allow weakness, false modesty, fear of other people, and timidity to extinguish this spark in us? That eating, drinking, planting, calculating creature we call man is not the representative of man but of his distortion and degeneration. "Him we do not respect; but the soul, whose organ he is, would he let it appear through his action, would make our knees bend." Emerson requires of us the moral courage to grant free expression to our soul. Let it flow into your actions, he calls to us: into your intellect, and it will appear as genius; into your will, and it will appear as virtue; into your affections, and it will manifest itself as love. "All reform aims, in some one particular, to let the soul have its way through us; in other words, to engage us to obey." To grant expression to the soul means to obey. It means to follow joyfully the voice of truth and of beauty, of love and of purity.

Are these novel truths? No, certainly not; and it is good that they are not, for otherwise they would not have this calm, eternal radiance. They are beyond old and new, beyond youth and age. In them is a power of immortal youth: "We are often made to feel that there is another youth and age than that which is measured from the year of our natural birth. Some thoughts always find us young, and keep us so. Such a thought is the love of the universal and eternal beauty. Every man parts from that contemplation with the feeling that it rather belongs to ages than to mortal life. The least activity of the intellectual powers redeems us in a degree from the conditions of the time."

The person accustomed to think historically will, when confronted with Emerson, speak of a resumption of the philosophical heritage of Plato and Plotinus. He is right—within his limits. But that is because there is a type of Platonism that is not a unique historical doctrine but a perennial attitude of the soul. Emerson is a Platonist in this sense. Platonic and Plotinic ideas recur frequently in his writings. But they are surrounded by an atmosphere that sets them far apart from their previous historical incarnations. We usually encounter Platonic mysticism in the immaterial air of late Classical or Christian monastic contemplation, where it appears as a rarefied spirituality and an inner vision of the soul. It has something of the spirit of the *Penseroso*:

> To walk the studious cloisters pale,
> And love the high embowèd roof,
> With antique pillars massy proof,
> And storied windows richly dight,
> Casting a dim religious light.

With Emerson Platonism leaves the cloister and the sanctuary and steps out into the open, into the sun, into wide blue spaces. "Come out into the azure! Love the day!" Emerson calls to us. The breath of the unspoiled nature of a broad, young land blows through the American's words of wisdom and beauty, quickening and hardening them. They arouse a sensation of joyous strength like a clear morning in summer. "We can love nothing but nature," Emerson tells us. His sense of nature is not elegiac, not sentimental; it is steeped in the strength, the purity, the health of flourishing life. It is no respecter of art, culture, society. It resembles the prairie wind. The smoke of cities, the dust of libraries, the incense-fumes of churches, the perfume of salons—all are swept away. "The spirit of the world, the great calm presence of the Creator, comes not forth to the sorceries of opium or of wine. The sublime vision comes to the pure and simple soul in a clean and chaste body." Emerson calls for men who can stand up to nature, people upright and firmly rooted as trees, clear and fresh as brook and stream. Nature liberates them from all history and all tradition. "We see literature best from wild nature. . . . No facts are to me sacred; none are profane; I simply experiment, an endless seeker, with no Past on my back. . . . If thou fill thy brain with Boston and New York, with fashion and covetousness, and wilt stimulate thy jaded senses with wine and French coffee, thou shalt find no radiance of wisdom in the lonely waste of the pinewoods."

At this point the affinity with Balzac of which we spoke turns into irreconcilable opposition. Balzac sought the play of the infinite cosmic energies in love, in artistic creation, in the mind. Its revelation in nature he did not understand. He views nature magically and alchemistically as the arcanum of matter. He interprets it symbolically as the antagonist of human energies and aspirations. He always conceives it as something other than itself, as an index of mind. He is not familiar with the contrary movement: the reimmersion of the mind in nature, the redemptive harmony with the stars, the clouds, and the winds. The tension of human existence occupied him too fully. Balzac is the man of the modern metropolis, the man of the industrial age who has become alienated from nature. What Emerson said of the literary men of Boston applies literally to him: that he "stimulated his jaded senses with wine and French coffee." (It is well known that the *Human Comedy* was produced by forced nocturnal labor under the stimulus of excessive coffee-drinking.) It was not given Balzac to find wisdom's radiant gleam in the broad solitudes of the pinewoods. The contrast that exists between Emerson and Balzac on this point has a symbolic significance.

The art and wisdom of continental Europe has been created, in the modern bourgeois era, by a type of man who has lost the sense of community with nature. The works produced by this type of man determine the physiognomy of our culture, and they also determine to a large extent the feelings of the few individuals who, at the heart of their individuality, have preserved that affinity with nature. Here we have one of the reasons for so much that is dull and joyless, that is without belief or hope in salvation, that is feverish, overheated, and lacerated by cynicism or tragedy in the age that has just passed. A Rousseau was bound to fail in his attempt to return to nature, since he read the Enlightenment's principles of reason into nature instead of opening himself to the voices of the universe. In Hölderlin the experience of nature is steeped in the sacred rites of an Orphic mystery religion; it has become myth. It is accessible only to the initiate. It is a nature consecrated and purified, remote and esoteric, burdened with metaphysics and refashioned by mythology—a precinct for the worship of a cult. The powers of nature are conjured here as in a mantic crystal. But it is not the way to a nature that is direct, free and wild, flowering and tempestuous. Nor is it to be found in Baudelaire, who builds himself landscapes of marble and metal from which he banishes the vegetation. Only in the great English poetry of the nineteenth century does the preestablished accord between man and nature sometimes receive a perfectly pure and forceful expression. It suffices to mention but one name: Wordsworth. A sonnet by Wordsworth, which is included in every English anthology, states in fourteen lines the whole essential truth regarding the soul, modern civilization, and the revelation of nature:

> The world is too much with us; late and soon,
> Getting and spending, we lay waste our powers:
> Little we see in Nature that is ours;
> We have given our hearts away, a sordid boon!

The sea that bares her bosom to the moon;
The winds that will be howling at all hours,
And are upgathered now like sleeping flowers;
For this, for everything, we are out of tune;
It moves us not.—Great God! I'd rather be
A Pagan suckled in a creed outworn;
So might I, standing on this pleasant lea,
Have glimpses that would make me less forlorn;
Have sight of Proteus rising from the sea;
Or hear old Triton blow his wreathèd horn.

It is, of course, also true for Wordsworth, if in an entirely different sense than for Hölderlin, that his feeling for nature is transfigured by religion, that it is natural piety. In an entirely different sense than for Hölderlin, because Wordsworth's religion is a Platonizing Christianity. And Wordsworth remains —like Hölderlin, though again in a different sense—remote from our world, the world in which, for better or for worse, we must live, even though we may see through its idols and know its curse. In pastoral simplicity, under the patriarchal living conditions of northern England's lake and hill district, Wordsworth found the tranquility of a life transfigured by contemplation. But to combine the message of nature's eternal revelation with labor and commerce, with industry and daily reality—that was perhaps only possible in the New World. This was the work of the American mind. Emerson performed it in his capacity as sage. But he knew that it would have to be ratified by a poet. One of his essays is entitled "The Poet." Poets, he says, should be lawgivers, the heralds and guides of our daily tasks. We have esteemed umpires and amateurs of beauty. But if you inquire whether their souls are beautiful and whether their acts are like fair pictures, you learn that they are selfish and sensual. Even the poets are content to write poems only from fancy, at a safe distance from their own experience. But the true poet is the complete man. He is the sayer and namer, the representer of beauty and truth. Each of us needs him and no one can tell how much depends for him upon the poet's advent. After all his disappointments, man still waits for the arrival of a brother who will put him in touch with the truth until he has made it his own. The people imagine that they hate poetry and yet they are all poets and mystics themselves without knowing it. But where is the poet of our age?

"I look in vain for the poet whom I describe. We do not, with sufficient plainness, or sufficient profoundness, address ourselves to life, nor dare we chaunt our own time and social circumstance. If we filled the day with bravery, we should not shrink from celebrating it. Time and nature yield us many gifts, but not yet the timely man, the new religion, the reconciler, whom all things await. . . . We have yet had no genius in America which knew the value of our incomparable materials. . . . Yet America is a poem in our eyes; its ample geography dazzles the imagination, and it will not wait long for metres."

By one of those beautiful and wonderful conjunctions which history provides by way of compensation, as it were, for so much that has gone wrong, a few years later the poet whom Emerson was watching for did make his appearance. *Leaves of Grass* is the creator's joyous and powerful reply to the sage. Whitman himself confessed that Emerson's essay had been one of the strongest impulses (or perhaps an anticipatory confirmation) for his work. And Emerson's famous letter of tribute (only a few months[4] after the publication of *Leaves of Grass*) brought the poet the gratitude of his greatest compatriot and contemporary, and brought him, too, his earliest acclaim.

Emerson and Whitman bring us the message of an America that perhaps lives on today only in secret and underground, but that has not lost any of its meaning for us on that account —an America before Americanism. Emerson's America has been displaced temporally by later history, but spiritually it is invincible—like Goethe's Germany. Emerson's America has annexed a new province for the soul. Wordsworth had consecrated a hemisphere to nature; Emerson embraces and

[4] Actually, only a few weeks.—TR.

affirms the whole of nature. Emerson belongs, like Cusanus, like Leibniz and Hegel, like Balzac and Goethe, among the representatives of a view of the world that Goethe calls "Totalism" and "Harmonism." Wordsworth listens only to those tones in nature that will blend into the chord of Platonic spiritualization. Emerson knows that nature "is no saint," but he sanctifies all of nature: the nature that eats and drinks and sins; and whose darlings are the great, the strong, the beautiful, and not the children of our law, not the pupils of the Sunday school.

To call Emerson, as has often been done, an immoralist, is a grave misconception. He is one of the pioneers of the modern ethic. He has overcome every trace of puritanism or moralism without on that account sinking into immoralism or mere idolatry of life; without lapsing into tortured paradoxes like Nietzsche, who wished to translate malice and cruelty into virtues because he believed that he must hate virtue. Emerson's wisdom is radiant with light and love, with harmony and beauty. It is true that Emerson's criticism of morality has many points of contact with Nietzsche's. But it moves in a completely different direction. Nietzsche looks from the present into the future, Emerson from the present into the eternal day. Nietzsche's thinking is a thinking forward, though it be in eons and even to the eternal return. Emersons' thinking is a thinking upward.

Emerson told his age hard truths, but he did not break with it. It is as divine and as full of promise to him as any age in history, as every age. Over against any romanticism of history, retrospective or messianic, he professes his faith in the "strong present tense," in an energetic present of the sense of life. Only one who takes history too seriously can feel that he is subject to a historical *fatum*. And only one who has lost sight of what transcends history can take history so seriously. Emerson puts everything in its place: "Trust thyself: every heart vibrates to that iron string. Accept the place providence has found for you, the society of your contemporaries, the connection of events. Great men have always done so, and confided themselves childlike to the genius of their age, betraying their perception that the absolutely trustworthy was seated at their heart, working through their hands, predominating in all their being." The "absolutely-trustworthy" dwells in our hearts. Platonically speaking it is the participation of the soul in the eternal being of the Ideas. This certainty gives Emerson's doctrine its wonderful power. Its unshakable foundation is called: "Self-reliance."

This does not mean "self-confidence," but rather to adhere to one's inner truth and realize oneself in it—without side glances, without considerations, and without concessions. It is the attitude of manly and great souls. "Whoso would be a man," says Emerson, "must be a nonconformist." And he adds: "He who would gather immortal palms must not be hindered by the name of goodness, but must explore if it be goodness."

Emerson's moral criticism is directed with bold candor at social, clerical, and conventional morality. But it can afford to be outspoken because it sees the constellations of moral beauty and goodness shining eternally within the soul and in nature. Constellations, not laws! Virtue, not virtues. The ascent of the soul does not lead to a special virtue but to the region of all the virtues. They are in the spirit that contains them all. The soul, says Emerson, requires purity, but is more than purity; it requires justice, but is more than justice; it requires goodness, but is something better than goodness—so that we feel a kind of descent and accommodation when we leave the sphere of moral nature in order to inculcate a virtue that it demands of us. To teach this moral nature within man to resound is the meaning of education. "Speak to his heart, and the man becomes suddenly virtuous." From this altitude a beautiful effulgence is shed upon all the virtues—"truth, frankness, courage, love, humility, and all the virtues"—and the eternal moral truth, too, appears in its traditional forms. "I do not know if all matter will be found to be made of one element . . . at last, but the world of manners and actions is wrought of one stuff, and, begin where we will, we are pretty sure in a short space to be mumbling our ten commandments."

So many words, the reader will ask, if after all this we are back again to the ten commandments? For this the expenditure of a prose style which, in Nietzsche's judgment, can be matched for perfection in the nineteenth century only by Leopardi, Mérimée, and Walter Savage Landor? Was the moralist Emerson nothing more in the end than a kind of staid country parson or village schoolmaster? But no! He was, again in the words of Nietzsche, "enlightened, discursive, complex, refined. . . ." But that is precisely Emerson's secret: he is complex and yet simple ("grandly simple" are the souls he admires), complex and simple as the world. For all of us the necessary path of development has been to become complex and refined, and our motto is—or was—the statement that Gide put in the mouth of one of his characters: "Ma valeur est dans ma complication." But we all know that we must pass through complexity to a higher simplicity. Emerson has both at once. Out of the bright, variegated strands of his essays the eternal truths of the soul emerge in simplest words. Thus he can set down the ten commandments again. Thus, amidst the excited uproar of modern ideological conflicts he can pronounce clearly, purely, and with earnest serenity the words: "Oh my brethren, God exists!"

1924

Unamuno

++

THE poet in exile—this is a situation that we feel to be typical of the Latin style of history. Elegiac in Ovid, heroic in Dante, theatrical in Victor Hugo, it is repeated in our own day by Miguel de Unamuno. When, in March 1924, Primo de Rivera banished the sexagenarian to Fuerteventura, a rocky island in the Canaries, he thrust him, surely unintentionally, into the glaring light of publicity. The world press reverberated with indignation. Intellectual antipodes like D'Annunzio and Romain Rolland united in protest. From one day to the next Unamuno had become a European figure. What is the significance of this man? What is his importance for Spain and for Europe?

Spain and Europe

Unamuno belongs with Ganivet, Azorín, Baroja, Maeztu, Rubén Darío, Valle-Inclán to the so-called generation of 1898, the generation which applied its energies after the debacle in Cuba to the spiritual and national regeneration of Spain. Actually, the efforts at renewal undertaken by the *regeneradores* had already begun before the colonial catastrophe. Reformers like Joaquín Costa (1841-1911) were precursors, and the line of ascendants can be traced—as Azorín has done—even further back. The problem of Spanish regeneration is as old as that of Spanish decadence. The importance of the events of 1898 lies only in the fact that they made the question of Spanish national existence visible by placing it squarely in the center of public discussion. That the leaders of the young felt bound to each other by a consciousness of belonging to the same generation, or were tak-

228

en, at least, as representatives of a common intellectual generation—this was the effect of the acute crisis.

So passionate an individualist as Unamuno cannot be squeezed into the frame of a community. That Unamuno's intellectual endeavors have been focused throughout his lifetime on the problem of Spanish destiny connects him, to be sure, with the men of 1898. But his struggle for the solution shows him from the outset as a fighter who relies only on his own resources.

Unamuno took up the problem for the first time in a series of five essays which were published in 1895 in the journal *España moderna* under the title of "En torno al Casticismo." The excellent French translation which Marcel Bataillon brought out in 1923 was entitled *L'Essence de l'Espagne* and retained the words *casticismo* and *castizo* in the text. And rightly so; they are untranslatable, being themselves an expression of that "Spanish essence" which Unamuno's book is concerned to expound and explain. *Casticismo*, a noun derived from the adjective *castizo* (racially pure),[1] is originally a literary concept and denotes the ideal of a stylistically pure Castilian. But it is founded on the mode of feeling of an aristocratic ruling caste which, in the course of its battles against foreign races and mixed breeds, developed a pride in purity of blood and authentic descent. *Casticismo* denotes a concept of tradition in which the qualification of blood has been raised to the level of the intellect and extended even to the shaping of language. Unamuno's book investigates the essence of Spain's national tradition, but it reaches beyond that to the question: what is the stand a modern nation must take toward its tradition? Thus *En torno al Casticismo* presents a double aspect: it is an introduction to the nature of Spanishness—of which we know so little and which we all too frequently confuse with a false, operatic romanticism—and the discussion of a problem of national education that concerns all the European countries.

[1] *Castizo* comes from *casta* (breed, race), which in turn is derived from *castus* (chaste, pure).

Unamuno contends against the traditionalists for the sake of the "eternal tradition." He looks for it in the living present, not in the dead past; in the suprahistorical or rather, as he puts it in a felicitous coinage, in the intrahistorical (*intra-histórico*). True tradition is a formal spiritual energy that is realized differently in every historical age and that transcends all its specific historical manifestations. What Unamuno is attacking is Historicism, or, in his own more profoundly accurate expression, "Temporalism." And he has coined the pregnant, liberating, and restorative phrase: "Those who live in history render themselves deaf to silence" ["los que viven en la historia, se hacen sordos al silencio"].

The supratemporal, the intrahistorical is at the same time, however, the sphere of the supranational, the eternally human. Only what is human is eternally *castizo*. That is why Unamuno demands of Spain that it become cosmopolitan. It must either become integrated or die in its isolation. Protectionism in matters of the spirit leads to petrifaction and death. On the other hand, to become accessible to foreign influences means to fertilize one's own substance. Ethnic consciousness and cosmopolitan sentiment, regionalism and Europeanism are not contraries but two vital impulses of an energetic patriotism that mutually determine and reinforce one another. Every higher organism arises from a more powerful differentiation. Castile created the Spanish nation, but only by submitting the Castilian spirit to that of Spain as a whole. This process has not yet been concluded. Hispanicization is still not complete. But Unamuno interprets the regionalism and particularism of his age as signs of a deeper national unity to come.

The Unamuno of 1895 is a resolute supporter of *europeización*, which was very controversial at the time. It was opposed by Ganivet, who in his *Idearium español* (1896) raised the warning: *Noli foras ire; in interiore Hispaniae habitat veritas.* This maxim, which employs a famous phrase of St. Augustine's, comes close to describing Unamuno's own later position. In an essay published in 1906, "On Europeanization," Unamuno confesses that despite all his pilgrimages through the landscape of modern European culture he himself is neither a European nor a modern. The two things most valued by modern civilization, science and life, have become "antipathetic" to him. The true Europeanization of Spain can only consist in Spain's maintaining its essential nature within the European community. It ought not merely to receive but also to give. It must try to hispanicize Europe (*españolizar a Europa*).

SCIENCE AND TRUTH

IN a short story, *La locura del doctor Montarco* [*The Madness of Dr. Montarco*], Unamuno presented a stylized portrait of himself. The physician Dr. Montarco, an upright, plain-dealing bourgeois, clever and original in his judgments, loyal to his profession, well versed in his branch of science, has the crotchet of writing all sorts of stories and articles—fantastic, humorous, ironic—but never anything about medicine. Although his cures are generally acknowledged to be successful, his literary endeavors are considered an eccentricity. They alienate his patients, who fear that they have put themselves in the hands of a fool, and make him the scandal of the whole town. He ends up in the madhouse as a victim of the human folly that he had assailed with his pen.

Unamuno is a professor of classical philology, but he has never written a line on problems connected with this discipline. In his book on Don Quixote he calls scholarship "an ill-disguised form of mental laziness" and scholars "an insufferable form of humankind." When a French critic, Camille Pitolet, expressed reservations about this view and about Unamuno's interpretation of Cervantes, Unamuno justified himself in an essay "Sobre la erudición y la crítica" ["On Scholarship and Criticism"] (December 1905).

He tells us that he took his degree in philosophy and literature, and that he then applied for a chair at a university—at first in the subjects of psychology, logic, and ethics, then in metaphysics. Both applications were turned down "on account of the independence of my judgment, which even at that time constituted my intellectual gift." He then tried classical languages. Two attempts to obtain a professorship in Latin failed. Finally he got one in Greek. A well-known scholar urged him to devote himself henceforth entirely to the study of Greek. "But I, fully aware that professors of Greek were not what Spain wanted most, did not bother with his advice at all, and this has been a source of steadily-growing satisfaction to me." He knew enough Greek, Unamuno continues, to impart to his students as much knowledge of it as they required. Beyond that he felt no obligation to bury himself in specialized scholarly studies. His country required other things of him. Not for this had God granted him his talents.

But it was not only the duty not to abandon his post in the struggle of the intellectuals for Spanish regeneration (though to do so would, in his opinion, have been treason to the fatherland) that kept Professor Miguel de Unamuno from his scholarly pursuits. It was rather the much more deeply-rooted conviction of the worthlessness of pure knowledge insofar as it is directed toward matters of an empirical or ideal nature. When he vents his rage at science it is always in a tone of contempt. Certainly scholarship offers a spectacle in which the important and the trivial, the sublime and the ridiculous, are mingled as in all human affairs. But Unamuno sees only the trivial. In the natural sciences he sees only technical utility and mindless materialism; in the Humanities only philological pedantry (a reproach he levels above all at the Germans). The study of history is, for him, primarily idle curiosity, with which little people drown out the question of the destiny of the soul.

Neither history nor science nor reason can supply the truth that the soul needs. What is truth? Unamuno has taken up the question in one of his essays—his philosophy favors the essayistic method. In order to get at the problem, he begins with a critique of the theory of truth that he learned at the age of sixteen from the *Filosofía elemental* of Bishop Ceferino Gonzales of Cordoba ("one of the people who have written the most stupidities in Spain"). As a Thomist the Bishop distinguished between metaphysical truth (objective reality of things insofar as they correspond to ideas preexisting in the mind of the Creator); logical truth (*adaequatio intellectus et rei*); and moral truth (conformity between what is spoken and the inner judgment of the speaker). Such thinking is ontological and thus unacceptable to Unamuno. For him moral truth is primary, and logical truth proceeds from it. The opposite of moral truth is called falsehood, that of logical truth, error. And the lie is graver. Better an error in which one believes than a reality in which one does not believe. Not error but falsehood kills the soul. How does one find truth? By speaking it. But the eternal, objective truth? By speaking, in each and every case, whether it is appropriate or not, the inner, the subjective, the moral truth. The so-called external, objective truth is only the reward of inner veracity and sincerity. "For someone who could always be unconditionally truthful and sincere nature would have no secrets."

Truth, says Unamuno in conclusion, is that which one believes with one's whole heart and soul and in accordance with which one acts.

The theoretical basis of Unamuno's thought is, as we see, the popular pragmatism of the period just before 1914. But fortunately Unamuno also has other and better things to give us. He is the prophet of Quixotism and Aeternism.

Quixotism

The first part of *Don Quixote* appeared in 1605. In 1905 Spain commemorated with great ceremony the anniversary of her greatest imaginative creation. Unamuno's *Vida de Don Quijote y Sancho . . .* [*The Life of Don Quixote and Sancho according to Miguel de Cervantes Saavedra, explained and elucidated*] was published in the same year. In his preface to the second edition (January 1913) the author emphasizes that his work only coincided by sheer chance with the anniversary, and that it was not a commemorative volume. Indeed, historical recollection forms no part of its purpose. Unamuno acknowledges the merit—*pro forma*, at any rate, for at bottom he despises and mocks them—of the critics and scholars who have concerned themselves with questions of the significance of the work in its own time, its relation to its era, and what the author intended to express by it. He himself has a different aim. He severs the book from its time, from its author, and even from its country so as to contemplate it *sub specie aeternitatis. Don Quixote* is the Spanish Bible; as such it demands and supports a mystical reading.

Unamuno does not want to be a "Cervantist" but a "Quixotist." Characters in literature have their own existence independent of their creators. Perhaps Cervantes himself did not always understand his hero (and understood Sancho even less). They are not, after all, arbitrary inventions. He received them from the genius of his people. They extend beyond him. They solicit interpretation again and again. Unamuno revives the mediaeval method of figurative scriptural exegesis on a changed basis.

His *Life of Don Quixote* has a religious background. It is supposed to pave the way for a holy crusade to deliver the tomb of Don Quixote from its captivity at the hands of the bachelors of arts, priests, barbers, dukes, and canon lawyers who are familiar to us from Cervantes' novel. It proclaims the holy crusade for the folly of belief against reason.

Unamuno follows the order of Cervantes' narrative. He will dwell on some chapters at length; others, which do not suit his purpose, he will pass over in a sentence. He assumes the privilege of selection, and he does not interpret the meaning but constructs a new one. Unamuno rediscovers all his favorite ideas in the novel—because he inserted them beforehand.

Cervantes' profundity is a gay pensiveness, and his wisdom is the ripe fruit of a life rich in pain and travail, of a loving, smiling humor. Unamuno complains, to be sure, that the atmosphere of modern Spain is filled with an oppressive seriousness, and that no nation today is so incapable of understanding and feeling humor as the Spanish. But he himself has expelled the humor from Cervantes' novel down to the last trace. And how could it be otherwise? He wants to breathe none but tragic air. The anxious struggles of the mind, the painful and passionate torments of the soul—this is the mood that he depicts with magnificent one-sidedness and the only one whose validity he is prepared to acknowledge. But great humor—the humor of a Shakespeare, a Jean Paul, a Cervantes—is precisely the heavenly and serene release, born of tears and laughter, from all tensions and rigidities. For that reason Unamuno's book is a splendid violation of the authentic Don Quixote. This can and must be said without disregarding the loftiness and amplitude of spirit that Unamuno has breathed into his legend.

It is the legend of a saint, or rather, of a savior. It is the life "of Our Lord Don Quixote." The points of comparison that Unamuno finds between the life of Don Quixote and that of Ignatius of Loyola—both were crazy about novels of chivalry and tempted by lust for worldly fame; the same episodes occur in the lives of both: the vigil of arms (Ignatius in 1522 before the altar of the Virgin Mary at Monserrat; Quixote in the courtyard of the inn) and solitary penance (Ignatius in the cave of Manresa; Quixote in the Sierra Morena)—such formal analogies in their histories are intended to give the knight-errant a place by the side of the founder of the Jesuit order. But fundamentally Unamuno exalts his hero above all the saints and makes him into a bringer of salvation.

He bears all the traits of the redeemer, and his foolishness is of the same kind as the folly of the cross. When Don Quixote, shortly after setting out, meets a pair of vagabond sluts at an inn, whom he takes to be noble ladies, and when they nurse his wounds and offer him food, the episode is transfigured by Unamuno after the manner of the gospels. Unamuno explains Don Quixote's encounter with the merchants in the same light. The knight demands that they acknowledge the peerless beauty of Dulcinea, whom they have never seen. And what does that signify? The merchants see and know only the material realm of earthly goods. The knight extorts from them a confession of the spiritual realm of faith—and so redeems them against their will. Don Quixote delivers the galley slaves. Why? Because he leaves the privilege of judgment in the hands of God. Because the execution of an abstract, impersonal justice by men, who are only human themselves, offends our sensibilities and because we feel the hangman's profession to be ignoble. Cervantes does not mention these reasons? That is because he relates only the external incidents. But the prophet of Donquixotism shows us their theological meaning.

Don Quixote's madness is truer and more pious than the sober understanding that has its feet on the ground of reality. Don Quixote is thrashed. But he declares the people thrashing him to be phantoms. His hagiographer elucidates: we should not let ourselves be vexed by what befalls us in this world of appearances. True faith is to hope in the essential and hold fast by it.

Well-aimed blows light upon the realistic and utilitarian standpoint of the modern world. There is Don Quixote's well-known adventure with the windmills. Sancho tries to hold him back. But Don Quixote was right! Today's windmills are locomotives, dynamos, turbines, machine guns, and all the other "giants" of technology. Only fear, a Sancho-fear, forces us to our knees before them. Only this fear makes us worshippers of steam and electricity. Don Quixote, however, sought salvation within himself and dared to attack the windmills.

Chivalry versus the arrogance of science! Don Quixote and Sancho find themselves alone in a wood at night. A dreadful noise is heard. In the morning it turns out that the source of the spectral sound was a fulling-mill. Sancho scoffs. But his master replies significantly: "Am I as a knight perhaps obliged to recognize and distinguish sounds, and to know which ones come from a fulling-mill and which do not?" No, such knowledge does not appertain to heroism. Provided that the knight shall listen to his heart and distinguish *its* sounds.

All the teachable subjects do not add one iota to the amount of good in the world. This is the quixotic lesson that Unamuno would like to preach to all Sancho Panzas even today. Today *Sanchopanzismo* is called positivism, naturalism, empiricism, and imagines that it can ridicule quixotic idealism.

Criticism of contemporary Spain is frequently interwoven in Unamuno's interpretation. Don Quixote's descent into the cave of Montesinos becomes, for the exegete, a symbol of his own immersion in the tradition of his people. And just as the knight-errant, with strokes of his sword, had to free the entrance to the cave from underbrush, out of which the startled ravens and crows flew up, so the interpreter of the national psyche must first clear away the debris and drive out the "traditionalists" who block the entrance to tradition and have never descended into its depths. "The tradition they invoke is not the true tradition: they call themselves the spokesmen of the people, but there is no truth to their claim."

Master Pedro's puppet theater is transformed, in Unamuno's reflections, into the Spanish parliament. Instead of the "Freeing of Melisandra" the play being performed is the regeneration of Spain, and the puppets move as Master Pedro pulls the wires. But unfortunately there is no knight-errant who will cut down those puppets, as Don Quixote cut down Master Pedro's, and smash the entire booth to bits.

Thus topical and polemical aspects are curiously interspersed among the religious, eternal ones. Nevertheless, the latter predominate. Don Quixote's desire for fame is the urge to become immortal. "Not to die! That is the basic root of quixotic folly. Anxiousness for life, for life eternal, is what has given you immortal life, my lord Don Quixote; the dream of your life was, and is, the dream of not dying."

From the literary point of view Unamuno's commentary cannot be considered entirely successful. He adopts too much and too little freedom toward his subject. Too little: for his adherence to the sequence of the chapters in the novel gives the work a jolting rhythm, like driving in a car over a ploughed field. An artistically wiser solution would have been to paraphrase Cervantes' book loosely and arrange it according to its inner logic, as dictated by the spirit of the interpreter. To forgo this solution probably meant a deliberate sacrifice on Unamuno's part for the purpose of making his commentary easier to use. The form he chose has the advantage, which the great majority of readers will undoubtedly appreciate, that for every chapter of Cervantes' narrative Unamuno's exegesis may be swiftly and effortlessly found. And the aim of the book—to lead the Spanish people more deeply into its greatest literary creation—justifies this form.

That this fidelity to the surface often conceals an all the more arbitrary wrenching of the sense should by now be clear. No one will dispute Unamuno's right to such a shift of perspective. There is a pleasure, albeit one not always free from contradictions, and a rare kind of intellectual stimulation, in viewing a great work of art through the eyes of an original and eccentric observer. But at the same time the illusory nature of Unamuno's enterprise cannot be ignored. What is it based on? We are supposed to let ourselves be persuaded into accepting a work of artistic imagination as a message of salvation. We are asked to exchange the realm of aesthetic freedom for the bondage of ideological dogmatism. Certainly, works of literature born of religious belief and conducive to it do exist. But to make a Bible of Cervantes' great novel is the way of error. Cervantes was a pious Catholic, and his hero dies as a Catholic Christian. Unamuno offends against this simple truth when he converts the questing and errant knight himself into a savior. The human wealth of the book is diminished by such a violent misconstruction. Like all very great works of literature, Cervantes' work contains an abundance of reference and a depth of meaning that may be pointed out by gentle hands but never squeezed into the Procrustes bed of a subjective conception. These reservations must be expressed. But having expressed them we are free to enjoy the moral energy, the prophetic pathos, the many ingenious significances with which Unamuno has imbued the figure of Don Quixote from the deep impulses of his own heart.

The Tragic Sense of Life

Unamuno's chief philosophical work is the book about the tragic sense of life.[2] To be sure, the book is philosophical only in the broadest sense of the term. Philosophy for Unamuno is not conceptual knowledge but the development of a personal outlook on the world that in turn derives from the sense of life and determines it. Life and reason are antitheses to him. Everything vital is irrational, everything rational, anti-vital. This antinomy forms the basis of the "tragic" sense of life. Pragmatism, which in its American home was a life-affirming meliorism or optimism, is transformed by the Spaniard into "tragicism."

Because of this pragmatic starting-point all higher and more refined operations of the mind are of course interrupted and diverted. The object of thought should not be the world of ideas but man, the "man of flesh and bone," the concrete individual. Not man as idea and ideal, not man as defined by Humanism, whatever its norms, but one's fellow-man in his reality, his contingency, his greatness and his misery. One perceives a relationship between this approach and the naturalism of Spanish art. It is Hominism, if this word may be allowed, not Humanism.[3] Unamuno reduces all search for knowledge to the vital situation in which man finds himself. He sees his existence threatened by transience, by want, by fate. He wishes to preserve it, wishes, in the words of Spinoza, *suum esse conservare*. The deepest instinct of human nature is to conserve its being and eternize it. Its deepest longing is the hunger for immortality, for the personal survival of the soul. Unamuno assents to Catholicism insofar as it is an institution that preserves and perpetuates the belief in immortality. Its rigid dogma enfolds this original "vital" urge like a protective sheath. But at the same time dogma means,

[2] *Del Sentimiento trágico de la Vida* (1st ed., Madrid, Renacimiento, 1913).

[3] In order to avoid the word Humanism, Unamuno occasionally borrows from the Portuguese the vocable *hombridad* (*Contra esto y aquello*, 1912, p. 81).

of course, an attempt at a rationalization which, as it does not satisfy the demands of rational thought after all, ends in compromises. Belief in immortality cannot justify itself to reason. Reason leads perforce to skepticism. Its incontrovertible motto in Unamuno's opinion is: the individual consciousness is extinguished at death. The vital consequence of this rationalism would be—as Kierkegaard also saw—suicide. What is left? The tragic conflict must be acknowledged and affirmed. Then from the abyss of despair a new certainty will arise, a certainty capable of sustaining our lives, our action, and our thinking. Whoever has endured this distress of soul, this dialectic of consciousness, will embrace his fellow-man with compassionate love. This pitying love will then radiate to everything that lives, and then to everything that exists. It will embrace the entire universe. And because love always personalizes its object, it will comprehend the cosmos as a consciousness, as a person. To the soul purified by pain the suffering world reveals itself as the suffering god. The soul commiserates with him and loves him, its feelings stirred by his love and his pity. God is "the personalization of the All, the eternal, infinite consciousness of the world; a consciousness in the grip of matter and struggling to free itself from matter." "We personalize the All in order to save ourselves from nothingness, and the only true mystery is the mystery of pain."

Unamuno's theological speculation loses itself in the antinomies incident to all forms of the idealism of consciousness. God to him is the sum total of all individual consciousnesses, yet separate from them as a personal consciousness. The individual soul is an idea of the divine mind, but this mind only realizes itself in and through the soul. God creates us and we create Him. To believe in God means to want God. But *is* this God? Does this eternal person that makes us eternal have a being apart from our desire? "Here lies something insoluble, and it is better that it should be so." In the last analysis the tragic sense of life in man does indeed constitute for Unamuno the sole foundation of God's reality. The fact is that idealism can never break through the confines of the immanence of consciousness. Only revelation can do that. And at this point Unamuno's religious speculation fails.

At this point, too, its contrast with Christianity is quite consistently revealed. Unamuno adopts from Christianity only the idea of the suffering God. But he gives a gnostic twist to the Christian idea of suffering by seeing the ground of suffering in the attachment to matter. Thus he arrives at the conclusion that it is man who must redeem God. Man should elevate everything that exists to the plane of consciousness in order that the word may be "resurrected." All of Christian dogma is twisted in this fashion, nor is the procedure less arbitrary here than in the exegesis of Don Quixote. Unamuno cannot submit to the Christian idea of God, but on the other hand he does not want to renounce Spain's popular Catholic piety. He claims Catholicism and even Dante for his tragicism. And so his religious philosophy as a whole leaves an impression of a vacillating, unreal, contrived, and extremely subjective system, incapable of generating any really persuasive power or flame of love.

Nevertheless it does contain, as I believe, a valuable, restorative, and deeply true element. I should like to call it Aeternism. Tragicism, the idealism of consciousness, misologism, and the gnostic idea of God's self-redemption in man—these are lines of thought, some more ancient than others, that can scarcely be expected to achieve any practical results in the struggle between Christianity and eternal paganism that marks world history. They are the residue of a faith that has been dissolved into pseudophilosophical reflection. But the genuine, strong, and irresistible impulse of Unamuno's religiosity is the craving for immortality. That in an age as subject to "temporalism" as our own this eternal need of the soul should again find expression—this we owe to Unamuno. Many of us are likely to be put off. But many others, so I believe, will feel a kind of inner relief at the knowledge that finally in our enlightened, skeptical, overrefined Europe, a voice can once more be heard that is not ashamed of being mocked by common sense and the cautious fuss of school philosophy. To speak of death and eternity is not considered proper in the intellectual world of Europe. But isn't this repression partly responsible for many of the afflictions we suffer from? Unamuno's belief in immortality is, to be sure, a far cry from that of a Goethe, with its transfiguring wisdom; of a Jean Paul, with its rapturous enthusiasm; of a Novalis, with its mystical fervor. Furthermore, Unamuno rejects the Christian doctrine of the *visio beatifica* in the next world because, in his opinion, it would permit the consciousness of self to be absorbed in God. Such an admission, needless to say, discloses an aspect of his belief in immortality that, from the standpoint of the mystical consciousness, is imperfect, immature, and all too human. The man whose religious psychology Unamuno expounds does not wish to renounce any part of his ego. His hunger for immortality is essentially nothing but the instinct of self-preservation. He does not want to die. He does not know that dying is the gateway to regeneration. It is indicative that Unamuno finds something tragic and "destructive" in sexual love because it means a surrender of self, hence a kind of dying. This singularism, which recoils anxiously from any relaxation or penetration of the ego and which identifies soul with selfhood, can of course never attain to those realities of the religious experience which are mentioned in the confessions of all the mystics. For that reason, something infelicitous, tormented, and disharmonious clings to this singularism even when Unamuno raises it to the mataphysical sphere. And here perhaps lies one of the roots of the "tragic" sense of life. The pious man whose refuge is God, be he Brahman, Sufi, or Christian, knows nothing of tragicism. And the Buddhist monk, when asked about the nature of Nirvana, replied: "Bliss unspeakable."[4] The chorus of all mystical souls bears joyful witness to the bliss of union with God. But they all went the way of renunciation and abnegation of self. They did not want to preserve the self but to lose it. But with Unamuno God ac-

[4] Rudolf Otto, *Das Heilige* [*The Idea of the Holy*].

tually only appears at the point where the person who hungers for being requires a guarantor of eternity so as not to despair.

The I and the Thou

Unamuno is not one of those writers who simply state their case because their minds are on the case and on nothing else. With Unamuno reflection upon his own ego and upon the resonance of his words constantly obtrudes itself. The relation between the I and the Thou does not run smoothly. The integration of the personality into the work as a whole does not proceed by a natural rhythm but by continual conflicts. Something violent, excessive, harshly eruptive, irritable, dissonant in the method of communication keeps calling attention to itself. The social function of the personality is charged with a high degree of tension. This is the root of the many essays in dialogue form. "I don't agree with that!" one such dialogue begins. "And why should I or anyone else be interested in whether you agree with what I have just said or not? Would you be so kind as to tell me that? Are you not aware of the enormous presumption and the no less immense vacuity of every negative utterance? If you have an idea of your own to oppose to my presentation, please do so; and insofar as you do it with wit, charm, acuteness, novelty, or power of suggestion, we shall all applaud, and I myself shall be the first; but. . . ." We see that it is not easy for the opponent. If he expresses a dissenting opinion without fulfilling all the conditions enumerated, he incurs the author's displeasure.

Ideological objections Unamuno rejects in any case: "Ideas are contemptible to me; I only value men." This playing-off of "man" against the "idea"—one of Unamuno's favorite themes—is typical of his Hominism. It permits him a freedom of movement, which he exploits in every direction, to satisfy, consciously or unconsciously, his powerful egotism. One might suppose that to tell people one doesn't give a rap for their ideas would be to disparage them. But Unamuno retorts that all that matters to him is emotional agitation, passion, ve-

hemence, pride, turmoil. For this is what is genuinely human.
And in this fashion, naturally, he secures for himself the right
to fling the lava of his temperament at the reader. He dismisses the reproach that he always speaks about himself. That
is what we should all do! We should turn our inner side out
and overwhelm our fellow man with it. All restraint is harmful. People are crustaceans. Everyone lives in his shell, in his
solitude. The writer should smash the carapace of his fellow
men, should incite them, wake them up. "The first requirement for writing effectively is: to have no respect for the reader, for he doesn't deserve any." Why not? Because, Unamuno
replies, I do not write for readers but for men, and if the man
in you who reads these lines isn't interested in them, then I
don't care a hang for all your righteousness. Unamuno
doesn't mince his words. Clumsy fools, nitwits, cowards, yap-
ping dogs . . . he is fond of throwing such epithets around. He
complacently confirms that he is repugnant to most of his
readers ("A mis lectores" in *Soliloquios y Conversaciones*).
So long as they read him! He despises the crowd. He flees
from it, praises solitude, and prizes holy silence. But then
why talk and write so much? Unamuno concedes the justice
of this remonstrance, but he is not embarrassed for an answer. In this respect his dialectic is highly revealing.

Couldn't one have both at once: to be alone and to stir the
crowd with one's words at the same time? "There are times
when I have wished—and may God punish me for it—to become suddenly deaf and blind and at the same to be endowed
with a voice as commanding as thunder which would drown
out the cries of the most unruly crowds, and to speak,
to speak, and to speak, calmly and firmly, word after word, in
imperious tones; and my phrases should descend, while
amidst the shrieks of the people holy silence would envelop
and protect me."

Alone and in public, simultaneously! And Unamuno compares himself to a dancer in the marketplace. I danced, he
tells us, but to a music that no one heard. People began to
laugh, they called me mad or extravagant, pronounced me

vain, reviled and stoned me. And in the end they went away. But a few, who took pleasure in my leaps, stayed. And today I dance before large multitudes. People applaud, clapping their hands in time to my dancing. And they imagine that I dance to their clapping. And they do not know that I do not even hear their applause. "And that is the advantage of dancing alone."

And yet another confession. Once more Unamuno has spoken and reaped applause. Doubts assail him. Is it possible that he has become an actor? Has even the sincerity on which he so often prided himself turned into a subject of rhetoric? "Would it not be better for me to go home and compose myself, to be silent and wait? But is that feasible? Tomorrow, shall I be able to resist? Is it not perhaps cowardly to desert? . . . Is the voice that calls to me: be silent, actor! the voice of an angel of God or that of a devil and tempter? O my God, Thou knowest that to Thee I sacrifice the praise as I do the blame!"

Unamuno is a confessor who is sometimes unable to rid himself of the notion that he is a rhetor, a dancer, or a mime. He would like to retire into the desert—"not for forty days but for forty months and even longer"—yet for what purpose? To forge a huge club, temper it in fire, stud it with nails, try it on the granite of the wilderness . . . and then smite the human crustaceans with it.

In *Don Quixote* the priest and the barber personify the opposition of the Philistine. Unamuno confides to us that he considers most of his readers as belonging to this race. "They will say—it seems as if I can hear them already—that I do nothing but hunt after ingenious paradoxes in order to acquire a reputation for originality, but I say to them: if they do not see and feel all the passion and mental fervor and profound restlessness and fiery longing that I have put into this commentary on the Life of My Lord Don Quixote and his Squire Sancho, if, I say, they do not see and feel this, than I pity them with all the strength in my heart and hold them to be the miserable slaves of common sense. . . ."

Such waverings, disparities, and excesses recur again and again in Unamuno's writing. Nor can these traits be ignored if one wishes to characterize his literary personality. He gives his fellow-men some hearty whacks and then draws them again to his bosom. He drives them off, stages a flight to Patmos in the presence of his audience, stresses what separates him from the rest of us, and then returns to vindicate his eccentricities, which he denies them to be—all of which would be unnecessary if he really did despise us. He forestalls criticism that he may invalidate it himself. He rears up imperiously, and then humbles himself again. And then he reflects once more on the arrogance implied in such voluntary self-abasement. In that case, he decides, it is still more honest to profess one's own nature, and true humility consists in not being humble. It is a *circulus vitiosus* of self-appraisal from which Unamuno never seems to escape. He makes it easy for his detractors to use this egocentricity as a weapon against him.

We have examined the reverse side of Unamuno's Hominism. But one would have to be emotionally callous not to see in these scruples, weaknesses, uncertainties, and frailties the pathos inherent in the drama of our humanity.

Excitator Hispaniae

In the character and effect of Unamuno there is something discordant. It is reflected, too, in the critical evaluation of his work in Spain. He has been frequently attacked and rejected. But then, he has been a fighter all his life. His way through the Spanish world of the last generation has been, like Don Quixote's, full of adventures, of challenges, and of defeats. That is part of the nature and honor of Quixotism. And it is this Quixotism alone that can afford the perspective from which Unamuno is to be truly appreciated. One can never do justice to Unamuno by measuring him against the norm of an artistic, rational, or human perfection. Spain has thinkers of finer-spun thoughts, poets of sweeter songs, creators richer in powerful images, and artists with a purer sense

of form—and yet Unamuno is unique by virtue of the
dynamism of his personality. He is an instigator of his nation.
He is an *excitator Hispaniae*, prodding and provoking, challenging and animating. Spain has him to thank, before many
others, for her awakening from her apathy, from that
"aboulia" of Ganivet's diagnosis. Without the blows of Unamuno's hammer and the strokes of his sword the Spanish
mind would not be today what it is and means for Europe.
The tribute of the great poet Antonio Machado remains valid:

> . . . el alma desalmada de su raza,
> que bajo el golpe de su férrea maza
> aun duerme, puede ser que despierte un día.
>
> .   .   .   .
>
> Tiene el aliento de una estirpe fuerte
> que soñó más allá de sus hogares,
> y que el oro buscó tras de los mares.
> El señala la gloria tras la muerte.[5]

["The unsouled soul of his race, which beneath the
blow of his iron club still sleeps, may perhaps
awaken some day. . . . He has the breath of a powerful breed, that dreamed beyond its homes and
sought the gold across the seas. He proclaims the
glory beyond death."]

1926

[5] From the poem: "A Don Miguel de Unamuno por su libro **Vida
de Don Quijote y Sancho**."

Charles Du Bos

++

IN THE "alten Westen" section of Berlin fifty years ago there was a boardinghouse, the Pension B. The refined solidity of the Hanseatic manner of life provided a frame of comfort. In the Munich office of the prematurely deceased Herr B. Thomas Mann had composed his first verses. The enchanting daughters of the house brought with them an air of the Atelier, the Secession, the Reinhardt stage. The atmosphere was international. In 1904 you could meet a young Frenchman there. He had something of a prince of the Arabian Nights about him. He was surrounded by an aura of luxury of which he seemed to be unaware. His name was Charles Du Bos. He must have had very good references, for he moved as freely in the financial aristocracy of the Mendelssohns as in the intellectual salons of Westend, which were no less exclusive. Only powerful magic gained admittance to the afternoon teas at Georg and Gertrud Simmel's and to the house of Reinhold and Sabine Lepsius. Simmel's philosophy was the last word in intellectual subtlety. It was considered "corrosive," but its seductiveness was all the stronger as it dealt with matters that had not come up in philosophy till then: the financial system or Chinese art. Georg Simmel collected lace because it represented "the highest spiritualization of material." His philosophy of history bore a dedication to Stefan George. Gertrud Kantorowicz, whose life was to end in the concentration camp at Theresienstadt,[1] and Margarete Susman (whose biography of Simmel unfortunately remained an unfulfilled wish) enlivened the salon with wit and charm. It was that fleeting moment when Simmel's analysis and the new

[1] Concerning her, see Ludwig Curtius, *Merkur*, II (1948), 474.

manner of George seemed to inhabit the same climate of the soul. Besides Simmel, the only man who counted intellectually was the young Bernard Groethuysen. He was equally close to Dilthey and to Simmel. The philosophical aphorisms that filled his conversation seemed to presage a work conceived in an entirely new mode of thought. They must have held the strongest fascination for Du Bos, for on the evening in November 1904 when he met Groethuysen, he accompanied him back to Berlin from Westend on foot, a walk of considerable distance. Groethuysen, who had removed to Paris before 1914 and lived through the war as an internee (Bergson's intervention ensured him a very mild surveillance), remained for decades a close friend to Du Bos. From the Simmels' it was only a few steps to the house of the Lepsiuses. Here painting and music predominated. Bach and Chopin resounded. Those who belonged to the innermost circle of the elect could meet Stefan George there. I have told about it elsewhere.

Charles Du Bos was twenty-two years old when he became acquainted with these precincts of cultured intelligence in Berlin W. and Westend: circles which were unnoticed by the public at large and were, in turn, at pains to stay aloof from Wilhelminian Germany. What did he have to offer? He used to say of himself that he was born at seventeen, meaning that he had awakened to the life of the mind at that age. That was in 1899. He was no precocious juvenile intellectual. He came to Oxford at eighteen and spent a year at Balliol.[2] There he discovered English poetry; then, in Florence, Botticelli and D'Annunzio. Around 1900 the link between Oxford and Florence was still Pre-Raphaelitism, that complex and aromatic world of beauty that embraced Rossetti and Ruskin as well as William Morris and Walter Pater. Its essence was presented by Rudolf Kassner in his first work, *Die Mystik, die Künstler und das Leben*, with the subtitle *Über englische Dichter und Maler im neunzehnten Jahrhundert. Accorde*

[2] Du Bos's mother was English, the daughter of an American woman. His paternal grandmother was Polish (née de Laska).

[*Mysticism, Artists, and Life; On English Poetry and Painters of the Nineteenth Century. Chords*] (Leipzig, Eugen Diederichs, 1900). It had an intoxicating effect on some young people in Germany at that time. "Germany is thought of as the land of dreamers," you could read there. "But when an English artist paints a dream, it is as if there were no other life." These dreams from the banks of the Thames, which could be relived in the Viennese writer's book, harbored worlds of mystery and joy. An exalting and transfiguring power emanated from them. To young people on the threshold of their twentieth year such images could become crystallizations of a high yearning. Youth that grows up without transforming images to guide it loses something that cannot be recovered. Of course it was the end of an era; but before the last tones faded, motifs and chords rose once more to a final intensity. All these things were alive in Du Bos. In Florence, Berenson had initiated him into the study of art history. He was planning to take a doctoral degree in Paris with a dissertation on Botticelli. But the professor at the University to whom he presented his plan turned him away on the ground that he had just assigned the topic only an hour before. Du Bos never had more than slight contacts with the academic world. The specialist seemed to him a comic figure on the world stage, especially when he had to deal with things of the mind in a professional capacity. He thought it a splendid inspiration that Ibsen should have made Hedda Gabler's petit bourgeois husband an assistant professor of the history of civilization.

Du Bos's financial situation seemed to relieve him from the worry of choosing a profession. He came from the highest social class where both wealth and connections were inherited. His father was a friend of the Prince of Wales and president of the *Union*, one of the two most exclusive clubs in Paris. Charlie—as his friends called him—was naturally also voted in. What Proust would have given for such a distinction—which he could never attain. He "didn't belong." Charlie belonged, but it meant nothing to him. He was a disappointment. Only after a great deal of persuasion would he condescend to show up at least for the ballotting. After a few years not even then. He enjoyed his freedom from the cares of having to make a living, but he only used it to pursue his inclinations toward art, poetry, and the world of ideas. Baudelaire's remark, "J'ai grandi par le loisir" ["I have grown through leisure"] he applied in retrospect to himself. In a late entry in his Diary he happens to mention once the social type of the young man of the world who freely chooses to give up his position in society in order that he may devote his life entirely to personal culture. This *mondain défroqué* is indebted to the sphere in which he grew up for one thing at any rate: from his twenty-fifth year he is definitely and radically immune to any kind of snobbishness. It is true that the specious values of "society" have probably long inhibited the development of the personality (that was how Du Bos explained his late awakening to himself). But once he has broken through to the true values, a reversal so complete takes place in him that he seizes upon truth with an earnestness unknown perhaps, in the same degree, to others. These reflections bear an unmistakably personal stamp. For it was precisely the imperturbable seriousness with which he treated the greatest as well as the most negligible intellectual matters that often provoked the laughter of his friends. Even I was somewhat taken aback when, after the first greeting in Pontigny, he asked whether I had recently been studying Plotinus ("Avez-vous récemment pratiqué Plotin?"). I had never done so. But the conviction that all the better people reach for the *Enneads* on occasion, as one now and again takes up *Hamlet* or *Faust*, was a touching and ingratiating feature of that earnestness about intellectual tradition that has become rare in our day.

From Proust's world, which touches that of Du Bos at so many points, we are acquainted with the "clubman" as a turn of the century Parisian type. At the time of his conversion to literature, Du Bos was a failed clubman. Later on he never got further than membership of the Pen Club, in which capacity he spoke in London in 1923. The famous critic Sir Edmund Gosse, who was then seventy-four years old, invited him to the Marlborough and made clear to him that the Pen Club was meaningless. The Marlborough Club was something else again: the only club in London which required the king's approval for a change in the rules. In the smoking-room Charlie was presented to an old gentleman who could remember seeing his father in the salon of the Princesse de Sagan, the very one who is mentioned in Proust's novel. Gosse was highly content (Du Bos less so), and now they could turn once more to literature, and in particular to Walter Pater, whom Sir Edmund had entertained thirty years earlier in those same rooms.

The First World War had thrown Du Bos's existence off its course. Financial catastrophes plunged him into poverty and debt. He was forced to coin the exquisite treasures of his spirit into a living. That was especially hard for him as he did not have an official stamp. A professorship was out of the question; he had not taken any examinations, hence did not belong to the ranks of the university. But he didn't belong to those of literature either. He fitted no category—he was *inclassable*. Besides, he was completely unknown. And, in addition, of a touching ineptitude. This began with a lack of manual dexterity, but it also made itself disastrously felt in his relations with publishers, journals, and the well-regulated game of the Paris *vie littéraire*, with its tacitly assumed compromises and conventions. Not only had Charlie never learned how to shave himself; he did not even know how to fill his fountain pen. So he had to carry an entire battery of pens with him and take them once a week to a stationery store for refilling. One was amazed that he could actually fill his beloved pipe by himself, but "he seemed even to smoke it with a slight affectation of realism," as M. Saint-Clair has so charmingly put it.[3]

[3] In her *Galérie privée* (Gallimard, 1947) there is a masterly portrait of Du Bos, but equally good ones of Groethuysen, Michaux, Malraux, Camus, *et al.*

Not only was he incapable of satisfying the most modest demands of the technical world, he was also unable to adjust himself to social and economic techniques. Once we boarded an overcrowded express and could only find seats in a first-class compartment (in which, by the way, was sitting an old friend of Charlie's, Edith Wharton, who, at once mundane and modern, wrote for the public orphaned by the death of Henry James). In an access of quite unfounded embarrassment Charlie explained to me that formerly he had, of course, used only the first class, but now. . . . Then, when we got out at the Gare d'Orléans, Charlie, not without a touch of ostentation, obeyed a prompting of his moral scrupulosity. He managed to create a traffic jam at the gate of the track by insisting on paying the surcharge for crossing over to first class, to the great annoyance of the functionary on duty as well as of the stream of people at our heels. However, on a trip from Pontigny to Avalon, while searching for a better hotel (the room that had been reserved for him in the *Chapeau Rouge* faced the kitchen), he could also succumb to the dangerous allures of the Post Hotel, because the rooms on the first floor gave off an inner courtyard ("une sorte de modeste patio") that was overlooked by an open gallery, "où avec mes incurables et nostalgiques visées claustrales, je vis un promenoir méditatif tout désigné" ["where, with my incurable and nostalgic monastic aims, I saw a covered walk just right for meditation"]. So Charlie rents this secular monastic cell and finds out too late that it has no electric light, that in order to breathe it is necessary to leave the window open and thus to be constantly disturbed by the coming and going of the guests, and on top of that to sustain "a well-trained assault of fleas."

After our early meeting in Berlin I had lost sight of him completely. When I saw him again at Pontigny in 1922 and 1924 we discovered so many admirations in common (the coordinates were set by Giorgione and Walter Pater) that we soon became best friends. At that time I was still in quest of a France founded upon the assumptions of a general European mind. For that reason it made me happy to know that Gide could not live without Goethe, Shakespeare, Dostoevski; that he loved Browning; that Larbaud was "naturalizing" Whitman and Joyce in France. But neither Gide nor Maurois nor Martin Du Gard nor Jacques Rivière (the prominent men at those "Décades") had any affinity with that which, for short, I will call "metaphysics," and which constitutes an essential element in German life. Du Bos possessed it. To his mind Novalis was more exciting than Laclos, Meister Eckhart more challenging than Stendhal. To be able to make this discovery at the time was overwhelming. But I soon noticed that no one at Pontigny saw Du Bos as I did. People did not seem to know what they had in him. And yet it was a very carefully sifted, very advanced French public that Paul Desjardins (1859-1940) summoned to Pontigny. In the struggles between church and state during the Third Republic Desjardins had attracted attention as the advocate of an unecclesiastical idealism, first by his book *Le devoir présent*[4] (1892), then by founding the *Union pour la Vérité*. "Perhaps you have never read Paul Desjardins," says a character in Proust.[5] "He is now transformed, as I hear, into a kind of preacher monk, but in the old days. . . ." During a long life Desjardins had been able to make many valuable contacts and collect valuable memories: as a boy he had carried Corot's paintbox; in 1886 he had attended the cinquecentennial celebration of Heidelberg University and sent witty dispatches about it to the Paris newspapers in the late style of Renan; he had offered Tolstoy the same armchair that the visitor to his studio occupied; Proust had been his pupil, Bergson his fellow-student; he was a friend of Marshal Lyautey. All these experiences, in one way or another, stood the

[4] It figures in the shipboard library of Gide's *Voyage d'Urien* (1893).

[5] *Du côté de chez Swann* I, 113. *Swann's Way* (New York, Random House, 1934) I, 92.

Décades at Pontigny in good stead. The intellectual elite that foregathered in the renovated Cistercian abbey under the motto of Saint Bernard (as a lay spiritualist Desjardins had had *pristina nec periit pietas* chiseled into the wall of the entrance hall), though receptive to the elegance with which Du Bos conducted the Décade on poetry and mysticism (as André Gide's Journal for 3 September 1922 attests), was nevertheless not prepared to admire him as I did at the time —and stated in a German periodical (*Die Literatur*, October 1925). The relations between Du Bos, who in conversation liked to call himself "France's last individualist," and Desjardins, who thought of the individual as "a legal fiction of the modern western world" (whose "dissolution" he believed he could detect in Proust), were strained, and this strain, though unavowed, has left traces in Du Bos's "Diaries."

Was it André Gide who brought Du Bos to Pontigny? The two had met in March 1911, at the home of Jacques-Émile Blanche (1861–1942),[6] which served as a residence for artists. With its garden that resembled a park and its spacious ease it reminded the visitor of one of those English country houses from which many of Blanche's models came. A connection was soon established. Their correspondence begins in May 1911. In October 1914, the friends found the relief organization *Le Foyer Franco-Belge*. This collaboration can seem surprising, however much it may do both of them credit. Neither the immoralist who had just charmed and outraged the public with his *Caves du Vatican*, nor the spiritual aesthete who entered rare moments in his unpublished journal as a composer notes down new combinations of sound, seemed to possess the qualifications for handling the administrative details of a social relief organization. Du Bos, to be sure,

---

[6] Cf. *Lettres de Charles Du Bos et Réponses de André Gide* (1950), p. 9. Gide's *Journal* for 27 March 1911 mentions only that Barrès was among the guests. From J.-E. Blanche's posthumous papers fascinating memoirs have been published (*La pêche au souvenirs*, 1949), but they only go up to 1914.

brought to the task a lifelong need to pry into other people's souls. To practice moral casuistry upon the living person, to bend confidentially over mental anguish, to receive confidences and confessions—that had always attracted him. Although not founded for this purpose, the *Foyer Franco-Belge* offered opportunities for such exchanges. Du Bos's friends have preserved a remark he is supposed to have made to a refugee from Belgium: "Madame, la complexité de votre cas me plonge dans la consternation."[7] This sentence, which one recalled with a mixture of tenderness, irony, and humor, contains many of Charlie's peculiarities: a certain solemnity, a certain ceremonious politeness, much stylistic gravity, and a great deal of unworldliness.

To the relief organization Du Bos devoted all his time and all his strength. He was ailing, he was weary, but he reveled in moral idealism. "Sous prétexte de perfection, il poussait toute chose à l'absurde: il avait aboli la notion du temps fort coûteusement pour lui et pour ceux qu'il secourait. Prenant sur son sommeil, il inventait de secrètes séances de nuit. . . . Par excès de zèle et absence de sens commun, il mettait le désordre dans tout ce qu'il touchait, compromettant ainsi l'existence de l'oeuvre" ["Under the pretext of perfection, he pushed everything to absurdity; he had abolished the idea of time at great cost to himself and to those whom he was helping. Cutting into his sleep, he invented secret sessions at night. . . . Through excessive zeal and lack of common sense he threw everything he touched into disorder, thus compromising the existence of the project"]. The restless Gide was already uncomfortable in the relief organization after a few weeks, as one can observe in his *Journal*: "Au Foyer Franco-Belge, pas un instant de solitude où reprendre sa forme personnelle et se détendre. Je me sentais bu par autrui (10 Nov. 1914). . . . Je suis distrait du Foyer; n'y retourne qu'après-midi et pour n'y trouver qu'une occupation insuffisante. Je suis las et m'échappe sans cesse. Je n'en puis plus (28 Sept.

---

[7] Saint-Clair. The following citation also from there.

1915). . . . Une lettre de Madame Théo me donne des nouvelles de Charlie Du Bos, à qui, finalement, l'on a enlevé la disposition des subventions. Il y avait longtemps qu'on aurait dû le faire (24 Oct. 1916)" ["At the Foyer Franco-Belge (Franco-Belgian Center), not a moment in which to assume one's own personality and relax. I felt myself *absorbed* by others. . . . I am diverted from the Foyer and now go there only in the afternoon to find little to do. I am tired of it and constantly break away. I can't stick it. . . . A letter from Mme Théo gives me news of Charlie Du Bos, from whom the attribution of the financial grants has finally been taken away. This should have been done long ago"].[8] By that time Gide had long since retired.

Social idealism had been a component of the intellectual situation of 1900. In England the University Settlements sprang up, in France the shortlived popular colleges in which Romain Rolland and even Jean Schlumberger took an active part. Du Bos himself had once interpreted . . . Emerson there. His loyalty to Ruskin must have had something to do with it. Social idealism was to lead Gide to Moscow, from which he retired as rapidly as he had from the *Foyer Franco-Belge*, only to declare at the end of his life: "le monde sera sauvé par quelques-uns." The elegant solution of an individualistic collectivism, which Gide for a time had recommended, had been "wishful thinking."

But for Du Bos, too, social idealism, like aesthetic spiritualism, could only be a transitional stage. When he came to Pontigny for the first time in 1922, the impression made on him by the abbey church was the strongest he had received since his youth in Florence: "l'église de Pontigny a réveillé en moi certaines portions dormantes de ma nature—et qui avaient besoin d'un symbole concret pour pouvoir sortir de la lethargie" ["the church at Pontigny has awakened certain dormant parts of my nature—which needed a concrete symbol to be able to emerge from their lethargy"]. In

[8] Trans. Justin O'Brien.

Pontigny, Vézelay, Auxerre, he rediscovered the France of the cathedrals, that is, of those celebrated by Walter Pater.[9] Before the churches Pater loved, his French disciple read again the mellifluous words with which, half a century earlier, the Englishman had praised the white God-castles of the Burgundian wine country—just as the youthful Proust communed with Ruskin's *Bible d'Amiens* before the Gothic of northern France. One could foresee even then that these emotional and artistic pilgrimages would lead Du Bos precisely to where Pater had conducted his Marius: into the Church. But Pater was able to find peace in that Anglo-Catholicism which offered a glorified resting-place to the English Pre-Raphaelites' dream of beauty. Du Bos having been born into the Church of Rome could only rejoin this community with its very different obligations. He accomplished this step, to the surprise of none of his friends, in July 1927, and a year later published extracts from his Diary in a luxury edition[10] (100 copies on imperial Japan, 700 copies on vellum). In this gesture an aesthetically-tinged individualism could be blended with the profession of a suprapersonal responsibility. On the last leaves of the costly impression the reader makes the acquaintance of the Abbé Altermann, who had brought Du Bos back to the Church and remained his spiritual director. Publication, it is safe to assume, ensued with the Abbé's consent.

It is curious that for the origin of the Diary, too, a priest is responsible, the Abbé and later Canon Mugnier (1853–1944), who had already had a hand in Huysmans' conversion. It is reported that at his death he left enough notes to fill 330 notebooks. Should they ever be published, they might also have a good deal to tell us about Du Bos. As a young priest the Abbé Mugnier already had connections in the best society. He received so many invitations that he seldom dined at home and that Forain could mock: "Quand l'abbé mourra,

---

[9] "Denys l'Auxerrois" in *Imaginary Portraits* (first published in 1887).

[10] *Extraits d'un journal.* 1908–1928 (Paris, Schiffrin).

on l'ensevelira dans une nappe" ["When the Abbé dies, they will bury him in a tablecloth"]. But his connections with literature were just as close, and among his friends he was known as "le vicaire de Notre-Dame des Lettres." To this wise and experienced friend the young Du Bos, in 1908, poured out his anguish: inability to write in spite of a strong influx of emotional experience. It was like a tormenting inner paralysis. He was deliberating whether to keep a journal, and the Abbé Mugnier actively encouraged him in this intention. Diaries, confessions, autobiographies had always attracted Charlie. Only the form of a diary enabled him to produce without planning, satisfied his need for completeness, flattered his mania for minute exactness (we shall see examples of it), and allowed him to catch the source of inspiration at the moment when it welled up. After 1919 he began to write critical essays, which were collected in the seven volumes of *Approximations* (1921–1937). The diary ceased to be his only form of expression. But it remained the essential one. The composition of the Journal became, by a process which can be traced, a rite of the soul's liturgy. It becomes the *raison d'être* of Charlie's existence, at once a mirror of the personality and an instrument of its perfection. But by this very fact, in time, it also acquires a set of inner contradictions and a dialectic subject to its own laws.

Du Bos lived for his Diary and spoke about it with his friends. Gide notes on 2 January 1922: "Je l'engage instamment à continuer son *Journal intime*, où certainement il livrera le meilleur de lui, qui trop souvent échappe à ses articles" ["I urge him insistently to continue his *Journal intime*, in which he surely will reveal the best of him, which too often escapes his articles"].[11] To Du Bos himself the Diary soon seemed provision and preparation for an autobiography. As early as 1923 (i, 257)[12] he is seeking a title for it.

[11] Trans. Justin O'Brien.

[12] Four volumes of the *Journal* have become available so far: i. 1921–1923 (1946); ii. 1924–1925 (1948); iii. 1926–1927 (1949); iv. 1928 (1950).

À la Recherche de moi-même? [*In Search of Myself?*] No, that won't work because of Proust. *La Traversée intérieure? En plongée?* [*The Interior Crossing? Submerging?*]. Neither satisfies. What about *Sondages?* Yes, that fits marvelously. To sound a depth—that's it. But Gide counsels against: "Non, cher, je ne puis vous dire que je goute ce mot de sondages qui a quelque chose de trop chirurgical. . . . On voit trop les amis disant: Avez-vous lu les Sondages de Charlie?" ["No, my dear, I cannot say that I like the word soundings, which has something too surgical about it. . . . It is too easy to see our friends saying: Have you read Charlie's soundings?"] The discussion is indicative of Charlie's relation to language. He, who had been so often operated on and was constantly ailing, had indeed found *sondage,* "sounding," in the Littré, but neglected to remember that a sound is also used in the exploration of wounds and inner organs.

In the same conversation Gide had also stated: "Faites bien attention surtout de laisser votre Journal tel qu'il est, de ne pas le transformer" ["Be careful, above all, to leave your Journal as it is, not to transform it"]. That meant that the idea of the autobiography had been unequivocally rejected. For Charlie it was painful. Fate has decided in favor of Gide. The diaries from 1921 on we possess only in posthumous form, in a written copy not revised by the author: so far, about 1500 pages of authentic testimony by a unique personality. This is something precious: far more valuable than the attempt, which Du Bos was probably contemplating, to supply an appendage to the confessions, self-revelations, and self-stylizations of world literature. The *Extraits* of 1928 are an anthology; the posthumous diaries, on the other hand, give us the genuine Du Bos—or at any rate, as much of him as he deemed worthy of registering. We must be grateful for the loyalty that saw to its publication. The documents in the case have been laid open.

The Diary was dictated to one of the self-denying secretaries who quickly rose to the position of family friends. Du Bos seems to have made handwritten notes only during the

years before 1914. Gradually a symptom developed that
Charlie designated "l'ivresse de la dictée" ("Saturday, the
4th of October, twelve o' five"). He was acute enough to perceive that the seeking and finding of phrases to match every
nuance of thought was bound up in him with a sensual and
emotional pleasure ("une volupté"); and that, as a consequence, the activity of dictating could lead to the temptation
of ascribing to this pleasure a heightened sense of the scope
and import of a momentary state of being. In other words:
the act of dictating engendered a euphoria independent of its
contents and thus ran the risk of falsifying the very thing that
the medium of dictation was supposed to catch and preserve
in all its spontaneity. The problems of dictation are more involved still, however, as a notation of 28 December 1927
("7h.30 soir") shows. Du Bos has laryngitis. He is deprived
of his voice, which M. Saint-Clair has described thus: "Avec
une voix agréablement timbrée, bien posée, sans beaucoup
d'inflexions, il avait une articulation impeccable, implacable,
une articulation de jugement dernier" ["Along with a pleasant
sounding, well-placed voice without many inflections, he had
an impeccable, implacable articulation, an articulation of
Judgment Day"]. He could dictate in a whisper, but then the
inspiring element of a subtly varied intonation which alone
has the power of inducing the "headiness" of dictation would
be missing. We observe that Du Bos, the virtuoso of conversation, is transformed while dictating into a virtuoso of the
monologue. What intoxicated him was to hear himself talk.
The sound of his voice made him sensible of the uniqueness
of his ego—"cette zone d'unicité qui en nous tressaille,
s'émeut, entre en vibration et communique à tout ce que nous
disons ces inflexions de la voix, cette continuité des ondes
sonores, ces caressants prolongements de la pédale . . ." (*Ap-
prox.* VI, 281ff.) ["that zone of uniqueness in us that quivers,
stirs, starts to vibrate and communicates to everything we say
those inflections of the voice, that continuity of sound waves,
those caressing prolongations of the pedal . . ."]. This should
be compared with the early admission (*Extraits*, 108; 5 Oct.

1920): "il y a des moments où je me sens moi-même comme pris à mon propre enchantement, et je ne parviens pas à me désensorceler" ["there are moments when I feel as though caught in my own spell, and I do not succeed in breaking the enchantment"]. At the time Du Bos put down this sentence, he had not yet started to dictate. But strange! when he later came to compare his older, handwritten journals (they go up to 1920) with the ones he had dictated, he found himself compelled to acknowledge the higher value of the former: "la lenteur impliquée dans l'acte même d'écrire induit à un degré de perfection artistique qui se perd d'autant plus dans le journal dicté que la rapidité est la norme. Du point de vue de l'art, depuis 1922 . . . j'ai infiniment perdu" (III, 387ff.) ["the slowness implicit in the very act of writing leads to a degree of artistic perfection which gets lost in a dictated journal so much the more as rapidity is the norm. From the point of view of art, since 1922 . . . I have lost a great deal"].

Of the early, handwritten Diaries[13] we possess only the fragments that were deciphered for the *Extraits d'un Journal* of 1928. Du Bos was right to prefer them to the dictated journals. They have a higher literary quality. That the writer admitted it to himself shows that, within certain limits, he was capable of self-criticism. But these starts were not followed up. He skirted, or so it seems to me, the basic problem. He did not analyze that "headiness" he enjoyed while dictating, did not submit it to "introspection" (*Introspections* is one of the titles he was considering for the contemplated autobiography). He must otherwise have discovered that it was his facility in improvising that intoxicated him; that intoxication of any kind conjures up pseudosublimities, pseudorealities, pseudovalues; and that virtuosity borders dangerously upon psychic automatism, which means running idle. Perhaps he might also have asked himself whether the attitude of improvised dictation was compatible with the conduct of an in-

---

[13] In the preface to *Journal* I (1946) we learn that the "little gray notebooks" had already become illegible by 1928. Even handwriting experts to whom they were shown were baffled by the task.

ner examination and depth analysis that is supposed to be
served by self-scrutiny and that alone can justify it. In order
to descend to the bottom of the soul and dive for pearls, a
state of composure must have been attained; nothing must
distract us from concentration upon the inner vision and from
the expenditure of energy necessary to trace it in words—
nothing, not even the sound of our own voice. When it is indispensable for heightening the emotional euphoria, we are
nearly at the point at which dictation turns into aria and the
virtuosity of parenthetical insertions into coloratura (by a
strange misapprehension Du Bos spoke of this as the
"polyphony" of his Diary). What always drew his mind like
a lodestar was self-absorption, the apprehension of pure inwardness. Can this be achieved otherwise than by silence and
solitude? Is it possible to have a meditation *à deux*? But this
was precisely the paradoxical situation in which the later
Diary originated. It required the presence of a devoted secre-
tary with the understanding and background for such taxing
work. Could she resist the spell of the modulations in which
exquisite insights were conveyed?

In a man of Du Bos's temperament the return to faith
could only aggravate the problematical aspects of the Diary
rather than settle them. Does he still have the right to confide
his inner states to dictation now that they transcend psychology and concern religion? Hasn't he been charged with a new
responsibility? And won't it have a crippling effect? He feels
an obscure urge he had hardly known before: to be silent—
"de me taire, de me tapir, de me terrer, de résoudre
mes propres problèmes sur le seul plan vital, en deçà et en
dehors de toute expression . . ." ["to be silent, to conceal myself, to burrow into the ground, to resolve my problems only
on the vital level, short of and beyond all expression . . ."].
He thinks of himself as a difficult case: "Que mon cas . . .
recèle en soi de germes d'insolubilité!" It dawns on him that
"simplicity" of spirit will forever elude him—"l'impossibilité
où je devine que je resterai toujours de rejoindre la complète
simplicité sur le plan de l'esprit" ["the impossibility, in which

I suspect that I shall always remain, of once more achieving complete simplicity on the level of the spirit"]. He must surely have been familiar, if not from the *Imitatio Christi* then from Walter Pater, who makes it his point of departure (in "Diaphanéité" in *Miscellaneous Studies*), with the ideal of *sibi unitum et simplificatum esse*. This was denied him. Perhaps it might be attained in an exalted hour while taking a stroll. Or it might suddenly shine forth at the turn of a solitary path in the woods—not in a library in the presence of a lady taking shorthand. In any event, Du Bos once did advance far enough to encounter silence as a demand. But he was unable to achieve it. The less so as his new adherence to the ritual and tradition of the Church was presenting him with a new emotional richness—"le journal religieux dont chaque matin je porte en moi tous les éléments" (IV, 183). The ideal would be to write a religious diary every morning ("et de préférence avant midi") and a psychological diary every evening.

Of course this idea could not be carried out. But that it could be conceived at all betrays—a want of psychology. From the conversion on, the Diary presents a mesh of the "merely-human" and the religious that cannot be untangled. Du Bos always liked to refer to his intellectual world as his "house of thought."[14] Now a new guest has entered this densely populated abode—Faith. One of the old residents is scrupulosity ("la maladie du scruple"). From this situation new tensions arise. What is *my* faith? To what extent is it real? "Il est très probable," replies Du Bos to his own question, "que j'ai au moins autant, sinon plus de foi, que neuf dixième des croyants . . ." ["It is very probable that I have at least as much, if not more, faith than nine-tenths of the believers . . ."]. Is this pride, as he has so often been told? No: —"je suis convaincu que dans mon cas il ne s'agit pas d'orgueil, ou du moins pas seulement de cela" (IV, 144) ["I am convinced that in my case it is not a matter of pride, or at least not only of that"]. How much is revealed by this qualification! How prematurely is self-examination broken off

[14] A coinage of Walter Pater's (in "The Child in the House").

here! One has the impression that religious experience is put at the service of self-reflection. When Du Bos is reminded by a verse from the Bible of the commandment to be meek, the result is the following entry: "La douceur—quel chapitre pour 'Introspections' que mon attitude si partagée envers elle toute ma vie durant" (IV, 144) ["Meekness—what a chapter for 'Introspections' this divided attitude toward it all my life!"]. Which does not deter him from presuming to state in the same dictation: "Je suis en pleine période théocentrique" (IV, 146) ["I am in the middle of my theocentric period"]. He had learned about Bérulle's theocentric mysticism from Bremond's recently published history of French religious sentiment and appropriated it with the naïveté of the novice. Once he goes so far as to dictate a prayer to God (IV, 157ff.) in which he begs for illumination. Woven into it are a characterization of César Franck's music and a quotation from "Thy Claudel."

The diaries that have been published so far end with 31 December 1928. Hence the entire last decade is still missing (Du Bos died on 5 August 1939). Du Bos's religious development during this phase remains hidden from us. What we can survey is merely the early history of his conversion and the initial reaction to it. What sort of a reaction is it? Predominantly, it involves a greater seriousness toward his own personality, which has after all gained in value through its new experiences. It has become familiar with signs of grace, which are expertly defined by the spiritual director ("en ce moment vous êtes l'objet d'une grâce actuelle," says the Abbé, IV, 105). This places a heavy weight of responsibility upon the personality, the first fruit of which is the *Dialogue avec André Gide*.

In the diaries of Du Bos and Gide and in the correspondence between them we can follow the history of this friendship, its deterioration, destruction, and resumption. There was also to be a sequel. When Jacques Rivière died in 1925, Du Bos indulged the hope of succeeding him as director of the *Nouvelle Revue Française*. He was cruelly disappointed on

March 10, when Schlumberger informed him that the choice had fallen on Gallimard. On April 28 he has an interview with Gide. He managed to conceal from Gide the depth of his disappointment—"la déception que j'éprouvais de sa totale abstention en ce qui me concerne dans la période de choix du directeur de la *N.R.F.*" ["the disappointment that I felt at his complete abstention concerning me during the period of the choice of a director for the *N.R.F.*"]. This did not become known till 1948 when the second volume of Du Bos's diary was published. Gide wrote to me on 21 June 1948 that this passage had opened his eyes to the reasons for Charlie's sudden coolness. Charlie's candidacy had never even been con-suitable.[15] Gide suspected, of course, that Charlie had suf-cope with practical difficulties," made him appear quite un-suitable.[15] Gide suspected, of course, that Charlie had suffered a certain disappointment, but that it had been such a "deep and lasting chagrin" he would never have believed possible. That was how Gide accounted for the fact that the *Dialogue avec André Gide*, "begun with enthusiasm," soon modulated to an entirely different key. "Curieux de voir un esprit aussi soucieux de droiture et d'équité à la merci des plus déformantes passions et si accessible à la flatterie!" ["It is strange to see a mind so anxious about right and justice at the mercy of the most disfiguring passions and so accessible to flattery!"]. Since then Gide has also expressed himself publicly about this episode. He had the last word in the dispute.

As early as 1924 (*Journal* ii, 233) Du Bos had diagnosed in himself "the sense of being always and altogether left out."[16] That makes it easier to understand the profound vex-

---

[15] For years Du Bos had entertained the idea of editing a review. It was to bear the—perhaps not very felicitous—title of *Textes*. It finally materialized as the shortlived Catholic quarterly *Vigiles* (published by Grasset, 1930–1931): "ce monument d'ennui," as Gide notes in his diary. The judgment is unfair. But the review might have been better.

[16] In English in the original.—TR.

ation of 1925. Nevertheless, his change of front with respect to Gide cannot be attributed entirely to this feeling. Gide's erotic confessions had always embarrassed Charlie. Charlie was a spiritualist long before he became a Catholic. He worshipped an ideal of spiritualization to which he tried to assimilate his heroes in painting and poetry ("my chosen ones," as he said on one occasion). The archangel among these angels was Keats. But even Keats is judged adversely once (1 December 1922) because in certain verses he had the audacity to describe nothing less than the "physical possession" of the beloved—"et si je trouve qu'il échoue, qu'entend-je par là, si ce n'est peut-être qu'il réussit? En tout cas il nous donne exactement ce je ne sais quoi de si merveilleusement déplaisant qu'est la chose sans plus" (*Extraits*, 133) ["and if I find that he fails, what do I mean by that unless it is that perhaps he succeeds? In any case he gives us exactly that certain so marvelously unpleasant something that is the thing itself"]. This astonishing utterance acquires a special accent as it does not come from the posthumous diaries but from the *Extraits* (1928). Du Bos considered it an opinion worth communicating. That only increases one's dismay on reading it. But for Du Bos's psychology it is not indifferent. Du Bos possessed a very refined and consciously indulged sensuality. For his well-being he required apricot jam and honey that had to be bought at Tanrade's (IV, 12); many cups of tea and chicken sandwiches, such as could only be obtained in the Bar de la Paix (IV, 22); or "un nombre respectable de tasses de thé accompagnées de quelques biscuits Déjeuner-Olibet" (this time in Versailles in the Trianon Palace, IV, 186). When he has his hair washed, it must be at Gustave's, "mon coiffeur de la Rue Royale." This procedure is so beneficial that it works wonders for the soul and gets combined with attendance at Mass (IV, 141): "Dans les périodes de langueur physique je devrais faire escale chez le coiffeur dès mon retour de la messe et avant même le petit déjeuner, tant le schampoing et la barbe m'apportent alors l'unique tremplin (je reconnais que l'image est curieuse, mais je n'en suis plus à cet egard à une curiosité de plus)" ["During periods of physical languor I would have to stop in at the hairdresser's on my way back from Mass and even before breakfast, to such a degree did shampoo and shave provide at the time my only springboard (I recognize that the image is odd, but I am past the point of worrying about one more oddity)"]. Once, on a sunny morning in September, I was passing by the Hotel Crillon. To my great surprise Charlie came out. Somewhat embarrassed, he explained that he had had to drink a glass of milk. Where else could one do it? He needed luxury. The area of the Avenue Henri-Martin (at most extended as far as "Les chers jardins du Trocadéro") is the section of the city "où j'aurai le plus plaisiblement, je devrais dire le plus luxueusement, médité" (IV, 46). One is reminded of Baudelaire's "luxe, calme et volupté." The province of *volupté* comprises, for Du Bos, the agreeable stimulation of a scalp massage as well as the tonic effect of tea; and, most of all, naturally, the pleasures of art, as we shall see.

So much the more remarkable, then, that the sphere of the erotic provoked so defensive a reaction. It appears again in his reaction to *Si le grain ne meurt*. Through Gide, he had already become acquainted with the work in 1923, one year before it was published, and was so overwhelmed by its artistic value that he forgot "the other factors of the problem." A "call to order" from Jean Schlumberger was needed to draw his attention to it (II, 264). On reading the book again in 1925, he takes offence at the "abstract decency" with which daring matters are treated in it: "Je disais à Paule ce matin que dans cette constante et si elegante stylisation du langage à ces moments-là chez Gide on se prend à dire: 'Une obscénité vaudrait mieux, serait en tout cas en un certain sens plus propre' " (II, 265) ["I was saying to Paule this morning that with that constant and so elegant stylization of language at these moments in Gide one is tempted to say: 'An obscenity would be better, would in any case be in a certain sense more appropriate' "]. In reading this one gets the same shock as at the lines about Keats. The remark about Gide dates from nearly a year and a half before the conversion. To note this is not without significance: the turning away from Gide is not to be accounted for solely by the turning toward the Church. It grows out of the realization—arrived at only very late—that Gide could not, after all, be numbered among the representatives of spirituality, of those who, for Du Bos, constituted the sacred precinct of literature. Gide had disappointed. And that was to have consequences.

Only one day after the last diary entry cited above, Du Bos decides to disclose to a publisher "qu'il se peut que je dispose d'un livre sur Gide (mes six leçons, ma conférence de Genève, mes chapitres sur 'Corydon' et 'Si le grain ne meurt . . . ,' ou je dégagerai ma position personnelle vis-à-vis de cette aspect de Gide) . . ."[17] ["that it could be that I have available a book on Gide (my six lessons, my Geneva lecture, my chapters on 'Corydon' and 'If it die . . . ,' where I shall define my personal position toward this aspect of Gide) . . ."]. On 28 April 1925 the Diary already records "la gêne que j'éprouve présentement à l'égard de mon ami Gide" (ii, 356) ["the embarrassment that I experience at present with regard to my friend Gide"]. Embarrassment turns increasingly into estrangement and the criticism begins: Gide knows nothing about the depths of life; he denies pain. The progress of this estrangement can be followed year by year in the Diaries. In 1927 the recognition has matured: "Gide n'est pas par définition un sujet mien" (iii, 218). What would have been more natural now than to set this subject resolutely aside? By such a resolution Du Bos would have spared himself and others a good deal of pain. He did not make it. With evident repugnance he "drags the cart out of the mud," even though he has to agree with his friends: "il est vraiment comique que les

---

[17] This is to be construed as an anticipation (hence "il se peut"). At that time, in January 1925, these texts did not yet exist. The remaining sections that make up the *Dialogue* (apart from the short piece on the *Symphonie Pastorale*) were not written till 1927 and 1928.

circonstances m'amènent à m'exprimer sur le problème de l'homosexualité" (III, 258–259). On 5 July 1927 Du Bos has reached a state of "total indifference to the subject" (III, 302). He condemns Gide for "rejecting the law of contradiction" and declares his three-fold bankruptcy: "la faillite du théoricien de l'homosexualité avec 'Corydon,' la faillite du romancier avec 'Les Faux Monnayeurs' ['The Counterfeiters'], la faillite de l'autobiographe avec 'Si le grain ne meurt . . .' ." On 14 July the verdict is rendered that Gide represents a combination of the "astral" and the "all-too-human," but that he has nothing of the "truly human." On 25 July Gide's *Isabelle* (1911) is dismissed ("une déception charmée"; III, 325). In January 1928 the intended book on Gide has become a "punishment" weighing heavily upon him (IV, 35). In March Du Bos feels certain that Gide's autobiography was written only "pour la confession pédérastique" (IV, 168). In August he believes he can detect Gide's "senility" (IV, 168).

It is understandable that as a recent convert Du Bos became inwardly estranged from his once admired friend and master.[18] But it remains regrettable, to my mind, that he felt the need to pronounce judgment on him in public—as the first offering to his newly-recovered faith. One can be freshly converted and yet not feel constrained to assume such a judicial office. It is distressing that the condemnation was made on artistic grounds, even though the motivation for it did not

---

[18] As recently as 1921 he had compared Gide's work to a richly indented peninsula: "Ouverte au vent du large, recueillant l'eau par tous les pores de ses innombrables petites criques, toujours reliée néanmoins à la terre ferme—telle m'apparaît à ce jour l'oeuvre d'André Gide: vigie avancée de l'esprit français, mais sur laquelle veille à son tour, tutélaire, la pure et mélodieuse mémoire de Jean Racine" (*Approximations* I, 57) ["Open to the sea wind, gathering in the water through all the pores of its innumerable little creeks, yet always connected with solid ground—such appears to me today the work of André Gide: advanced beacon of the French mind, but over which in turn watches, as guardian, the pure and melodious memory of Jean Racine"].

lie in aesthetics but in personal disappointment on the one hand and in moral disapproval on the other. Du Bos proved by his *Dialogue avec André Gide* that he lacked something essential to become what his friends had expected—a great critic.

The verdict on Gide—"threefold bankruptcy"—was an obvious misjudgment. It was not the only one. When Du Bos notes, in 1927, that he esteems T. S. Eliot highly but that compared to Middleton Murry he is merely a Matthew Arnold as against a Coleridge (III, 275), one is struck by "the want of a sense of proportion of things," to use a phrase of Henry James.[19] Thibaudet is rejected as "vulgar": "le malheur de Thibaudet, ce qui peut-être le rendra incurable, c'est que ses fameux Bourgogne développent, étalent sa vulgarité" (III, 328) ["the trouble with Thibaudet, that which will probably render him incurable, is that his famous Burgundies develop, display his vulgarity"]. Balzac remains alien to Du Bos (II, 280); instead he admires Gautier, whom he thinks Gide has always judged quite unfairly (III, 361), and Bourget.

Du Bos published his first book in 1922: essays on Valéry, Gide, Proust, Baudelaire, Flaubert and . . . Madame de Noailles, Jacques Chardonne, Bourget, Amiel. One is puzzled; the first row of names seems incompatible with the second. Authors of the first rank are indiscriminately mixed with those of the third. It is the same in the second volume (1927): Stendhal but also François Fosca; Shelley but also Guy de Pourtalès; Browning but also Maurois. Even more disappointing is the third volume (1929), whose twenty-one articles are devoted largely to inconsequential authors. Readers like myself were distressed, for we expected from Charlie books about the heroes we revered: a Keats, a Pater, a Browning, many others. We never got them. Why did he lavish so much time, attention, and energy on books of no particular merit? Their authors were his friends. Because Du Bos had

[19] For Du Bos's relation to English literature, cf. A. Ph. Bertocci, *Charles Du Bos and English Literature* (New York, 1949).

the feeling "que l'on ne dira pas sur eux juste les choses dont je voudrais qu'elles fussent dites" (III, 49) ["that no one will say about them just those things which I would wish should be said"]. But the claims of friendship must have been satisfied once the articles inspired by it had appeared in a periodical. Did it also require that they should be included in the series of *Approximations*? Yes! For Du Bos—as is clear from the letters we exchanged concerning *Approximations* III—regarded every one of his literary utterances as at the same time a document of the state of his soul at a particular moment (which is also why he arranged them chronologically); and of these evidences of the self not one must be allowed to go to waste. With this the standpoint of literary criticism has, of course, been abandoned. That this could happen with Du Bos was only because evaluative criticism was not his concern. He made use of it in only one case—in the *Dialogue avec André Gide*—and there it was a misuse. That was not appreciation but depreciation; not judging but damning. And it was not a question of art but of morality.

Several of the pieces in *Approximations* reproduce lectures on literature that Du Bos gave in the salons of his friends.[20] Four lectures on Walter Pater were delivered in 1923. Unfortunately only one of them was published (on *Marius the Epicurean* in *Approximations* IV). A society audience composed chiefly of ladies had first of all to be familiarized with the subject. An adaptation, a compromise was necessary. "Il faut que j'essaie de vous satisfaire tout en lésant le moins possible la memoire de quelque grand mort" (*Appr.* IV, 10) ["I must try to satisfy you while injuring as little as possible the memory of one of the gread dead"]. This constellation did not permit the subject to be enlarged on in all its fullness and depth. A tedious summary of the contents was in order. Then: "Mon seul objet dans les instants qui nous restent est de revenir sur certains des sentiments de Marius" (p. 28) ["My one object in the moments that remain is to come back

20 Further details in M. A. Gouhier, *Charles Du Bos* (1951), p. 17.

to certain feelings of Marius"]. First his piety. Pater compares it with that of the young Ion in the play by Euripides. Although he has only a few more minutes at his disposal Du Bos appends a quotation from the *Ion* that occupies two and a half pages of print. The final paragraph, in which reminiscences of Meredith, Joubert, Claudel, Newman, Edmund Gosse, and Alphonse Daudet have been interspersed, achieves an effective vibrato. But anyone who knows and loves Pater has not much to gain from this "approximation." And this despite the fact that since 1904 Pater had been a guiding star for Du Bos's spiritual way. His debt to him was so great that as late as 1929 he admitted that he would never be able to repay it.[21] He might perhaps have done so could he but have been relieved of the drudgery of lectures and other obligations. That was never to be granted him. His salon lectures were made easier for him by his enormously wide reading and his virtuoso ability to play on a keyboard of selected "texts" (which, to be sure, were frequently repeated). He had acquired the knack of leaping, by association, from one to the other of these secular gospels; but only at the cost of deeper penetration. He was aware of this deficiency: "Il peut advenir que l'on ne donne jamais davantage la sensation de dominer un sujet que lorsqu'on ne le domine que pour n'avoir pas été jusqu'au point où vraiment on l'épuiserait" (IV, 203) ["It can happen that one never more fully gives the impression of dominating a subject than when one only dominates it so far as not to have been at the point where it can really be exhausted"]. That is why the writings published in book form do not give an adequate picture of Du Bos's intellectual world. They are approximations, but they do not strike dead center.

To do justice to Du Bos, to derive pleasure and profit from the wonderful gifts of his spirit, one will have to judge him not as a critic or even as a psychologist. Most especially will one have to ignore the clerical-apologetic tendency of his later

---

[21] *Approximations* IV, 8 and 9.

years. The area in which he is, as I believe, incomparable, lies elsewhere.

Du Bos possessed something which he once praised in Watteau: an organization of the senses so fine that it reached the point of spiritualization. He might have said with Keats: "O for a life of sensations rather than of thoughts." Sense impressions held something inexhaustible for him. He was aware of it: "Le point de départ du travail de l'esprit est presque toujours chez moi une sensation, une sensation qui rélève la plupart du temps de la sensibilité intellectuelle, mais qui est aussi precise et aussi puissante que les sensations qui nous arrivent par les sens; l'intensité de la sensation est telle qu'elle se communique a l'âme tout entière, et sous la plénitude de l'afflux l'emotion jaillit aussitôt" (23 October 1917) ["The point of departure for the work of the mind is with me almost always a sensation, a sensation which depends most of the time on intellectual sensibility, but which is as precise and as powerful as the sensations which come to us through the senses; the intensity of the sensation is such that it communicates itself to the entire soul, and under the abundance of the afflux the emotion bursts forth at once"]. So far as sensation is equated here with "intellectual sensibility," a real condition is identified, although not perhaps quite adequately described. But is there a word for it in today's psychological terminology? I doubt it. Rather, what is meant is very likely something analogous to the "inner senses" of which the mystics have so much to tell us—not, to be sure, on the mystical but on the poetic level. This sensibility is as distinct from intellect as water is from fire. But it is suffused with spirituality. From this suffusion spring poetry and the poetic interpretation of the world. In sensation a feeling of fulfillment is given that is experienced with overwhelming astonishment—"cette stupeur comblée de la sensation et devant la sensation" (III, 115) ["that overwhelming astonishment of sensation and at sensation"]. An example: on a bright summer morning—it happened to be the day on which the Archduke Franz Ferdinand was assassinated—Du Bos is bending over a bed of

lilies in a palace park. In the white calyxes of the flowers he
"experiences" purity in its delightful sensuous fullness. The
petals are fleshy and thick, but without a trace of heaviness:
"une épaisseur immatérielle." Their odor—a flight of honey
such as ascends from the verses of Keats. And Keats also has
this in common with the lily—that the spiritual essence arises
from the density of the matter. But his poetry is also fruity:
"fullness, roundness, juiciness, down, saturation, and brilliance: he has all the qualities of the peach." A portrait by
Ingres: the face has the foamy, creamy consistency of a
custard: "onctueux, souvent l'on a besoin de cette épithète
pour les visages de femmes d'Ingres" ["unctuous, often one
needs this epithet for the faces of Ingres' women"]. These
faces are solid, certainly, "but they have the very special
solidity of a thick fluid that has reached the point of curdling:
a congealed fluctuation ('une fluctuation saisie')." By means
of such comparisons Du Bos's eye renders the individuality of
great painters visible. Just as he defines the state of con-
gealment in the faces of Ingres' women, so he draws our
attention to the fact that in Holbein the beards seem soft
as fur, the hands like formations of rock crystal (II, 216).
Such correspondences from the three kingdoms of nature
could become points of departure for a classification of
minds. Emerson, for example, belongs to the mineral kingdom: "Minéral essentiellement d'ailleurs: ses pensées les
plus fortes affectent les formes coniques des cristaux" (23
June 1918) ["Essentially mineral, moreover: his strongest
thoughts tend toward the conic forms of crystals"]. But
Novalis and Gide also seem to Du Bos to be "fascinated
by the mineral element." In Gide's early prose as in Novalis'
"Apprentices at Sais" he perceived the tendency toward a
beauty which might be related to that of a transparent
precious stone. Among painters Pier della Francesca, Vermeer, and Van Eyck belonged to this—very rare—mineral kingdom. In a letter to Gide (31 December 1925) Du Bos
reports on a lecture he had given in Milan: "Par de savants
rapprochements entre le cristal léopardien (exemplified by

Leopardi's 'Elogio degli uccelli') et votre cristal à vous, j'ai initié les Milanais à cette 'famille des cristallins' qui furent souvent le sujet d'inoubliables entretiens. Le public se montra particulièrement sensible à ce passage de la causerie, ce qui montre que pour subtils que soient nos jeux, et situés dans la zone du 'tresor réservé,' ils ne sont cependant pas tout 'intraduisibles' " ["By skillful juxtapositions between the Leopardian crystal and your own, I initiated the Milanese into that 'family of crystallines' that were often the subject of unforgettable conversations. The public showed itself particularly receptive to this passage of the talk, which shows that however subtle our games may be, and located in the zone of 'private treasure,' they are nevertheless not entirely 'untranslatable' "]. Subtle games? Indeed! And sometimes they were elevated to a kind of trifling that verged on sublime preciosity. If Hofmannsthal determines the poet as the slave of all living things, created in order to enjoy passively the infinity of appearances, Du Bos translates this definition into the concept of a point of intersection, a midpoint which does not place but is placed. This leads then to the distinction: "ici, disjonction des deux grandes races de poètes suprêmes: les situants et les situés." But now the distillation goes further: "Rossetti situe plutôt qu'il n'est situé; Baudelaire au fond est plus situé. Tout en prétendant toujours situer" ["here, division between the two great orders of supreme poets: the situating and the situated." "Rossetti situates rather than is situated; Baudelaire at bottom is more situated. Even while pretending always to situate"]. To witness such a game of distinctions at Du Bos's tea table was delightful. In print the effect is curious.

These sublime games had originally been intuitions, real certainties that induced a corresponding experience in the reader. Even so, the question of whether they were accurate could come up from time to time. A characteristic entry is (I, 301): "Ce matin en allant à pied à la gare de Vaucresson m'est venue une intuition peut-être juste, peut-être tout à fait fausse (et dont, si je m'en sers dans mon Pascal, il faudra user la plus grande prudence): la voici . . ." ["This morning while walking to the Vaucresson station an intuition came to me which is perhaps right, perhaps entirely wrong (and which, if I avail myself of it in my Pascal, must be used with the greatest caution): here it is . . ."].

The interpretation of the spiritual content with which a sensation was endowed seems to me not to have reached ultimate clarity in Du Bos. He could have found it in the concluding section of Proust's novel, which appeared in 1927 under the title of *Le temps retrouvé*. But Du Bos was absorbed just then with his religious life. And although he greeted the book with the highest admiration (III, 366), the hope he still cherished of becoming a "Christian Proust" alienated him from it again. Indeed, in the end he condemns Proust's "all-embracing, seemingly innocent, serenely indifferent amoralism" (IV, 148).

All I can see in this is a tragic misunderstanding, tragic in the sense of Goethe's verse:

Keins wird vom andern wünschenswert ergänzt.

[Neither is the other's desirable complement.]

Precisely in *Le temps retrouvé* (II, 24) could Du Bos have found the final victorious resolution of those experiences of spiritualized sensation that formed the nucleus of his creative interpretations of poetry and art. The shifting perspective of the towers of Martinville, the taste of a madeleine cake dipped in tea—these had been the determining childhood impressions of the narrator of *À la recherche du temps perdu*. In a late retrospect he sums up his account: "Il fallait tâcher d'interpréter les sensations comme les signes d'autant de lois et d'idées, en essayant de penser, c'est-à-dire de faire sortir de la pénombre ce que j'avais senti, de le convertir en un équivalent spirituel" ["I must try to interpret the sensations as the indications of corresponding laws and ideas; I must try to think, that is to say, bring out of the obscurity what I had felt, and convert it into a spiritual equivalent"].[22] Such experiences are truths that reveal themselves in a secret code. They form an "inner book" composed of unknown signs: "Pour sa lecture, personne ne pouvait m'aider d'aucune règle, cette lecture consistant en un acte de création où nul ne peut nous suppléer, ni même collaborer avec nous. Aussi combien se détournent de l'écrire, que de tâches n'assume-t-on pas pour éviter celle-là" ["To read the subjective book of these strange signs . . . no one could help me with any rule, for the reading of that book is a creative act in which no one can stand in our stead, or even collaborate with us. And therefore how many there are who shrink from writing it; how many tasks are undertaken in order to avoid that one!"].[23] But this is also the only book dictated to us by reality. "Les idées formées par l'intelligence pure n'ont qu'une vérité logique, une vérité possible, leur élection est arbitraire. Le livre aux caractères figurés, non tracés par nous, est notre seul livre" ["The ideas formed by pure intellect have only a logical truth, a potential truth; the selection of them is an arbitrary act. The book written in symbolic characters not traced by us is our only book"].[24] In this kind of a metaphysics of literature Du Bos's intuitive experiences also could have found their place.

One of Du Bos's household gods was the "Lady with a Tea Cup" by Utamaro. She hung over his standing-desk in the Rue de la Tour, holding a tray with a bowl of yellow porcelain as though she were bringing him his beloved tea. To read a page of Plotinus in a low voice beneath her glance—that would be refreshing. With such impressions he furnished his "house of thought." Like Walter Pater he saw in literature and art a retreat, "a sort of cloistered refuge from a certain vulgarity in the actual world."[25] For Du Bos, as it had for Pater, the meaning of life lay in "impassioned contempla-

[22] Trans. Frederick A. Blossom.   [23] Trans. Frederick A. Blossom.
[24] Trans. Frederick A. Blossom.
[25] Walter Pater, "Style" (in *Appreciations*).

tion." Giorgione and Baldovinetti, Van Eyck and Vermeer gave Du Bos a satisfaction that he was unable to find anywhere else. Giorgione was enthroned high above the rest. In him he found "the transition from emotion to form." With other painters—Poussin, for example—part of the emotion was sometimes left over and strayed about on the canvas. With Giorgione the emotion formed everything thoroughly—"not only the faces but also the hair, the clothing, even the ramparts." How delighted Charlie was when in 1935 he was able to see Giorgione's scattered paintings—the *Antonio Brocardo* (Budapest), the *Judith* (The Hermitage), *The Thunderstorm* (Venice), and *The Concert* (The Louvre)—all hanging on the same wall of the Petit Palais.

What Giorgione was in painting, Keats was to Du Bos in poetry. He occupied the innermost circle. Close beside him was the luminous Pater. Joubert and Maurice de Guérin were France's contribution to "spirituality" in literature. Henry James and Chekhov, George and Hofmannsthal were loved and revered. Shakespeare and Dante were paid homage, but from a greater distance. Goethe was for a long time a stranger—"le plus beau de mes étrangers." That changed, however, in his last years.

The sacred precinct of literature in which Du Bos performed the rite of eternal adoration contains almost exclusively figures of the nineteenth century. Classical Antiquity always remained distant and alien to him—"je n'ai pas un atome de grec dans ma composition." So, too, the French classics, except Pascal, and seventeenth century England, except Milton. His philosophical outlook was determined by Simmel and Bergson, who, however, were displaced after 1927 by Maritain and . . . Peter Wust. England was strongly predominant. Directly after Keats came Shelley and Browning. George Eliot and Thomas Hardy received the tribute that was denied to Balzac. The whole picture: an Anglo-aesthetic nineteenth century. With Du Bos Giorgione too was Pateresque. Only in relation to painting in the nineteenth century was Du Bos completely French; at the same time it was the only field in which he found Classicism and approved of it: in Ingres. But Delacroix and Corot, Degas and Renoir were loved no less sensitively. His matchless ability to interpret his impressions of painting is perhaps nowhere so brilliantly displayed as in the comparison, running to many pages, between Cézanne's flowers and those of Manet (IV, 133ff.). The interested reader will seek out these passages for himself.

In Zurich there was recently an exhibition of the art of the turn of the century. It seemed strange to a visitor who could still remember the Darmstadt artists' colony and the first volumes of the "Insel." It was all more or less "right" and it was all dead (which is in no way meant as a criticism—that is simply how museums are). Entombed in their showcases and labeled the objects looked as though they were shivering. And yet that era had a soul. For people whose language is German it speaks most audibly from the prologue to George's *Der Teppich des Lebens* [*The Tapestry of Life*] and Hofmannsthal's *Der Tod des Tizian* [*The Death of Titian*]. Both poems preserve the poignant sweetness (*Schmelz*) of a one hundred year-old history of the soul, a history that begins with Novalis' *Blütenstaub* [*Pollendust*] (1798): "The wings of the dove lined with silver and the green-gold of its pinions gleaming," or in the even more beautiful version of the Vulgate: "pennae columbae deargentatae, et posteriora dorsi eius in pallore auri." The history of this soul has never been told and probably no longer will be. But in the Diaries of Charles Du Bos much of its essence has been stored up.

I do not know of a more dignified way to conclude these pages than with a fragment from the year 1922 (I, 123): "Word for word quotations are a sign of spiritual magnanimity. They are entirely misunderstood, and it is good that this should be so, for it is the calling of spiritual magnanimity to be misunderstood. They are an indication of the fact, incomprehensible to most people, that all those to whom we owe a debt of the spirit accompany our thinking on all its ways. When one possesses a certain intellectual constitution one will not only not wish to avoid quotations—no, it cannot be done without feeling that we have cast aside with the most ungrateful brutality those especially, thanks to whose distant radiations we have attained to the very thought that we are about to express. The relations to the dead writers in particular are among the most poignant, the most solemn, but also the most consolatory that the spirit can maintain: I at any rate do not know of a day on which a number of them do not participate in my life with a degree of intimacy that moves even to tears."

1952

Ortega y Gasset

✦✦✦

I

JOSÉ ORTEGA Y GASSET is the founder and editor of the *Revista de Occidente*, which has rapidly gained a place for itself among the liveliest and most intelligent periodicals in Europe; professor of philosophy at the University of Madrid; and author of a series of essay collections that reveal him to be a brilliant and universal critic.[1] The originality of this criticism lies in the rare combination of sparkling vitality and power of organized thought. From Ionic philosophy of science to Cubist painting there does not seem to be anything in which this critic is not passionately interested. His intellectual curiosity is greater than that of a Remy de Gourmont, and his mind is infinitely more elastic than that of this last of the *Encyclopédistes*. This intellectual flexibility does not lead to anarchic impressionism, however, for it is controlled by a will to philosophical construction. Philosophical—the criticism of a Thibaudet might be so described. But with Thibaudet philosophizing is only a spice of pleasure, the Attic salt of his taste in culture. With Ortega philosophy does not function as irony and Humanism, but rather as a striving for order, a way to the hierarchy of values, constructivism.

Another trait of Ortega's originality is the manner in which he assimilates and brings together German and French culture. I do not know of any critic in Europe capable of writing with the same sympathy and the same understanding on Madame de Noailles and Simmel, Marcel Proust and Max

[1] *Meditaciones del Quijote*, 1914; *El Espectador*, three volumes (1916, 1917, 1921); *España invertebrada* (1922); *El Tema de nuestro Tiempo* (1923).

Scheler. Ortega can and does. And in language sparklingly pointed, nervously clear, sensitive, and unrhetorical. He is acquainted with and ranges over the entire impressive development of the German humanistic disciplines (*Geisteswissenschaften*). Mommsen and Eduard Meyer, Max Weber and Dilthey, Cohen and Rickert, Wölfflin and Worringer—all these names are as familiar to him as they are to us. There cannot be many foreigners who are so thoroughly conversant with the researches of German historians and philosophers and follow their work so carefully as Ortega. But this is augmented by the aesthetic-literary culture of nineteenth century France and the France of the present. So in Ortega the France of the *Nouvelle Revue Française* (to put it briefly) intersects with the Germany not of the poets (the contemporary poets) but of the thinkers. And the one amends, expands, and complements the other. What with us is at times professionally narrow and inartistic, what in France is intellectually limited, frivolous, and self-complacent—these opposing tendencies are neutralized in such a synthesis.

I cannot think of a better introduction to the problems of the Spanish mind than Ortega's little book *España invertebrada*, literally, "Spain without a backbone"—that is to say: the Spanish disintegration.

The brochure came out in 1922. It is an attempt to diagnose Spain's illness. Ortega defends himself against the reproach of pessimism. Spain's greatest need is clarity of insight. In Spain there are incessant debates about domestic conditions, but they lack a total perspective that would assign details to their proper places. The Spaniard's view is clouded by the fact that he has an exaggerated notion of Spain's past importance. He consoles himself for the unhappy events of the present with the thought that we did, after all, have a Cid. But this is the true pessimism: the idea that Spain was for a time the most perfect of nations and has been on the decline ever since. Ortega prefaces his diagnosis of modern Spain with an historical anamnesis. Taking his cue from Mommsen's *History of Rome*, he considers the formation of states

as a process of integration (synoikismos) that creates out of
originally isolated elements systems of an ever-increasing
unity, yet without completely annihilating these primary elements. So Rome's way leads from the Septimontium to the
Latin League, to the Italic union, to the colonial Empire. But
a nation's history comprises not only its formation and rise
but its decay and decline as well. Decadence means disintegration and as such is an essential component of the vital
process of a nation and its dynamics. What is the basis for
such a national evolution? The power to form a nation is a
creative gift like a talent for art or religion. Athens lacked
it; Rome and Castile, though far less talented intellectually,
were endowed with it. This gift does not have its basis in power, for otherwise Timur and Genghis Khan must have been
the greatest founders of nations. Besides power, an essential
requirement for the formation of states is the tendency to
communal life, "un proyecto sugestivo de vida en común."
To its subject tribes Rome meant a universal program for the
organization of life. It possessed a superior system of justice
and administration as well as a culture, created by the
Greeks, that enhanced human existence. For a nation, the
decisive factor is not that it has a past but a plan of life for the
future. The nation lives through its program for tomorrow.

The nation-building element in Spain has always been Castile. It was Castile that knew how to command, itself
and others. The spirit of Castile was directed from the first
toward great enterprises. It invented the idea of Spanish unity
during the struggle with the Moors, and having realized it set
itself new and more comprehensive goals: the diffusion of
Spanish energies over the entire globe. Castile and Aragon
united in order to conduct a global policy. Machiavelli paid
the closest attention to this procedure. His book on the prince
is a meditation on the deeds of Ferdinand the Catholic and
Cesare Borgia. What we call Machiavellianism is the intellectual commentary of an Italian on the actions of two Spaniards. Up to around 1580 Spanish life is a process of integration, which means concentration and accumulation of

energies. From that time on the reverse development takes place. The process of disintegration advances according to strict laws from the circumference to the center. First the Netherlands fall away and Milan is lost; this continues till, around 1900, the corpus of Spain has returned to its peninsular shape. At this moment a new process of disintegration commences inside the peninsula; particularism. Only thus can we understand the Basque and Catalan movements. Bilbao and Barcelona are the centers of economic power in the peninsula, and that is the reason why regionalism and separatism were able to take an aggressive form there. But psychologically, the ground is probably also prepared in Galicia, Asturias, Aragon, and Valencia. Nevertheless, particularistic tendencies can only take effect if the central power within society has itself been tainted with particularism, and that is what has happened in Spain. In the reign of Philip III Castile's vital process begins to stagnate. It becomes suspicious, narrow, conservative. For three centuries Spanish history is nothing but sleep, stultification, and egocentricity. The monarchy and the church replace national interests with their own private interests. Is it any wonder, then, if the elements of Spain's national community should ask themselves: why are we living together? And to this regional particularism must be added the particularism of the social classes. One of the prerequisites of a vigorous national life is social elasticity, which is the intensification of the individual life through participation in the life of the whole. This must not be taken to mean equality of ideas and needs, but mutual knowledge and mutual contact between the most diverse spheres of interest and the most varied strata of the population. Only a nation that is elastic in this psychological sense of the word will, at the decisive moment of its existence, be able to draw upon historical elasticity. In Spain today this elasticity has completely vanished. The politicians are not concerned about the country, the country does not care about the politicians. The soldier, the industrialist, the intellectual, the farmer, the worker, the aristocrat—each lives an hermetically-sealed existence and doesn't show the slightest interest in anyone else. After the Spanish-American war public opinion unanimously and resolutely demanded that all future enterprises requiring war should be renounced. In this way it lost all interest in the army. The army, in its turn, feeling itself isolated from the life of the nation, began to mistrust the politicians. It lived a life apart. In 1909 military action was required in Morocco. The populace ran to the railway stations to prevent the troops from being transported. But Morocco gave back to the soul of the Spanish army its inner cohesion and filled it with energy. How was this energy to be discharged? It turned on the nation itself. The army took command of the country. The particularism of the army led perforce to "l'action directe." Every particularism must lead to that, since it necessarily engenders an aversion to the institutions of the state. Usually it expresses itself as anti-Parliamentarianism. All levels of Spanish society, all social classes have in common this aversion to politicians. The psychological motive for the aversion consists in this: that the institutions of the state symbolize for each class the necessity of taking the others into account.

In Spain today we often hear the complaint that there are no men. But this is to overlook the fact that a man's impact upon society is never due to his personal qualities but to the social energies that the masses deposit in him. His personal talents are only the occasion for this social dynamism to become condensed in him. In periods of historical ascendency the masses feel themselves as masses, that is, as an anonymous collectivity which creates a symbol of its own unity in leading personalities on whom it lavishes its enthusiasm. It is then that people say, there are men. But when the masses refuse to follow the leading minority, nation and society start to decompose. The Spain of the present is an extreme case of such disintegration. The Spanish sickness does not consist in the corruption of law and government. That a society is immoral may be bad; but it is much worse when a society is not a society. That is the case with Spain. Neither in affairs of state nor of the mind does anyone acknowledge a hierarchy. The worst are rebelling everywhere against the best.

In history there is a constant alternation of two kinds of periods. In the one an aristocracy forms and with it a society; in the other this aristocracy decays and society falls apart. Hindu wisdom calls them Kitra epochs and Kali epochs.[2] In the Kali epochs the caste system degenerates. The lower castes rise because Brahma has fallen asleep. Then Vishnu assumes the dreaded shape of Shiva and destroys the existing orders. The twilight of the Gods commences. At last Brahma awakens, creates the world anew, and causes a new Kitra epoch to arise. We are at the end of a Kali epoch. In such periods the Kali system is felt to be intolerable. Nevertheless, organization and hierarchy are part of the concept of society. But the democratic ideology has put us in the habit of asking, what should a society be? instead of, what constitutes a society? The notion of what should be has muddied the analysis of social reality since the eighteenth century. And yet an elementary intuition suffices to understand it. The fundamental law of every social structure becomes operative whenever even a few people gather. Should one of them find a more expressive gesture, a keener thought, a richer emotional response with regard to a certain event, the others will spontaneously feel a desire to be like him. This is not a matter of imitation. When we imitate someone we are aware that we are not like him but only pretending to be. But here we are concerned with the wish to assimilate thoroughly and genuinely an alien mode of existence. The superior personality has an exemplary effect and awakens in the rest of us the wish to form ourselves upon it. In a man's mode of existence we sense a higher type of life; it transmits an intuition of values previously overlooked. This type becomes the model for the articulation and organization of a society and the development of a hierarchy. Every genuine aristocracy is founded

[2] Cf. Max Weber, *Religionssoziologie* [*Sociology of Religion*], vol. 2.

upon the effects of such a psychological power of attraction. It follows that society is by nature an instrument of perfection. If one nation lags behind the others it is always either because exemplary men are lacking or because the masses no longer form themselves on their example.

In the worst case both reasons coincide. That is what has happened in Spain. Owing to a tragic perversion of its instincts the Spanish people has for centuries detested the type of exemplary man: the Spanish sickness is aristophobia. Spain and Russia are similar in that both suffer from an obvious and chronic lack of outstanding individuals. In Spain the people have always done everything, and what they could not do was left undone. Spanish art exhibits a wonderful wealth of anonymous popular forms: in song, in dance, in ceramics. But it is poor in personal accomplishments. Occasionally an artist of genius has arisen, but his works remained isolated afterward; and even these infrequent geniuses were always half folk-artists. Spanish architecture reaches its high point in churches and public buildings. Private constructions are almost without exception rather poor and modest. Only seldom is a personal style achieved. Always and in every field Spain lacks an adequate elite. It is usual to see an advantage in the fact that feudalism did not exist in Spain. In reality it was a grave misfortune. As a matter of fact, Spain possesses the same historical structure as France, England, and Italy. All three of these nations—even if in very different ways— were constituted from three elements: the native stock, the Roman cultural heritage, and the Germanic invasions. The Roman factor is the neutral element, as it were, in the origin of the European nations. The native stock in each case is the matter that is decisively shaped by the Germanic element. The difference between France and Spain does not come from the difference between the native stock of the Gauls and the Iberians but from that between the Franks and the Visigoths. On the scale of historical vitality the Frank stood much higher than the Visigoth. The Visigoths were an older Germanic tribe. They had still shared in the communal life of the declining Empire. They were civilized, but for that very reason degenerate. They had become "alcoholized" so to speak by Roman civilization so that they could no longer embody the vital forms of the Germanic spirit in a vigorous fashion. The Roman spirit understands life in community only in the form of the state, the *civitas*. For the Germanic spirit the people consists of a few powerful leaders who, as conquerors, make their followers lords of foreign territories. The Roman is not the master of his glebe but its servant. He is a farmer. The German did not cultivate his land till relatively late. Roman law and Germanic seigniory are extreme antitheses, although both are bound up with the same consciousness of moral obligation. They represent different forms of the sense of justice. The Germanic sense is not interested in ownership but in lordship. He does not want to earn but to command, to judge, and to have vassals. To his way of feeling, right must be gained and defended, not inherited. The nations of modern Europe did not evolve out of a city-state like Rome but were shaped by Germanic seigniory. Hence it is a misfortune and not an advantage that the feudal system was so feebly developed in Spain. For Spain was thereby deprived of its leading aristocratic minority. This is evident in the so-called *Reconquista*, the struggle which lasted eight hundred years, to regain the Moorish parts of the country. Can one call something that takes eight hundred years a reconquest and be proud of it? Had feudalism existed in Spain, there would most likely have been a real reconquest, as in other countries there were crusades.

The entire course of Spanish history is so abnormal that reasons for it must be sought. Until thirty years ago people believed that the decline of the nation had set in only a few decades earlier. Costa and his generation then realized that the decline had already begun two centuries before. Ortega himself advocates the paradoxical view that the Spanish decadence was no less marked in the Middle Ages than in modern times. To be sure, there had been moments of apparent exuberance, and even hours of splendor and universal glory. But on the whole Spain has never enjoyed normal health. That is why one cannot really speak of decay but rather only of congenital constitutional defects. From the very beginning Spain has lacked the *aristoi*. An examination of the causes for the expansion of Spanish power and greatness between 1480 and 1600 only confirms this diagnosis. What was it that changed so decisively in Spain between 1450 and 1500? During this period only one fact of importance stands out—the unification of the peninsula. Spain was the first nation to concentrate all its capacities and forces in the fist of a king. While the power of France, England, and Germany was scattered among many single rulers and Italy was atomized in small city states, Spain shaped itself into an elastic, unified body. But quite as sudden as the rise of 1500 was the decline of 1600. Unity merely meant an artificial abundance of life; it had, after all, only come about because of Spain's lack of a strong feudal pluralism. The early unification must be regarded as a sign of diminished vital energy.

Spain's true greatness lies in the colonization of America. This was the work of the people, not of leading minorities, as was the case with the English colonies. The Spanish people engendered new peoples, but it was unable to confer that upon them which it did not itself possess: discipline and cultural goals. Spain is to the present day a nation of peasants. It suffers from the stagnation common to peasant countries. It has never been a modern nation. But in this day and age, when the modern era is coming to an end, we shall not need to lament this fact. In the new historical climate that is dawning everywhere today, other values will prevail than those of the so-called modern era. The modern tendencies are rationalism, democratism, mechanization, industrialism, capitalism. France, England, and, in part, Germany have realized these tendencies most intensely; Spain has not. But if the fertility of these tendencies should be exhausted, the small nations that have hitherto remained in the background or lagged behind would be presented with a new historical opportunity. The very phenomena of Spanish life that have hitherto been interpreted as symptoms of illness would then become the basis for an optimistic perspective. The ills from which Spain suffers may be arranged in three layers. The top layer would comprise abuses in politics and administration, religious fanaticism, and the so-called lack of culture. In the pathology of Spain they do not have the great importance that is ordinarily ascribed to them. The second layer would consist of the phenomena of decomposition, which have been advancing for centuries and which manifest themselves today as particularism and *action directe*. These are grave disorders, but they are results, not causes. They are rooted in the soul of the Spanish people itself, in that radical perversion that expresses itself in hostility toward all forms of superiority, in the obstinate apathy of the masses and their refusal to submit to any kind of leadership. To this fundamental evil must be attributed the fact that in the course of history the Spanish type of man has become lower rather than higher. The emotional rebellion of the masses, the hatred of the best, and the paucity of superior natures—these are the true reasons for Spain's fate. Can these value-destroying tendencies in the soul of the people ever change? They can, once they have entirely spent their force, once they have arrived at an insight into their own effects. There are indications, sporadic and feeble indications, that such a feeling is emerging in the Spanish masses. The possibility of Spanish ascent depends on whether these signs grow stronger and predominate. The most urgent demand of the moment is to work toward a new, unbourgeois type of man.

Ortega's piece belongs to that genre of sociological-intellectual analysis that is so abundantly represented in France (Taine, Renan, Barrès, Maurras) and that is all but undeveloped in Germany. We have Scheler's *Ursachen des Deutschenhasses* [*Causes of the Hatred for Germans*]. But in general this Romance form of creative criticism occurs infrequently with us. It is kept down by our ideal of specialization and objectivity which, like all ideals, has a positive and enhancing but also a negative, suspensive effect. We allot our intellectual problems to specialists in whom reverence for science becomes a reluctance to overstep boundaries and a hindrance to synthetic conclusions. That is why all our political parties lack suggestive formulas, persuasive programs, convincing ideas. That is why our democrats are shamefaced, our nationalists rough and crude. No one has an engaging system to put forth. It is incredible but true that Germany today, while facing its gravest historical crisis, has no national ideology capable of uniting the leading elite. Of course the fault does not lie only with specialization but equally with the wild proliferation of German individualism, with the particularism of the races, the creeds, the educated classes, and the groups with fixed ideologies. But these reasons are not an excuse. The Spanish example ought to make us stop and think. There are those who say, we are so deep that we cannot define ourselves. The only answer to that is: what cannot find expression does not really exist. There is a false inwardness that is nothing but a deficiency in the power to shape and to realize. What we feel for Germany must be translated into the language of the mind if it is to become kinetic energy.

But if we have been able to accomplish this only very imperfectly so far, it may be due to the tension that exists between vitality and culture, a disequilibrium affecting not only the German but the whole European spirit of the age. This is the basic idea of Ortega y Gasset's most important book, entitled *El Tema de nuestro Tiempo* [*The Modern Theme*].

Our time—for Ortega, this means the era the beginning of which we are now witnessing. As a disputatious philosopher, Ortega undertakes to illuminate its tendencies by a critique of the historical and philosophical epoch that is now drawing to a close. He seeks to formulate the historical imperative of our generation. The battle positions of the past no longer make sense to this generation. The dilemma between, say, progress and reaction no longer exists for it. What is struggling for expression in our time, the nature of its inner law, can best be discerned in the region of pure thought, in the new forms of scientific and philosophical knowledge. The delicate subject matter of knowledge reacts to the slightest vibrations of the vital sense. In science every epoch arrives at a consciousness of itself. This does not mean that all scientific truth is relative—such relativism was a typical form of nineteenth century thought. We must not relapse into it. Relativism is skepticism, and skepticism as a definitive attitude is the suicide of the mind. Relativism is valuable only as an attempt to do justice to the variety and constant flux of life; but it is an unsuccessful attempt, for it sacrifices truth for the sake of life. On the other hand Rationalism, the authoritative mode of thought in Europe since the Renaissance, renounces life to save truth. It is incapable of seeing a meaning in the varied configurations of history and considers it the index of human errors. It would regulate life according to principles. Thus an absolutism of reason that kills life is set in opposition to a relativism of life that dissolves truth. Both attitudes of mind have become equally impossible for us. Thinking and living will not tolerate being set in opposition to each other. Thinking is a vital function like respiration and the circulation of the blood. The thinking consciousness is an instrument of life and at the same time it has the function of enabling us to see things as they really are. Hence, on the one hand, it is ruled by the vital need of the individual and his subjective benefit. On the other hand it consists in an accommodation to things, in submission to objective truth. The same also holds true for the will. Every act of will is the expression of organic energy, but it is also the acknowledgment of an objective norm by virtue of which we prefer a higher value.

This double character of the life of the mind is repeated in every field of activity. The subjective and the objective element mutually determine each other. I cannot think a biologically useful thought unless I think the truth. Life possesses a transcendent dimension in which it goes beyond itself in order to participate in something that is no longer life. Life, as Simmel has said, is at the same time always more than life. The vital functions which are realized in objective laws we call culture. The phenomenon of human life thus has two sides: the biological and the spiritual. In the movement of culture both sides must find their expression. The result of this is a double imperative: life should be culture, but culture should also be life. An uncultured life is barbarism, devitalized culture is Byzantinism. The culture of our time is an unlived culture. Our rationalism has lost its confidence in reason. The same is true of our morality. A morality that is objectively correct but leaves us cold, does not spur us to action, is subjectively immoral. We have a systematized culture but we lack the corresponding vital impulses. What the English call *cant* is merely one form of the cultural hypocrisy general everywhere in Europe. The events of the last decade have compelled Europe to review its position with regard to cultural values. It concluded that it did not believe in its own culture. This discovery has been called a culture crisis. What we need is a new balance between culture and the vital sense, a reordering of the relations between them. European history is the story of a progressive differentiation between culture and life ending in complete separation and opposition. That is the joy and the sorrow of Europe. It is the specifically European experience that Asia has never known. It is a development that began on the day when Socrates discovered reason in the public squares of Athens. From Socrates to the present the history of the European mind has had only one meaning: to put reason in the place of spontaneous life. Today the reverse of this movement is taking place. Socrates discovered the line at which the power of reason begins; we have reached the boundary where it ends. We have passed through the cycle of rationality and rediscovered spontaneity. We are confronted with the task of reintegrating culture with life. It is only since Nietzsche that European man has discovered the autonomy of the values of life. Up until then they had always been veiled by the ideal of a beyond; at first by the religious beyond of Christianity, then, since the eighteenth century, by the cultural beyond of philosophy and science. Culturalism is a Christianity without God, for the kingdom of culture is no less transcendent, with respect to the reality of life, than the Christian's state of bliss. Science is something that can never be perfected in this life. The values of knowledge and of morality are not perfectible even within an endless process of history. For culturalism the meaning of life is always in a better tomorrow. Our real existence has meaning for it only as a passage to a utopian future. The eighteenth century French idea of progress is the preliminary model for the nineteenth century German idea of culture. This culturalism is a form of illusionism. It creates an artificial separation between that which can only exist together: science and respiration, morality and sexuality, justice and the endocrine processes. The aseptic philosophy of culture appears to us today as hypocrisy toward life. The system of values that dominated European existence as recently as thirty years ago has lost its power to attract and its power to shape. Only thirty years ago people still lived for culture. Science, art, justice were undisputed ends in themselves. They alone conferred cultural legitimacy upon human existence. Today we feel otherwise.

The transformation in the European sense of life can best be learned from the new art of our day. In all the countries of Europe, with astonishing unanimity and as though by common consent, the youngest generation is producing an art today that shocks and scandalizes its elders and that even friendly critics do not understand, so that they imagine they are being confronted with a gigantic farce which is spreading over Europe and America like a conspiracy. It is easy to see why! In all previous stylistic transformations in art it was only the aesthetic objects that changed. New forms of beauty were discovered, but throughout these transformations the relations between man and art remained the same. Today we are witnessing a much more radical alteration, not only in the objects of art but in the subjective attitude toward it. Art is no longer taken seriously, so to speak. The religious pathos with which aesthetic pleasure had been invested for the last two centuries has vanished. Art as the basis of life, as the focal point of existence, seems impossible to the present generation. For the new sense of life art only possesses its grace and magic when it is a game and nothing but a game. This shift of emphasis in the realm of aesthetics is the counterpart to the new, joyous and festive sense of life that has arisen in opposition to the nineteenth century's ethic of work. Culturalism rated human performance by its results. Its perspective was economic and utilitarian. In assessing achievement today, we prefer values which, like those of sport, are pure luxury, pure expressions of energy; and we value the same anti-economic attitude, on a much higher plane, in intellectual creation, in political and moral heroism, in religious sanctity. The sad demeanor of work and the pathetic reflections on the duties of man and the sacred tasks of culture have lost their power of conviction. The nineteenth century experienced existence as a hard workday. The youth of the present seems to approach life in a sort of holiday mood.

In politics too a corresponding change has taken place. Here a downward trend has set in. There is less politics than in 1900. No one expects salvation to come from politics any more. We no longer quite understand that in our grandfathers' time people fought at the barricades over constitutional reforms. The word freedom does not intoxicate us any more. For that reason Ortega believes that the age of revolutions is concluded. Political utopias no longer exercise any attraction. We see through their chimerical character. The politics of ideas is being succeeded by a politics of affairs and of men. Above all, however, politics is disappearing from the foreground of human interests. It is becoming a trade like any other, indispensable, but minus the accents of pathetic emotion. People no longer die for political ideas.

It follows that cultural values are not dead but have shifted their rank and place. Their claim to exclusive validity is extinct. Perhaps because of this the antinomy between culture and life, between rationalism and relativism, will become soluble. In reality, both positions are untenable. The subject is not a transparent medium, an immutable, pure ego; but it is no less untrue that the registration of reality on the part of the subject means a falsification of this reality. If a sieve is inserted in a stream, it will let some things pass through and hold others back. It accomplishes a choice, a selection, but not a deformation. Man behaves in exactly the same way in regard to reality. As the eye and the ear perform a choice among the vibrations of the ether, so does the soul of each individual among truths, and so likewise does the soul of every people and of every era. All peoples, all eras participate fully in the truth. Every collective and every individual soul apprehends reality from a point of view accessible only to itself. If different people contemplate the same landscape from different angles, this does not mean that all these views are illusory but rather that each of them is legitimate. "Cosmic reality is constituted in such a way that it can only be perceived from a certain perspective. Perspective is one of the components of reality. Far from distorting reality, it organizes it rather. . . . The *species aeternitatis* of Spinoza does not exist. It is a fictitious and abstract point of view. . . . This way of thinking leads to a radical reform of philosophy and—what is more important—of our sense of the world. The individuality of every subject was the insurmountable obstacle encountered by the intellectual tradition of the past in its attempt to justify the claim of knowledge to the attainment of truth. . . . Now we see that the difference between the worlds of two subjects does not imply the falseness of one of these worlds; on the contrary, it is just because what each one sees is a reality and not a fiction that its aspect must be different from the one observed by someone else. This difference is not a contradiction but a complement. . . . Every life is a point of view upon the universe." The only wrong perspective is the one that considers itself to be exclusive. If every standpoint yields truth, it means that every truth is tied to a place from which it is understood. Hence every truth is tied to a place in space or in time. This localization in space-time is thus a *sine qua non* of truth. It is not merely a mode of perception but belongs rather to the essence of reality. The greatest error that knowledge can commit therefore is to look for a truth that is not tied to any place. That is utopia in every sense of the word. To desire to see something without seeing it from a certain place has always been utopian and uchronic. Each system lays claim to being valid for all ages and for all men. That seems primitive to us today in the same sense as the painting of the Quattrocento. The great philosophies are not images of the world but horizon lines. They determine the horizon of their creators. Only if one were to juxtapose all these perspectives would one possess the absolute truth in all its infinite variety. This sum of all perspectives is omniscience, is God.

These are the basic features of Ortega's perspectivism. He himself discerns in this mode of thinking a philosophical analogy to the physics of Einstein. Be that as it may, one thing may be said: that this perspectivism is indeed the appropriate and convincing expression for the new mental attitude of our time. It is the organizing scheme for the twentieth century form of consciousness. It represents perhaps the sole possibility and the sole instrument by which we and our successors might manage to cope with the multiplicity of vital meanings and cultural values that the intellectual syncretism of the age brings us. We shall not be able to do otherwise than to think perspectivistically. We already do so today, though without being aware of it. But we have only to gain if we raise this process to the level of consciousness. This effort is already being made in many different ways, in many areas, and from many points of departure simultaneously. The art of a Proust, the philosophy of a Keyserling, the studies in *Weltanschauung* and theory of types in Scheler's sense—disparate as these things may seem, they all possess, in their conscious or unconscious tendency toward perspectivism, a common orientation. From this point of view much of the intellectual history of the nineteenth century appears in a new light. In Emerson's universalism, in Sainte-Beuve's relativism, in Nietzsche's psychology ("Every instinct has its perspective. . . .") are revealed to us the seeds of a direction of thought that today has become conscious. We cannot pursue these connections further here or even hint at the unexpressed possibilities and implications contained in perspectivism. My only concern was to trace a few of the lines connecting Ortega's ideology with our intellectual environment. Like all discoveries of the mind, perspectivism, too, has its polygenesis. But it was the Spanish philosopher who first saw it clearly, characterized it, and made it known. He added to it the positive sign of the modern sense of life.

That perspectivism should have been originally formulated by a Spaniard might at first seem surprising. But on closer consideration the fact acquires its historical significance. Spain is geographically and mentally the eccentric country. It provides an excellent observation post for a spectator of Europe. Undisturbed by rivalry, by hatred, or by egocentricity, he will grasp the movement of the various national mentalities more clearly than they can themselves. Yet he will always retain the consciousness of his own particularity. He belongs to a race whose artistic gifts bear their most perfect fruits in the depiction of the concrete human being, in the psychological realism of the portrait. He has been educated by a literature whose masterpieces exhibit the contiguity of various perspectives on life: dream and life in Calderón; Don Quixote and Sancho Panza. He possesses in the painting of El Greco the magnificent example of a fantastic heightening of reality through perspective distortions by the mind and eye of genius. Perhaps perspectivism is the necessary perspective of Spain.

And would perspectivism itself, then, be but one perspective among others? This final conclusion Ortega has not drawn. But it imposes itself inevitably. I see no negation in this but rather a stimulus that will lead us further. Ortega himself after all is a long way from having said his last word. I conclude these reflections with the verses dedicated to him by Antonio Machado ("Al joven meditador José Ortega y

Gasset," in *Poesias completas,* 1917)—may they convey to
the reader something of both the Castilian dignity and the
strict music of this poet:

> A ti laurel y yedra
> corónente, dilecto
> de Sofía, arquitecto.
> Cincel, martillo y piedra
>
> y masones te sirvan; las montañas
> de Guadarrama frío
> te brinden el azul de sus entrañas,
> meditador de otro Escorial sombrío;
>
> y que Felipe austero,
> al borde de su regia sepultura,
> asome a ver la nueva arquitectura,
> y bendiga la prole de Lutero.

[May laurel and ivy crown you, favorite of Wisdom, architect. May chisel, hammer and stone
serve you; may the mountains of the cold Guadar-
rama present to you the azure of their entrails, oh
meditator of another somber Escorial; and may
stern Philip appear at the edge of his royal tomb to
see the new architecture, and bless the offspring of
Luther.]

1924

II

TODAY, as thirty years ago, Germany faces the task of putting the entire material and economic apparatus of its existence in order. We have excellent technicians and experts for
this purpose. We are the nation of experts, after all. But re-
pairing the material damages of war is not enough. On the
level of mind, too, an enormous operation is needed. The
devastation of our culture did not begin only with the Second
World War, but in 1933. The results are that today's genera-

tion of thirty-year-olds no longer has any notion of what a cultural life that is functioning normally looks like. Culture, like electricity, needs conductors, contacts, transformers. It is spiritual energy, but it requires a very complicated and sensitive system of equipment. Does anyone in Germany today think about how this system is to be repaired? Do we have a group of eminent experts for this task as well? Let us be truthful enough to answer: No! Where were the experts between 1933 and 1945? Not in the colleges and universities, not in the muzzled press and bridled literature. Are they to be found today at the innumerable conferences that are supposed to drown out with their speeches Germany's inner emptiness? The "culture festivals" of our cities, the programs of our theaters and concert halls, the noisy commemorations of all kinds cannot mend the dreadful injuries of the last sixteen years. They are only a symptom of the general lack of direction, and they conceal the risk that we may content ourselves with a pseudoculture as under the regime that has just ended. This officially organized pseudoculture is flourishing in the Germany of today. That is one of the reasons why today the thoughts of José Ortega y Gasset have again become very relevant for us.

There are other reasons too.

In 1916 Ortega wrote: "It is a sad war—not only a cruel war. The French are performing their duty sadly, be it said to their credit. But I should prefer to see duty performed somewhat more gaily. . . . I distrust a sad heroism. The Germans are also fighting sadly, though in a different way. They are fighting with rage, with haste, and—forgive the naïveté— with an excessive desire for victory. Is what I say really as naïve as it appears at first glance? The German state is suffering the same fate in this struggle as the German textbooks on war. Should the war be lost, then what the state has done and what the textbooks said will not be good for anything any more. And yet it should be good for everything. A people must not only know how to be victorious; it must also know how to be defeated. It is a sign of spiritual poverty not to be prepared to see in defeat one of the aspects that life can assume."

These are trenchant phrases, caustic and salutary. They are judgments as little pleasing to the victor as to the vanquished and, finally, to the neutral, painstakingly concerned with preserving his neutrality. These are the words of an independent mind. Defeat is a trial like every historical event. What counts is how the nation and the individual react to this trial. Some react with bitterness. That was the reaction of France in 1871 and of the "national" Germany in 1919. Such reactions usually lead to a self-poisoning of the body politic. Today the German public frequently reacts with self-pity. That is weak and effeminate. The manly reaction is to see in defeat one of the aspects that life can assume. Such a reaction is fruitful, for it points to the tasks that lie ahead. It releases energies of will. To understand life as a task—a new task in every situation—is a fundamental feature of Ortega's philosophy.

With that I come back to the task of reconstructing the system of spiritual culture. When cultural devastation has been systematically practiced for twelve years, the damages cannot be repaired in four or five. To do that will require extensive and dedicated labor, for which a decade is not enough. It will only succeed if we take as our starting point the world of before 1933, in other words, a time that has nearly been forgotten.

Spiritual culture is a vital continuity embracing centuries and millennia. It is an error to suppose that it can be rebuilt out of the stunted remains of the mere present—a desperately impoverished and ravaged present. We must reforge the broken links with the past. "To forget the past," writes Ortega in a book published in 1942, "produces the result we are witnessing today: the relapse of mankind into barbarism." But, we might add, there is a tradition of the European mind. We must find an approach to it again. That is more important and more effective than all educational reforms and all experiments.

During the 1920s, Ortega had many and enthusiastic readers in Germany. They found in his work the analysis of our age of the masses, the diagnosis of our spiritual condition. In this thinker philosophy impinged upon the reality of our existence.

Philosophy presents itself to us as a science that can be studied at a university. It is a subject. It is a profession. There are people who are occupied with it in an official capacity, often throughout their entire lives. Is this the only form of existence for philosophy? Does not something dubious cling to it? What have our personal experiences to do with this socially classified, "decontaminated" form of philosophy? I would like to see the German student who has not had the same experience as Goethe's Faust: "I have studied philosophy through and through with ardent effort. Here I stand now, a poor fool." We have all felt the same way. With what hopes we went into our first course in philosophy. And how disappointed we were when we came out. It cannot be otherwise when philosophy is made a branch of learning and a subject for examination.

It was not always that, however. When Socrates conversed with the young men in the squares of Athens, asking them insidious questions with amicable irony, philosophy was something quite different. It was life. A form of life elucidated by questioning and thinking. It was philosophy *in statu nascendi*. It had not become all-knowing as yet. Socrates made the challenging admission that he knew nothing.

Why did Socrates have this inspiring effect? Because he spoke of questions that concerned the conduct of life and because these questions were terribly urgent to him. He could speak of them during an evening's revels and his auditors would hang upon his lips. We are carried away to the same extent as the speaker is himself transported. There must be an exuberance in him that communicates itself to us. Genuine philosophical activity is rooted in a vital enthusiasm. It springs from a new contact with life: a rapturous contact. I allow Ortega to speak for himself: "I regard philosophy as the general science of love. Within the spiritual cosmos it represents the strongest tendency toward universal interrelatedness." Ortega then employs a bold metaphor. "Sexual satisfaction," he writes, "seems to consist in a sudden discharge of nervous energy. . . . In analogous fashion philosophy is a sudden discharge of mental activity." In the movement of thought a progressive clarification takes place. It may culminate, in a Plato or a Hegel, in an explosive illumination. From a theoretical formula immense light flows out over the broad perspective of the world. This formula may prove to be wrong. Perhaps all formulas are wrong. But from their ruins philosophy rises again and again as an eternal urge of the mind.

That enthusiasm for living philosophical thought should be restored to us by a Spaniard was one of the surprises in which the intellectual world of the twenties was so rich. Spain is a country which, during its efflorescence in the sixteenth and seventeenth centuries, brought forth magnificent poetry and painting—but no great architecture and no great philosophy. When the Spanish world-empire sank before the hegemony of France under Louis XIV, the country's power of cultural creation perished with it. Spain seceded politically and spiritually from Europe. It became provincial. European Romanticism discovered it as scenic décor. So it remained throughout the nineteenth century. Spain was the land of the Alhambra and of the bullfight. It was the opera-land of *Carmen*. It was only around 1900 that a spiritual awakening took place in Spain. The renewer of contemporary painting is the Spaniard Picasso. He was born in 1881, Ortega in 1883.

The cultural awakening of Spain is one of the few gratifying events of the twentieth century. And it is of no little significance. Spanish is a universal language, which has an enormous field of expansion in South America. Ortega's books are published simultaneously in Buenos Aires and in Madrid.

Spain had the good fortune not to be touched by the First World War. It was able to derive economic profit from this circumstance. Madrid, around 1930, was a charming mixture of ultramodern luxury and historical patina. An elite of Spanish society was becoming receptive to new modes of life and new ideas. The *Revista de Occidente*, which Ortega edited, took charge of supplying the modern ideas. It transmitted the best of foreign intellectual production. But the elegant city of Madrid was situated on the rugged Castilian plateau. A high blue sierra closes off the horizon, at the foot of which lies the gray castle of God and the monarchy, the Escorial, one thousand meters above sea level. It is the granite embodiment of Philip II's stern dream of dominion. On the terrace in front of the enormous façade the eighteen-year-old Ortega would pace up and down, studying Kant. In 1906 he is in Berlin, in 1913 we find him in Marburg as a student of the great neo-Kantian, Hermann Cohen. In 1932, for the Goethe centennial, he writes about Weimar and Jena. He was ecstatic over what the University of Jena meant between 1790 and 1825: a "fabulous wealth of the highest intellectual incentives." "Thousands of miles removed and still further removed by my difference of race, I cannot hear that name without trembling, I, a little Celtiberian, raised upon a barren Mediterranean plateau."

The encounter of Mediterranean sunshine and Nordic-German climate of thought—and the fertile tension in this encounter—is one of the biological premises for Ortega's intellectual work. One of the tasks Ortega set himself and accomplished was "to enrich the Spanish mind with the torrent of Germanic thought." Nevertheless, Ortega is anything but a mere student and offshoot or continuator of German philosophy. He absorbed it, from Leibniz to Husserl, from Kant to Scheler, as a stimulus in the physiological sense. The stimulus provoked a reaction, a response of the organism. Ortega's thinking found its identity in the collision with the world of German thought. Every true philosopher is born with an original intuition, which later reveals itself to him as his mission. It is a nucleus of thought, which unfolds through concepts and is strengthened by opposition. This productive opposition is the role played by German philosophy for the young Ortega, the Celtiberian from the Escorial.

The Celtiberians are the oldest population of the Iberian peninsula to whom a name can be given. For we know nothing of the Paleolithic peoples who created the cave paintings of Altamira. The Iberians in all likelihood came from North Africa and were related to the Berbers. The Celts, who migrated from the North, intermingled with them. Then came— as settlers, traders, founders of cities—Phoenicians and Greeks, as conquerors, Romans, Vandals, Goths, Arabs. But all of them were foreigners, so to speak. The Celtiberians are the aborigines. The historians of Antiquity relate that they were the only people who worshipped death. A cross-section of Spanish culture would show that it consists of many layers piled one on top of the other like the layers of the earth's crust. But the deepest, most enduring layer is the Celtiberian. It is the primitive rock of Spain. It comes to light whenever the Spaniard searches for his fundamental nature. It is pre-European, nihilistic, wild. All this reverberates when Ortega designates himself a Celtiberian. Many of the most brilliant pages in his work are devoted to the analysis of Spain. They have been collected in a volume entitled, in the German edition, *Stern und Unstern. Gedanken über Spaniens Landschaft und Geschichte* [*Fortune and Misfortune. Thoughts on Spanish Landscape and History*]. To immerse oneself in this book is to imagine that one is driving in an automobile along the magnificent motor roads of Spain. One recognizes the changing aspects of the Spanish earth and receives from Ortega a running commentary on them: a chain of descriptive formulas that illuminate like flashes of lightning.

For Ortega is a stylist of dazzling elegance and colorful profusion. Whether he is speaking of Andalusia or the Argentine woman, of the golf course in Madrid or a restaurant in Biarritz—his sentences shoot off like arrows and hit the target squarely in the center. We feel that we are seeing all things for the first time and, what is more, seeing them in their true shape. Ortega's vibrant sentences trace clear profiles. The things of the world take on sharp contours, and in these contours they reveal their essence. Ortega's art of language might be described as universal characterization.

This art is cognitive prose, and its form is the newspaper article or the essay. This is a scandal to the official philosophers. Ortega has answered them: "The newspaper and periodical article is an indispensable form of the modern spirit, and whoever looks down on it from pedantry hasn't the faintest idea of what is going on historically today." Ortega's early books are reflections on men, books, paintings, landscapes. But however varied the themes, they are always inspired by the same motive: an intellectual love of the world, an *amor intellectualis*. And the aim is the same: to bring all of these things, in the most direct way, to their greatest fullness of meaning.

These works of Ortega's youth radiate a bright, virile enthusiasm. The profusion of life and world that they exhibit seems overwhelming. But the energy of the thought and the accurate handling of the language are equal to this abundance. The happiness of the spectator[3] is a hunter's happiness. He stalks the game and brings it to bay. A festive luster plays about these books. The thirty-year-old thinker sees the dawning of a new age, one that will be richer, more complex, saner, nobler, and that will open up infinite possibilities of experience.

Fullness of possible experience—but dominated by the power of thought. The point at which vitality and reason meet and intersect—that is the creative center of Ortega's philosophy. This is where the contact takes place, where the sparks are emitted. This is the focal point in which all incident rays converge. It is the locus of tensions and decisions.

Let us try to visualize this clearly. A simple example may serve to orient us. In a volume of Ortega's writings we find a letter to an Argentinian student. It reads: "The impression produced by a generation can only be completely favorable

---

[3] A possible allusion to *El Espectador*, the review which Ortega wrote and published.—TR.

when it arouses two things: hope and confidence. The youth of Argentina with which I am acquainted inspires in me—why should I not say it?—more hope than confidence. It is impossible to achieve anything significant in the world unless strength and discipline are combined—these two qualities. The new generation rejoices in a magnificent dose of vital energy, which is the primary condition for every historical enterprise. That is why I have hope for it. But at the same time I suspect that it is completely lacking in inner discipline —without which energy disperses and evaporates. That is why I have no confidence in it. Intellectual curiosity is not enough if one wants to arrive at things; intellectual rigor is needed in order to master them. . . . I should like to discern in your youth groups the strictest demands for inner discipline. But I see exactly the opposite: a hasty effort to reform the world, society, the state, the university, everything external, without preliminary reform and construction of the inner world. On this point I shall never see eye to eye with you. Everything that impels young people to give up the marvelous cosmic sport that is youth; to leave it in order to occupy themselves with the so-called serious things—politics, world reform—is harmful. However serious these things may be—nevertheless, he is the victim of a mere prejudice who unhesitatingly believes that what is serious is also what is important and essential." To the pretended dignity of the so-called serious things Ortega opposes the concept of play in the sense of sport. An activity that has been forced upon us we have the right to perform badly without being ashamed of it. But a game must be played as well as possible. "Just because it lacks external seriousness, because there is no compulsion, it possesses spontaneously a strong inner seriousness." A sublime game of this type is mathematics, ethics, philosophy.

Vital strength and inner discipline: here we have the required synthesis of life and reason in the elementary form of guidelines for young university people. Of course, only for the young people of Argentina.

Let us take a different case: a process of greater historical dimensions. What could have caused the polarity of life and reason, which is one of the chief themes of Ortega's philosophy? Two conditions were necessary: the belief in life and the belief in reason. These two forms of a single faith that excludes religious revelation are of fairly recent date. Christian philosophy of the Middle Ages was a compromise between reason and revelation. But around 1600 reason made itself independent. Two great thinkers personify this process: the founder of modern natural science and the founder of modern philosophy, Galileo and Descartes. An epoch in the history of philosophy begins that has been termed the era of the great rationalist systems. Rationalism is the intellectual attitude of the modern world. But Goethe is already at a point outside rationalism. He is, as Ortega has put it, the first to discover the immanent values of life. The second is Nietzsche. "To Nietzsche we owe one of the most fruitful discoveries that have been made in our era: the distinction between ascending and descending life, between life as success and life as failure." With this, rationalism has passed its peak. Europeans begin to have doubts about the extent of the validity of reason. They incline toward relativism, i.e., toward an attitude of mind that is willing to surrender the belief in an absolute truth in order to respect the fullness of life. Rationalism proceeds in the opposite fashion. It would forgo life in order to save truth. Ortega recognizes this conflict but he overcomes it by a new attitude. He cannot content himself with a human existence that has been deprived of the organ of reason nor with a truth that has been removed from the stream of life. There is no intellectuality without vitality. On the other hand, life, as Simmel rightly observed, is always more than life. It contains a transcendental function. Therefore, the two forces, life and reason, must not be set in opposition. They must interpenetrate each other. A double commandment obtains: life shall be spiritual but spirit shall be vital. To put it another way: culture is only valuable to the extent that it is lived. The mere profession of faith in culture, the mere belief in it, which surrounds it with religious devotion and can degenerate into culture-worship, has no value. The task of our time consists in integrating reason with biology. Pure reason must be replaced by vital reason.

Ever since the animating effect of Bergson there has been a whole series of philosophies called philosophies of life. They have varied greatly in quality. Although unable to eliminate conceptual thought entirely, they set intuition, inner vision, and similar notions alongside it, if not above it, as sources of knowledge.

Ortega's philosophy has nothing to do with these philosophies of life. He adheres firmly to the strict discipline of the concept, he adheres firmly to reason. But he endeavors to incorporate the vital element into reason. He demands a vital reason. It appears in his work as a virtually new dimension of reason. He enforces this demand with the greatest severity, and he has turned with the same severity against all the philosophical directions that have thriven in the last decades—so, for example, against the phenomenology of Husserl and Scheler, but also against the existential philosophy of Heidegger. Whether he has succeeded or will succeed in substantiating, developing, and triumphantly defending the system of vital reason I do not know. I would not and could not live without philosophy, but I am not a philosopher and do not wish to be one. I am a historian and a critic. My subject is literature, and philosophical literature belongs to it. My vital reason forces me into the role of spectator. From this standpoint I follow the intellectual curves of Ortega's thought with passionate interest.

In the past decade it was not always easy to stay on his tracks. The political upheaval that gave rise to the Second World War also spread to Spain. The Spanish Civil War drove Ortega into exile, first to Paris, then to Argentina. He went into exile, but not, be it noted, as an adherent of Red Spain but as an independent, proscribed by both parties. The postwar years he spent in Portugal. Recently he has returned to Madrid to found a free institute for philosophy and the

Humanities. A few of Ortega's books, it is true, were still published in Germany during the Second World War. But a comparison of these texts with the original reveals that certain passages, unacceptable to the Germany of that era, have been omitted. Ortega speaks at one point of the "bestiality of our time" which nothing in the past can equal. That could not be printed in Germany in 1943, although Grillparzer had already summed up the way of the nineteenth century in the formula: "From humanity through nationality to bestiality." From 1944 to 1948 we were cut off from Spain intellectually and postally. Now and then a book by Ortega would reach us after all—from Switzerland or the United States. But it will still be some time before we are able to read everything he has written in these last years.

The polarity of reason and life had determined the thought of the young Ortega. But in 1929 he came to know the writings of Wilhelm Dilthey. He devoted four years to studying them. This tardy encounter with Dilthey cost Ortega, as he says, ten years of his life. As I understand this sentence, Ortega found in Dilthey a historical and philosophical approach to the world of the mind that would have spared him a good many detours. The essay on Dilthey dates from 1933. The work *Über das Wesen geschichtlicher Krisen* [*On the Nature of Historical Crises*] comes from the same year. This was followed in 1935 by another on *Geschichte als System* [*History as System*]. In other words: Ortega's philosophy is turning to a new great theme—history. Vital reason is displaced by historical reason. At bottom, the issue is the same, only the perspective has been altered.

Life, our own and that of others, is immediately given to us. It may be viewed, felt, experienced, accomplished. But it can never be entirely subsumed in thought. The concrete offers an insuperable resistance to the abstract. It is the same with history. It is the realm of chance events. It is chance that a Napoleon was born. And it is chance that Corsica was sold to France by the Genoese in 1768 so that Napoleon was born a Frenchman. The historian can afterwards endeavor to construct a significant pattern out of the facts of history. That is why history has been described as rendering sense to the senseless. The enormous matter of the past must be ordered and reduced to manageable compass. In late Antiquity and in the Middle Ages the succession of the four world-empires was used for this purpose, the Roman empire being considered the last of them. Later this sequence was replaced by the very unsatisfactory division into Antiquity, the Middle Ages, and the Modern Period. Then Spengler and—with an improved method—Toynbee introduced the civilizations themselves as subjects of the historical process. Toynbee's theory of history is the most recent and most impressive synthesis we possess. Along these lines the historical material can be mastered and the contingency of events comprehended. But what no one will ever succeed in proving is that the course of history possesses a logical necessity. Hegel, of course, made a profound attempt to do so. But he had to invent a new logic for the purpose, in which the concepts were endowed with movement. And then he attributed the movement of history to this system of logic. This is the reproach that Ortega directs against Hegel. He himself repeats Hegel's attempt by other means. For Ortega, history, not physics, is the fundamental reality. The stars, plants, and animals have a nature. Man does not have a nature but a history. For that reason the task of thought is to elevate history to a system. The evolution of man is not merely change; it is growth. Every stage preserves the ones that preceded it. Therefore, man only understands himself when he understands the entire past. History is, or should be, the systematic knowledge of the fundamental reality that is my life. However, every intellectual activity that puts us in touch with reality is reason. Hence history must become a rational science. When it has completed its work, it will mean a "new revelation."

These are very bold ideas. Utopian ideas. But Ortega would not consider that an objection.

Let us turn back. Ortega's philosophical starting-point is the fundamental situation of man. If I ask myself what I, as a thinking human being, find present, the answer can only be: I am I and my surroundings. All reality which is not that of my life is secondary reality. My life consists in the fact that I see myself constrained to exist in a certain surrounding world or situation, in a certain "circum-stance" as Ortega says. There is no life *in abstracto*. I am not present to myself merely as a thinking consciousness, as idealism has taught since Descartes. Living means, rather, to be the prisoner of an unalterable environment. One lives here and now. In this sense life is absolute actuality, bound to a particular point in space and time. Everything I do is determined by this unique situation. And my life consists of what I do. One is what one does. At every moment we are faced with the necessity of deciding what we wish to do. Among possible courses of action man must choose those that he conceives as his task. Man is his task. But most men flee from this task because it is inconvenient. They fail their own being, they falsify themselves. The authentic man realizes the project that he carries within himself.

For Ortega the highest moral imperative is sincerity. The absoluteness with which he argues for it leads to extreme consequences. Whatever I cannot sincerely assent to from vital personal sentiment I must discard. Hence there are no eternal models. There are no classics. "A Greek statue," writes Ortega, "seems perfect to me, but this Greek perfection leaves me dissatisfied. And what happens to me, happens to everybody, although hardly anyone is able to see that it is happening to him. The classics exercise a harsh terrorism over the poor souls of today who are so unsure of themselves. . . . The classical life consists of commonplaces."[4]

[4] "La vida clásica se compone de tópicos." *Topos* is the Greek term for commonplace. There is a rhetorical and a philosophical topics. The first mediaeval encyclopedia, the *Etymologiae* of Bishop Isidore of Seville (d. 636) treats the topic as "a simply admirable achievement" (*mirabile plane genus operis*). More on topics may be found in my book *European Literature and the Latin Middle Ages*. In English the word topic has faded to the meaning of "subject of conversation."

These are sentences that sound incisive and irrefutable. One might say, recalling Ortega's racial metaphor, that the Celtiberian is speaking through them.

Even in his early writings Ortega had criticized the belief in culture and the bigoted cultural idolatry of the modern world. But at that time he was still very much interested in the contemporary movement in literature. He wrote on Proust and on Góngora, whose tercentenary in 1927 was so significant for modern Spanish criticism. But gradually symptoms of an estrangement from literature begin to appear. It found expression in 1932 in an article on and against Goethe that attracted much notice. Toward French literature, too, Ortega has adopted a critical outlook. It is, in his opinion, the "normal" literature, but—like everything normal—without summits and without abysses. He is suspicious of Pascal. In 1937 he writes: "Long ago I learned to be on my guard when I hear someone quoting Pascal. That is an elementary hygienic precaution." Rousseau, on the other hand, ruined a century and a half of European history with his insane theory of the natural goodness of man, until after endless catastrophes (which may not yet be concluded) we have learned to rediscover the simple truth with which almost all previous ages were familiar, namely, that man is by origin an evil beast.[5] Ortega has also commented with mordant asperity on Paul Valéry. These are some of Ortega's judgments on French literature. For the last three hundred years France has thought of itself—perhaps correctly—as the land in which one writes best. But "it was also the most reluctant to convince itself that nowadays one cannot live by literature any more."

The philosophers, when they understand themselves properly, have always been the enemies of the poets. The pre-Socratics inveighed against Homer, and Plato wanted to banish the poets from his Republic. Ortega for his part has declared: "We have become accustomed to speak of poetry

[5] I might add that this truth was discovered by Bias of Priene, one of the Seven Sages of Antiquity. It seems to have been lost to later Greek philosophy.

without great pathos. When someone says that poetry is not a serious matter, it is only the poets who are offended." In Germany, too, we have examples of great poets being called to order by philosophers. It cannot be otherwise. For a magnificent intolerance is part of the essence of philosophy. It is part of its nature that it can take nothing seriously besides itself. But the philosopher finds poetry as a component of the world. He has to take it into account. I can imagine a sparkling essay by Ortega in which literature is put on trial. He opens his *Reflections on Technology* with the following sentences: "One of the themes that will be most actively discussed in the next few years is the meaning, advantages, liabilities, and limits of technology. I have always been of the opinion that it is the writer's mission to discern in advance for his readers what will become a problem years later, and to furnish them betimes with clear ideas on the issues so that they can enter the tumult of battle with the serenity of spirit of one who in principle has already decided. 'On ne doit écrire que pour faire connaître la vérité,' said Malebranche, turning his back on literature. For a long time now Western man, whether he takes cognizance of it or not, has ceased to expect anything from literature and craves once more to have clear and distinct ideas about things."

Every philosophy puts forward a totalitarian claim. But only that philosophy can command our respect that knows it is doing so and admits it. Ortega fulfills this expectation. Philosophy, he teaches, possesses a violence that is part of its essence and that is in marked contrast to the pacific demeanor assumed by the philosophical fraternity almost since its first appearance on the scene. Philosophers are generally too polite to discuss this point openly. But the very fact that philosophy exists signifies a permanent and irreconcilable offense to the rest of mankind. It means nothing else, after all, than that without philosophy man is little better than a beast. Where philosophy does not reign, there reigns somnambulism. We all of us who do not philosophize pass our days in a kind of twilight state.

A harsh verdict! But we shall know how to bear it. It is not proved and not to be proved that all men must philosophize. Ortega once spoke, in a critique of the modern natural sciences, about the "terrorism of the laboratories." We could now retort that he teaches a terrorism of clear ideas. This is a spectacle that we rarely get to see. There is something exciting about it, as there is about every procedure in which thought commits itself to an extreme position.

Let us take a few final steps in philosophical knowledge under Ortega's guidance. His first problem had been the antagonism between life and reason. The formula for resolving it was to be the concept of vital reason. Life in its immediacy was then shown to be an aspect of history. Now the task called for was: the system of historical reason. What position, however, is due to natural science in the scheme of human thought? What is the world of physics? Does it affect the reality of our existence? Not at all! Physics is a theoretical system that may have a certain relation to reality but is first of all an intellectual construction. These theories are not real, and reality is not theoretical. Thus the physicist lives in a self-created world of ideas. He is related to it as the reader of a novel is related to the imaginary world that the book presents. A world of this kind we call a "poetic world." It is a product of the imagination, an "inner world." But is physics anything else? Its concepts are constructions of the mind. Physics, philosophy, poetry, religion—they are all inner worlds, creations of the imagination which, according to Ortega, is the "chief organ" of our intellectual apparatus. The world of knowledge is therefore only one of the many inner worlds that man has produced. How are these worlds related to each other and in what do they consist? These are questions that hardly get asked. And yet their solution would be of the greatest importance. Ortega formulated the problem clearly fifteen years ago. Anyone who has some familiarity with the history of philosophy will notice that the problems under discussion have already arisen in Hegel and Schelling. Earlier, Ortega had formally arraigned philosophical idealism, he had mocked the "knights of the spirit." But this system of inner worlds that the creative imagination generates out of itself is, in other formulations, exactly the same as what Hegel called objective spirit. There are inescapable problems in philosophy. They represent the encounter of the mind with itself.

Everything Ortega has written so far bears a programmatic character. It is stimulating and provisional. Will he weave the many threads he has spun out into one fabric? That is our question to him.

1949

Ramón Pérez de Ayala

✦✦✦

THROUGH Unamuno and Ortega the intellectual problems of contemporary Spain were discovered for German readers. But Spanish poetry and the Spanish novel are still little known. That is why I should like to call attention to the work of a man who has, for decades, as poet, as critic, as novelist, been producing an extensive body of work distinguished by strength and full-bloodedness, by magnificent originality and complex spirituality. I am speaking of Ramón Pérez de Ayala, whom the Spanish Republic sent as ambassador to London in 1931.

Of the nineteen volumes of his Collected Works (Editorial Pueyo, Madrid) only one has hitherto been translated into German and, so far as I know, it was promptly forgotten after publication. It is the novel *A.M.D.G.* (Berlin, 1912). The original appeared in 1910. To be sure, this novel occupies a particularly significant place in Ayala's complete work, for it is the first, if not in date of publication, then in respect of subject matter, in a series of four autobiographical novels which also includes *Tinieblas en las Cumbres* (1907), *La Pata de la Raposa* (1912), and *Troteras y Danzaderas* (1913). Although Ayala did not expressly consolidate them into a tetralogy, they do in fact form a unity which sets them off distinctly from his later works and constitutes as it were their solid and ample foundation. Standing out as further groupings within the total oeuvre are three volumes of poetry: *La Paz del Sendero* (1904), *El Sendero innumerable* (1916), *El Sendero andante* (1919); four volumes of essays: *Herman, Encadenado* (1917), *Las Máscaras,* I and II (1917ff.), *Política y Toros* (1918); and lastly a series of large novels, which in distinction to the autobiographical group may be designated objective epics: *Belarmino y Apolonio* (1920), *Luna de Miel, Luna de Hiel* (1924), *Los Trabajos de Urbana y Simona* (1924), *Tigre Juan* (1928), *El Curandero de su Honra* (1930). Finally, several collections of short stories round out the imposing edifice of Ayala's work. The most important are *Prometeo* (1916) and *El Ombligo del Mundo* (1924).

A.M.D.G., that is to say, *Ad majorem Dei gloriam*, bears the subtitle: *Life in a Jesuit College*. It presents the childhood of Alberto Díaz de Guzman—this is the name that Ayala gives to the stylized literary reflection of himself. The novel carries the story of the hero up to the threshold of adolescence and of his days as a university student. It is the sad tale of a richly endowed youth who has been abandoned, in the sensitive years of his formation, to the mortifying mechanism of the Jesuit boarding school. A student novel, then, if you will, except that the tyranny of the secondary-school masters attacked in German novels of a corresponding type is replaced by the sinister anonymity of an institution which is deeply rooted in Spanish history and which, at the same time, subserves an intellectual struggle for power with its basis in very real factors. Even closer than to the German school novel is the work's resemblance to Joyce's *A Portrait of the Artist as a Young Man*, which is also, of course, a settling of accounts with Jesuit education. But whereas in Joyce the experiment ends with the resolute and definitive rejection of any and all religiosity, Ayala's hero remains painfully suspended between the voluptuous, narcotic self-annihilation of mysticism and the tormenting mortification of the personality through asceticism. The depreciation of the world and reality by means of a higher world of the beyond, now enticing with sweet ecstasies, now terrifying with the nightmare of eternal punishments, represents a violation and subjugation of the vital instincts from which Albert will only be able to liberate himself in long years of struggle and suffering.

Ayala's work is too rich for me to describe in a few pages the gradual sequence of metamorphoses which it has undergone up to the present. I shall have to content myself with the merest indications.

Albert's years at the boarding school are followed by a period of self-searching and testing, a whole segment of life filled with experiments of an intellectual and vital kind. They are the apprentice years of a modern intellectual who knows that he was born to be an artist. Art and fame are the young man's guiding stars, but even they grow dim amidst the furious convulsions of tempestuous youth. Albert vacillates between aestheticism and pessimism, between advances toward a great love and descents into a shallow and vulgar assertion of the instincts, between serious efforts at work and self-development and ironic, antisocial humor.

Uprooted from his Asturian homeland, he plunges into the intellectual and social bustle of Madrid, and here, for the first time, he begins to face the historical, national, and literary realities of his country. These experiences are reflected in the novel *Troteras y Danzaderas*, which undertakes a criticism of Spanish literature, culture, and politics. This work struck readers as a *roman à clef* when it was published and, like the earlier *A.M.D.G.*, created a sensation which had strong repercussions in Spain. For foreign readers, these personal allusions are either hardly noticeable or noticeable only here and there as surmises. All the more important, for us, are the typical and symbolic aspects of the book. In precise and highly telling outline, recalling the realism of a Velazquez and perhaps even more of a Goya, the various social spheres and intellectual milieux of the Spanish capital are presented to us: the corruption of politics, the threads of which converge in the hands of cynical opportunists whom the anarchy of the Bohemians opposes as impotently as does the idealism of the young academic intellectuals; the world of the pleasure seekers where wealthy young idlers, gamblers, and adventurers meet with prostitution in every degree, from the expensive courtesan to the brutal and apathetic whore; the world of the theater and of the circus; finally, the stratum of the deracinated intellectuals, in touch with all sorts of criminality as well as with the possessors of power and wealth. In this book the attitude of Ayala's hero Albert is mainly that of a spectator. Only two manifestations of Madrid life provoke him to a strong personal reaction, to a productive dissent; one is the literary activity, the other the efforts at cultural renewal on the part of the young academic intellectuals. Spanish lyric and dramatic poetry, which since Romanticism has been hardening into convention and rhetoric, is here utterly condemned. This melodramatic theatricality, this inwardly false, because unlived, sentimentalism, may enjoy a momentary success with the public; but Albert's artistic sense scourges it for its remoteness from nature and from life, for its intellectual poverty, and draws from this dissent a strengthened conviction of the necessity for a new literature, one nourished by the sources of experience and by the whole wealth of the European cultural tradition. If, in contrast, the representatives of a generation of young academics, trained at German universities and having as their goal the cultural and political renewal of Spain, are painted in more favorable hues, Ayala nevertheless confronts even them with fundamental criticism. It is criticism directed at pure intellectuality; it is mistrust of the philosophical and sociological approach to problems, which exhausts itself in perpetual linguistic confusion; it is, in the last analysis, the reaction of the artist whose concern is for the people, for humanity whole and entire, against the merely cerebral view of the problems of life. The pseudoromantic poet and the philosophical theoretician, these are the two representatives of Spanish intelligence to whom Ayala knows that he is unalterably opposed. During his apprentice years in Madrid, his hero becomes convinced that the entire artificial life of the big city has a pernicious effect upon the best energies of the nation; and he endeavors to return to the simple life, close to nature and to the people, of his rural homeland.

But this negative criticism, though often verging on despair, does in the end liberate the will—by now conclusively restored and unassailably fortified—to self-affirmation, self-assertion, self-creation. In constantly new variations this theme is treated in the great objective novels. Between them and the autobiographical group lies, or so one would like to suppose, a decisive experience of conversion and rebirth of which the author does not reveal anything to us but whose effects we feel on every page of his mature work. Here all the iridescent mists of aestheticism and intellectualism finally dissolve. From this nebulous sea of diffuse sensibility, which at times reflects delusory images of the far away, at others, like a dull flux and oppressive burden, blocks the path to freedom and action, the sun rises in triumph. The poet has now found the way to the elements of nature. Water and fire, air and earth become vast pregnant symbols of the same sort and significance as the two fundamental elements of mankind: pure femininity and vigorous masculinity. Now dramatic destinies take shape, no longer seen from the perspective of the effete intellectual but from the energetic consciousness of a matured manliness, which transfigures heroically and tragically all the natural forms of life and stands with its feet firmly planted upon fertile ground.

In *Belarmino y Apolonio*, which is rated particularly high by French criticism, we are once again transported to the imaginary provincial town of Pilares, in northern Spain, which has the same central significance for the totality of Ayala's work that Dublin has for Joyce. Here, with obvious love and consanguine sympathy, the poet reimmerses himself in the authentic, intact popular culture of his native region—a world full of colorful, vital profusion and odd types —whose geographical remoteness becomes transformed for the reader into a temporal remoteness of centuries. Here we palpably grasp the unity of life, almost entirely free from class struggle, of the Spanish people, a unity which encompasses feudal aristocracy and manual laborers, clergy and notables, peasants and students in a living community founded upon the soil, and in which the stereotyped daily events of a *Piccolo mondo antico* are brought together as on the stage of a Baroque *theatrum mundi*. In this novel Ayala's humor, that

smiling pleasure in the eccentric and grotesque rooted in ancient Spanish tradition, works to especially gratifying effect,
although here too humor finds its complement and resonance
in absorbing and moving tragedy. In the two characters who
give their names to the novel, the versifying shoemaker Apolonio and the philosophizing shoemaker Belarmino, we again
meet the two representatives of Spanish intellectualism
against which the harshest criticism of the Madrid novel was
directed. Only here they are both endowed with the amia-
ble traits of native singularity and transferred from the area
of satire into the region of a humorous and serene observation
of mankind. Nevertheless, anyone familiar with Ayala's entire
output will rediscover in Belarmino the Socratic folk sage
who has already been drawn sketchily in other narratives and
whose harmless mania of a philosophical system based upon
systematic twisting of the Spanish vocabulary suggests, for
all the character's touchingly human traits, the deeper-lying
intentions of the author.

If the erotic problem was a theme frequently raised in
Ayala's other early works, in the two novels which belong together, *Luna de Miel y Luna de Hiel* and *Los Trabajos de
Urbano y Simona*, it becomes the subject of a fundamental
investigation. A web of ideological motives, intricate yet quite
clearly discernible to the attentive reader, determines the construction of these works. Ayala always tends to model the
fables of his novels upon classical motifs of world literature,
be it the Odyssey, the Biblical account of creation, Shakespeare or Calderón. In the novels about Urbano and Simona,
motifs from the late Classical erotic pastoral romance of
Daphnis and Chloe cross with others derived from *La vida
es sueño*. Two twenty-year-olds, conducted by the wills of
their families but also by their own inclination to betrothal
and marriage, both reared in careful, or ought we to say criminal, innocence regarding all matters of life and love, must
make their way on their own and without any direction—unless it be that of the birds and beasts of the field—from a rap-
turously shy, tender devotion to the full realization of a sen-

sual and spiritual love. Misled and deceived by parents and teachers, they must learn to perceive within themselves the voice of the eternal powers of nature and to understand it. The colors of a pastoral idyll are mixed here with an impassioned and incisive criticism of our moral conventions and decorous lies, with the scourging of that entire system of education which traditional clerical morality has imposed upon our society.

Here a word must be said about Ayala's erotic philosophy. If he exposes and castigates the hypocritical treatment of the problem of the sexes with prophetic wrath, no one is further removed than he from a hedonistic or loose conception of the love life, or from one contaminated with the artificial values of romantic effusion. In close conjunction with the treatises on sexual education by the great Spanish physician Gregorio Marañón,[1] Ayala pleads for a reestablishment of the ideal natural form of erotic relationship. With a vigorous, heroic, and severe ethos he proposes a theory of love and marriage which might be designated the normality of genius were the notion of the normal, especially in this area, not discredited by feeble banalities. Ayala's protagonists must suffer many setbacks, must take many a wrong road before they grasp the norms eternally prescribed in nature and the soul and embody them with renewed innocence. But they always aspire to the ideal type of the wholly feminine woman and the wholly virile man, to ideal fulfillment in one lifelong amorous association, to authentic marriage and paternity exempt from everything problematical. The love-bond for begetting the new, pure, vigorous child and for propagating the generations, through whom all values are transmitted—this is the stirring and impressive message of the Spanish writer, and not only in the novels discussed. It is likewise the source of his criticism— also expounded on a scientific basis by Marañón—of Don Juan and Donjuanism, that singular form of erotic anarchy which has been traditional in Spain for hundreds of years and

[1] Cf. his *Aufsätze über das Geschlechtsleben* [*Essays on the Sex Life*] (Heidelberg 1928).

is today again the subject of a particularly lively debate. In the two-part novel, *Tigre Juan* and *El Curandero de su Honra*, the Don Juan problem receives especially searching treatment.

To the superficial reader, Ayala's novels might appear the products of a literary regionalism, but in fact his Pilares only happens to be the site of his existence, a site from which his clear gaze takes in the whole of nature and the cosmos. The poet's Asturian homeland, with its mountain peaks and green meadows, with its veils of mist and its ancient, stagnating villages, nevertheless borders on the ocean, and the roar of its waves can be heard as an elemental force in every one of his works. Pilares or Congosto are more than picturesque or archaic provincial towns; they are also more than the navel of the world (cf. *El Ombligo del Mundo*), as their resident parish-pump politicians and coffee-house intellectuals suppose. They are universally valid symbols of man's dwelling place on earth, of this dwelling place which can make the Franconia of a Jean Paul or the Asturias of Ayala the scene of a hell or a paradise. Not many among the Spanish writers of the present are cosmopolitan in the same degree as Ayala, not only in spirit but in their actual lives. His work again confirms the proposition that the highest intensity springs only from the tension between native roots and a cosmopolitan attitude of spirit.

Inasmuch as he struggles for the new man, the new Spain, the new ethos, Ayala joins the ranks of those minds who have a message to bring to the entire world of our culture. He belongs with the very few novelists whose view of the whole has not been cramped by the ordinary exercise of their craft. He has held himself strictly accountable for the meaning of his work as an artist. His criticism of Spain culminates in the diagnosis that his country, alternating between brutal life of the instincts and foggy dream existence, has hitherto neglected to grasp this real world with the combined powers of sense, soul, and mind. He remarks on occasion that art can serve the goal of a Spanish renaissance more effectively than philosophy and sociology because art provides the Spaniard with the refinement and development of his emotional and spiritual sensibilities. But beyond this goal lies one even further, higher: the vicarious experience of alien destinies, the endurance of tragic careers, in the last analysis the reception and assimilation of all great art implies a heightening and intensifying of the personality, a deepening of the ethos, a strengthening and broadening of the sense of humanity, or shall we say quite simply: a way to virtue, a way to salvation.

The essence of Ayala's work reveals itself ultimately as a powerful ethical force. All struggles and sorrows, all doubts and weaknesses were only the preparation for the bursting forth of a new, vigorous humanity, in which will and idea, instincts and feelings find at last their full, strong accord, an accord which sets down the eternal norms of human existence in a courageously-won new classicism.

1931

James Joyce and

His Ulysses[1]

++

THE *Portrait of the Artist as a Young Man* gives us the self-portrayal and self-analysis of this artist, who in private life is named James Joyce. It shows the forces that influenced him: Irish destiny, i.e., political, cultural, and religious opposition as an atmosphere of life; upbringing in a Jesuit boarding school; the home, poisoned by economic failure with all its humiliating consequences. In these surroundings the drama of Stephen Dedalus's soul is enacted. The stresses of puberty drive him into the arms of a streetwalker, into the dark rapture of sin; he is extricated by a three-day period of devotional exercises in school; Ignatian meditations on the four last things are undertaken; the detailed and concrete representation of the material and spiritual torments of hell plunge the boy into an agony of terror and remorse; he confesses and begins a new, pious life.

But he withers in drought, his faith expires. When invited to join the Order, Stephen declines. He knows he will not be able to fit into any social or religious order. Not for him the wisdom of the priests—he must learn his own wisdom. He will realize the truth of his name, become Daedalus, the winged man who had soared hawklike above the sea toward the sun. "His throat ached with a desire to cry aloud, the cry of a hawk or eagle on high, to cry piercingly of his deliverance to the winds. . . . He would create proudly out of the freedom and power of his soul, as the great artificer whose name he

[1] This discussion was published in 1929. Joyce lived from 1882 to 1941.

327

bore, a living thing, new and soaring and beautiful, impalpable, imperishable."

Stephen studies at the Catholic university in his native city. Aristotle and Aquinas are his masters in philosophy. His sense of literature is shaped by the Italians of the thirteenth century, the English of the sixteenth, Newman's prose, and the modern drama of Ibsen and Hauptmann.

He goes his way in solitude. With analytical coldness and sarcastic derision he judges family, friends, country, morality, and faith. His attitude toward the Irish national Renaissance, toward Irish language and literature, is one of harsh rejection. In solitary moments of philosophical intuition and poetic inspiration the ecstasies of the spirit are revealed to him. We witness something that has never been depicted in literature before, the genesis of a poem: transformation of vision into rhythm and rhyme.

He must break his ties with his country. On an early spring evening, leaning upon his ashplant, he observes the swallows passing in the sky. Like the men of the most distant ages he senses an augury in their flight. His cane becomes for him the curved staff of the augur. "And he felt that the augury he had sought in the wheeling darting birds and in the pale space of sky above him had come forth from his heart like a bird from a turret quietly and swiftly. Symbol of departure or of loneliness?"

The proud, arrogant solitude of his soul drives him to break with his mother: he refuses to go to Easter confession. He breaks with his friend: "I will not serve that in which I no longer believe, whether it call itself my home, my fatherland, or my church: and I will try to express myself in some mode of life or art as freely as I can and as wholly as I can, using for my defence the only arms I allow myself to use—silence, exile, and cunning."

Poor, lice-ridden, loveless, but harboring a wild, bold dream of life and beauty, Stephen goes into exile, in the Latin quarter of Paris.

Sin — art — mind — revolt — exile — solitude — pride: these are the seven fundamental tones in the melody of Stephen's life.

We shall find all of them again in *Ulysses*.

But the way to *Ulysses* goes through *Dubliners* and *Exiles*. It is the way from lyric to epic and dramatic expression. In the *Portrait* this step-by-step sequence in the mode of artistic expression is presented as a psychologically necessary progression. It is the way from purely personal emotion to representation nourished by personality and from there to an impersonal creation with a life of its own.

Joyce had begun as a lyric poet, like Stephen.

The epic poet develops in reaction to the new environment: Dublin; to the misery of existence in the big city. In the *Portrait* we read: "It was toward the close of his first term in the college when he was in number six. His sensitive nature was still smarting under the lashes of an undivined and squalid way of life. His soul was disquieted and cast down by the dull phenomenon of Dublin. He had emerged from a two years' spell of reverie to find himself in the midst of a new scene, every event and figure of which affected him intimately, disheartened him or allured and, whether alluring or disheartening, filled him always with unrest and bitter thoughts."

This is the germ of experience out of which the short stories in *Dubliners* grew. It is a series of photographically precise vignettes of Dublin life. Those who know the city claim that its atmosphere has been re-created with suggestive power. The reader is led through various milieux: middleclass society, political clubs, pimps, drunkards are exhibited in sharply-outlined sketches, only seldom perceptibly tinged with personal emotion.

But the book is at the same time the preliminary study and masterly preparatory exercise for *Ulysses*. Not only that a number of characters appear here for the first time whom we shall meet again in *Ulysses*. But that through *Dubliners* Joyce developed the capacity to use Dublin in his later great work as the symbolic scene of his human tragicomedy. In *Ulysses* Dublin figures as the focal point of all human and cosmic relations. In order to make it that, Joyce had first to record it demographically, as he did in *Dubliners*. Indeed, the connection is still closer. Padraic Colum tells us that the description of a day in the life of Leopold Bloom had originally been planned as a short story within the frame of *Dubliners*. Almost all the pieces in the collection are, after all, stories whose time span is limited to the course of a few hours or of a single day. It is easy to reconstruct such an original form of *Ulysses*: Bloom, or the portrait of a Jewish advertisement canvasser in Dublin. *Ulysses* would then be the synthesis, as it were, of this "Ur-Bloom" and Stephen Dedalus. In *Ulysses* the lives and worlds of both are combined and their paths brought together.

But *Exiles*, too, constitutes an important link in the history of the origin of *Ulysses*. Motifs from the *Portrait of the Artist* turn up again: the unbelieving son's break with his devout mother; exile; the question of Irish culture. The fundamental ethical problem of the play, however, is: can people who are intimately bound up with one another subsist on a basis of perfect sincerity? Richard Rowan, his wife, and his friend have tried this experiment. But the more they wish to reveal their inmost selves to one another, the more impenetrable and inscrutable to one another they become. Two psychological components are at work in this drama: a compulsive urge for sincerity verging on exhibitionism and an awareness of the unbridgeable loneliness of every soul, verging on despair.

Richard Rowan forces his confession of guilt upon his wife, for "she must know me as I am." The strongest motive in the composition of *Ulysses* seems to me to have been an analogous need for self-disclosure or—what amounts now to the same thing—the disclosure of the whole nature of man. The shock effect of *Ulysses* derives not least from the fact that the book breaks through all inhibitions. Moreover, it does so— and this is what is new—by method. Certainly, there are enough books today that intrude into all the zones of sexuality. But never has the entire region of the sexual and excretory functions, and the sensual and emotional reactions that these physiological phenomena may provoke, been scrutinized with such cool scientific thoroughness. These motifs have already been touched upon in the *Portrait*. Stephen tries systematically to mortify his five senses: "To mortify his smell was more difficult as he found in himself no instinctive repugnance to bad odors, whether they were the odors of the outdoor world such as those of dung or tar or the odors of his own person among which he had made many curious comparisons and experiments." Certain scenes in *Ulysses*, which need not be discussed here, stem from this area of experience. So does the obscenity of speech, which in its unsurpassed matter-of-factness must be seen as an ab-reaction of Stephen Dedalus to his adolescent experiences. As a little boy he had already discovered that there are ugly words that one must not utter around the house. Vulgar scribbles, indecent expressions haunt him, burrowing into his imagination and gradually acquiring a compulsive power that shatters all restraints. Now in *Ulysses* all of this is exposed, making the book a museum of sexual psychology and scatology.

Larbaud points out that the models for this objective treatment of taboo areas must not (or not only) be sought in the French Naturalists but rather in the Jesuit moral theologians. He is most probably right. But the influence of Jesuit methods goes much further. To define its limits more precisely would be a tempting project for a specialist. It is known that through the sensual evocation of dogmatic truths the *Exercitia Spiritualia* act with the highest psychological skill upon the imagination of the believer. The subject of meditation is rendered palpably evident by the method of the *compositio loci*, concentrated successively on each of the senses, so that the result is a continuous, sharply-outlined image. Joyce gave an excellent sample of this method in the *Portrait of the Artist*, in the description of Hell which he puts in the mouth of a priest. In *Ulysses* he once explicitly alludes to this method. Moreover, the scrupulous attention paid throughout the entire work to geographical locations (the characters can be followed step by step on a map of Dublin) as well as the question and answer form of the catechism employed in the seventeenth chapter can probably be traced to Joyce's intellectual training under the Jesuits. Perhaps only a Jesuit is capable of doing full justice to these formal merits of Joyce.

Without a doubt the outsider can only with difficulty distinguish between the specifically Jesuit, the Scholastic, and the Catholic element in Joyce. But the imprint of these spiritual powers adheres to Joyce as the *character indelebilis* to the priest. Stephen—even in *Ulysses*—thinks in scholastic terms. Entities, entelechies, forms, and modalities occupy his mind. He exalts Aristotle at the expense of Plato. Dogmatic formulas, such as consubstantiality, serve him as the conceptual dress for his personal problems. Liturgical texts turn up associatively again and again in the fabric of Stephen's consciousness. He has lost his faith and he has no desire to recover it. But this break with the mother church has simultaneously meant a break with the mother of flesh and blood. He refused the dying woman's request to pray. This conflict accompanies him throughout the entire book, throughout his entire life. It is not contrition, for in that case he could repent. But it is a dull, nagging pain.

And there are the other sins, the immodest, unspeakable sins of the imagination and of lust: *The Sins of the Past*; they rise again, assuming masklike shapes and voices. And they appear in the spectral dance of the fifteenth chapter, the Walpurgisnacht and Pandemonium of *Ulysses*. The outward scene is a brothel. But we soon feel that we have left the "real" world for a realm of monstrous and terrifying superreality; a witches' sabbath of dreams and spirits, an orgy of vicious and blasphemous hallucinations that makes Flaubert's *Temptation of Saint Anthony* seem tame and literary by comparison. The whole scene culminates in the perversions of a black mass. Critics have argued about the value and meaning of this chapter. I believe it can only be explained with reference to the profundity of the Catholic consciousness. I see in it neither grotesque humor nor the superiority of a novel artistic experiment nor icy nihilism, but the choking despair of the apostate creature. It seems to me to occupy the same place in the plan of *Ulysses* as the depiction of Hell in the *Portrait of the Artist as a Young Man*. This *is* hell: sin that knows only of itself and nothing of God.

These are the Catholic elements in Joyce's creation. To be sure—a negative Catholicism that knows only the Inferno. It is significant that in the *Portrait*, of the four last things, only the first three—death, judgment, hell—are considered. Paradise is missing in the sequence of meditations. It is missing in *Ulysses* too; it is missing in the art and mind of Joyce. What has become of Stephen's boyhood dream of an ineffable new beauty? What of the "seraphic life" to which he had been transported by his poet's reveries?

The young Stephen had wanted to write books. "Letters were going to be the titles. Have you read his F? O yes, but I prefer Q. Yes, but W is wonderful, O yes, W." They were books that would be written on green oval leaves, copies to be sent after the poet's death to all the great libraries of the world. But these dreams were not realized. Stephen goes to Paris to study natural science. On his return he becomes a teacher at Mr. Deasy's private school. Carries on encyclopedic studies at the National Library on the side, "reads two pages of seven books every evening," associates with literary men and journalists. The editor of the *Evening Telegraph* asks him to write "something with a bite in it" for his paper. "You can do it. Give them something with a bite in it. Put us all into it, damn its soul." But music attracts Stephen too. He is thinking of having his voice trained.

His companions look upon him as an eccentric who suffers from fixed ideas. According to them his mind has been unbalanced by visions of hell. His tragedy is, he can never be a poet. They say that he wants to write something in ten years.

These are the hints from which we must gather the emotional change that separates the Stephen of the *Portrait* from the one in *Ulysses*. But let us not forget that in *Dubliners* the meanness of life, in the *Portrait* the linkage of the soul to the animal body, are already present as fundamental experiences. Since then, to be sure, Stephen's soul has received a fresh wound from the death of his mother and from the remorse connected with it. Perhaps this might explain the bitterness of *Ulysses*: the fact that the poet's dream of beauty has had to yield to the hostile and destructive forces of cold analysis, derision, parody, and blasphemy. And yet, deep inside, the poet has not changed. Even as a boy, on the streets of the city, amidst the noise of drunken men and bargaining women, he had borne his feelings "like a chalice safely through a throng of foes." So in the chapel of the Jesuit boarding school he had carried the censer. And at the beginning of *Ulysses*: "The nickel shaving-bowl shone, forgotten, on the parapet. Why should I bring it down? Or leave it there all day, forgotten friendship? He went over to it, held it in his hands awhile, feeling its coolness, smelling the clammy slaver of the lather in which the brush was stuck. So I carried the boat of incense then at Clongowes. I am another now and yet the same. A servant too. A server of a servant." Joyce himself has informed us through Stephen's mouth of his conception of the artist's identity through changes in time: "As we . . . weave and unweave our bodies, from day to day, their molecules shuttled to and fro, so does the artist weave and unweave his image. And as the mole on my right breast is where it was when I was born, though all my body has been woven of new stuff time after time, so through the ghost of the unquiet father the image of the unliving son looks forth. In the intense instant of imagination, when the mind, Shelley says, is a fading coal that which I was is that which I am and that which in possibility I may come to be. So in the future, the sister of the past, I may see myself as I sit here now but by reflection from that which then I shall be."

A knowledge of Stephen's inner and outer biography (which corresponds to a great extent to Joyce's own) is necessary in order to understand *Ulysses*. But we must not forget that Stephen is not the main character in *Ulysses*. It is

Leopold Bloom. Yet even Bloom not as an individual but as a type. Above and beyond his definition by milieu, race, and moment in time, Bloom grows into a universally valid embodiment of human nature. That is why he bears "binomial" appellations. "Everyman or Noman." He is the "Everyman" of the mediaeval morality, but at the same time the "Noman" (Utis) that Ulysses hides behind from the Cyclops.

With that we come to the problem of Joyce's symbolism. There is a twofold symbolism in *Ulysses*. As Valery Larbaud informs us—and the initiates confirm—the whole work is constructed on a complex scheme of symbolic relations: each episode corresponds simultaneously to a particular science, art, organ of the body, color, and technique. As an example Larbaud cites the fourth chapter, which takes place in the editorial offices of a newspaper. This chapter, according to Larbaud, corresponds to the art of rhetoric, to the lung, the color red, the technique of the enthymeme, etc. It is immediately evident that this scheme has analogies in mediaeval modes of thought. These modes were realized literarily in the theory (and practice) of multiple (threefold, fourfold, sevenfold) scriptural exegesis; ritually in the liturgy; pictorially in the sculpture of the cathedrals. Joyce appropriated this symbolism from the Middle Ages by the same act and with the same intellectual attitude as he did the Thomistic-Aristotelean method of reasoning.

But *Ulysses* also contains a second kind of symbolism: the construction, plot, and characters of the work form a parallel to the *Odyssey*.

The two systems of symbols are interwoven, first with each other, and second, with the matter of the book: the report on the experiences of Stephen Dedalus and Leopold Bloom from the 16th of June, 1904, 8 o'clock in the morning, to the 17th of June, 3 o'clock in the morning.

To understand *Ulysses* completely one would have to grasp precisely how this double symbolism has been carried out. But we lack the key to the first system: a carefully worked-out scheme of concordances. It exists, but only in the possession of the author and a few of his intimate friends. So far criticism has not been concerned with this system of symbols.

All the more has the Homeric symbolism been written about. Its main lines are easy to perceive. How far one wishes to go in the interpretation of details is a matter of taste. A more interesting question is, why did Joyce use this symbolism? Why did he name his book *Ulysses*? Odysseus was Joyce's favorite hero as a child. As an adolescent he read the *Odyssey* again and again, comparing his own experiences and surroundings with those of the epic. Thus we can understand that he was ambitious to revive the figure of his hero. Needless to say, this implies the claim of being esteemed as the new Homer. There is no indication that Joyce would reject such a claim.

It is not solely a matter of Odysseus and Homer, however. Joyce apparently has a strong affinity with Greek mythology. The Daedalus symbol stands beside the Homeric and clarifies it. Odysseus and Daedalus have much in common: intellectual superiority, the gift of invention, sagacity, and the fate of exile and wandering. Joyce found both of them reflected in his own nature. He has identified himself with Daedalus. Over the *Portrait of the Artist* stands an inscription from Ovid "Et ignotas animum dimittit in artes," and the same book ends with the sentence: "Old father, old artificer, stand me now and ever in good stead."

He is at once Daedalus and the son of Daedalus. He is the son who is seeking his father. He is Telemachus.

He identifies himself with Odysseus and is simultaneously the spiritual son of Odysseus. As son he is Stephen, as father he is Bloom. That is why the symbolism of *Ulysses* leads up to the moment when Bloom recognizes in Stephen his spiritual son.

And here we touch on another fundamental theme of *Ulysses*—the father-son complex. In theological terms: the consubstantiality of father and son. This concept from Catholic dogma is also one of the "motifs" of *Ulysses* and intersects with the other systems of symbolism.

The choice of the *Odyssey* scheme is thus only a special instance of the symbolic thinking that, in general, dominates Joyce's mind, and that resides in all of us from time immemorial. It serves the artist Joyce as a means of clarifying and shaping his problems, both emotional and technical.

It is closely bound up with the problem of personality. I can regard myself as Daedalus or as Odysseus. I am I, but I am also the other and yet another. Such displacements of consciousness are normally experienced by all of us in dreams. But in Joyce they are a perfectly regular form of mental progression. The brothel chapter in *Ulysses* offers any number of examples. And in his most recent *Work in Progress*, the "hero" is in the first place Adam, but at the same time he is Noah, Napoleon, the Archangel Michael, etc., and is either called by one of these names, or quite simply named H.C.E. (= Here comes Everybody; but simultaneously = H. C. Earwicker). This is nothing but the next logical development in the form of consciousness and the technique by virtue of which Bloom is at the same time Odysseus.

JOYCE wants to present an *integral* representation of human experience (external and internal experience). He reproduces the stream of consciousness without filtering it logically or ethically.

Association in its various forms plays a principal part in this endeavor. Usually Joyce omits to explain the origin of an association. That is one of the reasons why his work is so hard to understand. I shall give a typical example. After midnight Bloom and Stephen stop to rest in a cabman's shelter. A knife is lying on the table. Stephen asks Bloom to take it away: ". . . oblige me by taking away that knife. I can't look at the point of it. It reminds me of Roman history. Mr. Bloom promptly did as suggested and removed the incriminated article, a blunt, hornhandled knife with nothing particularly Roman or antique about it to the lay eye, observing the point was the least conspicuous point about it." The incident occurs on p. 590 of *Ulysses*. The reader, like Bloom, will not comprehend why the knife should remind Stephen of Roman history. Nor does the author resolve the question.

But if we read *Ulysses* once more from the beginning, we shall find the key on p. 25. Stephen is teaching a class in school. Pyrrhus. His death. "Had Pyrrhus not fallen by a beldam's hand in Argos or Julius Caesar not been knifed to death." Here we have the explanation for the origin of the association "knife—Roman history."

In *Ulysses* such processes of consciousness are simply noted, stenographically recorded.

Once two or more things have been associated, one can stand for the other in the further course of the stream of consciousness. Stephen sees two women on the beach. He recognizes one of them as the midwife, Mrs. Florence McCabe. "One of her sisterhood lugged me squealing into life. Creation from nothing. What has she in her bag? A misbirth with a trailing navelcord, hushed in ruddy wool. The cords of all link back, strand entwining cable of all flesh. That is why mystic monks. Will you be as Gods? Gaze in your omphalos." Hence, navelcord—contemplation of the navel—sequence of generations—first beginning—creation from nothing. From there Stephen's meditation moves on to the original mother, Eve. "Naked Eve. She had no navel. Gaze. Belly without blemish, bulging big, a buckle of taut vellum, no, whiteheaped corn, orient and immortal standing from everlasting to everlasting. Womb of sin." The image of naked Eve summons up the idea of a heap of white corn.[2] This explains the stenographic notation of consciousness a hundred and fifty pages further on: "Eve, Naked wheatbellied sin," and similarly later: "Orient and immortal wheat standing from everlasting to everlasting" (232). The result is the relationship: navel—body—(sin)—wheat.

From this, initially meaningless, chain of associations a significant symbolism emerges quite by itself. "Navel," as we

---

[2] The comparison is Biblical. "Umbilicus tuus crater tornatilis: nunquam indigens poculis. Venter tuus sicut acervus tritici vallatus liliis." Song of Solomon: 7:2.

have seen, means self-contemplation. The Greek word for it is omphalos. The island of Delos was called ὄμφαλος θαλάσσης. Ireland is an island. We should Hellenize it, suggests Mulligan. From the combination of these ideas we can understand Stephen's musing: "To ourselves . . . new paganism . . . omphalos"; and Mulligan's sentence: "Billy Pitt had them[3] built, when the French were on the sea. But ours is the omphalos."

Even further: navel of the sea—birth—the sea as mother —the wine-colored sea—blood. "Isn't the sea what Algy[4] calls it: a great sweet mother? . . . Epi oinopa ponton." And Stephen: "Tides, myriadislanded, within her, blood not mine, oinopa ponton, a winedark sea."

The sea—primal element, lifegiving and deathbringing— washes round the symphony of experience that is *Ulysses*. The motif of the drowned man runs through Joyce's work as it does through Eliot's *Waste Land*. In reality: Mulligan has saved the life of a drowning man by artificial respiration. A boatman reports on another, who was not saved. "There's five fathoms out there. It'll be swept up that way when the tide comes in about one. It's nine days to day."—The motif is then given a literary reflection; Stephen is taking up *Lycidas* with his pupils.

> For Lycidas, your sorrow, is not dead,
> Sunk though he be beneath the watery floor.

In Stephen's meditation on the beach both these motifs are mingled: "Five fathoms out there. Full fathom five thy father lies.[5] At one he said. Found drowned. A corpse rising saltwhite from the undertow. . . . There he is. Hook it quick. Sunk though he be beneath the watery floor. . . . A seachange this, brown eyes saltblue. Seadeath, mildest of all deaths known to man. Old Father Ocean."

Stephen is not a hero, could not save anyone from drowning: "You saved me from drowning. I'm not a hero however."

---

[3] The watch towers.   [4] Algernon Charles Swinburne.
[5] Ariel's song from *The Tempest*.

He cannot save anybody. He could not save his mother from dying: "A drowning man. His human eyes scream to me out of horror of his death. I . . . with him together down . . . I could not save her. Waters: bitter death: lost."

Stephen meets his sister. At home there is bitter poverty. He cannot help. "She is drowning. Agenbite. Save her. Agenbite. All against us. She will drown me with her, eyes and hair. Lank evils of green death. —We. —Agenbite of inwit. Inwit's agenbite. —Misery! Misery!"

These examples are a concrete illustration of how a motif is at once presented by the reality of external events, reflected in literary form (Milton, Shakespeare), and expanded by Stephen into a symbol of the problems of his own life: death, distress, grief, remorse. For in the last quotation the seadeath-theme blends into that of remorse: "Agenbite of inwit."

Remorse, or rather the pangs of conscience, the again-bite (re-mords) of conscience (inwit) is one of the factors that dominate Stephen's inner life. And Stephen-Joyce gives it the name of the Middle-English devotional tract by Dan Michel of Northgate, *Againbite of Inwit*. Like a musical leitmotif this name recurs significantly again and again in *Ulysses*.

We see, then, that in its associative structure Stephen's thought, the thought of a student of the Jesuits, always shows a tendency toward philosophical and theological speculation. Joyce characterizes the persons in his book by exhibiting the different directions taken by their individual processes of association.

Bloom's consciousness goes in ways entirely distinct from Stephen's. Bloom is a canvasser of advertisements. His ideal is "improvement all round"; amelioration of the world through reason and benevolent accord. No violence! No revolutions! Let tolerance and convenience be spread. Every man should have a comfortable, moderate income of around 300 pounds per annum. Bloom is a lover of life, of women, of music—all after his own fashion, of course: utilitarian, sensual, philistine. His associations match his outlook. Commercial slogans haunt him. He reads in the newspaper:

What is home without
Plumtree's Potted Meat?
Incomplete.
With it an abode of bliss.

This returns, in disconnected verbal fragments, all day long.

More food for thought is given him by the announcement for a model farm in Palestine, Agendath Netaim. Berlin Agency: Bleibreustrasse 34. He finds the prospectus at a pork butcher's, reads it carefully, later recalls the name of the firm again ("Agenda what is it?"), etc.

Sensuously sentimental melodies trail after him. The operetta *Rose of Castile*. Roses, language of flowers, women; my wife, Mrs. Marion Tweedy Bloom, was born in Spain; last rose of summer, last rose of Castile . . . and the banal motif goes on in this way.

Women. Their odor—perfume. The postscript in Martha Clifford's letter: "What kind of perfume does your wife use?"

Eroticism in music. In cosmetics. In literature. At a secondhand book dealer's Bloom asks to see some indecent books. *The Sweets of Sin*—that ought to be something. And he reads a few sentences that speak of "queenly shoulders" and heaving embonpoint, of expensive underwear, and finally of a certain Raoul for whose enjoyment all of it is intended. Traces of his reading rise to the surface later in his stream of consciousness: "Hands felt for the opulent, felt for the curves." Bloom acquires this promising work for his wife.

For she had just that morning got finished with her latest trashy novel, *Ruby: the Pride of the Ring*. One of the words in it had puzzled her: *metempsychosis*. She had pronounced it "met him pike hoses." But he explained to her what it meant. Transmigration of souls. The Greeks believed that people could be transformed into animals or trees. "What they called nymphs, for example."

This little occurrence of a feminine-philological character sticks in Bloom's consciousness. "Met him pikehoses she called it till I told her about the transmigration. O rocks!" At noon he encounters a blind stripling and helps him across the street. Poor young fellow! Terrible. Life a dream for him. Where is God's justice there? Or is it just after all? And are we punished in this life for the sins of a previous life? "Karma they call that transmigration for sins you did in a past life the reincarnation met him pikehoses. Dear, dear, dear." Finally, at night, Mrs. Bloom, half asleep and thinking about her husband: "that word met something with hoses in it and he came out with some jawbreakers about the incarnation he never can explain a thing simply."

Mrs. Bloom's emotional structure is simple and massive: for her only sex exists. In her nocturnal reflections she passes in review the entire chain of her adventures. The first time? Yes, that was that time in Gibraltar (they called her señorita). With the handsome Lieutenant Mulvey. My husband knows, knows about most of them; but not all.—

From the variegated fabric of *Ulysses* I have detached a few strands. If the reader has kept up with me he will now be in a position to understand the following passage, which reproduces Bloom's reflections after he has been sexually aroused (the object is not, as one might suppose, Mrs. Bloom, however, but an adolescent flapper named Gertie MacDowell): "O sweetie all your girlwhite up I saw dirty bracegirdle made me do love sticky we too naughty Grace darling she him half past the bed met him pike hoses frillies for Raoul to perfume your wife black hair heave under embon señorita young eyes Mulvey plump years dreams return next in her next in her next."

This passage is a good example of the coalescence of several series of associations; and of the difficulty of Joyce's text. But these difficulties can be solved. One must only have the patience to read the book very precisely until one has become familiar with all the psychological cues. That is not an easy task, in view of the dimensions of *Ulysses*. But Joyce's art can be fully appreciated only by someone who has analyzed the immense motivic intricacy of the work. *Ulysses* is an intellectual puzzle. All one sees at first is a chaos of irregularly formed building blocks. But with patience we can consolidate them into a magnificent picture. And then we shall not cease to be astonished at the sheer infinite variety of relationships and possible combinations revealed by such a task.

So far I have spoken only of the reproduction of the stream of consciousness. But in the same way as the associations, the events and characters can only be apprehended clearly by using a synoptic procedure.

At the beginning of the book Bloom is contemplating his garden. Ought to be manured and newly planted. Could sow peas, lettuce. Always have fresh vegetables. "Still gardens have their drawbacks. That bee bluebottle here Whitmonday." We understand nothing at first. But on p. 155 Bloom is thinking of the young medical student Dixon: "Who dressed that sting for me in the Mater and now he's in Holles Street where Mrs. Purefoy." And after several hundred more pages we learn that on 23 May 1904 (Whitmonday) Bloom was stung by a bee in the left intercostal region below the diaphragm. These are the drawbacks of a garden then. But that is not enough. The same bee sting is parodied in comic epic style. "And the traveller Leopold was couth to him [Dixon] sithen it had happed that they had had ado each with other in the house of misericord where this learning knight lay by cause the traveller Leopold came there to be healed for he was sore wounded in his breast by a spear wherewith a horrible and dreadful dragon was smitten him for which he did do make a salve of volatile salt and chrism as much as he might suffice."

Finally the motif is introduced into the apocalyptic infernal Sabbath of the fifteenth chapter. Among the grotesque specters that appear in this nightmare we find a "Brother Buzz." The word "buzz" occurs soon after in one of Virag's speeches and immediately awakens in Bloom the recollection: "Bee or bluebottle too other day butting shadow on wall dazed self then me wandered dazed down shirt good job I. . . ." Virag's reply, consistently with the atmosphere of the chapter, converts the incident into something comically suggestive.

In this way a trivial fragment of experience is treated as a musical theme, so to speak, and presented in a series of variations. This is one of the techniques Joyce has taken over from musical composition. Of course the analogy is only partial. The literary variation differs from the musical in this particular: that the theme is incomprehensible on its first entrance and unfolds its significance only in the course of the variations.

We can soon observe how it works in the "potato-theme." It enters toward the beginning of the book, when Bloom is getting ready to leave the house. "On the doorstep he felt in his hip pocket for the latchkey. Not there. In the trousers I left off must get it. Potato I have. Creaky wardrobe. No use disturbing her." So, he does not have his latchkey with him. It is still in his other suit. But if he opens the creaky wardrobe he will disturb Mrs. Bloom, who is not awake yet. Everything clear but for "Potato I have." This is on p. 55. Later in the day Bloom is looking for something in his pockets. "Try all pockets. Handker. Freeman. Where did I? Ah, yes. Trousers. Purse. Potatoes. Where did I?" Combining both passages we get: Bloom is carrying a potato around in his hip pocket. Whatever for? The answer is to be found on p. 404. The whole page consists of nothing but torn scraps from the conversation of a large group of people. These scraps have been strung together without any differentiation as to the speakers. From the hubbub of voices we detach the following fragment: "Spud[6] again the rheumatiz? All poppycock, you'll scuse me saying."—So, one of the speakers believes that potatoes are good for rheumatism, a belief labeled nonsense by his interlocutor. Now we know why Bloom carries a potato around, and why he carries it in his hip pocket.—In chapter 15 his mother's ghost appears to him. She is dismayed at the condition she finds him in, looks for her smelling salts, rummages through the pouch of her striped, slate-gray petticoat: "A phial, an Agnus Dei, a

[6] Slang expression for potato.

shrivelled potato and a celluloid doll fall out." So Bloom has taken over the belief in the healing power of the potato from his mother. That Bloom really does need the potato talisman we only gather from his words on p. 496, however: "I have felt this instance a twinge of sciatica in my left glutear muscle. It runs in our family."

Both the bee-sting and the potato theme are a superb contribution toward the characterization of Bloom. Medicine, hygiene, cosmetics are among his main fields of interest. That is why the bath and the purchase of soap play such a large role in his daily round. He is very much preoccupied with his health ("if his nose bleeds you'd think it was O tragic"). He has picked up a vast knowledge of popular medicine, so that he is called "Mr. Knowall" by his acquaintances, is introduced in a parodistic passage as "Professor Luitpold Blumenduft," knows how to write prescriptions, and sees to the distribution, among other useful books, of a medical advice sheet, *Expel that Pain*. The "new nine muses" of this modern Jewish Greek are: Commerce, Operatic Music, Amor, Publicity, Manufacture, Liberty of Speech, Plural Voting, Gastronomy, Private Hygiene, Seaside Concert Entertainments, Painless Obstetrics and Astronomy for the People (463).

The muse of "Painless Obstetrics" is so typical of Bloom because two of his chief interests merge in this ideal figure: the bringing about of a condition for mankind in which pain, poverty, war, sickness, race prejudice, and intolerance are eliminated, in other words, the new Jerusalem ("the new Bloomusalem in the Nova Hibernia of the future");—and, secondly, his interest in the mysteries of generation and birth.

Our analysis of the Omphalos-complex has already shown that birth is one of the central themes of *Ulysses*. This applies to Stephen as well as to Bloom. An entire chapter (the fourteenth) takes place in a lying-in hospital and provides the occasion for detailed discussions of "the gravest problems of obstetrics and forensic medicine." Generation and fertilization are debated not only from the medical and juridical, but also from the medicynical and theological standpoint. *Per deam Partulam et Pertundam!*

The theme of birth can be designated as the locus where all the fundamental motifs of *Ulysses*, and indeed of Joyce's entire conceptual world, intersect.

This is the point from which the complex of the father-son problem unravels. But the problem of sexual polarity—of the relation between the male and the female principle—is intricately intertwined with it as well.

This second theme comes up for the first time in Bloom's consciousness when, in the morning, he sees an announcement of a theatrical representation. "Leah tonight; Mrs. Bandman Palmer. Like to see her in that again. Hamlet she played last night. Male impersonator. Perhaps he was a woman." Hamlet played by a woman. Perhaps he was a woman? Bloom raises the question to himself probably without being aware that a commentator on Shakespeare advanced the same hypothesis, as we learn on p. 190. In this way the androgyne-motif is introduced. Is the polarity between man and woman perhaps not absolute? Can a man be a woman at the same time? Give birth? The literary theme of male pregnancy enters. Stephen: "Boccaccio's Calandrino was the first and last man who felt himself with child." In nature it is not possible, but "in the economy of heaven, foretold by Hamlet, there are no more marriages, glorified man, an androgynous angel, being a wife unto himself." The cynical Mulligan seizes upon these words of Stephen's and outlines the plan of a satirical comedy *Everyman His Own Wife*, but is himself later teased about his corpulence by the medical student Dixon, who asks him whether it indicates "an ovoblastic gestation in the prostatic utricle or male womb."

In the grotesque mummery of the fifteenth chapter Bloom is then presented as "a finished example of the new womanly man." He exclaims, "O, I so want to be a mother," and with the assistance of the midwife Mrs. Thornton bears eight fine boys "with valuable metallic faces." Later he appears as a whore, while the brothelkeeper Mrs. Bella Cohen changes into the male brute Bello. The latter two transformations can be explained as hallucinatory realizations of the perverted masochistic and fetishistic instincts which are part of Bloom's makeup. The development of these perversions is due to his experiences at puberty, and especially to his having played the part of a woman on the stage.

These are little defects in Bloom's moral character. But fundamentally he is of a benevolent, even lovable nature. He is kind to old women, to the blind, to beggars and animals. And he has strong family feelings. He often thinks nostalgically of his poor father, who took his own life. He mourns for his son, little Rudy, who died at eleven days old. Now he is the last of his race. "No son."

Bloom is without a son—Stephen without a father. Although his bodily father, Simon Dedalus, is still alive, Stephen has renounced him along with the rest of his family. He denies physical paternity altogether. Fatherhood has no meaning save as spiritual generation. "Fatherhood, in the sense of conscious begetting, is unknown to man. It is a mystical estate, an apostolic succession, from only begetter to only begotten."[7]

Stephen is in search of his (spiritual) father. That is why he is Telemachus. Or, in Christian symbolism, *the eternal son*. That is why his problem is to be united with the father: "The son striving to be atoned with the Father." That is why he reflects on the dogma of the consubstantiality of father and son. That is why he is preoccupied with the heresies of Arius and Sabellius. He even interprets Hamlet with reference to these problems: the ghost of the King is Shakespeare himself, and Prince Hamlet is the embodiment of Shakespeare's son, Hamnet, who died at eleven years old.

Finally, Stephen finds himself likewise in the situation of

---

[7] That fatherhood can only be conceived pneumatically and theomorphically is an idea of Christian speculation that goes back to Paul: "Flecto genua mea ad Patrem Domini nostri Jesu Christi: ex quo omnis paternitas in coelo et in terra nominatur" (*Eph.* 3:15).

the prodigal son: "Filling my belly with husks of swine. Too much of this. I will arise and go to my," which equals "I will arise and go to my father and say to him: Father, I have sinned in heaven and before thee." Here the theme of sonship merges with the theme of remorse.

The son is the Logos, the word. If Bloom is entirely on the side of life, stands for instinct, revolves around woman, then Stephen is the man of the spirit, which destroys life but overcomes it at the same time: "In woman's womb word is made flesh but in the spirit of the maker all flesh that passes becomes the word that shall not pass away. This is the postcreation."

The icy coldness of pure mind envelops Stephen like an impenetrable aura. His thought transcends earthbound reality in every direction. He wants to shake off history like a nightmare. He broods upon the metaphysics of potentialities that never became actualities. He meditates on the collapse of time and space and on the reciprocal relation of these two systems of order.

The relativizing of all fixed categories is perhaps the most comprehensive theoretical perspective from which to contemplate Joyce's work. Relativity of space and of time, of the actual and of the potential, of the personality, of sexuality, of life and of death. It is only through this mode of vision that Joyce was able to shape the Walpurgisnacht of the fifteenth chapter, in which inanimate objects speak, the dead or absent appear, bestial and human, male and female forms are mingled and transposed. But also the symbolism and the parody, indeed ultimately the entire composition of *Ulysses* is founded upon aesthetic relativism.

To show this graphically, I should like to analyze the technique of two chapters of *Ulysses*.

The eleventh chapter (pp. 245–279) exhibits a special technique that Joyce employed only here. The scene is the Ormond Restaurant in Dublin. The two waitresses, Miss Douce (haircolor: gold)[8] and Miss Kennedy (haircolor: bronze),

8 Curtius has reversed the colors.—TR.

both in black satin blouses, are looking out of the window, watching the viceregent of Ireland passing by with his wife and procession. —The house porter brings them their tea, and makes a rude remark, which is resented as "impertinent." The porter mutters the word under his breath. —Simon Dedalus enters, tearing splinters off his thumbnail. —Miss Douce makes an off-color remark; Miss Kennedy blushes at it and chides. —Dedalus takes his pipe out of his pocket and blows into it, producing two hoarse flute tones. —Bloom is strolling meanwhile through the streets of Dublin. —Miss Douce trills a tune from the opera *Rose of Castile*. —Miss Kennedy is sitting in the corner, reading. Lenehan tries to arouse her attention. —Miss Douce tells of the piano player who had been there today. She pities him on account of his blindness. A diner's bell rings shrilly.—The tuner has left his tuning fork. Somebody strikes it: a slow dying call. —Lenehan attracts Miss Kennedy by a whistle and a call. —Singing is heard and piano accompaniment. —Boylan pays. A coin rings as it falls on the table. —The clock strikes. —Benjamin Dollard sings: love song of a warrior. —Then Cowley sings: Farewell of a girl standing on the deck of a ship, her veil waving in the wind.

That is a small selection of the incidents in this chapter. It was necessary for an understanding of the technique.

For at first we do not understand anything at all. I reproduce the beginning of the chapter in the typographical arrangement of the original, only with numbers added.

1.) Bronze by gold heard the hoofirons, steelyringing.
2.) Imperthnthn thnthnthn.
3.) Chips, picking chips off rocky thumbnail, chips.
4.) Horrid! And gold flushed more.
5.) A husky fifenote blew.
6.) Blew. Blue bloom is on the.
7.) Gold pinnacled hair.
8.) A jumping rose on satiny breasts of satin, rose of Castile.
9.) Trilling, trilling: Idolores.

10.) Peep! Who's in the . . . peepofgold?

11.) Tink cried to bronze in pity.

12.) And a call, pure, long and throbbing. Longindying call.

13.) Decoy. Soft word. But look! The bright stars fade. O rose! Notes chirruping answer. Castile. The morn is breaking.

14.) Jingle jingle jaunted jingling.

15.) Coin rang. Clock clacked.

.   .   .   .

16.) Boomed crashing chords. When love absorbs. War! War! The tympanum.

17.) A sail! A veil awave upon the waves.

So it continues throughout the entire next page. But what does this apparently senseless introductory text that fills two whole pages, mean?

It constitutes an overture: it presents, arranged in a disconnected series, some of the main themes of the following twenty-two pages.

I elucidate:

1: Bronze by gold, Miss Douce's head by Miss Kennedy's head, over the crossblind of the Ormond bar heard the viceregal hoofs go by, ringing steel (246/7).

2:—Imperthnthn thnthnthn, bootsnout sniffed rudely, as he retreated (247).

3: Into their bar strolled Mr. Dedalus. Chips, picking chips off one of his rocky thumbnails (250).

4: O, Miss Douce! Miss Kennedy protested. You horrid thing! And flushed yet more (250).

5: He blew through the flue two husky fifenotes (250).

6: Blue Bloom is on the rye (251).

7: Kennygiggles, stooping her fair pinnacles of hair (249).

8: (Miss Douce) sighed above her jumping rose (250).
—combines with: their blouses, both of black satin (248).

9: Gaily Miss Douce polished a tumbler, trilling:
—O, Dolores, queen of the eastern seas! (251).

10: —Peep! Who's in the corner? (251).

11: Tink to her pity cried a diner's bell (252).

12: From the saloon a call came, long indying. That was a tuningfork . . . (253).

13: Lenehan's lips over the counter lisped a low whistle of decoy.
—But look this way, he said, rose of Castile (253).
This combines with:
—The bright stars fade. . .
A voiceless song sang from within, singing:
—. . . the morn is breaking.
. . . birdnotes chirruped bright treble answer (253).

14: Jingle jaunty jingle (251).

15: Coin rang (254). —Clock clacked (255).

16: Over their voices Dollard bassooned attack, booming over bombarding chords:
—When love absorbs my ardent soul. . .
—War! War! cried Father Cowley. You're the warrior. . . . Sure, you'd burst the tympanum of her ear, man, Mr. Dedalus said. (259).

17: Softly he sang to a dusty seascape there: A Last Farewell. A headland, a ship, a sail upon the billows. —Farewell. A lovely girl, her veil awave upon the wind. . . .

Joyce's procedure ought to have become plain. We see that the two pages of apparently senseless text form a complete and carefully worked out composition—which, needless to say, cannot be understood until the entire chapter has been read, and read very thoroughly. This literary technique is an exact transposition of the use of motifs in musical structure or, to be more precise, of the Wagnerian technique of the leitmotif. With this difference, however, that a musical motif is complete and aesthetically satisfying in itself; and that I can enjoy listening to a Wagnerian leitmotif with pleasure even if I do not know the meaning (Valhalla? Walsungs?). The

351

word-motif, on the other hand, remains a senseless fragment and only receives its meaning from the context. I cannot make anything of "Horrid! And gold flushed more." This profound distinction between the nature of word and sound Joyce has deliberately ignored. For that reason his experiment remains questionable.

In the twelfth chapter Joyce has employed yet another technique. The whole chapter is in the form of a first-person narration. The narrator, whose name we are not told, earns his living as a "collector of bad and doubtful debts." On a business errand he runs into his friend Hynes. Both repair to Barney Kiernan's tavern, there to meet the "Citizen": a drinking companion and gabber, Giltrap by name. They are joined by others; there is lots of drink and talk. The scene ends with an altercation between Giltrap and Bloom. The Citizen makes anti-Semitic remarks and finally resorts to violence by hurling an empty biscuit box at Bloom. All these incidents are related by the narrator in a highly realistic manner. But his report is constantly interrupted by parodic episodes, which are, of course, never marked off as such. There are perhaps thirty such interpolations all told. They vary in length from a few lines to two, and once even to four, pages. Their connection with the monologue is that the incidents, topics of conversation, and items mentioned in the narrator's report are used as motifs for stylistic amplification.

In addition, the handling of the parodies ranges from "authentic"-sounding pastiche to caricature, fantastic grotesquerie, and blasphemous travesty. The parodied styles range in like manner: legal jargon; heroic epic; minutes of a theosophical society; Ossianic lament; scientific, literary, fashion, and sports journalism; schoolboy composition; grammar lesson; church ceremony; Catholic credo. For the most part the parodic pieces are a satire on the "Celtic Renaissance"; the movement in whose intellectual, cultural, and political atmosphere Joyce had grown up.

But thus every one of the eighteen chapters has its own technique and would require separate analysis. One thing all the chapters do have in common, however—and all our analyses have borne this out—: each passage, each sentence, each phrase only becomes comprehensible with reference to another. Here too Joyce's creation reveals its affinity with music. *Ulysses* must be read like a score; it could be printed like one. In order really to understand *Ulysses* one would have to have the entire work present in one's mind at every sentence—which is virtually impossible. But what does that signify measured against the power of sustained mental effort that the author had to have at his disposal in order to keep track during the conception and execution of his work of its thousands of correspondences, and to rivet them together into a totality hard as steel? Considered merely from this standpoint *Ulysses* must appear as an absolutely unparalleled, as a gigantic achievement.

It is clear that the relativizing of all categories of existence and thought would also have to invade the language. Words and names are linked associatively, distorted, twisted out of shape. *Bloom* is apocopated to *Bloo*, lengthened to *Bloohoom* and *Booloohoom*. Contamination with *who, whose, whom* results in the declension *Bloowho, Bloowhose, Bloohimwhom*. By way of *greasy* and *sea* we get *Greaseabloom* and *greaseaseabloom*. *Bloom—Blume—flower* lead to *Blumenduft* and *Don Poldo de la Flora*. His first name leads to *puffing Poldy, Jolly-poldy, Leopoldleben, Sir Leo Bloom, Lionelleopold*. A misprint changes the hero to *Boom*, and that is what the author then calls him, "to give him for the nonce his new misnomer."

This treatment of language results in innumerable, more or less good puns: *Lawn Tennyson*; *Margaret Mary Anycock* (*Alacoque*); *Beau Mount and Lecher*; *San Tommaso Mastino*; *Thursdaymoomun* (*Desdemona*).—The playing with language leads to syllable reduplication and word compounds: "Just mix up a mixture of theolologico-philolological. Mingo, minxi, mictum, mingere; pornosophical philotheology."—In addition, languages are mixed: "She trudges, schlepps, trains, drags, trascines her load; grandoldgrossfather."

Sometimes the language relapses into inarticulate sounds. "His mouth moulded issuing breath, unspeeched: ooeeehah: roar of cataractic planets, globed, blazing, roaring wayawayaway-awayawayaway."—Syllables are permuted: "Plumtree's Potted Meat" (Plumtree—meat—pot) yields "peatmot—trumplee—montpat—plamtroo."—Essex and yes becomes "Yessex."—Lydia Kennedy + George Lidwell produces "Lidlydiawell."—*Talafana, alavatar, hatakalda, wataklasat* are theosophical kitchen Sanskrit.

In Joyce's most recent work, *Finnegans Wake*, the destruction of language is completed.

With which literary genre is *Ulysses* to be classed? The book is chronicle ("this chaffering allincluding most farraginous chronicle") — novel — drama — epic — satire — parody — summa. It is a new *Inferno* and a new *Comédie Humaine*. The fifteenth chapter is a cross between the *Tentation de Saint Antoine*, the Apocalypse, and the Walpurgnisnacht. The composition as a whole corresponds to the *Odyssey*, but at the same time recalls Rabelais and the Elizabethans. Symbolism and Scholasticism bring it into proximity with the Middle Ages. It is the all-inclusive and yet utterly singular, magnificent, cruel, exalting and depressing work of a man who is solitary, proud.

1929

T. S. Eliot

✦✦

I

1

Let us begin with the positive facts. A small volume is lying before me, *Poems*, by T. S. Eliot.[1] The dust jacket contains a note on the author: "Thomas Stearns Eliot was born at St. Louis, Mo. in 1888. He received his A.B. at Harvard in 1909 and his A.M. in 1910. He studied subsequently at the Sorbonne, at the Harvard Graduate School, and at Merton College, Oxford. He has lived in London where he became a master at Highgate School, and lecturer under both the Oxford and the London University Extension Systems. He has contributed to several English papers, among them, the 'Athenaeum.' From 1917 to 1919 he was Assistant Editor of the 'Egoist.' He published *Prufrock* in 1917 and *Poems* in 1919—this volume assembles the contents of the two, together with a number of other poems, and is the first volume to be published in America, where heretofore it has been exceedingly difficult to obtain his poems."

Groping a bit further bibliographically, we come upon *The Criterion*, a quarterly. The editor is T. S. Eliot. The first number appeared in October 1922, published by R. Cobden-Sanderson in London. It contained contributions by George Saintsbury, Dostoevski, T. Sturge Moore, May Sinclair, Hermann Hesse, Valery Larbaud—and a poem by the editor entitled *The Waste Land*. The work was published separately, with additional notes, in 1923.[2] Since 1926 *The Criterion* has

[1] Alfred A. Knopf (New York, 1920).
[2] Hogarth Press (Paradise Road, Richmond, Surrey).

been continued by Eliot as *The New Criterion*.[3] It is in a class by itself among the literary periodicals of the globe. Other publications of Eliot's that I am familiar with are: 1. *The Sacred Wood, Essays on Poetry and Criticism*,[4] 2. *Homage to John Dryden, Three Essays on Poetry of the Seventeenth Century*,[5] 3. *Poems 1909–1925*,[6] 4. various contributions to the *Nouvelle Revue Française, Commerce*, etc.

In France Ramon Fernandez has written on Eliot (1925, in the *Nouvelle Revue Française*);[7] in England his influence on recent literature has been strong, according to the testimony of Edwin Muir (in *Transition, Essays on Contemporary Literature*).[8] But despite my literary sympathy for Fernandez and Muir, I cannot think that they have viewed and appreciated Eliot correctly.

The Waste Land is Eliot's most important work up to now. I have tried to translate it.[9] In my translation I was particularly concerned to reproduce the rhythms and the changes in the rhythms. Coleridge once said that, to please him, a poem had to have either "sense" or "music." These are indeed the two approaches to the arcanum of poetry. They issue in the one adyton. But the point of departure is different. And yet both are legitimate. A line of verse that causes us to vibrate musically, that excites us with its rhythm and haunts us with its melody—must be a good line, even if its meaning is still hidden from us. Think of Hofmannsthal:

> Den Erben lass verschwenden
> An Adler Lamm und Pfau

[3] Faber & Gwyer Ltd. (London).

[4] Methuen & Co. (London, 1920).

[5] Hogarth Press (London). [6] Faber & Gwyer (London).

[7] *The Waste Land* was translated into French by Jean de Menasce and published in the first issue of *Esprit* (F. Rieder & Cie., Paris, 1926).

[8] Hogarth Press (London, 1926).

[9] My translation appeared in 1927 in the *Neue Schweizer Rundschau* (newly reprinted in the *Neue Rundschau*, 1950), and now in T. S. Eliot, *Ausgewählte Gedichte. Englisch und deutsch* (Suhrkamp, Frankfurt).

Das Salböl aus den Händen
Der toten alten Frau.

[Let the heir squander on eagle, lamb, and peacock
the anointing oil from the hands of the dead old
woman.]

A long time may pass before the meaning of *The Waste Land*
has become clear to us. I do not pretend to have solved all its
riddles. But even on the first reading, years ago, it captivated
me with sudden dazzling flashes of mystery and music, with
a resonant happiness. This is the path I followed; this is the
path on which I should like to guide a few readers.

Criticism, after all, always remains a risk. Evaluation cannot be grounded. The ground exists, no doubt, but only as intuition. This can leap across as a spark. It can be transmitted,
but not communicated. That is the beauty of criticism. It is
an act of creative intellectual freedom. Of course intuition can
be subsequently motivated. But this motivation will only convince those who are already favorably disposed. The fundamental act of criticism consists in irrational contact. True criticism never seeks to prove, it seeks only to show. Its metaphysical background is the conviction that the world of the
mind is organized around systems of affinities.

2

But I do not wish to be misunderstood. Intuition is an
unfortunate term. It is constantly in the mouths of people who
are otherwise starving. I am "against intellectual nourishment
through intuition," to use Franz Blei's estimable coinage.
What we would like, after all, is that intuition and intelligence
should be brought together. Hence we combat the superstition that poets must be stupid, men of letters uncultured, and
scholars obtuse. Eliot is especially interesting to me because
he unites criticism and poiesis in one person. He confirms me
in the conviction, which I recently found again in Marichalar,
that in the twentieth century criticism is an ingredient of all

superior intellectual production. Examples? Here they are: Gide, Proust, Valéry, Larbaud, Joyce, Ayala, Ortega. . . . They are all artists of intellectualism, all establishers of awareness. Mere "creativity," or whatever else goes by this label, is no longer enough. Do I mention only foreign names? I could mention German ones as well. I go so far as to claim priority for us Germans in this respect. We once had a Novalis, a Friedrich Schlegel. This is where the new world begins, where consciousness means a creative heightening of life; where myth is wedded to method; where for the first time the synthesizing mind crystallizes and mirrors itself in ironic-mystical fashion. After that we had Nietzsche, who has not been discovered as a critic even now, when we mummify him as a hero or work him up as scholarship. We still have criticism today, even if—as good old custom requires—it is not acknowledged or is not allowed to be acknowledged as such. We simply want to have only poets. But how is one to do justice to a Franz Blei or a Borchardt if one doesn't take them as critics, as creative critics (and hence also destructive)? If we could bring ourselves to erect a temple of criticism on the German Parnassus—only utopian dreamers could demand a section for criticism in the German Academy of Literature—then the rank of Alfred Kerr might at last be properly ascertained; this sovereign intellect and founder of values who, from a historical standpoint, has been the sole but perfectly adequate justification for the existence of hundreds of bad plays: that is, to say that they were bad, to say it with such brilliance and trenchancy; and to use the occasion to say so many other, more interesting things that have nothing to do with the matter.

It is not merely a western European, it is, we may hope, also a German phenomenon that criticism is assuming a new and productive function within the economy of the intellectual energies of our age. It cannot be otherwise if we wish to accept this age, with its exploration of consciousness, its syncretism, its emerging ecumenical, cosmopolitan culture.

3

And if it really were an epoch of Hellenism? Would that be so bad as people often suppose? Those five or six hundred years from Menander to Lucian, from Theocritus to Plotinus, from Callimachus to the *Pervigilium Veneris*, those ages of Alexander, of the Ptolemies, of the Julians and the Antonines —should they really still need "saving"? Many a later age, and not the worst, has turned with longing toward their ripe abundance, their autumnal sweetness, toward the breadth of vision and freedom of choice of late Antiquity, where every desire could find its wisdom.

This is the horizon against which I see Eliot's poetry. Eliot is an Alexandrian poet in the strictest sense of the word—as such a poet can and must look today. He is first of all an erudite poet. He knows the languages, the literatures, the techniques. His works are adorned with the jewels of quotation, with reminiscences of his reading. He does precisely what the Alexandrians and Romans did, except that he indicates his sources directly in a footnote. His poetry draws its sustenance from the late Latins, the Trecentisti, the Elizabethans, and the French Symbolists. Philologists might learn from his work the artistic significance of this technique of mosaic: how personal experience is enhanced, suffused, illuminated when it is registered by the discerning memory. Ages and styles coalesce into magical substance. It is the poetry of an expert, and only the expert will get the best out of it. But to be an expert, an expert in literature, would be contemptible only if literature itself were contemptible. For literature without tradition is destiny without history—uncomprehended, unpossessed. Only original geniuses could take offense at this idea or maintain even further that literature and life are antitheses. Literature is a form of life: a form by which it can be enjoyed, known, and overcome.

Poetry of this kind operates with the highest awareness of its art. It knows all the means and all the effects. According to his purpose Eliot will choose free verse, blank verse, rhymed verse. The rhythmic curve feels out precisely the curve of the emotion. In *The Waste Land* nothing is chance or pure inspiration. One might have that impression because the poem is so obscure. But this obscurity, too, is deliberate. It is one of the stylistic elements of all secondary poetry. It is present in Hellenism, in the troubadours (where, as *trobar clus*, it was held in high esteem); it is present in Dante and in Mallarmé. The purpose of this obscurity is to scare off the superficial reader, but it is also to reinforce the symbols, to deepen the mystery. It was this obscurity that prompted the troubadours, and Dante as well, to comment on some of their own works; so that when Eliot appends notes, he is only taking up again a time-honored practice.

Finally, Eliot has a third trait in common with the Alexandrians: his learning in mythology. Eliot himself tells us that he is indebted to the anthropological research of Frazer and Jessie Weston for the title, plan, and symbolism of his work. We shall go into that later. Apart from anything particular we are fascinated by the general situation that for the poet, with his sensibility and receptiveness, the miracle-plant of eternal religion can spring from the soil of philological and historical scholarship.

Our religion, inasmuch as we still have one, is a spiritualized religion. The religions of the ancient world, however, were predominantly religions of life. Even after the great god Pan had died, they were not yet dead. They survived through centuries and millennia, partly in the form of heresies which sought an accommodation with Christian dogma, spiritualizing on gnostic principles the old life cult; partly in secret fellowships; and partly as customs, legends, and traditions which had been emptied of meaning and had lost the memory of their origin. The Church has always done everything in its power to repress and extirpate them: by force (through persecutions of heretics); by method (through eradication of documents, reinterpretation of traditions); by reform (under which must be included both Reformation and Counter-

Reformation). What this work of annihilation destroyed cannot be estimated. But it could not destroy everything. Again and again a longing for the mysteries made itself felt, for a religious consciousness which should embrace nature as well as spirit, for a new initiation into the cult of the life powers. Goethe hinted at it in his poem *Die Geheimnisse* [*The Mysteries*], in Faust's rejuvenation, in the journey to the Mothers. Novalis, in his *Hymnen an die Nacht* [*Hymns to the Night*], proclaims a Christianity in which Dionysian enthusiasm is united with Catholic Mariolatry; a Christianity in which all the beauty of Hellas, all the wisdom of the East is not only preserved but actually realized for the first time:

> Die Sternwelt wird zerfliessen
> Zum goldnen Lebenswein.
> Wir werden sie geniessen
> Und lichte Sterne sein.
> Die Lieb' ist frei gegeben
> Und keine Trennung mehr.
> Es wogt das volle Leben
> Wie ein unendlich Meer. . . .

[The starry world will dissolve into golden wine of life. We shall drink it with joy and become bright stars ourselves. Love is freely given, and separation at an end. Life billows in all its fullness like an infinite sea. . . .]

It is that third kingdom, that everlasting gospel of Christianity, which had already appeared to the heresies of Antiquity and the Middle Ages as the light at the end of their journey.

From debris and oblivion the scholarship of the last hundred years has rescued much that the tradition of the Church had consigned to extinction. In ecclesiastical history men like Harnack have brought us the insight—in H. v. Soden's fine formulation—"that heresy is not a caricature but a component of Catholicism."[10] Classical and Oriental philology,

---

[10] From which it would be possible to conclude, of course, that one must be a Catholic and a heretic at the same time.

in close collaboration, have shed new light on our view of postclassical syncretism. Research in ethnology and anthropology—stimulated by Jacob Grimm, advanced by Wilhelm Mannhardt's *Feld- und Waldkulte* (1875–1877)—has recognized and interpreted the survival of pre-Christian religious practices up until our own times. Upon Mannhardt is based Sir James George Frazer's *The Golden Bough* (from 1890 to 1922, several editions and revisions), and Frazer's work was carried on and expanded in valuable studies like Jane Harrison's *Themis* (1912) and Jessie L. Weston's *From Ritual to Romance* (1920).

A strong influence has been exerted by this English branch of studies in comparative religion (in England customarily designated by the misleading term anthropology) upon recent English literature. Without a knowledge of these connections *The Waste Land* cannot be understood at all.

Impressive as is the achievement of modern work in comparative religion, it has, by the very nature of the case, been accomplished from the point of view of the modern scientific consciousness, which in its main varieties of liberalism, historicism, and positivism, is essentially irreligious or at most religious only in a pallid moral sense. The aim of comparative religion is to confront customs, explain myths and rituals, delimit spheres of religious conceptions, establish influences. It hands its material over to libraries and museums. But this material was alive once, these conceptions were certainties, these rites had power, and these mysteries were the gate by which the adept ascended to higher planes of life. The monuments of comparative religion are nothing but the petrified and fragmentary remains, in stone or script, of a religious life that had its reality only in covenants and cults, and that was consummated in initiation, apotheosis, ecstasy, and the transcendence of life and death. They are evidences of a race of men still bound to the earth and to the stars, and they can reveal their significance only to those who, even in these "times without gods," have preserved some trace of these primary religious powers. They resemble shriveled flower bulbs, which can blossom into life if planted in a bed of warm soil. This warm soil is the soul of the poet.

4

What is the result of such a fertilization? Well, surely no rebirth of ancient mysteries. We can no longer raise altars or cultivate gardens to Adonis. That a poet like Eliot may once again hear echoes of a long vanished world does not make him either a priest or an initiate. No, he is a poet and a man of this age, and he knows its thoughts and its dissensions, its restless city-life, its wage slavery, its suburban ugliness, its prostitution, and its snobbishness. But Psyche is alive even in this world. Even in this desolate land the soul lives and can pray with the Psalmist: "Deus meus, Deus meus, ad te de luce vigilo. Sitivit in te anima mea, quam multipliciter tibi caro mea in terra deserta et invia et inaquosa" ["O God, thou art my God; early will I seek thee: my soul thirsteth for thee, my flesh longeth for thee in a dry and thirsty land, where no water is"—Psalm 63]. The soul can abate nothing of its wishes, its hopes, its fears. It thirsts for the waters of life, it cowers at the darkness of death:

> Animula vagula blandula,
> hospes comesque corporis,
> quae nunc abibis in loca,
> pallidula rigida nudula,
> nec ut soles dabis iocos!

["Dear wandering, charming little soul, guest and companion of the body, whither will you go now, pale, rigid, naked little soul, and not crack jokes as you used to do!"]

This soul is not only at home in our age but in every age. And if she cannot find an echo amidst the noise of our time, she puts her ear to the shell that resonates with the song of vanished ages, there to hearken to the voice of her longing.

To sum up: Eliot is not a religious poet, but in our Americanized age—the age of the Sweeneys[11]—he has rediscovered the primary form of religious symbolism and used it to express Psyche's passion and longing.

It will now be necessary to state some of the main conclusions reached by the English studies in comparative religion on which Eliot has drawn. The work of Mannhardt and Frazer directed attention to the significance of the vegetation cults. The Syrian Adonis, the Phrygian Attis, the Egyptian Osiris are vegetation gods. The death and resurrection of these deities symbolizes the cycle of growth and decay in nature. The fertility of nature is conceived as dependent upon the vital curve of a god or godlike being, and occasionally even of a king or priest-king.[12] Such a being is inhabited by the cosmic life-principle. Tree-cults, rain magic, maypoles, harvest festivals are all associated with it.

Miss Weston, known to specialists for decades as an authority in the complicated field of Grail studies, and inspired by Frazer, Jane Harrison, Leopold von Schröder *et al.*, was able to demonstrate—convincingly, to my mind—that the Grail legend derives neither from a Christian legend nor from a folkloristic *märchen* motif (the enchanted cup or vessel), but rather from an ancient nature cult which, at the time of the Hellenic-Christian religious mingling, was incorporated into the symbolism of the cult of the Eucharist and then sur-

[11] Sweeney is the name Eliot gives to the American man of practical reality. He is a recurring figure in Eliot's poems and also appears in *The Waste Land*.

[12] According to Frazer, monarchy is of magical origin. Traces of it in Roman religion are the legend of Numa and Egeria as well as the priestly offices of the *rex sacrificulus* (in Rome) and above all of the *rex nemorensis* (by the lake of Nemi). The latter institution, with its highly archaic features, is attested as late as the period of the Empire, and constituted the starting-point for Frazer's investigations. Renan treated it in his drama *Le Prêtre de Némi* (1885). In England and France, too, the monarchy preserved vestiges of the magical conception for a long time. As recently as the seventeenth century one of the King's functions was to cure scrofula by the laying on of hands. The republic means a "dis-enchantment" of the state.

vived esoterically for centuries until, merging with the cycle of Celtic legends about King Arthur and his Round Table, it penetrated, along with this cycle, the matter of the courtly romance, finally to lose altogether, in its latest versions, its original meaning, owing in part to the misunderstandings of uninitiated jongleurs, in part to a systematic correction in the sense of clerical orthodoxy.[13]

The original version of the Grail legend tells of a young hero who comes to a barren land in which the water has dried up and nothing can grow. The lord of the land, the ailing fisher-king, inhabits a mysterious castle whose knights receive material and spiritual nourishment whenever the miraculous vessel of the Grail manifests itself. Spear and cup are always seen in connection with the appearances of the Grail. The task of the hero—regardless of whether he succeeds or not—is to heal the fisher-king and so to redeem the parched land, which is withering because of the king's infirmity.

What is this infirmity? Some versions veil it in euphemism, others say it outright: it is the loss of male potency, in other words, it has the same meaning as the mutilation of the Phrygian Attis and the mortal wounding of the Syrian and Cyprian Adonis by the boar.

Why do lance and cup appertain to the symbolism of the Grail and of the fisher-king? This combination of symbols is unknown to Christian literary and artistic tradition. Attempts have been made to prove their origins in the spear of Longinus and the chalice of the mass. But these attempts have been unsatisfactory. The question is resolved simply if lance and cup are taken as life symbols, as male and female sexual symbols. This symbolism antedates Christianity and lies outside it. It belongs to the magic archetypal symbolism; but there it is further associated with two other symbols: the sword and the dish.

[13] As might have been expected, official Grail scholarship, working only with philological and literary-historical methods, has rejected Miss Weston's conception.

The ensemble of these four symbols may have an esoteric efficacy and validity even today. Exoterically, however, it has sunk to the lowest level: it is found in the suits of playing cards. The Tarot pack had 870 cards, distributed among four colors: hearts=cup; diamonds=spear; spades=sword; clubs =dish (also pentagram). Initiates are still familiar with the meaning of these symbols. There are good indications that playing cards were imported from Egypt by the gypsies.

I mention all this only to explain the significance of cartomancy—Mme. Sosostris—and the Tarot pack in Eliot's work.

But what does the fisher-king mean? He is one of those semihuman, semidivine creatures on whose vitality the fertility of the land depends. He is a life and vegetation daemon. The fish is a life symbol of utmost antiquity (corroborations for which can be found in psychoanalysis). The Temple of Astarte in Ascalon was surrounded by flocks of doves and by fishponds. It was prohibited to catch the fish—except for certain ritual meals at which fish was eaten by the priests and initiates in order to unite with the lives of the gods. These meals were held on Friday as the day sacred to Astarte and later to Venus—hence *venerdì, vendredi*. The Jews, probably during the Babylonian exile, adopted the custom of eating fish on Friday.

The secret of the Grail lies in the fusion of ancient life-cults with the Christian mysteries, a fusion that was probably a component of an esoteric tradition. It happens that we possess a document attesting this tradition, the so-called Naassene sermon, which was transmitted by Bishop Hippolytus (220) in his *Philosophumena*, a polemic against heretics. The Naassenes combined the (Iranian?) myth of the celestial original man and his son—from which the Biblical expression "son of man" also seems to be derived—with the Attis cult and the belief in Christ as chosen to fulfill the entire process of cosmic redemption. They taught that the beginning of perfection was the gnosis of man, but that the gnosis of God was perfect perfection.[14] They distinguished between the little and the great mysteries. The former are those of fleshly generation. "When men have been initiated into these, they should cease for a while and become initiated into the great, heavenly mysteries . . . , for this is the gate of heaven and the house of God, where the good God dwells alone, into whose house no one impure shall enter."[15]

This is followed in the document by an Attis hymn. The conclusions reads, however: "And of all men we alone are Christians and fulfill the mystery at the Third Gate."[16]

The question that has interested students of comparative religion in this text is, of what and how many strata of various provenience does it consist, and how many redactors have worked on it. For the study of comparative religion this is worth knowing. But for religion it is worth knowing that this text reproduces a unified experience, albeit one drawn from many sources, of a pagan-Christian fellowship in the mysteries. What to the eye of history appears as syncretism is, regarded phenomenologically, a *complex oppositorum*; a unity in multiplicity; a life. And of this age-old life of the mysteries the Grail legend is a last—or provisionally last—literary residuum. Who can tell whether the heretical esotericism that brought destruction upon the Order of the Templars may not be related to it in origin?

5

No one who understands poetry will suppose that Eliot's work is nothing but an ornamental tissue of motifs from comparative religion. The only reason why Eliot could employ these motifs was that they expressed certain essential elements in his own psychological situation, reinforcing and concealing them at the same time. But this situation comprises more and other things as well. Eliot's poem is motivated by the two great afflictions of the soul—sexual love and death.

[14] *Hippolytus Werke*, ed. Wendland, vol. 3 (1916), 78.
[15] *Ibid.* p. 97. [16] *Ibid.* p. 102.

These are the poles around which revolve the thoughts and struggles of all those who cannot rest content with the traditional solutions of Christianity and the available stores of worldly wisdom. Eros and Thanatos are the gods of the hooded gaze before whose images the modern soul prays, laments, questions, and sacrifices. Eliot is modern because he sees and speaks of everything physical, defiling, anxious, horrible, and grotesque that has to do with love and death. To label this as materialism would be a grave misconception. Materialism and spiritualism are no longer antitheses in our world. What contemporary poet is still capable of separating body and soul? Perhaps this very separation, which seemed so certain to past centuries that it was taken for granted, was itself a symptom of decay. And perhaps the very fact that it is no longer valid for us affords a guarantee that a new type of man is developing who has once more achieved integration.

Anyone who still refuses to see the reality, the ugliness and the beauty of this flesh-spirit human condition to which we are bound will have little to say to us today. Whether this reality and unity is experienced as more depressing or more elating in character will undoubtedly always be a matter of personal temperament and type. With Eliot the depressive element predominates. He is of those for whom everything earthly reeks of the charnel house. The rat plagues and torments his imagination. He has an obsession with decay that expresses itself partly as poetry, partly as cynicism—both are manifestations of suffering. This earthly residue which is "impure" does not signify a delight in filth. It represents the old Christian consciousness of sin in the modern soul. And like this consciousness it goes hand in hand with a spirituality that longs for seraphic worlds. It would be enough to cite Baudelaire in this connection. We ought to be more careful generally in our use of the word realism. There is a kind of realism that seems to be a necessary component of ecstatic religiosity. One has only to think of Tintoretto. The putrescent horrors depicted in his *Last Judgment* in Santa Maria dell'Orto are brought to mind by certain of Eliot's verses.

Others make one think of Brueghel. There are drawings by him that could be set beside the last section of *The Waste Land.*

The waste land, the desolate, barren, rocky, terrible land, is our age. This at any rate is one side of the symbol that cannot be ignored. It is an age of self-despair, in all its hopelessness, its deadly lassitude, its memories of the song and story and beauty of former ages which it is almost too ashamed of itself to dare to recall. It reduces all grandeur to a common grimace. It thought it could rise to heroism through war. But the outcome is the banality and ugliness of daily life to which the demobilized soldier returns. This age has turned the ancient arts of magic and divination into the sordid practice of card reading; has made of the Phoenician sailor an unshaven Smyrna merchant trading in currants. Eliot's poem is a lament for all the misery and fear of this age. It breathes the same air of desperation that constitutes the substratum of Proust and Valéry: that sense of universal collapse that prompted Joyce to introduce "the End of the World" into the hallucinatory procession in one of the scenes of *Ulysses.* It is the mood of the concluding lines of Eliot's poem:

> This is the way the world ends
> This is the way the world ends
> This is the way the world ends
> Not with a bang but a whimper.

All this had to be suffered, suffered to the bitter end. The pangs of thirst, the barren stony wastes, the horrors of death had to be spoken. Like the Sybil in Petronius, a poet would have to say: "I want to die." The way to rebirth lies only through this mortal agony.

This mortal agony is already lit up, in Eliot, by the first faint dawning of a new consciousness. I am referring to that new consciousness of our age which knows the synthesis beyond the antitheses. It is, properly speaking, a mystical consciousness. The last section of *The Waste Land* may be read as a journey to the hereafter. Such things are being written again. Psyche wanders through unearthly regions. The "little life in dried tubers" has a presentiment, however obscure, of future germination. He who has felt his life to be united with the general rhythm of growth, who has recognized his own passion in that of the ancient vegetation gods, has passed through the gates of death into the land of the beyond. Death and life are no longer antitheses to him. He has come to know a third condition that is neither

> Your shadow at morning striding behind you
> Nor your shadow at evening rising to meet you.

The old distinctions no longer apply. Past and present are contemporaneous. The seer who once sat at the gates of Thebes is the same who is present in the shabby room of the London typist. He, Tiresias, has experienced in his own person the changes of time and the changes of sex—"venus huic erat utraque nota." He knows that the division into male and female is not permanent either. The original man—Adam as well as the Anthropos of the Gnostics—was not aware of it. Individuation is an illusion. All the women in the poem are, according to Eliot's explanations, the same woman, just as the one-eyed merchant of the Tarot cards melts into the trader in currants Mr. Eugenides and into Phlebas the Phoenician.

All this seems unreal. But even this ultimate antithesis between "reality" and "unreality" must be abolished. What is unreal need not on that account be a fiction. It simply belongs to a different level of existence. There are many such levels. The modern poet is familiar with this superreality. He sees the dead streaming across London Bridge, sees Elizabeth and Leicester on their gilded barge, he sees the cities in the land of the beyond; and our cities become unreal:

> Jerusalem Athens Alexandria
> Vienna London
> Unreal.

The more often I read Eliot's poem, the more sense and music I discover in it. What I have said about it is only a fragment. . . . Eliot's aesthetic theories especially ought still to be discussed. But that would have to be done in connection with his critical writings. I shall save it for a later occasion. May it suffice if I have led a few readers to the poet.

1927

II

WHEN E. M. Forster, during a convalescence in 1917, was looking for something to read that would not be patriotically uplifting, he picked up Huysmans' *À Rebours*. It was refreshing, he found, to move in a world that lived for its sensations and excluded the will. "Was it decadent? Yes, thank God!" Then he turned to a recent volume of poetry: *Prufrock and Other Observations*. These poems also had nothing to do with the spirit of the "great age." They sang of private experiences of a depressing kind. "The author was irritated by tea parties and not afraid to say so, with the result that his occasional 'might-have-beens' rang with the precision of a gong."

Prufrock was followed by *Poems* (1919). Around 1920 Eliot was discovered by the English literary avant-garde. He was propagated by the highbrows, ignored by the Establishment. A slender volume of critical prose, *The Sacred Wood* (1920), demolished the household shrines of Victorianism: Swinburne, Pater, Meredith, Shaw. Eliot's influence grew from 1922 on, when he could edit his own review, *The Criterion*. With the January 1939 number, Eliot took leave of his readers. In his "last words" he observed that the "European mind" that the review had sought to promote had become invisible. Literary culture was on the decline. "It will require a harder trial than anything we have hitherto experienced before life can be renewed. . . . For the immediate future, and perhaps for a long way ahead, the continuity of our culture may have to be maintained by a very small number of people." Today, in the English-speaking countries, Eliot possesses, both as poet and as critic, an authority for which there are few analogies. This authority is not contested even by those who are far removed from Eliot in their political and ecclesiastical convictions. His *Four Quartets* (New York, 1943; London, 1944), are for England the most important work of poetry of the period since World War II, as *The Waste Land* was for the period after World War I. The curve of Eliot's literary success can be deduced from the editions of the *Collected Poems*: 1936–1937–1939–1941–1942–1944 (March and December)–1945–1946 (January and November), etc. Eliot belongs to the literary generation that might be called the survivors of two world wars, as Tacitus after Domitian's reign of terror speaks of the few who "have not only survived others but as it were themselves" ("non modo aliorum, sed etiam nostri superstites sumus").[17]

His work is alive. But at the same time it already belongs to history. Eliot has been compelled by his own development to contemplate himself historically. We can discern this in the way he manages and rectifies his own production. *The Sacred Wood* bore the subtitle *Essays on Poetry and Criticism,* in marked contrast to *For Lancelot Andrewes* (1928), *Essays on Style and Order.* In the preface to this volume Eliot protested against "certain conclusions" that had been drawn from *The Sacred Wood* and professed himself "a classicist in literature, a royalist in politics, and an Anglo-Catholic in religion." But in 1934 and 1936 he was already in retreat from this program.[18] So from time to time he will revise or abandon positions that were intended for a certain moment and

[17] For Eliot's sixtieth birthday (26 September 1948), there was published *T. S. Eliot. A Symposium compiled by Richard March and Tambimuttu,* with contributions by some forty authors (*Editions Poetry London*).

[18] *After Strange Gods,* pp. 27-28. Preface to *Essays Ancient and Modern.*

have "served their turn."[19] But he has likewise suppressed polemical utterances which he enunciated not without some smugness in his early years and which one does not like to miss because they are so indicative. *Homage to John Dryden* (1924) has a preface, later eliminated, in which one could read: "I have long felt that the poetry of the seventeenth and eighteenth centuries, even much of that of inferior inspiration, possesses an elegance and a dignity absent from the popular and pretentious works of the Romantic Poets and their successors. . . . I hope that these three papers may, in spite of and partly because of their defects, preserve in cryptogram certain notions which, if expressed directly, would be destined to immediate obloquy, followed by perpetual oblivion." An author who writes like that feels a need to let the world around him know what he thinks of it. Since then Eliot as a critic has imposed, formally at any rate, an ever greater restraint upon himself. He no longer speaks about himself. A remark like, "I am a timid person, easily overawed by authority," he would not be likely to set down any more. He has become representative, and maintains in his style, too, the dignity and detachment of the representative function.

The reader who comes upon Eliot's verses for the first time will find them obscure, as Mallarmé, George, and Valéry were found to be obscure. This is due in part to their intellectual content. English and American critics have done much to expound these texts philosophically and theologically; others will follow. But these interpretations have only a relative value. They reduce a sequence of images to a concatenation of sterile concepts. The poetic substance evaporates in this transfer. For the presentation of philosophical ideas the suitable medium is prose. Poetry formulates emotions that cannot be communicated by other means. These emotions

---

[19] The text of the poems seems to be unchanged. In the first edition, however, "The Hippopotamus" bears a motto from Ignatius of Antiochia which is omitted in the *Collected Poems* (1936)—probably because Eliot's position regarding the Church has changed.

may be aroused by the time of day or the seasons of the year or, also, by contact with metaphysical problems. In this sense a poetry of ideas does exist. But it does not matter what sort of ideas these are, just as it does not matter what landscapes inspire a poet to write. You can describe the landscapes geographically, you can classify the ideas philosophically. But you won't get much closer to the poetry that way. Moreover, a certain obscurity acts as an aesthetic charm. The artist may use it as a stylistic device. That is how it was used in Góngora, in Mallarmé; frequently in Dante. One ought not to forget that Eliot recommends Dante as a model for poets. Like Dante, Eliot has a certain tendency to mystify the reader. A certain amount of deliberately intended obscurity remains in both. We may leave it at that. One of the commentators believes that in the line

> O keep the Dog far hence

the dog signifies humanitarianism. I doubt it. But the identification of this animal strikes me as quite as inconsequential as that of the Dantean *Veltro*. The panther, lion, and wolf in the first canto are symbols that can easily be interpreted. But when Eliot writes

> Lady, three white leopards sat under a juniper-tree
> In the cool of the day, having fed to satiety
> On my legs my heart my liver . . .

it would be a mistake to try to interpret the three beasts. In these lines an image is built up that demands to be looked at like a Gothic tapestry. At the same time they seek to convey a definite emotion: horror with a note of the macabre, heightened by the accent of whiteness, coolness, maidenliness. Such is the effect on the reader who knows how to receive verse. If, in addition, he is a specialist in literature, he will be reminded of certain models. The white leopards derive from Dante's pard "with the spotted skin." The allegorical lady has many relatives in Dante. The eating of the heart occurs in the *Vita Nuova*. And the juniper tree? Elijah sat under it "and

requested that his soul might die" (I Kings 19:4). This use
of literary allusions and reminiscences is a peculiar feature
of Eliot's poetic technique[20] and one of the reasons for his
obscurity.

The Waste Land and *Four Quartets* occupy the center of
current Eliot-exegesis. The explicators concentrate their efforts on the philosophical contents (like the Rilke-exegetes
with us). Hence the early poems are somewhat neglected. But
from a purely literary point of view just these are of particular
interest. The earliest piece, *The Love Song of J. Alfred Prufrock* (first published in an American periodical in 1915),
is in Eliot's work what *A Portrait of the Artist as a Young
Man* (1916) is in Joyce's. A fictional character is built up out
of the material of the poet's personal experience. In its 130
lines musical themes are sounded that the later work will
bring back in manifold variations. An October afternoon. The
evening is spread out against the sky like a patient etherised
on an operating table. We walk through the byways of cheap
vice:

> The muttering retreats
> Of restless nights in one-night cheap hotels
> And sawdust restaurants with oyster-shells.

A tea party. The women speak of Michelangelo. Yellow fog
licks at the windows. Prufrock's inner monologue discloses
banal sorrows. Should he declare himself to his lady? He is
inhibited and feels worn out. His hair is growing thin, his days
are empty, he thinks of himself as old. Once it was otherwise. Then he could hear the mermaids singing. But now?

> I do not think that they will sing to me.
> I have seen them riding seawards on the waves
> Combing the white hair of the waves blown back
> When the wind blows the water white and black.
> We have lingered in the chambers of the sea
> By sea-girls wreathed with seaweed red and brown
> Till human voices wake us, and we drown.

[20] This would require a separate discussion for which there is no
room in what follows.

On this muffled note of despair the poem ends. Drowning. . . . Death by water is one of the strands in the pattern of *The Waste Land* (Section I, Section IV), and in *Four Quartets* it returns in the form of annihilation by the elements. But also the effective image at the beginning of the poem ("a patient etherised upon a table") is employed again later. The pressure of existence is a wandering

> through the stone passages
> Of an immense and empty hospital
> Pervaded by a smell of disinfectant.
> (The Family Reunion)

Section IV of "East Coker" transposes surgical procedure to the theological level. The operation has become sacral.

The rest of the poems of the early period contain a masked procession of satirical figures in which two groups may be distinguished: a Boston family and educational tradition already in decay ("The Boston Evening Transcript," "Aunt Helen," "Cousin Nancy"); and its opposite, a set of socially rootless Bohemians:

> But this or such was Bleistein's way:
> A saggy bending of the knees
> And elbows, with the palms turned out,
> Chicago Semite Viennese.

An international caravan of shabby tourists passes before us: Burbank with his Baedeker; Hakagawa visiting museums; Princess Volupine "sinning" and giving receptions in Venice; Mr. Apollinax, on a tour of America, invited to tea by Mrs. Phlaccus and Professor Channing-Cheetah; Rachel Rabinovitch dining at Sweeney's. Sweeney is the protagonist of this section of Eliot's work. He might be called Aristophanic in the sense of the *Poèmes aristophaniques* of Laurent Tailhade. The function of these poems consists in demonstrating the questionable and trivial nature of the modern world through typical figures. These are not dramatic characters but tragicomic marionettes. Their shadowlike and grotesque contortions are the screen on which Eliot has projected his nervous reactions.

In saying this we are proceeding on the assumption that a poet's work, apart from its artistic value, is also a psychological document; that it expresses his "personality." But this is precisely what Eliot disputes. The essay "Tradition and the Individual Talent" (1917) contains the thesis of the impersonality of the poet. The poet does not have a personality to "express" but only a particular medium in which impressions and experiences combine in a particular way. Experiences that are important for his poetry may play a very small part in his personality; and the reverse is also true. The essay on Hamlet (1919) elucidates: "The only way of expressing emotion in the form of art is by finding an 'objective correlative'; in other words, a set of objects which shall be the formula of that particular emotion; such that when the external facts, which must terminate in sensory experience, are given, the emotion is immediately evoked." That is the theory. We will not ask whether it is logically tenable or even whether it could be explained psychologically on the basis of Eliot's personality. In any case certain data of the "medium" (not to say: personal experiences) can be read out of the poetry; and they constitute an inner coherence that may be formulated as the sense of the misery of existence and its ironic treatment. This misery is made up of the unpleasantnesses of everyday life. A wedding-trip looks like this ("Lune de Miel"):

> Ils ont vu les Pays-Bas, ils rentrent à Terre Haute:
> Mais une nuit d'été, les voici à Ravenne,
> A l'aise entre deux draps, chez deux centaines de punaises;
> La sueur aestivale, et une forte odeur de chienne.
> Ils restent sur le dos écartant les genoux
> De quatre jambes molles tout gonflées de morsures.
> On relève le drap pour mieux égratigner.
> Moins d'une lieue d'ici est Saint Apollinaire
> En Classe, basilique connue des amateurs
> De chapiteaux d'acanthe que tournoie le vent.

Ils vont prendre le train de huit heures
Prolonger leurs misères de Padoue à Milan
Où se trouve la Cène, et un restaurant pas cher.
Lui pense aux pourboires, et rédige son bilan.
Ils auront vu la Suisse et traversé la France.
Et Saint Apollinaire, raide et ascétique,
Vieille usine désaffectée de Dieu, tient encore
Dans ses pierre écroulantes la forme précise de Byzance.

Seedy hotels, cheap restaurants, slovenly waiters are part of the scenery of this existence (cf. for example "Dans le Restaurant"). Even when the three Magi, grown old and gray in the meantime, relate their journey to Bethlehem, they remember the high prices and the discomforts of the trip:

And the villages dirty and charging high prices:
A hard time we had of it.
At the end we preferred to travel all night. . . .

In the everyday life of London the underground can become the symbol of the dreariness of travel and its gloomy hopelessness:

The desert is not remote in southern tropics,
The desert is not only around the corner,
The desert is squeezed in the tube-train next to you.[21]

Images of degradation and decay are recurrent patterns in the fabric of Eliot's poetry. They appear in the earliest poems and are still present in the *Four Quartets*.

I have spoken of neurosis. The only prose piece in the first collection of poems is entitled "Hysteria" and goes: "As she laughed I was aware of becoming involved in her laughter and being part of it, until her teeth were only accidental stars with a talent for squad-drill.[22] I was drawn in by short gasps, inhaled at each momentary recovery, lost finally in the dark caverns of her throat, bruised by the ripple of unseen muscles.

[21] Developed and transformed in *Four Quartets*, p. 10 and p. 19.
[22] Cf. "undisciplined squads of emotion" ("East Coker").

An elderly waiter with trembling hands was hurriedly spreading a pink and white checked cloth over the rusty green iron table, saying: 'If the lady and gentleman wish to take their tea in the garden, if the lady and gentleman wish to take their tea in the garden. . . .' I decided that if the shaking of her breasts could be stopped, some of the fragments of the afternoon might be collected, and I concentrated my attention with careful subtlety to this end." A ruined afternoon-tea (as in *Prufrock*) amidst a seedy, battered décor: a fragment of lived time that crumbles into atoms. Offscourings of existence.

Scraps of refuse float on the stream of memory:

> The memory throws up high and dry
> A crowd of twisted things;
> A twisted branch upon the beach
> Eaten smooth and polished
> As if the world gave up
> The secret of its skeleton. . . .

Gerontion looks out of his window on

> Rocks, moss, stonecrop, iron, merds.[23]

The desert of *The Waste Land* displays only rubbish and a heap of broken images (ll. 20–22). Later (ll. 177ff.) we see empty bottles, sandwich papers, cardboard boxes, cigarette ends being borne on the Thames. The scraps are not eliminated but galvanized by the poetry. They symbolize the stale remnants of used-up time: "the butt-ends of my days and ways—the smoky candle-end of time—the burnt-out ends of smoky days." These formulas of the early poems are a prelude to the statement in "East Coker":

> Twenty years largely wasted, the years of *l'entre deux*
> *guerres.*

Life appears as

> A casual bit of waste in an orderly universe.

[23] *Merd* is an archaic and Latinate vulgarism that has disappeared from the language since Ben Jonson.

In both cases the motif has been contracted into a synthesizing formula in which aspects of long stretches of life are summed up. We find it again in "The Dry Salvages" (1941). Just as in *The Waste Land* we saw refuse floating on the Thames, so the American river carries its cargo of dead negroes, cows, and chicken coops. But here the motif is transposed into a different key by the verse

> Time the destroyer is time the preserver.

The stream of time degrades and destroys, but also preserves. A symbol of decay has been raised to the metaphysical level.

A central symbol of the theme of decay is the house. In "Gerontion" (1920) it is a shabby tenement:

> My house is a decayed house
> ....
> An old man in a draughty house.

In "Lune de Miel" and *The Waste Land* the dilapidated church is a variant of the decayed house:

> There is the empty chapel, only the wind's home.
> It has no windows, and the door swings.

For an American like Eliot or Henry James, who has reemigrated to England and the English tradition, the country seat of the English aristocracy is a type of residence which contains an especially strong emotional charge. It signifies permanence, the link between the generations, the legacy but also the burden of the past. *The Family Reunion* is the tragedy of a family, but it is also the tragedy of a house. Wishwood is the family seat of the Monchenseys. The widowed Lady Monchensey lives for the house:

> I keep Wishwood alive
> To keep the family alive, to keep them together,
> To keep me alive, and I live to keep them.

Nothing in the house may be changed. The eldest son should find everything on his return as he left it. But when he comes home, he notices in the old house only the effects of decay:

> I am the old house
> With the noxious smell and the sorrow before morning,
> In which all past is present, all degradation
> Is unredeemable.

Three of the *Four Quartets* take their titles from English country houses to which centuries of tradition attach: "Burnt Norton" in Gloucestershire; "Little Gidding" in Huntingdonshire, associated with the memory of Nicholas Ferrar and Charles I; and "East Coker," named after the home of Eliot's ancestors in the sixteenth century. The poem is inspired by the device of Mary Stuart: "En ma fin est mon commencement." It concludes:

> In my end is my beginning

And begins:

> In my beginning is my end.

A logical aporia of the concept of time is expressed in the rhetorical form of antithesis and its inversion. But the idea is elucidated by the fate of houses. They "rise and fall, crumble, are extended, are removed, destroyed, restored, or in their place is an open field, or a factory, or a by-pass. . . . Houses live and die." A theme of decay (the crumbling house and the I that is linked with it) is elevated here to metaphysical dignity.

Decadence means fascination with all the symptoms of declining life. Baudelaire discovered this psychological state for poetry, and the Symbolism of the later nineteenth century took up his inheritance. The decadent can feel a magical attraction toward decay; he can approve it and enjoy its sterile pleasures as the lure of the abyss. But he can also suffer under it. One section of the *Fleurs du Mal* is entitled "Spleen et

Idéal." George translated it as "Trübsinn und Vergeistigung" ["Dejection and Sublimation"]. The sense of decadence was a form of modern psychological suffering incident to the age. To succumb to the attraction of forces hostile to life was only possible if one's own vital powers had already been stricken. For the artist this meant: the drying up of his creative power. One of the main themes of Mallarmé's poetry is the sterility of his Muse. Lack of fertility is a central motif of *The Waste Land*. Eliot drew upon a repertory of timeless folkloristic elements for the decorative trappings of his poem. The ancient vegetation cults popularized by Frazer and Jessie Weston's interpretation of the Grail legend contributed to its imagery. There were those who wanted to see in *The Waste Land* the "disillusionment of an entire generation." Eliot pointedly rejected this view: "I may have expressed for them their own illusion of being disillusioned, but that did not form part of my intention." The work may be regarded as the final formulation of the decadence-motifs we found in the earlier poems. But that does not exhaust the content of the work, and its beauty lies beyond all theoretical analysis. The intellectual themes are only the framework for a sequence of images and moods which gives us pleasure. What strikes us as poetic is the telescoping of time and space: the mythical age of Tiresias and the banal London of every day:

> And I Tiresias have foresuffered all
> Enacted on this same divan or bed;
> I who have sat by Thebes below the wall
> And walked among the lowest of the dead.

The poetic relativizing of reality and time is the specifically modern element in *The Waste Land*—a sense of time that we also find in Joyce. Contemporaneity of all times—that also means depriving time of its reality, an ir-realizing of time. From this awareness it is but a step to the contemplation of time from a metaphysical and religious point of view. This step is accomplished in the *Four Quartets*.

The four "Quartets"—altogether about 900 lines—are considered to be the high point of Eliot's work up to the present. For about two decades now Eliot has been a professing Christian. The Anglican Church is to him "the Catholic Church in England," whereas he designates the Roman Church in England as a "sect." It is the position maintained a century ago by Pusey and his supporters, whereas Newman dissociated himself from them. In *Thoughts after Lambeth* (1931) and other writings Eliot defends this idea of the Church, which seems illogical to Continental thinking. The "Quartets" are the poetic expression of Eliot's religious experience. It is significant that he has chosen a title drawn from musical theory. Such a title cannot and should not make any assertion as to the content of the work. It urges the reader to concentrate on the technical achievement, that is, on how the musical themes are combined. And yet Eliot's concern is not artistic—"the poetry does not matter," as we read in "East Coker"—but religious. This contradiction reveals an antagonism between the poetic and the religious sphere. That is why the problem of poetic expression recurs as one of the themes in the *Quartets*.

This religious poetry is neither a hymn nor a confession of faith. It is the private monologue of a meditating and suffering spirit. Into the matter of the poetry have entered all the motifs, images, and symbols with which Eliot's earlier work has made us familiar. But they are varied and renewed by the selection of four different settings; by the four elements, here used as a system of reference (as they already were to some extent in *The Waste Land*); by the aporias of being and time, which have occupied philosophical speculation since the pre-Socratics (fragments from Heraclitus are prefixed to the work); and finally by the aporias of the mystical consciousness (starting from St. John of the Cross and Juliana of Norwich). A very complex mixture! It is almost impossible to speak of the contents of the *Quartets* otherwise than in the form of a continuous commentary, which would be out of place here. We can do no more than indicate, in a few key phrases, the themes of the individual sections so as to convey at least a rudimentary notion of the content, construction, and method of the work.

Each quartet has five movements. "Burnt Norton I" begins with a reflection on the relativity of the three dimensions of time. The scene changes to the park of a country house. A rose garden. The rose is a symbol of paradise adopted from Dante. It enters Eliot's work for the first time, if I am not mistaken, in *The Hollow Men*:

> Sightless, unless
> The eyes reappear
> As the perpetual star
> Multifoliate rose
> Of death's twilight kingdom
> The hope only
> Of empty men.

In the rose garden of "Burnt Norton" children are heard laughing among the leaves. Perhaps they derive from the blessed children in Dante's celestial rose (*Paradiso* 32, 40-48). The metaphysical is supposed to be assumed into the temporal, into the *hic et nunc* (as was Tiresias into the daily life of London); it should light up as an instant of timelessness in time, to disappear again at once.

"Burnt Norton II" takes its departure from the correspondence between microcosm and macrocosm. The aporias of movement follow (Goethe: "Versinke denn! Ich könnt auch sagen: steige!" ["Descend again. I could as soon say, rise!"]). —"Burnt Norton III." The "dark night of the soul" (John of the Cross). —"Burnt Norton IV." A moment of illumination. —"Burnt Norton V." Can words, which move in time, encompass what is outside of time? To give an idea of how such subjects are handled poetically, I subjoin the conclusion of the piece:

Desire itself is movement
Not in itself desirable;
Love is itself unmoving,
Only the cause and end of movement.
Timeless, and undesiring
Except in the aspect of time
Caught in the form of limitation
Between un-being and being.
Sudden in a shaft of sunlight
Even while the dust moves
There rises the hidden laughter
Of children in the foliage
Quick now, here, now, always—
Ridiculous the waste sad time
Stretching before and after.

"East Coker I." Beginning and end are the same. Decaying houses. Ghostly presence of past generations. "I am here or there, or elsewhere. In my beginning." —"East Coker II." Late autumn and spring are telescoped. Disturbance of the cosmic order. Then technical reflection:

That was a way of putting it—not very satisfactory:
A periphrastic study in a worn-out poetical fashion,
Leaving one still with the intolerable wrestle
With words and meanings. The poetry does not matter.
It was not (to start again) what one had expected.
What was to be the value of the long looked forward to,
Long hoped for calm, the autumnal serenity
And the wisdom of age? Had they deceived us
Or deceived themselves, the quiet-voiced elders,
Bequeathing us merely a receipt for deceit?
The serenity only a deliberate hebetude,
The wisdom only the knowledge of dead secrets
Useless in the darkness into which they peered
Or from which they turned their eyes.

Vain questionings! The only wisdom is the wisdom of humility.

"East Coker III." The darkness swallows up everything, cosmic spaces and prominent contemporaries. Give yourself up to the darkness of God! Wait without hope, without love, without faith. Then the darkness will become light. You must go by the way of ignorance. —"East Coker IV." Meditation on Good Friday. The Passion as redemption by the wounded surgeon.—"East Coker V." Technical reflection:

> So here I am, in the middle way, having had twenty
> years—
> Twenty years largely wasted, the years of *l'entre*
> *deux guerres*—
> Trying to learn to use words, and every attempt
> Is a wholly new start, and a different kind of failure
> Because one has only learnt to get the better of words
> For the thing one no longer has to say, or the way in which
> One is no longer disposed to say it. And so each venture
> Is a new beginning, a raid on the inarticulate
> With shabby equipment always deteriorating
> In the general mess of imprecision of feeling,
> Undisciplined squads of emotion. And what there is
> to conquer
> By strength and submission, has already been discovered
> Once or twice, or several times, by men whom one cannot
> hope
> To emulate—but there is no competition—
> There is only the fight to recover what has been lost
> And found and lost again and again: and now, under
> conditions
> That seem unpropitious. But perhaps neither gain nor loss.
> For us, there is only the trying. The rest is not our
> business.

"The Dry Salvages." I. The river, brown god of primitive times. The worshippers of machines do not honor him. The river is in us, the sea is around us. The howling of the sea. The ground swell measures a time "older than the time of chronometers." —II. Fishermen in peril of the sea. Endless sailing. Growing older. The past has a different pattern. No development! Uncertain nature of experience. Agony of others and our own. —III. Life as a railway journey, a sea voyage. Borrowings from Hindu mythology. —IV. Prayer to the Virgin. —V. Rejection of modern superstitions. Then:

> Men's curiosity searches past and future
> And clings to that dimension. But to apprehend
> The point of intersection of the timeless
> With time, is an occupation for the saint—
> No occupation either, but something given
> And taken, in a lifetime's death in love,
> Ardour and selflessness and self-surrender.
> For most of us, there is only the unattended
> Moment, the moment in and out of time,
> The distraction fit, lost in a shaft of sunlight,
> The wild thyme unseen, or the winter lightning
> Or the waterfall, or music heard so deeply
> That it is not heard at all, but you are the music
> While the music lasts. These are only hints
>   and guesses,
> Hints followed by guesses; and the rest
> Is prayer, observance, discipline, thought
>   and action.
> The hint half guessed, the gift half understood,
>   is Incarnation.
> Here the impossible union
> Of spheres of existence is actual.

"Little Gidding." I. Mood of midwinter spring. The house to which you have made a pilgrimage was once a chapel. The dead speak here with tongues of fire. "Here, the intersection of the timeless moment is England and nowhere. Never and always." —II. Air, earth, fire, water: forms of death.—Meeting with a departed spirit (reminiscent of Dante's meeting with Brunetto Latini), who was a master of words and now reports on the terrors of the hereafter. —III. Meditation on sin, on the Civil Wars of the seventeenth century and its martyrs. —IV. Purification through Purgatory as instituted by Divine Love. —V. The way of poetry and the way of action lead to death. We die and live with the dead. The close:

> We shall not cease from exploration
> And the end of all our exploring
> Will be to arrive where we started
> And know the place for the first time.
> Through the unknown, remembered gate
> When the last of earth left to discover
> Is that which was the beginning;
> At the source of the longest river
> The voice of the hidden waterfall
> And the children in the apple-tree
> Not known, because not looked for
> But heard, half-heard, in the stillness
> Between two waves of the sea.
> Quick now, here, now, always—
> A condition of complete simplicity
> (Costing not less than everything)
> And all shall be well and
> All manner of thing shall be well
> When the tongues of flame are in-folded
> Into the crowned knot of fire
> And the fire and the rose are one.

The Quartets are a paradoxical undertaking. Christian certitude, the deepest and strongest bond of our tradition, is presented in the most subjective form of experience and language imaginable. The great mystics speak a much simpler and warmer language than Eliot. The poet could reply that he does not intend to convey mystical insight, which he lacks, but only such religious experience as he has realized. But the Quartets force the reader to pose the question of their religious relevance. One can, of course, reject this question as illegitimate. This leaves the reader with the option of taking the poems as a confession—but wasn't poetry supposed to be impersonal? Or, finally, one can attend exclusively to the poetic values, letting the subjective as well as the objective religion take care of itself. This would, of course, mean surrendering Eliot as a religious poet. These things must be said in the interest of clarity. The critic, at any rate, cannot evade the question of how he is to apprehend this poetry. And the poet must have asked himself similar questions. The need for such distinctions and definitions only occurs, as we know by experience, in the face of a work or an attitude of mind which, in its very substance, presents a commingling of various spheres. The nature of time, of space, of movement, of generation and death, are philosophical problems and as such not confined to Christianity. Purgatory and the Passion are components of Catholic dogma. The "dark night of the soul" belongs to a different sphere again—the *via purgativa* of the mystics. Finally, the "technical" reflections on the possibilities of poetic language are intrusions, however valuable in their own right. What holds these essentially distinct spheres together is the pathos of a personal spiritual situation. It is the emotional coherence of a tense, individual spirituality. From this point of view the philosophical and religious motifs recede into indifference, without the significance of the poem evaporating on that account into the psychological. For it is not a matter of soul (psyche) but of mind (nous). What we experience are not states of emotion but stations of the mind on its pilgrimage. On this view the personal elements would also be the vehicle of an objective content. All these questions exceed the bounds of what a commentary can supply. So far as I can see, they have not been raised as yet. But they will be raised in the future. The very fact that the Quartets compel such questions is proof of their significance. It testifies to their reserves of what Bergson calls *l'énergie spirituelle*.

Regarded purely artistically, the Quartets seem to me an end which there is no going beyond. Eliot himself will not be able to employ this particular combination of elements again:

topography, conceptual antinomies, dogma, mysticism, poetics. The very appearance of the "technical reflection" (not yet present in *The Waste Land*) and its insistent recurrence lends the Quartets the character of a borderline case. The juxtaposition of logical paradoxes, "hints" and visions, and ascetic exercises seems to admit of no continuation or further development that would not be self-imitation—and that means: a manner. The Quartets as a work of art are the thrust of an isolated artist; a daring ascent to uncharted heights which from below sometimes looks like presumption. The last works of Mallarmé have this terminal character. So have *Ulysses* and *Finnegans Wake*. Why does modern art bring forth such structures? Why must it? These are questions which we can do no more than raise here.

It might be surprising that the poet of such chaste and subtle chamber music should also write for the stage. Perhaps in composing *The Rock* and *Murder in the Cathedral* he was reminded of the liturgical origins of modern drama. The desire to revive English verse drama and restore it to the stage may have been an influence as well. *The Family Reunion* takes the step toward a tragedy on antique lines. I consider Eliot's works for the stage the most dubious part of his production.[24] They have passages of fine poetry. There is only one thing missing: the indefinable aura of life. From the stage, living people must speak to us. Eliot's characters are elegant puppets. A poetic theater cannot be created by knowledge of art. The introduction of the chorus, the three unities, the Eumenides can produce shudders but not tragic horror. The tragedy of Aeschylus' Orestes is convincing because it involves characters of heroic-archaic stature. But Eliot has placed them in the setting of contemporary English aristocracy, and this attempt was bound to fail. The Monchensey family is "society" as the newspaper reader imagines it. "Orestes' " uncle and aunt speak and behave like people of their class in the amusing potboilers of Angela Thirkell. Clytemnestra is celebrating her birthday.

[24] *The Cocktail Party* (1950) represents a great step forward.

390

Ivy: And when will you have your birthday cake, Amy.
        And open your presents?
Amy: After dinner:
        That is the best time.
Ivy: It is the first time
        You have not had your cake and your presents
            at tea.

In a comedy of manners this tone might be convincing. In a tragedy it sounds false. And when after Clytemnestra's death the birthday cake is brought in and the candles are—symbolically!—blown out, the effect on the reader is one of unintended mirth. In *The Family Reunion* everything is calculated according to the best models. It is a fruit of design, not of necessity. Tiresias' transplantation to London could be poetically convincing, but not that of the Eumenides to Wishwood, even if they provoke an agreeable shudder in the spectator. One need not, like Harry, have committed a murder to feel the compelling urge to escape from this milieu, in which every natural impulse is stifled by convention and conformity. E. M. Forster said maliciously, in 1928, about the essays *For Lancelot Andrewes*: "The argument draws no clear line between literary and social tradition, and one has a feeling at moments that the Muses are connected not so much with Apollo as with the oldest county families." But the Monchenseys are no Atrides, and Eliot is no Aeschylus. Attic tragedy is not a transportable institution.

The Family Reunion is an experiment which has its basis in a specific aesthetic. It is indicated as by a catchword in the subtitle of *For Lancelot Andrewes*: *Essays in Style and Order*. Style and Order! That was the battle-cry in the struggle against Romantic and post-Romantic anarchy (I disregard here its application to Church and State). Eliot felt that it behooved him to recall English poetry to disciplined craftsmanship in art—as had been done in France in 1850 by Gautier, in 1920 by Valéry; in Germany around 1890 by George. Eliot's literary criticism stresses this aspect.

One of the critic Eliot's favorite terms is "precision." He praises the "careful and precise" workmanship of a Ben Jonson, the "deliberate and conscious" craft of a Marlowe. He defines the artist's activity as concentration on a task, "which is a task in the same sense as the making of an efficient engine or the turning of a jug or a table-leg." Precision, then, means clean technical handiwork in the sense of good craftsmanship. Turning on a lathe or wheel is a metaphor drawn from the manual arts. Those who demand careful elaboration of the poet have always compared his work to that of the sculptor, the goldsmith, the potter or the carpenter. It is the conception of poetry as craft. To understand its roots we must go back to classical antiquity. This sort of historical reconsideration is as indispensable to literary criticism as it is to philosophy. One of the reasons for the low level of current criticism is its unwillingness or incapacity to satisfy this professional requirement.

The formal-artistic conception of poetry first arose during the Hellenistic age, which has been called the period of "Greek modernism," and is the symptom of a far-reaching cultural transformation that cannot be dealt with here.[25] The ideal of the "erudite poet" originated in Alexandria, at the court of the Ptolemies. Poetry was in the safekeeping of grammarians and philologists. Here arose the new poetry and poetics of Callimachus. The ancient commentators were already of the opinion that it had nothing in common with that of Homer and Pindar.[26] For that very reason it is akin to the modern sensibility, and Valery Larbaud was right when he said in 1925 that the fame of Callimachus, who has six hundred readers in all of Europe, will survive that of our best-known contemporaries. Callimachus offers a "refined" and exquisite art in miniature forms for connoisseurs. A Greek poet of the Augustan age compares it to chased metalwork.[27]

[25] Felix Jacoby, *Die griechische Moderne* (1924).

[26] Hermeias, in his commentary on Plato's *Phaedrus*, p. 245 A.

[27] Crinagoras (*Greek Anthology* IX, 545). The same metaphor,

Such metaphors now become popular. Horace advises the poet to "file" his verses, that is, to polish them, although he knows that smoothness is often achieved at the expense of strength ("sectantem levia nervi deficiunt"). "Polish!" Boileau orders the poets:

> Vingt fois sur le métier remettez votre ouvrage:
> Polissez-le sans cesse et le repolissez!

["Put your work back on the frame twenty times:
Polish and repolish it incessantly!"]

The danger in this aesthetic is prettiness: a complacent turning of elegant trifles. Rivarol scoffed: "J'avoue en mon particulier que j'estime autant celui qui n'a fait en sa vie qu'un bilboquet d'ivoire que Phidias élevant son Jupiter Olympien ou Pigalle sculptant le Maréchal de Saxe. In tenui labor" ["I confess that for my part I value the man who in his life has only made an ivory bilboquet as highly as Phidias raising his Olympian Jupiter or Pigalle carving the Maréchal de Saxe. In tenui labor."] The flood tide of Romanticism washed the dainty little knickknacks away. But when it had ebbed Gautier once more bade the poet:

> Sculpte, lime, cisèle.

His own poems were meant to emulate enamel painting and gem carving (*Émaux et Camées*).

The view of poetry as craft leads to the measuring of a work by the standard of formal perfection. It is tested for beauties and "faults," each element is dissected and analyzed. Horace proclaimed generously that if a poem evinced many fine passages ("ubi plura nitent in carmine"), a certain number of "flaws" might be overlooked ("non ego paucis offendar maculis"). But the ideal is still faultlessness, which leads readily to mere correctness. Eliot counts bad writing, care-

---

joined with that of filing, is also employed in the Augustan age by Dionysius of Halicarnassus (*De Thucydide* XXIV).

less writing, among the "faults" of the Elizabethans and recommends, as a good exercise, "a line by line examination of almost any Elizabethan play, including those of Shakespeare." In another passage he returns to the "minute and scrupulous examination of felicity and blemish, line by line." And he recapitulates: "I wish that we might dispose more attention to the correctness of expression, to the clarity or obscurity, to the grammatical precision or inaccuracy, to the choice of words . . . in short, to the good or bad breeding of our poets." These demands are, of course, fully justified pedagogically. But the proposal of a line-by-line examination of Shakespeare has a different aim. It contains a judgment on Shakespeare. In the name of whom? And Shakespeare's "faults"? The three witches in *Macbeth* are an example of "correct supernaturalism," but to introduce Banquo's ghost into the same play was an error for he belongs "to a different category of ghosts."[28] The formalist method of judging poetry has been distorted here into an ideal of correctness that we cannot go along with. The overestimation of technique is subject to Plato's verdict: "But he who, having no touch of the Muses' madness in his soul, comes to the door and thinks that he will get into the temple by the help of art—he, I say, and his poetry are not admitted; the same man disappears and is nowhere when he enters into rivalry with the madman" [Jowett's tr.]. In Aristotelian terms, Eliot is a "highly gifted" rather than a "manic" poet (*Poetics*, Chap. xvii, 1455b 32). Is he a great poet or a great *poeta minor*?

Yet it would be unjust to limit Eliot's aesthetics to the formalism of correctness, to the intellectualism of "precision." One must not overlook the fact that it also has spiritual roots. Precision for Eliot is a matter of emotional discipline, of intellectual order, clarity, breeding. He requires order even of the emotional constituents of poetry, of "experiences" and "feelings." He finds the structure of Dante's poetry in an ordered scale of human emotions. ". . . Dante's is the most compre-

[28] Shakespeare's rhetoric "is a vice of style, a tortured perverse ingenuity of images" (essay on Marlowe).

hensive, and most ordered presentation of emotions that has ever been made" (1920). "We talk as if thought was precise and emotion was vague. In reality there is precise emotion and there is vague emotion . . . every precise emotion tends towards intellectual formulation."[29] The need to have only disciplined emotions would be understandable in a Yogi. But in a Christian saint? Between ascesis and psychic training is a borderline which it is dangerous to cross. Especially dangerous to artists! The effort to achieve spiritual discipline can kill spontaneity and paralyze the creative powers.

The criticism of the thirty year-old Eliot affects the tone of haughty superiority with which a new generation erects the new tables. This tone can manifest itself in the carefully measured and aloof courtesy of the dandy ("Monsieur Paul Valéry, a writer for whom I have considerable respect . . ."), but also in a provoking lack of respect. Bergson's philosophy is classed among the "follies and stupidities of the French."[30] Milton's heaven and hell are "large but insufficiently furnished apartments filled by heavy conversation." Dickens is a "decadent genius," and Sainte-Beuve is dismissed as "the voluminous Frenchman." Goethe and Coleridge represent the "most dangerous type of critic," the one who is actually born to create, but who through some weakness in his creative gift strays into criticism; hence, Hamlet becomes a Werther in the one, a Coleridge in the other. "We should be thankful that Walter Pater did not fix his attention on this play." Charles Whibley gets a good mark as a critic for having read Petronius and Herondas, but "the suspicion is in our breast that Mr. Whibley might admire George Meredith." All this was very refreshing in 1920. The permanent value of *The Sacred Wood* lies in the intensity and the intellectuality with which the problems of literary criticism are treated. "There is no method but to be very intelligent." Golden words. The critic's

[29] Eliot's reproach against Coleridge is: "his feelings are impure."
[30] Eliot's judgments on France often display a certain irritation. In *The Criterion* (December 1928), he writes once: "The French are an insolent people, and inclined often to repudiate their best friends."

task is simply to "elucidate." Impressionistic criticism is rejected, but—and this is more significant in view of Eliot's later development—so is the doctrinaire criticism of a Horace, a Boileau, "even of a Dryden." For even he was not a completely free mind compared with, say, La Rochefoucauld. The Neoclassical critics always tend to construct rules instead of performing analyses, which is the real profession of the free intelligence. Its contemporary representative is Remy de Gourmont, whom Eliot mentions in the same breath with Aristotle. Gourmont's versatility was indeed fascinating, like that of a Diderot. He taught how to "dissociate" ideas, an exhilarating occupation, but not in the long run. Eliot later tacitly dissociated himself from Gourmont as he did from his intellectual antipode Maurras. He also renounced the cult of the "free intelligence." But one requirement of his early criticism he would perhaps still acknowledge today: that the critic and the poet should possess an awareness of the two-and-a-half thousand years of the European literary tradition. "Tradition cannot be inherited; and if you want it you must obtain it by great labor. It involves, in the first place, the historical sense, which we may call nearly indispensable to any one who would continue to be a poet beyond his twenty-fifth year; and the historical sense involves a perception, not only of the pastness of the past, but of its presence; the historical sense compels a man to write not merely with his own generation in his bones, but with a feeling that the whole of the literature of Europe from Homer and within it the whole of the literature of his own country has a simultaneous existence and composes a simultaneous order." This traditionalism is no longer the awe-inspiring sanctuary of Winckelmann, Goethe, and Schopenhauer: "the figure of which Walter Pater and Oscar Wilde offered us a slightly debased re-edition. And we realize better how different—not how much more Olympian—were the conditions of the Greek civilization from ours. . . . If Pindar bores us, we admit it; we are not certain that Sappho was *very* much greater than Catullus; we hold various opinions about Virgil; and we think more highly of Petronius than our grandfathers did." Antiquity, then; but as felt by the modern sensibility, with an emphasis on the Latins and a mistrust of "classics." This is assuredly not the only position toward Antiquity that a person of artistic sensibilities can adopt nowadays, but it is a natural point of departure, unburdened by didacticism: the attitude of the amateur. We see: *The Sacred Wood* has excellent things in it.

But this open-minded Europeanism of 1920 remained an unfulfilled promise. Eliot concentrated his efforts more and more on the revision of England's poetic tradition from 1580 to 1780. His reevaluations of the Metaphysical Poets, and of the Elizabethan, Jacobean, and Caroline dramatists (who admittedly meet with only little interest on the Continent)— these are the achievements of a great critic. They have already become part of the permanent heritage of English literature. They complete Eliot's intellectual anglicization. But this anglicization at the same time meant a de-Europeanization. From France during the last thirty years Eliot has accepted only Maritain and Maurras: Thomism and *Action Française*. From Spain and Germany nothing. As guest professor at Harvard in 1932 the critic Eliot pronounced the bold judgment that Goethe "dabbled in both philosophy and poetry and made no great success of either." Was Eliot trying to demonstrate the fallibility of his criticism *ex cathedra*? It is true that he also sacrifices Shelley, Keats, and other great writers on the altar of his taste, as refined meanwhile by Dryden and Dr. Johnson. Do the Neoclassical standards of value really exact such asceticism? I am reminded of the penitent Wagnerians mentioned by Proust: "Je n'avais, à admirer le maître de Bayreuth, aucun des scrupules de ceux à qui, comme à Nietzsche, le devoir dicte de fuir dans l'art comme dans la vie la beauté qui les tente et qui, s'arrachant à *Tristan* comme ils renient *Parsifal* et par ascétisme spirituel, de mortification en mortification parviennent, en suivant le plus sanglant des chemins de croix, à s'élever jusqu'à la pure connaissance et à l'adoration parfaite du *Postillon de Long-jumeau*"[31] ["I had not, in admiring the Bayreuth master, any of the scruples of those people whom, like Nietzsche, their sense of duty bids to shun in art as in life the beauty that tempts them, and who, tearing themselves from *Tristan* as they renounce *Parsifal*, and, in their spiritual asceticism, progressing from one mortification to another, arrive, by following the most bloody of *viae Crucis*, at exalting themselves to the pure cognition and perfect adoration of *Le Postillon de Longjumeau*"].[32] The splendid merits of Eliot's criticism are offset by a rigorism that can go to the extreme of a sterile negativity and that will undermine the authority of this critic. This must be regretted by all those for whom the task of criticism consists in preserving the continuity of the European tradition.

It is difficult to determine what are the ultimate roots of Eliot's critical rigorism and exclusivism. Although he recommends clean theoretical distinctions and sometimes gets himself trapped in a glassy intellectualism, we never obtain complete clarification on this point. Does he wish to set up an aesthetic orthodoxy beside the clerical? He has approved in principle "the Roman and Communist idea of an index of prohibited books," deplored the "spirit of excessive tolerance," and declared any large number of freethinking Jews "undesirable." Of Shelley he says: "I find his ideas repellent . . . and the man was humorless, pedantic, self-centered, and sometimes almost a blackguard. He makes an astonishing contrast with the attractive Keats." But Keats too. . . . On the famous conclusion to the *Ode*:

> Beauty is truth, truth beauty,—that is all
> Ye know on earth, and all ye need to know

Eliot says, this "statement of equivalence" seems meaningless to him. "But on re-reading the whole Ode, this line strikes me

[31] Popular opera by Adolphe Adam (1803–56).
[32] Trans. C. K. Scott Moncrieff.

as a serious blemish on a beautiful poem; and the reason must be either that I fail to understand it, or that it is a statement which is untrue." Poor Keats! The "meaningless equivalence" of truth and beauty was already to be found in Shaftesbury, who said: "Beauty is truth." The source of the idea is of course Plato. Eliot is probably too much of an Aristotelian to be susceptible to Platonic thought. But his animadversions on Keats and Shelley testify to a dogmatism the studied modesty of whose phrases ("I fail to understand it" and similar expressions in other essays) cannot conceal an even more deeply-seated arrogance. It would be impolite to use such words were it not that the same author pleads for Christian humility in his poems.

A Christian moralist has a perfect right, of course, to condemn literature which he considers to be pernicious or heretical. But then he must do so from the standpoint of clerical orthodoxy, not of literacy criticism. Or he must separate the two spheres, as Fénelon did when he wrote: "Catulle, qu'on ne peut nommer sans avoir horreur de ses obscénités, est au comble de la perfection pour une simplicité passionnée" ["Catullus, whom one cannot name without horror at his obscenities, is the summit of perfection for a passionate simplicity"]. But one has to be a Fénelon to be able to speak with such loftiness and clarity. In Eliot's attitude, especially in the *Four Quartets*, we believe we can always detect a residue of Jansenism and Puritanism. Behind it is an unresolved antagonism between artistic and religious behavior as a perhaps unavoidable form—and therefore not subject to criticism—of the spiritual conflicts of our time. This position would suffice to assure Eliot a place among the significant manifestations of our epoch. It explains the response which his work has found in the Old World as well as the New. But to Eliot's censure of the age, to his lay theology I prefer his poetic work, most of all *The Waste Land*. He is the discoverer of a new tone which can never be forgotten. He has heard the mermaids singing.

1949

Toynbee's Theory
of History

+++

THE individual understands himself to the extent that he learns to understand his personal history. In order to comprehend our civilization, we Europeans need the consciousness of our history. This is an essential correlation. It was expressed by Goethe and Hegel at the beginning of the nineteenth century. All philosophy before Hegel (the sole exception is Vico) considered history as something totally alien to thought, if not actually contrary to reason. It was Hegel's Copernican feat to have recognized in this element, alien and opposite to mind, a form of the mind itself. History, for Hegel, is mind that has become alienated from itself and taken the form of contingent happening. It is only in this way that mind can display its complete range of forms. The pure happening of history is a text that must be translated back into the language of the concept. In this manner "happened" history becomes "conceptual" history. This is the return of the mind upon itself. In the conclusion to the *Phenomenology of Mind* (1807) these ideas are set forth in exalted, hymnic prose.

Hegel wrote at a time when German philosophical speculation stood at its zenith. Philosophy elevated history to the dignity of mind, but annexed it at the same time. A prospect upon a new land had been opened, but a limit had also been transgressed. The feet of those who should bury philosophy were already at the door (*Acts of the Apostles* 5:9). The age of philosophy was succeeded by the age of history. History made itself independent. In 1826, Leopold Ranke conceived as his mission "the discovery of the legend of world history." At the age of ninety he crowned his life's work with a *Weltgeschichte* (1881–1888). Viewed from without, universal history to Ranke meant history of power; from within, however, it meant "participation in the knowledge of the All"; the key to the piously venerated mystery of the universe. Jacob Burckhardt could no longer share the consciousness of such an initiation; no more than he could share Ranke's affirmation of power. The subjects of his histories were not states but civilizations. But he shared Ranke's aversion to philosophical speculation. The greatness of Ranke and Burckhardt did not become fully discernible until the twentieth century, the age which invented—not without a passing note of resignation—the concept of historicism. Certainly, no previous age had possessed such a wealth of historical knowledge and insight. But was it "conceptual" history? Spengler claimed to supply it, but failed.

Toynbee's theory of history (this is perhaps the best rendering of the title *A Study of History*) ushers in a new phase of historicism. Historicism is placed at the service of reconstruction, as Troeltsch had already demanded that it should be. What Hegel had anticipated by intuition and distorted by logic is developed in Toynbee with sovereign freedom. The immense amount of historical information accumulated throughout a century of historical research is here set forth in a carefully conceived form and with transparent coherence: not for the purpose of aesthetic gratification (although that too is afforded the reader), but of shedding light on the question: where do we stand? what are the chances of a civilization threatened by destruction? "The owl of Minerva flies only when night has fallen," says Hegel. "Night is coming on!" the Sibyl calls to Aeneas in the Underworld: "nox ruit, Aenea" (*Aenead*, VI, 539); and these words stand on the title page of Toynbee's *A Study of History*.

It is a comparative morphology of the twenty-one societies or civilizations that have reached complete maturity on our planet up to the present. They are comparable because the course of their development permits a series of phases to be observed. These phases recur in every civilization and in the same sequence. This sequence proves to be the fundamental law of history for which historians have been searching since Comte. It represents an evolutionary scheme that is rendered comprehensible and distinct by a system of original concepts. The reader must first acquaint himself with this system. I shall attempt to explain it.

Civilizations are vital phenomena and as such are subject to four main phases: genesis, growth, breakdown, and disintegration. Growth means differentiation and integration—as it already does in Spencer's theory of both biological and social development. Accordingly, we also find in Spencer the concept of disintegration as a symptom of dissolution. How do civilizations originate? The naturalistic theories believe that the genesis of civilizations can be traced to biological or geographical factors. Such explanations fail to account for the spiritual life either of the individual or of the civilizations. The creative process is set in motion by a spiritual event. Myth represents it in the image of the encounter between two superhuman potencies: Yahweh and the serpent in the Biblical story of creation; God and Satan in the Book of Job and in the Prologue to Goethe's *Faust*; the Voluspa Saga and Greek mythology also offer analogies. When modern science explains the origin of the planetary system in the encounter of a star with the sun (Sir James Jeans), the underlying conception is the same. This star intrudes into a state of rest or stability like the devil into the earthly paradise or the divine order. It functions as a stimulus that provokes a reaction, were we to translate this cause and effect relation into the language of physiology and psychology. We find this relation again at every level of existence: in the wager between Mephistopheles and Faust and in the passage from the Yin to the Yang, as the two fundamental opposing principles are called in Chinese thought. A bipartite formula corresponding to these analogies has been invented by Toynbee to describe this stimulus-reaction relation that plays a part in the genesis of all civilizations: challenge and response. "Challenge" can apply to a declaration of war but also to an athletic contest. It introduces an ordeal the outcome of which is, and must always be, unpredictable. It can end in success ("victorious responses") or failure. Such physical ordeals are in the first instance a contention of external forces. But even in them spiritual energies are already called into play. The ordeals can also be of a purely internal kind, however. Every task that life sets me contains the possibility of success and failure. This series of trials ending in achievement and confirmation is the stuff of our daily life. Toynbee's formula corresponds to one of man's most fundamental experiences.[1] The conceptual schemata of Toynbee's theory which we have examined so far were borrowed from the theory of evolution, from biology, mythology, and physiology. They must now be further transposed into the language of human morality. To do so becomes possible and even necessary because for Toynbee the creative individual—above all the genius and the mystic —is the bearer of cultural growth. "All acts of social creation are the work either of individual creators or, at most, of creative minorities." This statement sums up one of the chief elements of Toynbee's theory. It has a close affinity with the philosophy of Bergson.

The explanation of the growth of civilization through the action of creative elites meets with a great difficulty: how does the minority succeed in carrying the majority along with it? The difficulty is further increased when we fix our attention on the minorities instead of the creative individuals. The latter are men like ourselves, only they have something we lack: the creative gift, the inner vision. We may illustrate this with an example to which Toynbee would probably not object. In the Christian community of Corinth, "enthusiasts" (*pneumatikoi*) appeared, boasting that they had special gifts. "Effects of power" were supposed to emanate from them such as cures and miracles, but also prophecy, gnosis, and speaking

---

[1] According to A. Portmann it could already be constitutive of the biological nature of man (*Eranos Jahrbuch* 15 [1948], 40).

in tongues. The apostle Paul saw himself constrained to take a position in a letter toward these "gifts of grace" (*charismata*) (I *Cor.* 12). He acknowledged their validity, teaching that they were all operations of the holy spirit. "And God hath set some in the church, first apostles, secondarily prophets, thirdly teachers, after that miracles, then gifts of healings, helps, governments, diversities of tongues. And yet show I unto you a more excellent way. Though I speak with the tongues of men and of angels, and have not charity, I am become as sounding brass. . . ." The creative spirits in the early apostolic communities were charismatics. They disappear from the Church by the second century, yielding to official ministers entrusted with the care of authority, tradition, and orthodoxy.

The "creative individuals" of Toynbee and Bergson are privileged souls or charismatics. In every phase of civilization their number is minimal but also probably constant. What changes in accordance with the phase of civilization is their influence. The "creators" can achieve their effect in two ways. The kindling of creative energy through direct personal contact is the "ideal" or "inspirative" way. It is insufficient by itself to achieve its purpose. But there is also another method of transmission, which makes use of a faculty that is generally available even among ordinary people and primitive societies: imitation. Toynbee uses the Greek word mimesis for it, and we shall retain it in order to distinguish imitation as a social phenomenon from other forms. In primitive, static societies the elders, the ancestors, and the dead are the objects of mimesis. If by means of "social drill" mimesis can be directed toward the "creators," there will be progress in the civilization. Only thus can the inert masses be moved to follow in the footsteps of the "pioneers." Only thus—I might add—does education become meaningful.

The pair of concepts, "challenge and response," led us into the realm of moral experience. But to follow the development of Toynbee's thought, we must now contemplate a phenomenon from the realm of *mystical* experience: ecstasy.

Ecstasy removes the mystic from the normal state of consciousness, but also from the social community. This withdrawal, however, is only the first step in a two-beat rhythm. In his ecstasy the mystic has beheld divine truth. He therewith receives his mission, which is to gain converts to it. He returns to men and to renewed action on a higher plane. This is the rhythm of "withdrawal and return." The formula designates a further step in the growth phase of civilizations. Like "challenge and response," it has been chosen with a view to its applicability to the most various levels of existence: the experience of the mystic but also the growth, decay, and regeneration of plant life. It describes the cyclical changes of seed and fruit, sowing and reaping, spring and autumn, from which the vegetation cults of the ancient world arose (Adonis, Osiris, Dionysus). The grain of wheat later serves the apostle again as a parable: "But some man will say, How are the dead raised up? Thou fool, that which thou sowest is not quickened, except it die. . . . So also is the resurrection of the dead. It is sown in corruption; it is raised in incorruption; it is sown in dishonor; it is raised in glory. It is sown a natural body; it is raised a spiritual body" (I *Cor.* 15:35ff.). A mythical variant of the motif is the story of the foundling. A newborn child of a king is cast away, then miraculously saved. At last, having grown to manhood, he returns to enter into his kingdom. Oedipus, Perseus, Romulus, Jason, Horus, Moses, and Cyrus are examples. In the story of Jesus the motif recurs as the flight into Egypt. The rhythm of "withdrawal and return" is also discernible, however, in the forty-day fast, the transfiguration on Mount Tabor, the death and resurrection, and the promise of the second coming. Human analogies can be found in the careers of Paul, Benedict, and Mohammed; but also in the history of creative minorities.

We perceive that the concepts of Toynbee's cultural morphology have been so formed that they extend from the mechanical to the mystical. They have "cosmic dimensions." The rhythms and oscillations of history are the pulse beats of the universe. At this point a metahistory, a metaphysics of history would have to supervene. Perhaps we may expect one from the volumes still outstanding.

Thus far we have been considering the theoretical aspect of the genesis and growth of civilizations. The curve of their decline may be divided into two phases: breakdown and disintegration. Initially, breakdown means nothing more than cessation of growth. The first symptom to appear is a "time of troubles." This is the term used by Russian historians to designate a period of anarchy in the seventeenth century known to us through drama (Schiller's *Demetrius*) and opera (*Boris Godunov*). It is the miniature model for Toynbee's "time of troubles," which lasts in Egypt from c. 2420 to 2070, in China from 634 to 221, in the "Hellenic" civilization from 431 to 31, in the "Orthodox Christian" civilization from 977 (outbreak of the great Bulgarian war) to 1372 (battle of Chernomen). The times of troubles are succeeded by a universal state. This is an institution by means of which a declining civilization secures a "reprieve," that is, a postponement of its date of expiration. The most familiar example of a universal state is the Roman Empire. The "Orthodox Christian" civilization creates it in the form of the Ottoman Empire, China in that of the Mongol and later of the Manchu dynasty, etc. The universal state is always followed by an "interregnum." For this concept German history from 1256 to 1273 serves as the miniature model. In Europe we had an interregnum of world-historical dimensions from c. 275 to c. 675. The Visigoths defeat the Emperor Valens at Adrianople in 378. In the fifth and sixth centuries the Roman Empire dissolves into successor states. The leading role falls to the Franks. But the power of the Merovingian dynasty collapses around 650. The Austrasian majordomo Pepin of Heristal gains power over the entire kingdom by the battle of Tertry in 687. This is the decisive event in the rise of the House of the Pepins or Carolingians. It signifies the replacement of the "Hellenic" (Graeco-Roman) civilization by western (European) civilization. Nevertheless, according to Toynbee, the genesis of this civilization is not due to the Germanic invaders but to the Roman Church. The Church was the only creative power in the crumbling shell of the Empire. Many historians would like to regard the alleged "infusion of new blood" or the comitatus system as the Germanic contribution to the mediaeval synthesis. They are wrong, according to Toynbee. The "primitive Teutonic liberties," if they existed at all, were rudimentary institutions such as may be found among almost all primitive men at almost all times and places, and did not survive the *Völkerwanderung*. The *Teutons* did not destroy the Hellenic civilization; "rather, they only completed the work of destruction, as it had already died inwardly" (Eduard Meyer). The Catholic Church, although established within the Roman Empire, not only survived it but became the matrix for the newly evolving civilization of the West. Here too we have a special case of a general law: a universal church forms the intermediate member between a declining and a rising civilization.

So much for the external stages in the breakdown of civilizations. What are the internal reasons for it? The creative impulse, as we have seen, is transmitted by way of social drill: "the dull ears that are deaf to the unearthly music of Orpheus' lyre will follow the piping of the rat-catcher of Hamelin." This method of transmission is in danger of becoming mechanical. Growth is predicated upon flexibility and spontaneity, but social mimesis tends toward automatism. If the initiative of the creative minority fails its followers will start to mutiny. The minority reacts by using violence. The piper exchanges his pipe for a whip. The creative minority turns into a "dominant" minority.

As long as minorities remain creative they release new social forces. Ideally, new institutions ought to be created for them. Usually, however, the new force must avail itself of an old institution, the new wine be poured into old bottles. The consequences are disturbances in the form of revolutions and social enormities. The latter are "penalties" imposed upon a society that has failed in its task of bringing into harmony the old institution with the new social force. From this point of view, Toynbee furnishes astonishing analyses of two social forces that have only become active in the last two centuries: Democracy and Industrialism. These two forces impinged upon the institution of slavery, which had already contributed to the decline and fall of the Hellenic Society and had been reestablished in America since the sixteenth century. At the end of the eighteenth century it seemed on the verge of extinction, when it was revived by the Industrial Revolution in England, which greatly increased the demand for the raw material produced by the slave labor of the plantations. Slavery was not legally abolished in the British Empire till 1833, in the United States till 1863. In the Southern States it had developed into a monstrosity that had to be cruelly expiated by the Civil War. It "did not pay"—as little as does the anachronistic institution of war. War too has been given a new lease on life by Democracy and Industrialism. The era of civilized wars came to an end at the close of the eighteenth century. The French Revolution gave rise to the first cycle of "modern wars." Modern war has become "total" war, ever since the "local or parochial states" of the eighteenth century became nationalistic democracies. The first example of total warfare was given by the victorious North Americans at the end of the War of Independence (1776–1783), when they expelled the supporters of the mother country—men, women, and children—from their homes. The example is significant because the victorious colonists were the first democratized nation of our Western society. Another consequence of democracy is universal compulsory education, which was welcomed as a blessing. Its results have been disappointing, however. The content of education becomes the more impoverished the more it is removed from its traditional cultural background and made available to the masses. Moreover, education is no longer valued as an end in itself but only for its practical utility. Finally, modern semi-education has bred an irresponsible press (Northcliffe) which unscrupulous politicians in turn have been able to put into the service of propaganda (Hitler). Hence, those countries in which the ideals of democratic education have been realized are continually in danger of falling into intellectual enslavement. The higher religions are a response to the challenge presented by the disintegration of civilizations. They bear the message of the one God and the brotherhood of mankind. But thanks to an irony of history they also breed intolerance and persecution, since the spiritual pioneers of religious unity seek to achieve it by the quickest way possible. The monotheistic reform instituted by Ikhnaton in Egypt in the fourteenth century B.C. seems to be the oldest example of that fanaticism which Lucretius scourged in a famous line, "Tantum religio potuit suadere malorum" ["to such evil could religion persuade"], and which since the sixteenth century has gained fresh momentum. All the phenomena which have been considered so far belong to the first phase of the decline of civilization, that of "breakdown." The final stage, that of "disintegration," presents new images, or at any rate new features in the image on which we have cast but a fleeting glance. Not all civilizations "die." There are some—like the Egyptiac or the Chinese— that pass into a state of "petrifaction." This may perhaps be the destiny in store for our own Western civilization: a totalitarian universal state, a planetary despotism in which technology would continue to develop and the higher activities of the spirit would perish. It is true that there are still the Christian churches. Have they been reserved for a new martyrdom that will save us from technology?

The emergence of a "dominant" minority has its counterpart in the formation of an "internal" and "external" proletariat. Like the "time of troubles" and "interregnum," "proletariat" in Toynbee's work is an historical concept modeled upon a unique event—the *secessio plebis*—which has then been expanded and made generally applicable. Proletariat, then, only denotes a social group that is "in" a society but not of it. The essence of a proletariat consists neither in poverty nor humble birth but in the resentment that springs from the consciousness of "not belonging." Within the Roman Empire both the oldest Christian communities and the Germanic war-bands constituted an "alien underworld"—the former an "internal," the latter an "external" proletariat. In the end phase of every civilization the dominant minority creates a universal state, the inner proletariat a universal church, and the outer proletariat war-bands. Schism, therefore, is the product of two negative movements. The dominant minority seeks to retain by force a privileged position that it no longer deserves. The proletariat reacts to fear with hatred, to violence with violence. Let us take a closer look at the individual factors. In a dominant minority we can distinguish types of greater and less value. The Roman universal state owes its long duration to innumerable, usually anonymous soldiers and civil servants who were active in it from the time of Augustus on. In the age of the Severi, Roman jurists translated the Stoic ethic into the language of Roman law. The golden chain of Greek philosophers from Socrates (d. 399) to Plotinus (d. A.D. 270) is another example of the function of a part of the dominant minority in the creation of values. A corresponding role is played by the Confucian literati in the Chinese universal state of the Han dynasty (202 B.C.–A.D. 221). Dominant minorities are capable, then, of producing excellent administrators. It is to them that we owe the fifteen universal states disclosed by our comparison of the twenty-one civilizations. The class of the politically able has its counterpart in that of the intellectual leaders. The significance of Greek philosophy for the Roman state is parallel to the immense advance in astronomy which was seen in the Babylonic Society in the eighth century B.C., which also saw the beginning of the war between Babylon and Assyria. At that time Babylonic scholars discovered that the three known cycles—day and night, the lunar phases, and the solar year—fitted into the vaster cycle embracing all planetary movement. The annual birth and death of vegetation thus had its correspondence in a recurrent birth and death of all things that was not to be measured by solar years but by cosmic years. Plato and Virgil (Fourth Eclogue) adopted this astrological determinism.[2] It still survives today—2700 years after its discovery—in a degraded form. Chinese counterparts are the ritual morality of Confucius and the paradoxical wisdom of the legendary Lao-Tse.

The internal proletariats, too, exhibit a wide diversity of types. In the Graeco-Roman society we find citizens of Greek city-states who were uprooted by political and economic struggles (Thucydides' description of the upheavals at Corcyra is classic); conquered peoples; and, last of all, slaves. The second Punic war uprooted the Roman peasantry, first by the devastation wrought by Hannibal and then by the long terms of Roman military service. The work of farming the land had to be performed by slaves. During the last two centuries B.C. all the lands along the Mediterranean coast supplied the demands of the Italian slave-market. The immediate reaction of the proletariat was an explosion of violence; Jewish uprisings against the Seleucids and the Romans from Judas Maccabaeus (166 B.C.) to Bar Kochba (A.D. 132); the Mithridatic wars; Spartacus. But suicidal violence was not the only "response" of the Graeco-Roman proletariat. We also find the nonviolent, "gentle" response: first in the Jewish martyrs who are commemorated in the second book of the Maccabees (chaps. 6 and 7); and then in Christ's crucifixion and the behavior of the first witnesses (*Acts* 5:34ff.). A similar response was that of Orthodox Judaism (represented today by the Agudath Israel as opposed to the Zionists) to the destruction of Jerusalem. The "gentle" resistance of the early Christians to the cult of the Caesars finally compelled the Empire to capitulate to a spiritual force that it had not been able to coerce. The rivals of Christianity were other higher religions which corresponded to the various regions from which the internal proletariat was derived. The Iranian half of the Syriac world contributed Mithraism; Egypt the cult of Isis. The worship of the Anatolian Great Mother Cybele is per-

[2] Virgil: "Magnus ab integro saeclorum nascitur ordo" ["The great cycle of the ages begins anew"].

411

haps a vestige of Hittite society and may originally have come from the Sumerian world (Ishtar).

The internal proletariat of our Western society also presents a great diversity of types. In the last four hundred years the labor force has been recruited from the disintegrating civilizations. African negroes and yellow coolies have worked the plantations in the overseas countries like the slaves from the Mediterranean coasts in Roman Italy. In every community that must adapt its life to that of an alien civilization there is a need for a social class to serve as a transformer. This is the class of the deracinated intelligence ("intelligentsia" in Czarist Russia). It supplies merchants, diplomats, schoolmasters, lawyers. This liaison class is hated by its own people (like the "Quislings" during the Second World War) and despised by the foreigners (like the Indian "babu" by the English "sahib"). The deracinated intelligence of our society is produced in part from that society's own body. Its origins go back to the religious wars of the sixteenth and seventeenth centuries. French Huguenots were scattered from Prussia to South Africa, Irish Catholics from Austria to Chile. The Revolution of 1789 brought with it the emigration of the aristocracy. Since then have followed the liberal émigrés of 1848, the Russian "White" émigrés of 1917, the Italian and German democratic émigrés of 1922 and 1933, and the Austrian Catholic and Jewish émigrés of 1938. Like the emigration, the industrial proletariat is also produced from the body of our own society. The industrial revolution, which around 1830 was greeted with enthusiasm, has conjured up the specter of unemployment.

The chronicle of European revolutions from 1789 to 1933 is written in blood. Of the "gentle" responses we find only vanishing traces (Quakers, Mennonites, Anabaptists). We shall seek in vain for a new religion. The system of Karl Marx springs from the religiosity of the ghetto, Yahweh having been replaced by "Historical Necessity," the Chosen People by the Proletariat, and the Messianic Kingdom by the dictatorship of the Proletariat. At present, however, religious Communism seems to have been defeated by the conservative national Communism of Stalin. On the other hand the planned economy is spreading to the so-called Democracies. It looks as though Capitalism and Communism were becoming different names for the same thing. If this is true it means that Communism has forfeited its prospects of becoming the revolutionary universal religion. It is only a local variant of nationalism. The failure of a new religion to develop among the internal proletariat can probably be explained by the continuing effects of Christianity. Machiavelli, Hobbes, Voltaire, Marx, Nietzsche, Mussolini, and Hitler have not been able to dechristianize Western civilization. Instead, Gandhi has assimilated Christian elements and the American negroes have adopted the religion of their Christian oppressors. Perhaps the apostate Western civilization is destined to be reborn as a *Respublica Christiana.*

The external proletariats likewise come into existence by an act of secession from the dominant minority. The resulting schism is marked physically by a frontier. As long as a civilization is growing it radiates outward and its frontiers are indeterminate. It penetrates all the primitive societies it encounters. Coins have been found in England, sarcophagi in Afghanistan, bearing the stamp of Hellenic art. They are products of mimesis, i.e., of the power of attraction of a higher civilization. But when a civilization ceases to grow its charm evaporates. It no longer exercises its charm on the cultural level but only in economics and politics. Its technical improvements (gadgets) continue to be imitated: as a violent defense against violence. It is at this moment that the *limen* or threshold, which was a buffer zone, becomes a *limes* or military frontier. At the height of its growth Greek civilization was surrounded by a girdle of buffer zones. In the north, Thessaly and Aetolia were still half-Greek, Macedonia and Epirus a quarter Greek, and Thrace and Illyria were barbarian lands. In Asia Minor the western coast of Ionia was screened from the barbarians by the diminishing Hellenism of Caria, Lydia, and Phrygia. In southern Italy [Magna

Graecia] there was a similar gradual transition. Our own civilization, in its first phase, exerted an analogous attraction with the conversion of the Normans, Magyars, and Poles. The conversion of England by the missionaries of Gregory (596) was also peaceful. But in long wars against the populations of the Celtic Fringe in Ireland and Scotland the English acquired habits of oppression and "frightfulness," the stages of which are marked by the Synod of Whitby (664) and the invasion of Ireland (1171). These habits were carried across the Atlantic and practiced at the expense of the North American Indians. Today the Northwest frontier of India affords the only example of a struggle over an undetermined *limes*. During the Hindu time of troubles (1175–1575) this frontier was broken through again and again by Turkish and Iranian war-bands. It was sealed under the rule of the Moguls. The British attempt to conquer Afghanistan ended in 1842 in a military disaster that far surpassed the Italian defeat in Abyssinia in 1896. The independent India of the present day will have to face the problem anew. But the external proletariats are less of a threat than disintegration from within. Up to now civilizations have never been destroyed by an external agency but by suicidal behavior. We breed our own barbarians (*Fasci di Combattimento, S.A.*, etc.).

In general the universal state is built by the dominant minority of its own society. At times, however, this minority deteriorates so rapidly that the construction of this state must be provided by aliens. It will be accepted gratefully even then, for it means a material improvement at any rate on the "time of troubles." Iran has supplied one universal state to the Orthodox Christian civilization in the shape of the Ottoman Empire, another to the Hindus (the Mogul Empire). The concept of the Orthodox Christian society is an historiographical innovation of Toynbee's that offers some difficulties.[3] But it is a key position, a covering construction, first for Byzantine and Russian, then for Turkish history. The Orthodox

[3] For criticism, see N. H. Baynes, *Byzantium. An Introduction to East Roman Civilization* (Oxford, 1948).

civilization emerges from the "post-Hellenic" interregnum at first on the Anatolian Plateau. This region had never been fully Hellenized. From the middle of the ninth century on, the center of gravity of the Orthodox society shifted from the Asiatic to the European side of the Straits. Since then its original stem has remained in the Balkan peninsula. But in modern times it has been greatly overshadowed by its Russian "offshoot." In the usual versions, the history of the Eastern Roman Empire appears as a unity from the founding of Constantinople to the conquest of the city by the Turks more than eleven hundred years later. Actually there are two different institutions, separated from each other chronologically by an interregnum. The Roman Empire in the West came to an end, as we know, in 476. According to Toynbee, the same fate overtook the Roman Empire in the East after the death of Justinian. There followed an interregnum of a century and a half, an epoch of dissolution in which the remains of a dead society were eliminated and the foundations of a new one laid. The Arab threat to Constantinople was twice successfully repulsed (673–677 and 717–718). Orthodox Christendom responded to this challenge by a political "expedient." The expedient was the "evocation of a 'ghost' of the Roman Empire in the Orthodox Christian World" by Leo the Syrian (717–741), which was successful, whereas Charlemagne failed in a similar attempt in the West. But Leo's "success" resulted in the aggrandizement of the Byzantine State at the expense of the Orthodox Church and the consequent internecine hundred years' war between the Eastern Roman Empire and Patriarchate on the one side and the Bulgarian Empire and Patriarchate on the other. "This self-inflicted wound was the death of the Orthodox Christian Society in its original form and its original home." The Bulgarian war was a fratricidal conflict between the two great powers of the Orthodox Christian world. It is the fatal turning-point in the history of this civilization—not the conquest of Anatolia by the Seljuks in the eleventh century, nor the invasion by the Latin West in the thirteenth century, nor the Turkish assaults

415

in the fourteenth and fifteenth centuries. The Orthodox Christian Civilization did not succeed in creating its own universal state, but was compelled to accept it at the hands of the Turks. The penalty imposed upon it for the *Pax Ottomanica* (1372–1768) was religious discrimination. Only the Osmanlis were allowed to govern and to bear arms. The Byzantine Christians were degraded to the position of traders. But as such they made themselves indispensable and soon regained entrance to the capital from which they had been evicted by Mohammed II. The Vlachs from Rumelia became grocers, the Greeks merchants, the Albanians masons, the Montenegrins hall-porters, the Bulgarians gardeners. The Phanar, the northwestern corner of Constantinople, was conceded to the Greeks. It was the seat of the Patriarch as well as of the wealthy merchants. The Phanariots enjoyed trade relations with the West and a close knowledge of Ottoman administration. When the power of the Ottomans began to decline after the second unsuccessful siege of Vienna (1683), the Phanariots moved into the leading positions in the state. At the end of the eighteenth century, it looked as if Western pressure would confer a new ruling class upon the Empire, consisting of the victims of centuries of racial and religious oppression. The Phanariots might have taken the administration of the Ottoman Empire into their own hands had they not let themselves become infected by Western nationalism, itself an aftereffect of the French Revolution. The first explosion of Greek nationalism (Alexander Ypsilanti, 1821) provoked a Turkish counterblow. All non-Turkish elements were expelled from the remaining areas of the Ottoman Empire; the last to go were the Greek Christians of Anatolia in 1922. The transplantation of the Orthodox civilization across the Black Sea (Saint Vladimir, 980–1015) and the vigorous development of this "offshoot" on virgin soil has an analogy in the Japanese offshoot of the Far Eastern civilization. Although interest in Byzantine history, art, and culture, has grown by leaps and bounds in the last decades, the Orthodox Christian civilization has not yet entered the consciousness of a "liberal education." This is no doubt partly due to the fact that it produced no classics. The main reason, however, is perhaps to be sought in its failure to leave behind a body, as it were. This was devoured by the Balkan States and Turkey. But we have seen that from the beginning the Orthodox civilization was subject to frequent changes of ground and shifts in the center of gravity. The presence of an extremely vigorous offshoot beside the withered original stem and, finally, its indistinct emergence from the Hellenic end-phase under Justinian aggravate the difficulty of recognizing the physiognomical outline of this society. It must be found in religion, and the parts of Toynbee's work dedicated to the Universal Churches have not yet been published. For us the essence of Byzantine culture is most tangible in Russian art (icons), literature (Leskow), and theology (Berdyaev).

The social aspect of the disintegration of civilizations has its counterpart in a schism in the soul. This section of Toynbee's work will perhaps interest the historian less, the psychologist and religious person so much the more. "Among all the almost infinitely various manifestations of Human Nature, the Soul alone is capable of being the subject of spiritual experiences and the author of spiritual acts." In the disintegration phase of society the soul's response is no longer creative. It has only the freedom to choose between active and passive behavior. On the level of personal behavior, in its endeavor to express itself,[4] it can choose the passive way of abandon (*akrateia*). It gives free rein to its spontaneous inclinations and lives "according to nature" in the delusive hope that the mysterious Goddess will restore from the fullness of her gifts its lost creative powers. The active alternative is the effort at self-control (*enkrateia*), in which the soul seeks the mastery over nature and the passions through spiritual training (*askesis*). On the level of social behavior the social drill of mimesis is either passively surrendered through truancy or actively replaced by martyrdom. When we pass from the plane of behavior to that of feeling we notice that

[4] Self-expression is not creativity!

417

the Promethean élan characteristic of growth has turned into an impulse to flight from the forces of evil: into a painful consciousness of failure. The passive expression of this situation is a "sense of drift"; the active a "sense of sin." In the domain of social feeling there is a loss of the "sense of style" that is inherent in any growing civilization. The soul abandons itself to formlessness. In the melting-pot of promiscuity incompatible traditions and values are mixed together. This composite style results in syncretism in philosophy and religion. The active contrast to this passive reaction is the striving for a unity of style and a unity of form which should supplant the formless chaos with a universal, eternal order. The same disintegrative tendencies that affect behavior and feeling also operate on the plane of life. Here too the unitary movement characteristic of growth is replaced by pairs of alternatives. We again encounter here the contrast between violent and gentle forms of response. The violent reactions are archaism (passive) and futurism (active). The gentle reactions are detachment (passive) and transfiguration (active). The movement characteristic of the growth stage of civilization is the transfer of the field of action from the macrocosm to the microcosm. In the disintegrative stages a mere linear transfer in the time-dimension is substituted for this movement: symptom of an evasion of the real task. Toynbee defines as archaism all actions and doctrines that call for a "back to." In archaism the objects of mimesis are no longer the creative personalities but the spirits of the ancestors: it is a relapse into the condition of primitive mankind. Futurism repudiates any mimesis at all, thus avoiding the static immobility of archaism, only to fall prey to the senseless motion of a convict on a treadmill or a mouse in a cage. The archaistic and the futuristic utopias alike are unrealistic and unattainable. Cato is presented as a converted archaist, Saint Peter as a converted futurist. Cato's archaistic policy failed. But his Stoic death was more dangerous to Caesar than his active resistance. Peter, though the first to hail Jesus as the Messiah, wanted to understand His kingdom as of this world, and earned a harsh rebuke from the Savior (*Matth.* 16:22). On the Mount of the Transfiguration he relapsed into his prosaic misconception (*Matth.* 17:4). Even in Gethsemane he drew his sword (*John* 18:10). Finally he denied his Master. Even after the Ascension he still protested against the divine command (*Acts* 10:9–16). But the "incorrigible futurist" Peter found the way to "transfiguration" at last as Cato found the way from archaism to "detachment." Transfiguration and detachment mean a genuine spiritual change. Detachment is developed as an ideal of life by the Stoics (apathy, i.e., invulnerability); by the Epicureans (ataraxy, i.e., imperturbability); and by the Buddhists (Nirvana). It is a way that leads out of this world. Its antithesis is the religious ideal of transfiguration. While the attitude of "detachment" is a sheer withdrawal, transfiguration, in the sense of a *Civitas Dei*, accords with the rhythm of "withdrawal and return." A few further references for the sake of clarification!

Abandon found its modern prophet in Rousseau. A modern case of desertion is the nerveless surrender of the newly-won principles of Liberalism by the European intellectuals. The sense of drift manifests itself in the belief in chance (*Tyche*) or necessity (*Ananke*) as determining powers. Tacitus was already uncertain which of the two should be regarded as the causal factor in history (*Annals* vi, chap. 22). Modern historians have still not resolved the dilemma. The man who sees himself adrift on a rushing stream will regard it as chaotic disorder (*Tyche*). But the rudderless ship, "struggling" against wind and waves (a Platonic simile), appears to the physicist as the object of the orderly effects of waves and currents (*Ananke*). The Goddess of Chance—*Tyche*—to which Hellenic statesmen built temples, was "even in the twentieth century, when she had begun to show her teeth, the oracle of British foreign policy." Tyche and Ananke are two ways of looking at the same thing: the soul's relinquishment of self-determination.

The doctrine of Original Sin has a certain external affinity with fatalism. It emerges in Greek Orphism, an artificial substitute for the higher religion which the declining Minoan civilization failed to bequeath to the Hellenic. Plato harshly rebukes the "mendicant priests and diviners" who follow the books of Musaeus and Orpheus and teach that release and purification from evil can be obtained through sacrifices and rites which liberate the dead as well as the living from the "torments of the world beyond the grave." In Virgil's *Georgics* (Bk. II, 489–514) we find a purer echo of this Hellenic sense of sin. The Sumerian penitential psalms afford still another example. The expected modern analogue has not appeared as yet. On the other hand the symptoms of "promiscuity" are all the more evident. Promiscuity already manifests itself in ancient Rome in the "vulgarization" of the dominant minority. Nero contented himself with imitating the proletarian variety artist. Commodus appeared in the arena as a gladiator, and Caracalla even adopted the dress and manners of the common soldiers. "But in A.D. 1946 an Englishman had no need either to read Gibbon or to book a berth on the Trans-Siberian express in order to study the process of proletarianization; he could study it at home. In the cinema he would see people of all classes taking an equal pleasure in films designed to cater for the taste of the proletarian majority, while in the club he would find that the black ball did not exclude the Yellow Press." Vulgarization through the internal proletariat goes hand in hand with barbarization through the external. Barbarians can become familiar with the civilization of a dominant minority either as hostages (Theodoric, Abd-al-Karim) or as mercenaries. Two examples of the role of mercenaries in world history: [1] The twenty-four years of the first Punic war (264–240) were hardly so terrible for Carthage as the subsequent four years of the revolt of the mercenaries, which constitutes the frame for Flaubert's *Salammbô*; [2] "At the time of writing [of Toynbee's book] the military strength of the French Republic resided in White African manpower drawn from the Carthaginian recruiting-grounds in the Maghrib and Black African manpower drawn from trans-Saharan sources. . . . Was it France's destiny, under the increasing strain of an effort to maintain her weakening position in Europe, to serve as the military vehicle through which the valley of the Rhine was to fall under the dominion of barbarians from the Senegal? To an Englishman in his armchair this suggestion might appear to be nothing more serious than a rhetorical question that had been drafted in a National-Socialist Ministry of Propaganda. On the other hand to any native of the Rhineland who had not been living abroad between the autumn of 1918 and the 30th June, 1930, the picture of a Europe cowed by African bayonets would suggest a grim reality with which he was already acquainted through his personal experience." This reflection touches on events from a still uncompleted chapter of the European decline. A prognosis is impossible in such cases. But at this stage in history we can watch the parallel processes in other civilizations by which a dominant minority sinks into barbarism while the barbarians are making their fortunes at its expense. An example of this process is the symbiosis between Germans and Romans in the Empire. At first the Germans assimilate themselves in customs and choice of names to the Romans. From about the middle of the fourth century they retain their own names. Germanic modes begin to spread. Three edicts of Honorius (between 397 and 416) forbid the wearing of trousers, fur coats and long hair within the precincts of Rome. From the fifth century on the Romans in Gaul assume Germanic names.

The most interesting manifestation of promiscuity in declining civilizations is religious syncretism. It occurs when a dominant minority develops philosophies during a time of troubles and when these philosophies collide not only with each other but also with the new higher religions introduced by the alien members of an inner proletariat. In the Hellenic Society the generation of Posidonius (c. 135–52 B.C.) seems to mark the beginning of an epoch in which the several schools of philosophy which had hitherto been in controversy emphasize what united rather than what divided them. In the first two centuries of the Roman Empire, Stoics, Peripatetics, and Academicians subscribe to much the same doctrines. A similar adjustment is reached during the Han Dynasty between Taoism and Confucianism. The religion of Zoroaster and Judaism had mutually interpenetrated to such an extent by the second century B.C. that modern scholarship can scarcely disentangle the different strands. In the interior of a Universal State the adherents of the schools of philosophy and the devotees of the popular religions usually converge. The religions commend themselves in the first instance to the dominant minority's notice by adapting their divinities to that minority's style of art. Mahayana Buddhism, Mithraism, and the cult of Isis and Cybele all proceeded in this fashion. But Christianity alone went so far as to express its creed in the language of Hellenic philosophy. In the synoptic gospels Jesus is regarded as the Son of God, but in the prologue to the gospel of John, the Savior of the World is called the Logos. The religion of the incarnate dying God is wrapped in a garment of philosophy.[5] The Alexandrian Christian Fathers continue this practice. The complementary and opposite movement is the approximation by the dominant minority of its philosophy to the alien religion of the proletariat. A classical example of it is the introductory scene of Plato's *Republic*. The dialogue takes place in the Piraeus, in the house of a resident alien. Socrates has walked down to the port in order to observe the festival in honor of the Thracian Goddess Bendis. The religious curiosity which drew him there was still alive in Athens nearly five hundred years later when several Epicureans and Stoics asked a foreigner: "May we know what this new religion is that you preach?" (*Acts* 17:19).

[5] Our theologians rightly reject the attempt "to derive Johannine thought with the aid of philosophical-idealistic interpretations from the thought of the Greeks" (*Theologische Literaturzeitung* [1948], p. 23). But Logos is a Greek word and a Greek idea, as John must have known when he wrote: "In the beginning was the Logos."

Platonism had developed in the third and second centuries in the direction of religious skepticism, but Posidonius, the Syrian from Apamea, opened the gates of the Stoa to popular religious beliefs and customs to an extent that would have astonished even his predecessor, the aristocrat Panaetius of Rhodes. Thus already at the turn of the second century B.C. a new religious mood announces its arrival in the sensitive organ of philosophy. The toleration of alien cults in the era of the universal state is found as an administrative practice with the first emperor of the Han Dynasty in China and with Gallio, the proconsul of Achaea, who rejected the complaints of the Jews of Corinth against Paul (*Acts* 18:12–17). This Marcus Annaeus Gallio was a brother of the philosopher Lucius Annaeus Seneca, whose religious attitude so closely approaches that of Christianity that mediaeval theologians could allow themselves to believe in an exchange of letters between Paul and Seneca. But there is nothing surprising in the harmonies of tone between "two pieces of spiritual music created in the same age under the inspiration of the same social experience." Thinkers like Seneca inhabit an intellectual march between the philosophy of the dominant minority and the religion of the proletariat. Such a position can be no more indefinitely maintained than a military *limes*. The philosophies burst into bloom at one moment only to sink into superstition at the next. Belief in demons and magic takes possession of the minds in senile Platonism as in senile Confucianism. Perhaps an analogous degeneration is in store for modern philosophy. The "red line" that runs from Hegel through Marx to Lenin will perhaps follow a curve similar to that golden chain which led from Plato through skepticism to the "medicine man" Proclus. . . . "Such is the miserable end of the philosophies of the dominant minority. . . . In the last act of the dissolution of a civilization the philosophies finally dry up and wither away, while the higher religions keep alive and in consequence become the defunct philosophies' residuary legatees. . . . When philosophies and religions meet, the religions must

423

increase while the philosophies must decrease." Unfortunately we must refrain from entering here upon a discussion of Toynbee's criticism of philosophy.

The counterbalance to syncretism, as has previously been indicated, is a tendency to unity. Behind the flicker of ephemeral phenomena the world is apprehended as an eternal unity. An intimation of this kind is an active element in the genesis of all universal states. Alexander assembled Persians and Macedonians at a banquet at which he prayed to the Gods for "concord" (*homonoia*) and for the common participation of both peoples in the imperial government. Plutarch reports as one of Alexander's sayings: "God is the common father of all men, but he makes the best ones peculiarly his own." If this saying is authentic, it may be regarded as a preliminary anticipation of the Augustinian *Civitas Dei*. The longing for a "world order" breathes through the Latin poetry of the Augustan age. In a mature universal state we find a supreme personal monarch and a supreme impersonal law. The ruler then appears as the earthly equivalent of a supreme God like Amon-Re or Marduk-Bel. In the states in which "Law is king of all" (Herodotus III, chap. 38, quoting Pindar), the personality of God is obliterated as the "law that governs the Universe" comes into sharper focus. Christianity's concept of God is being displaced in the West by natural science, just as Marduk-Bel was displaced in Babylonia in the eighth century by the worship of the planets. In China, though the concept of law has taken hold, the Godhead has nevertheless been supplanted by an "Order" which appears as a magical sympathy between the behavior of man and that of his environment. The Emperor is the "Son of Heaven." Yet the concept of the divine personality is so pale that the Jesuit missionaries were confronted with a difficult problem when they had to translate the word *Deus* into Chinese. The reverse is the case where the principle of universal unity is envisioned as an omnipotent Godhead. Then the law is conceived as an expression of the divine will. Just as the universal state comes into existence when a "King of Kings" makes himself sole monarch, so the diverse gods of a pantheon gradually merge into *one* God, whose uniqueness is his essence. The Persian monarchy, which overshadowed Judaea politically, influenced the conception of the God of Israel, as the Book of Daniel (c. 166–164 B.C.) attests (chap. 7:9–10). Yahweh was in origin a local divinity who inhabited a volcano in northwest Arabia. But he is also a "jealous" God whose first commandment runs: "Thou shalt have no other gods before me." He was both provincial and exclusive. What is surprising is that the same Yahweh retains his intolerance when, after the overthrow of the Kingdoms of Israel and Judah and the establishment of the "Syriac" universal state (Achaemenian Empire, 525–332), he steps out into the wider world and, like his neighbors, lays claim to the worship of all mankind. In this ecumenical phase of Syriac history Yahweh's persistence in maintaining his intolerance was an anachronism. Yet it was precisely this trait in his character that helped him to his triumph. The Jewish, Christian, and Islamic conception of God has been derived historically from the tribal and provincial God Yahweh, but its theological content bears a much closer resemblance to an Amon-Re or a Marduk-Bel, who reigns over the whole universe, or even to a Stoic Zeus or Neoplatonic Helios. But neither the philosophical one God of the Greeks nor the omnipotent and omnipresent supreme divinity of Egyptian or Mesopotamian provenience could compete with Yahweh, for he was a "living" God. "For who is there of all flesh that hath heard the voice of the living God speaking out of the midst of the fire, as we have, and lived?" (Deut. 5:26) —this is the boast of the Chosen People. This quality of being "alive" enabled Yahweh to overcome his primitive provincialism. His intolerance, moreover, enabled him to triumph over his rivals (Mithra, Isis, Cybele) who were ready to enter into a compromise with any other cult. Toynbee's philosophy of history leaves us with the conclusion that only a renewal of Christianity can save our civilization from disintegration. Not, however, in the sense that it should give birth to another "civilization," which would then take its place among those of the past, but in the sense of the genesis of an historical body of a new kind.

I have attempted to trace the main outlines of Toynbee's theory of history. This is the equivalent of projecting a map upon the dimensions of a postage stamp. But outlines can be recognized even on a postage stamp.

Toynbee's *Study of History* concerns every one who is intellectually alive and every such person will respond to it. This has never happened before with a work of philosophical history. Spengler, who might be compared, had almost no impact outside of Germany. But in the English-speaking world Toynbee's work has already reached the number of editions of a best-seller.[6] Even now no intellectual discussion of our time can afford to neglect it. And yet its influence has only just begun. In Germany it will be received all the more gratefully as our view of history, after a period of German-provincial followed by National Socialist indoctrination, has become unduly narrow. It may be foreseen that the response of official historical scholarship—and not only in Germany—to the "challenge" of Toynbee's *Study of History* will be one of protest. Scholarly criticism usually reacts to a revision of first principles by demonstrating that this or that is "incorrect." The significance of a universal theory is not affected, however, by corrections of detail: that is a fundamental law of progress in scientific knowledge. For the rest, we may leave it to Toynbee himself to try conclusions with the profession of history. Of the still unpublished sections of his work the last is expected to deal with historiography up to the present (*The Inspirations of the Historians*).

In Aristotle's *Metaphysics* God is the thinking of thinking

---

[6] The first three volumes of the work were published in 1934 and were also available in German libraries. I know of no reference to them in any German scholarly publication. Volumes IV to VI came out in the summer of 1939, too late for us to take cognizance of them. Fortunately, in 1946 the abridgment by D. C. Somervell was published. By December 1947, one hundred thousand copies of it had been sold in the United States alone. The ball has started to roll.

and at the same time the Prime Mover, i.e., the cause of all movement. But he is himself unmoved. How then does he move others? He does so through the power of spiritual attraction that emanates from him. He moves "by being loved." This profound conception is the philosophical parallel to the myth of Orpheus. He too moves by spiritual attraction: the animals obey his lyre. That spiritual attraction can become a moving force; that it can exercise its power as charm (Lat. *carmen*—French *charme*)—this gentle drawing of the mind is a truth that Toynbee sets in a new light. The "Creator's" power of attraction is a special instance of it. Needless to say, to create in this sense is something different from the fabrication of pictures and books, an activity that has sunk today to the level of mere self-expression ("creative writing" in Anglo-Saxon literary jargon, "Gestalten" in German) and that loses itself in discussions of no interest to anyone except the participants.

Toynbee's work makes world history more interesting and more absorbing than we could have imagined. This is not the result of simplification, which does violence to the facts or ignores them, nor of subjective "synthesis." The opposite is the case. The reader must take cognizance of broad areas of pragmatic events which he had never known existed. He learns to think not only in continents but in civilizations and millennia. Nothing is omitted and yet only the essentials are presented.We are given the *whole* of history. For the first time the survey is complete. This changes a great many things. "History," Ortega once said to me, "is perhaps a discipline which has not yet had its classics." Thus far the twentieth century had left the synoptic presentation of history to dilettantes like Wells or to constructors of systems like Spengler. Now for the first time an historian of modern training has taken the matter in hand. A sovereign view of the whole evolves here from precise knowledge of details. A new methodology for the humanistic disciplines is announced in this work. The growth of scholarship too proceeds only through creative individuals.

I imagine that Toynbee's view of history could become, in the next decades, a common possession of all thinking people —by way of "inspiration" and social mimesis. The positive effects which such a change in the state of consciousness would have are incalculable. One desirable negative effect would be the elimination of all those outmoded private historical constructions that occlude the vision today. Hitherto, history, even in its "scientific" form, has been a domain of free, unbinding opinion. One might learn the historian's craft and apply it to a tiny plot of historical ground. But one did not look beyond the pale. Or rather, the pale was the enclosing horizon. That is going to change. It will be a liberation.

1948

Jorge Guillén

+++

BETWEEN the two world wars there were three poets whose work I was inspired to translate: Paul Valéry, T. S. Eliot, and Stephen Spender. After many years Jorge Guillén is the fourth. One translates not what one wants to but what one must. There are poems that appeal to one like women. But there are appeals that die without an echo. They fade into the unspoken. They heralded possibilities that were not realized. Jorge Guillén in one instance employs the antithesis of existing and persisting. More than a mere appeal is required if the gulf is to be bridged. The appeal must strike again and again, must penetrate deeper and deeper, persist, draw us out. Then the dams will burst. Related elements embrace, recognize, affirm each other. Thus and thus only do I conceive the activity of translation. It is the response to the challenging power of creation. It is the most valid form of assent.[1]

Jorge Guillén (born in Valladolid in 1893) has taught Spanish literature in Paris, at Oxford, in Seville, and more recently in the United States, where he still lives. He is to be found among the contributors to the *Revista de Occidente*, the review founded by Ortega in 1923. A prose meditation under the heading of "Air—Breath" (*Aire—Aura*, October 1923) perceives in the atmosphere the beginning of transcendence ("the air is not human; the air is heaven") and illustrates this distinction with the image of Christ's ascension. Then poems appear in the *Revista*, as well as the translation of Valéry's *Cimetière marin* (June 1929). The poems are collected in 1928 as *Cántico* (seventy-five pieces); augmented

---

[1] This essay introduced a selection of translations from Guillén's poetry published under the title of *Lobgesang* by the Arche-Verlag, Zurich.

editions follow in 1936, 1945, 1950. This last edition contains 334 pieces and is described as the "first complete edition." Guillén is the creator of a single work, and that work a single "song of praise." As presently available, it encompasses the results of three decades of creation.

According to Aristotle, all poetry is originally either praise or blame. Goethe too determines poetry as "mankind's song of praise, which the Godhead loves to hear." The literature of the last one hundred years cultivated blame in all its subspecies rather than praise. Indeed, the neutral concept of blame may be used to cover all the accusations which each of twenty or thirty naturalisms, expressionisms, existentialisms of all countries and continents have brought together as an indictment against man, life, existence. The sum of these depositions represents the evidence for that European nihilism diagnosed by Nietzsche: "You must either eliminate your venerations—or yourselves." Modern literature has discharged its historical mission by eliminating all venerations. Twenty years ago Gottfried Benn drew up a balance-sheet, "nach dem Nihilismus" ["after nihilism"]. It was premature; for the "revolution of nihilism" followed on the heels of his account. Since then the problem has not been reformulated.

Naturally Aristotle's classification is somewhat primitive. Literature, like life, cannot be subsumed under a system of neat disjunctions. Such a system fulfills its purpose if it serves as a provisional means of sifting and sorting. The literature of nihilism becomes interesting at the point where "praise" blossoms out of negation and despair, like the vernal flower out of the rubble of our cities. Lyric poetry sometimes springs from ruins, and we have seen hymns sprout like lilies from disease wards—precisely in the poems of Benn.

But it seldom happens that a work of twentieth century poetry is, like Jorge Guillén's, a song of praise and nothing else. Here everything is played in a major key, everything exults and rejoices in the sun. Here are no dissonances, no neuroses, no "flowers of evil." The inconceivably lofty works are glorious as on the first of days. Some readers will first have to accustom their eyes to these cataracts of light. Here is a region without tragedy, without bitterness, without accusation. Where else can it be found in modern poetry? Stefan George sounded this note one time only:

> Hegt den Wahn nicht: mehr zu lernen
> Als aus staunen überschwang
> Holden blumen hohen sternen
> Einen sonnigen Lobgesang.

[Do not cherish the illusion: to learn more than from excess of wonder, gracious flowers, high stars, a sunny song of praise.]

George was aware of this possibility but his law directed him to other paths; he had to follow them. Valéry consecrated a hymn to dawn and extolled the mathematical beauty of Greek columns:

> Nous allons sans les dieux
> À la divinité.

[We go forward without the gods toward divinity.]

But his serpent addresses the sun as a blemish:

> Soleil, soleil! . . . Faute éclatante

[Sun, sun! . . . brilliant flaw]

and extends this indictment to the entire realm of being:

> Que l'univers n'est qu' un défaut
> Dans la pureté du Non-Être.

[That the universe is only a defect in the purity of non-being.]

Of course, it is the perspective of the serpent. But that of M. Teste, Valéry's intellectual hero, is not very different.

In blazing contrast is Jorge Guillén's affirmation of being. It is sole and singular in modern literature. Maurras once decreed that "poetry is ontology."[2] Should this statement be correct, Guillén's poetry would be a striking example of it. But fortunately it is as independent of every philosophy as it is of every passing intellectual fashion. Not even the Essentialism that is currently being brewed on the left bank of the Seine, now that Existentialism has been consumed, will be able to change that. The poetry of Guillén is self-sufficient utterance. It needs no philosophical commentary, although it might well serve the philosopher as a text for his meditations.

"Beyond" (*Más allá*) is the title of the poem that opens the carefully planned composition of the *Cántico*. The situation out of which it grows is a morning awakening. To the intrusion of the light of the rising day, the soul responds with joyous wonder. It is the sensuous and intellectual astonishment at the fact that something *is* ("that not rather nothing is," as Scheler put it). This invasion of being carries with it a blissful assurance that knows nothing of care or existential anxiety. It summons the soul to concord and harmony with thousands of voices. Its will to being responds to the being of the universe. A movement of rejoicing ascends, rises higher and higher, surpasses all bounds. "Further on"—this is the literal translation of the title. Can a single lifetime, a single age satisfy such a hunger for being? The soul demands more (*La Florida*): astral dimensions, ageless presences, mountains of raw eternity:

> Yo necesito los tamaños
> Astrales; presencias sin años,
> Montes de eternidad en bruto.

The matutinal awakening to the world is a theme for which Guillén constantly finds new melodies ("Der Morgen kam,"

[2] He relied for this view on the authority of Boccaccio and found approval for it in Maritain, who may thus number Boccaccio among his intellectual progenitors. Cf. *Europäische Literatur und lateinisches Mittelalter* (2nd edition, 1954), pp. 233ff. [*European Literature and the Latin Middle Ages*, trans. Willard R. Trask (New York, 1953), p. 227].

we hear in Goethe; "Der junge Tag erhob sich mit Ent-
zücken. . ." ["The morning came; The young day rose with
delight. . ."]. Awakening in the soft darkness of the night . . .
then a tearing, a shock, a vertical intrusion . . . and, already,
vertiginous delight in the restored world. World and soul have
attuned themselves once more to the same pitch:

> Otra vez el ajuste prodigioso.

[Once again the miracle of adjustment.]

The miraculous precision-mechanism of the soul! Guillén's hymnic affirmation of being contains nothing frenzied,
turbulent, or chaotic. With mathematical precision the rays
operate

> Que al mediodía ciñen
> De exactitud.

[Which encircle noon with exactitude.]

Autumn is an "island of severe profile" which allows "the in-
decisive wave" to be forgotten. The love of line is proclaimed.
It culminates in the perfection of the circle, which is also the
"secret of the sky." For it is there that the circle turns into
the arc of the sphere. The line is completed in space; not
in the infinity of space, however, but in its palpable rounding
—in volume, the fulfilled shape of space. In this determination one of the most characteristic features of Guillén's poetic
world is revealed. Translation can give only approximate
values here:

> ¡Oh concentración prodigiosa!
> Todas las rosas son la rosa,
> Plenaria esencia universal.
> En el adorable volumen
> Todos los deseos se sumen.
> ¡Ahinco del gozo total!

[Oh miraculous concentration! All roses are the
one rose, plenary universal essence. In adorable

433

volume, all desires are summed up. Ardor of total
delight!]

The path from the initial point of emotional impact to the
imperative function of line and from there to the fulfilling
presence of volume is one of the forms in which Guillén's
experience of being manifests itself. But at the same time it
is symbolic of the movement described by the incipient vibration of feeling in its gradual effort to become the poem. It is
the way "toward the poem" (*Hacia el poema*), "toward the
name" ("hacia el nombre"). In the analysis of this way and
this movement toward, Guillén's theory of poetry is to be
found. Its origin is a rhythmic pulse, as yet bare of any content and any expression. Trusting to it, the poet extri-
cates himself from the confused dream. Words flock to him,
"determined to light up in vivid volume" ("decididas a ilumi-
narse en vívido volumen"). Sound takes on profile, form becomes a "life-belt":

Hacia una luz mis penas se consumen.

[Striving toward light my efforts are consumed.]

The world beheld by the eye wishes to be repeated and confirmed in a valid poetic utterance, which contains it as a possibility ("forma de ese mundo posible en la palabra"), as all
life strives toward its utmost realization (*Vida extrema*).
To live the whole, but also to say the whole ("si del
todo vivir, decir del todo") is the poet's task. Life merely
lived is life incomplete, and requires transforming into precise
outlines, pure fullness of form:

Forma de plenitud precisa y casta.

Form in this sense is nothing but the apex of a dynamic curve;
the splendor of its legitimate sway. It is a final result, beyond
beauty and ugliness,

Por sí se cumple, más allá del gusto.

[Complete in itself, beyond taste.]

The movement of ascent toward something and "beyond it" recurs here. It signifies recovery and preservation of the luminous vision. The vital process of such poetry begins as the beating of a pulse that is simultaneously impulse: it is actualized in a combination of words ("el inicial tesoro de una frase"). Poetry becomes a limiting function, the ultimate flower of life:

Gracia de vida extrema, poesía!

Thus it participates in a universal process which presents itself to the experience of the poet as both internal and external. All being aspires to transcendence; it longs to soar beyond itself. The white pomp of the clouds over the ocean seems to evaporate into gray, but only "in order to gain crimson edges." A bush unfolds in the springtime. Slowly the bud begins to blush. Does it merely turn red? No, the flower is quivering with impatience; it wants to accomplish its own name: *lilac* (meaning both the shrub and the color).

As the cloud seals itself in crimson, as the bud matches its color to its name, so the poet enhances the things of the world by naming them as Adam did in the Garden of Eden, in the words of the Scripture: "And man gave names to all cattle, and to the fowl of the air, and to every beast of the field." According to ancient belief, things do not attain their true essence until they have been named. When Adam gives the animals names, he exercises his dominion over all creatures. To name the nameless constitutes the office and dignity of the poet. In this way he takes part in the work of creation:

Ser henchido de ser jamás empieza
Ni termina. Amor: tú siempre añades.
Creo en la Creación más evidente.

[Being filled with being never begins or ends. Love, you are constantly adding. I believe in the most evident creation.]

435

An archetypal memory of the first garden of creation pervades the poetic work of Jorge Guillén:

> Es la luz del primer
> Vergel, y aun fulge aquí,
> Ante mi faz, sobre esa
> Flor, en ese jardín.

[It is the light of the first orchard, and it still shines here, before my face, upon this flower, in this garden.]

With the newly-arranged garden of his "Song of Praise," Jorge Guillén takes his place in the first rank of contemporary poets.

1951

Remarks on the
French Novel

✦✦✦

NATIONS, like individuals, are distinguished by their gifts. As early as the twelfth century France supplied all of Europe with verse romances and narrative matter. In the nineteenth century, which for France begins in 1789, it outdoes the other nations in three fields: painting, the novel, and revolution. From David (1748–1825) to Cézanne (1839–1906) French painting dominates, as did Italian in the Renaissance, Spanish during the Baroque. It is not as though a talent of genius came to the fore from time to time; no, an abundance of first-rate masters is found together in a small area; they relieve each other, form schools, invent formulas, set the pace for all of Europe. Whoever wishes to learn how to paint must do so in France. The revolutions of 1789, 1830, 1848, 1871 have ostensibly nothing to do with painting and literature; in actuality, a great deal. The "Great Revolution," to which Napoleon put an end, became the French myth of the nineteenth century. The later revolutions model themselves upon it, take up its motifs, lead the nation constantly to reflect anew upon the phenomenon that is society. The France of the Ancien Régime had been composed of estates of the realm, in which the Third Estate (the bourgeoisie) was of no importance. That changed after 1789: not because of the Declaration of the Rights of Man but because of the confiscation of Church property valued at three billions. The state declared it national property, but then sold it again to the highest bidders. Among the buyers were wealthy bourgeois, but also peasants, craftsmen, and day-laborers. The result was not only an enormous shift in the distribution of wealth, but also a great number of new owners whose property was protected by law. The concept of private ownership with unlimited rights of disposal was one of the achievements of the French Revolution. It made the purchasers of nationalized land into the staunchest supporters of the new regime. At the same time, the redistribution of property meant a reordering of society.

The effect of these changes was that society emerged in a new way as a historical potency and a determining factor. It was no longer a rigid body of estates, but one that had become mobile through money. The spread of the Industrial Revolution from England to the continent hastened this process. Society, its patterns of movement and its laws, was discovered in France as a vital force between 1800 and 1848 and reflected in the novel. The reaction of German scholarship to this discovery was Lorenz von Stein's *Geschichte der sozialen Bewegung in Frankreich von 1789 bis auf unsere Zeiten* (1850) [*History of the Social Movement in France from 1789 to Our Own Day*]. "Movement"—this word was first used in France after 1830 to denote events of a political and social character. One distinguished between a "party of movement" and a "party of resistance." Since that time we speak of intellectual, artistic, religious "movements," thereby employing a term from the era of the French Revolution. The transfer of political concepts to art and literature is a nineteenth century French mode of thought. In 1827 Victor Hugo commended Romanticism as "liberalism in literature," and after 1871 Émile Zola believed he could prophesy: "The Republic will be naturalistic, or it will not be." His last, unfinished cycle of novels proclaims a new, fourfold gospel: fertility, work, truth, justice.

The first volume of this cycle *Fécondité*, appeared in 1899. France was shaken at the time by the fevers of the Dreyfus Affair, which was a civil war without arms. The founding of the *Ligue de la Patrie française* (January 1899), in which Maurice Barrès took part, was a symptom of reawakening

French nationalism. Charles Maurras developed it into royalism. As a program that meant the Counterrevolution. This change of front by a section of the French intellectuals had been prepared by schools and authors of very diverse origin and direction, who had only one thing in common: their esteem for French tradition. Even the greatest novelist of the nineteenth century was invoked as a witness. Balzac had defended the monarchy and the church. If one analyzes his political ideas, one finds, to be sure, that his fundamental notion was a politics of "national energy" above and beyond all parties, systems, and traditions. But around 1900 his authority could be cited in the struggle against the "errors of the French Revolution."

The strong politicizing of literature produced as a counter-effect an escape from politics into "pure art." The slogan of the ivory tower comes from a forgotten poem by the great critic and mediocre poet Sainte-Beuve, in which, in 1837, he had characterized the heads of the Romantic movement. He contrasts the combative Victor Hugo with Alfred de Vigny, who around 1826 was considered by connoisseurs as the greatest poet of the circle. But he had soon lapsed into silence:

> Vigny, plus secret
> Comme en sa tour d'ivoire,[1] avant midi, rentrait.

This escape from politics could take various forms. In Flaubert it is part of a nihilism of values that affects all departments of life with the sole exception of art. In *L'Éducation Sentimentale* (1869), he casts a critical spotlight on the Revolution of 1848. The hypertrophic dreams of his youth had shattered against reality. He represents the "disillusioned romantic" who unmasks the idols (the parrot of the old serv-

---

[1] *Turris eburnea* comes from the *Song of Solomon*, chap. 7, as part of a description of feminine beauty according to oriental taste: "Thy neck is as a tower of ivory." The Lauretan litany applied the term to the mother of God. Liturgy and mysticism have contributed many effective images to French Romanticism.

439

ant in *Un Coeur simple* is paradigmatic). Another Norman, Barbey d'Aurevilly, holds aloft through all changes in literary trends the banner of Romanticism even into the closing years of the nineteenth century; a late-Romanticism grown blustering and reactionary, to which Catholicism appears as the weatherbeaten balcony from which one can spit down on the modern masses. In the art of Villiers de l'Isle-Adam, which is to be rated higher, Symbolist elements are already present by the side of Romantic ones. In his novels he gives analyses of an Americanized world of the future; in the metaphysical drama he celebrates an idealism in flight from the world and superior to it. His feelings anticipate the emotional pressures of the age of the masses, but "for those who are worthy of it," he believes, there will always be solitude: "il y aura toujours de la solitude pour ceux qui en seront dignes."

Lonely, uncomprehended by his contemporaries—except for Balzac—Stendhal grew toward his posthumous fame, which with a sure instinct he had predicted for 1880 or 1890. Nietzsche became the executor of this prophecy. One admired on Nietzsche's tracks the boldness of Stendhal's psychology or the calculating lust for power of his Julien Sorel. Stendhal has his roots in the last years of the eighteenth century, but his critical intelligence alienated him from the nineteenth century, which in 1921 was to be branded the "stupid" century by Léon Daudet. Nevertheless, even the solitary Stendhal becomes comprehensible only against the background of history, which in three consecutive acts showed Napoleon's heroic adventure, the hypocrisy of the Restoration, and finally the dullness of the bourgeois monarchy. Napoleon, Italy, opera were Stendhal's passions; Italy—and thus opera—was opened up to him by the campaigns of the Corsican general. To him Italy is the country which alone permits the grand passion to flower. His Italian novellas give Stendhal a place among the earliest discoverers of the Renaissance. At the same time, Italy is the name for everything he loves—the positive counterpart to the France he detests.

Stendhal was able to set down a novel of five hundred printed pages like the *Chartreuse de Parme* in fifty-two days because he was carried away with his subject and because writing—including that of diaries, biographies, promenades in Rome, autobiographies—was for him the most fascinating of occupations. Balzac too wrote rapidly. His tempo is feverish haste. He is harassed by publishers and creditors, but also by the abundance of his inspiration—by the two thousand characters waiting to be brought to life. His style does not have the innate naturalness of Stendhal's. Where he wants to be emphatic or imposing, he can mistake the tone. But his lapses are like the slag from a stream of lava. No author of the nineteenth and twentieth centuries can even remotely match him in power. With Stendhal we have the feeling that he writes for his private pleasure without making a fuss about it. With Balzac it is quite otherwise. He regards himself as the explorer, anatomist, physician, legislator of society, of this "second nature," which he wishes to encompass in a titanic synthesis. His *Human Comedy* seeks to rival Dante's *Divine Comedy*. The lives of its main characters are interwoven among several dozens of novels. This artistic device could be imitated by modern and even contemporary novelists. But they could not wrest Balzac's secret from him. We shall have to start further back.

How does a novelist proceed? He finds a hero; endows him with traits capable of arousing our sympathy; guides him through the complications of the search for adventure, love, profession or calling; has him acquire the knowledge of men and the world which he, the author, possesses; conducts him to the haven of marriage or the maturity of death. This scheme underlies the mediaeval romances of chivalry, *Don Quixote*, Fielding's *Tom Jones, Wilhelm Meister*, and, in our own day, Romain Rolland's *Jean Christophe*. But the hero can also be set into a nearer or a more distant past on the model of the ancient epic. We find tendencies in this direction in France in the seventeenth century. But it was Romanticism

441

that first awakened the historical sense. Walter Scott and Manzoni are the European representatives of the historical novel. All these novels—with the exception of *Wilhelm Meister*, which cannot be gone into here—seek to entertain, which does not exclude an occasional appeal to the heart and mind of the reader. Since Balzac the novel has become more pretentious. It proposes to give lessons in sociology and psychology. With Flaubert its pretensions become even greater: on the basis of its formal qualities it demands to be evaluated as an absolute work of art and thus to compete in dignity with epic and tragedy. In Balzac, the elevation of the novel to a source of knowledge is not to be understood in a literal sense. It simply reflects the strongly marked interest of the writers in France since 1830 to be valued as indispensable and qualified collaborators in the civilizing task of the nation, if not of humanity. Victor Hugo and Lamartine, but even Vigny in his later years, behaved as though they were leaders of the people. The Messianism of Saint-Simon and Fourier had seized the poets and writers. Today this trait looks utopian and antiquated. The demands of Zola to be recognized as a sociological and moral authority were even more earnest and pressing. He believed that he must found "naturalism" on modern science. We ignore this attempt today because that science is outdated. But even in the twentieth century he has disciples who assign social and cultural analysis to the functions of the novel or make it the vehicle for other subjects of inquiry. This type of didactic novel is a carry-over from the nineteenth century because today the need for exact anthropological and other kinds of orientation can be better satisfied by several dozen highly developed special disciplines than by the consumption of novels. Since around 1870, the intrusion of scientific instruction into the novel has constantly increased—and not to the benefit of this genre. The furnishing of precise information about stock transactions or exotic cultures has pushed the intrinsic requirements of the novel—a hero and a fable—into the background. The writer concentrated on "observing" the so-called "reality," on gathering and transcribing all sorts of material. In this way he thought he could seize life. And at the same time he believed that he was standing in the succession of Balzac.

That was a misunderstanding. Henry James (1843–1916) and Paul Bourget (1852–1935) are the two novelists who studied Balzac's technique most carefully. It did not help them at all. In vain Henry James asks himself: "How did he do it?" Why does life itself look out at us from the creations of Balzac despite the fact that he himself, the galley-slave of work, never "lived?" What was Balzac's secret? The psychologist Bourget believes he is to be grasped as an "analytical visionary." But psychology fails for the simple reason that experimental subjects who have the stuff to be a Shakespeare or a Balzac do not occur in its textbooks and laboratories.

Balzac's secret is the secret of the genius to whom the totality of life has been given in an unfathomable way. In other ages he would have written epics or dramas. He was a poet, "since the poet prefigures the world through anticipation" (Goethe). In the nineteenth century and in France he had to write novels. But those who thought that they could enter upon his inheritance were the victims of a self-delusion. The conjunction of Balzac's creative power and the form of the novel was a happy chance that occurred once and could not be repeated.

The novel is a literary genre without a binding formal tradition. This has advantages and disadvantages. It is elastic as rubber. It can be adapted to any material and any period. We have had prehistoric, historic, and contemporary novels, but also rapid-motion projections into the future. The novel can enter any present, any temporal current or temporal mode. Jules Verne and others fulfilled the dreams of technology long before the engineers. But if the *Voyage around the World in Eighty Days* was superior to the transportation system of 1873, it has been surpassed by today's aeronautical techniques. We may see in this a parable of the danger that threatens the novel: the most modern at any given time is also the most quickly dated. Novels age faster than lyric poetry or historiography. Of the massive production of novels in nineteenth century France, which was given a strong impetus by the introduction of the serial novel in the press, the largest part has been forgotten. Who still reads Octave Feuillet or Augustin Filon, to whom Walter Pater consecrated essays? An additional burden on the novel that threatens its survival is its length. It is at the discretion of the author. He can present his material in 500 or 5,000 or 50,000 pages—a decision in which not only the exigencies of art but frequently also the conditions of the market are involved. The novel is the most commercialized genre of modern literature. It has become a commodity. But at the same time it suffers from an inner crisis the beginnings of which are indicated by Flaubert's posthumous work *Bouvard et Pécuchet* (1881). The question: what should the novel do? what can it do? has been raised by criticism. Joyce gave his response in *Finnegans Wake* (1939); Gide found another solution in *Thésée* (1946). These works are very different from one another; both are highly personal and their formulas cannot be transferred. The main body of novelists follows the tried and true recipes of the nineteenth century without being aware that there is a crisis of the novel. Meanwhile America brings out abridged editions of Victorian authors. In the nineteenth century three-volume novels and five-hour operas were esteemed. The public to which *Hamlet* and *The Brothers Karamazov* are offered as films is no longer prepared to expend the time required for the epic breadth of an Anthony Trollope or a Thomas Hardy, with its basis in old-fashioned, detailed description and narration. The dimensions of Proust's and Joyce's novels have an entirely different basis, which may be called microanalysis. It cannot be filmed. But it is not the only path to the future. The most recent narrative works of André Gide and Gottfried Benn demonstrate the will to energetic compression, and attain thereby a heightened expressive power. They confront the critic surveying the production of the nineteenth century with the questions: is the ideal novel the one in which nothing superfluous occurs? Was the nineteenth

444

century novel padded? Shall we be getting a slim, athletically-trained type? Do we not already find it in Benjamin Constant's *Adolphe* (1816)? How is it related to the novellas of a Mérimée or a Maupassant? Let us conclude with these questions. Interrogation is not the worst way of taking leave of a subject.

1949

The Young Cocteau

COCTEAU has collected the poems of seven years: 1916–1923. These two dates stand for the twenty-fourth and the thirty-first years in the life of the poet. Most of these poems were already published in the volumes *Le Cap de Bonne Espérance*, 1916 to 1919; *Poésies*, 1920; *Vocabulaire*, 1922; *Plain-Chant*, 1923. New in this collection is the *Discours du Grand Sommeil* (1916–1918): sounds "de cette langue morte, de ce pays mort où mes amis sont morts" [of that dead language, from that dead country where my friends are dead].

IN THE earliest of these poems there are lines like:

> é é ié io ié
> ui ui io ié
> aéoé iaoé
> auia ou aoé
> io io ioiu

or stanzas like:

> Des chromatismes
> jamais vus
> empêchent
> la tuberculose.

[Chromatisms never seen prevent tuberculosis.]

The reader asks: is this supposed to be serious? To which one might reply that there are situations in which the division of the world into what is serious and what is not breaks down. It no longer applies. In our practical affairs we need well-defined limits. Poetry may have to shatter them. This can produce splinters. Vowels fly up like dust. Trains of thought break apart. Images whirl about. Words mesh into uncontrolled phantasms. Cocteau's early poems are outbursts, eruptions—evasions. They tear into bits all the architectonics of language. Why? To make room for the new poetic mystery.

FOR poetry is a struggle with mystery. Its object is the occult. Not feeling, not atmosphere. Not subjective embellishment, but rather objective exposure of the world. To be a poet is to perceive the mysterious quality of the universe, to track it down in all its connections, to incise it deeply upon the record of language.

ANYONE receptive to this enchantment knows, when he puts Cocteau's anthology down: *ecce poeta*. Cocteau is a true poet: his relationship to poetry is that of a lover.

> Et rien
> ni les malentendus de vocabulaire ou de race
> ni la preuve par neuf cent fois refaite
> et toujours fausse
> ne troublent plus notre vieil amour, poésie.
>
> Me voici seul avec ton jeu d'échecs,
> poésie, o mon amour,
> meilleur que l'amour si triste
> quand il n'y a plus
> rien d'autre à faire que l'amour,
> quand il n'y a plus rien d'autre à faire
> que de ne plus faire l'amour.

[And nothing, neither misunderstandings of language or of race, nor the proof redone a hundred times and always incorrect, any longer troubles our old love, Poetry. Here I am alone with your game of chess, Poetry, oh my love, better than the love that is so sad when there is nothing else to do but make love, when there is nothing else to do but make love no longer.]

THESE lines show the poet to be cured of the convulsions of language-revolutionizing. He has found his own note, a pure melodiousness, a command of line that is as tender as it is sure. He will go on from this newly-acquired territory, will expand his realm, will adapt himself to the inherited forms of his language and its poetic tradition. Picasso—to whom Cocteau dedicates an ode—can permit himself to draw like Ingres. Cocteau now has the right to build stanzas like Malherbe (and a greater right than had Moréas):

> Voilà pourquoi la mort également m'effraye
> Et me fait les yeux doux;
> C'est qu'une grande voix murmure à mon oreille:
> Pense à mon rendez-vous;
> Laisse partir ces gens, laisse fermer la porte,
> Laisse perdre le vin,
> Laisse mettre au sépulcre une dépouille morte;
> Je suis ton nom divin.

[This is why death both frightens and seduces me. It is that a powerful voice whispers in my ear: Remember our rendezvous. Let these people leave, let the door be shut, let the wine ebb away, let the dead remains be deposited in the tomb. I am your divine name.]

We shall not be able to get around that much misused term: classicism. No sooner pronounced than it becomes distorted, dissolves in clouds of associations, releases iridescent mists of misunderstanding. Baleful effect! Against which antidotes must be employed at once.

Cocteau's classicism is no desertion and no capitulation. It is a form of self-realization—an enhancement. Here are three quatrains that ought to make any misunderstanding impossible:

> J'ai peine à soutenir le poids d'or des musées,
> Cet immense vaisseau.
> Combien me parle plus que leurs bouches usées
> L'oeuvre de Picasso.

Là, j'ai vu les objets qui flottent dans nos chambres,
    Trop grands ou trop petits,
Enfin, comme l'amour mêle bouches et membres,
    Profondément bâtis!
Les Muses ont tenu ce peintre dans leur ronde,
    Et dirigé sa main,
Pour qu'il puisse, au désordre adorable du monde,
    Imposer l'ordre humain.

[I can scarcely support the golden weight of the museums, that immense vessel. How much more than their worn mouths the work of Picasso speaks to me. There I have seen the objects that float about our rooms, too large or too small; in short, how love mingles mouths and limbs profoundly built. The Muses have included this artist in their round and guided his hand so that upon the charming confusion of the world he could impose human order.]

THIS classicism is no cautious retreat, but rather an assertion of self. Classicism can signify defeat or triumph. We have examples of both. With some poets, the turn to classicism is the manifestation of a decline in vitality. They have a way of acknowledging order that is a bad omen. They become reasonable in an alarming fashion. Cocteau remains charmingly unreasonable. His poetry, even though it makes use of classical forms, retains the bewildering and softly intoxicating fragrance of the era which today is the present for a few thousand people. I do not say "of the twentieth century," for there exist today, side by side, very different eras which all purport to be the twentieth century.

THERE is a volume of drawings by Cocteau. He calls these leaves *Poésies graphiques*. He is right. And with equal right the reader of these poems can say that their beauty is graphic in nature. They look as though they had been etched upon glass with a diamond. They have the elegance and the unpredictability of linear convolutions. Their aesthetic is that of the curve. They describe daring trajectories in the sky of fantasy. Cocteau works with his pen like the illustrator with his crayon. He reminds us that "to write" originally meant "to scratch." In his works writing and sketching have become a lyric theme:

> L'écriture des églantines
> Est un vrai fantôme grivois. . . .

[The scripture of the eglantines is truly a bawdy apparition.]

or:

> La Sainte-Vierge avait envoyé ce dessin
> D'un bleu miraculeux à chaque camarade.
> Ils n'en soufflèrent mot avant d'entrer en rade:
> C'etait un petit peu à gauche sous le sein.

[The Blessed Virgin had sent this drawing of a miraculous blue to each of the soldiers. They didn't breathe a word about it before entering port: it was slightly to the left under the breast.]

Line is less substantial and more permanent than color. It remains when color has faded. Color is earthbound. Line governs even amidst the solar systems. Line is more expressive than color. It fixes the accidental truths of contour and the eternal truths of mathematics. It can connect everything with everything; it has at its disposal the unconfined freedom of the abstract and the total accommodation to the given. It is the universal system of symbolism. In Cocteau's work the metaphysics of line is an aspect of poetic beauty. The somnambulant assurance of line is an element of his classicism.

WHAT does poetry actually deal with? With flight, with war, with play, with love—with everything; and yet, fundamentally, it always deals with the same thing: with the poetic world as the most real, the only true world. The current conception of reality is effaced here with one stroke of the pen. Suddenly all laws are suspended and with that everything has become possible—the sovereign act of liberation. The realm of reality is now infinite; it also embraces that which is above the real. Cocteau does not belong to the school of surrealism. But he does belong to that older, eternal poetic school whose credo Baudelaire formulated three generations ago when he wrote: "Deux qualités littéraires fondamentales: surnaturalisme et ironie . . ." ["Two fundamental literary qualities: supernaturalism and irony. . ."].

Poetic supernaturalism is an esoteric tradition of European poetry. It flashes up in works as widely disparate from one another as those of Blake, of Novalis, of Rimbaud. It is also present in Baudelaire, but only rarely and indirectly—less in the *Fleurs du Mal* than in his prose. Take, for example, the following: "Comme je traversais le Boulevard, et comme je mettais un peu de précipitation à éviter les voitures, mon auréole s'est détachée et est tombée dans la boue du macadam. J'eus heureusement le temps de la ramasser; mais cette idée malheureuse se glissa, un instant après dans mon esprit, que c'était un mauvais présage; et dès lors l'idée n'a plus voulu me lâcher; elle ne m'a laissé aucun repos de toute la journée" ["As I was crossing the Boulevard, and as I was hurrying a little in order to avoid the carriages, my halo came off and fell into the mud of the pavement. Fortunately I had the time to pick it up; but then an instant later this unfortunate thought slipped into my mind, that it was a bad omen; and from then on the thought would not leave me; it has given me no peace all day"].

Poetic supernaturalism must not be confused with mythology, theology, mysticism. Perhaps it has roots in common with them. But its growth tends in another direction. It is naïve, and it is irresponsible. It is not concerned with the meaning of life. It does not speculate on this world or the higher world; for, in its eyes, both blend into one another. It only desires to hold fast images—pictures of things that neither science nor religion will admit, but that are there nonetheless. They would be homeless did poetry not take them up. Baudelaire's prose poem about the aureole and *Dos d'Ange* by Cocteau reveal themselves to be related:

> Une fausse rue en rêve
> Et ce piston irréel
>
> Sont mensonges que soulève
> Un ange venu du ciel.
>
> Que ce soit songe ou pas songe,
> En le voyant par dessus
>
> On découvre le mensonge,
> Car les anges sont bossus.
>
> Du moins bossue est leur ombre
> Contre le mur de ma chambre.

[A false street in a dream, and this unreal piston are deceptions raised by an angel come from heaven. Be it a dream or not a dream, on viewing it from above one discovers the deception, because the angels are hunchbacked. At least their shadow against the wall of my room is hunchbacked.]

Cocteau's poetic world is densely populated with angels. But these angels have nothing in common with their romantic forebears. They are not pious and not ideal. They interfere in banal affairs, appear suddenly here or there, a winged race, something between spirits and birds. They are not of the earth, though they can settle upon it for fleeting moments. They can live inside man as well:

> . . . l'ange informe,
> intérieur, qui dort
> et, quelquefois, doucement
> du haut en bas s'étire.

[. . . the shapeless angel, within, who sleeps and, sometimes, gently stretches from head to toe.]

Of the same angel it is said:

452

Il dit: Je n'entre pas en toi.
Je ne sors pas de toi.
Je somnole intérieur.
Je me réveille aux harmoniques.

[He says: I will not enter into you. I will not go out
from you. I drowse within. I awaken to harmonies.]

In this poetic reality all spheres touch one another—as in
dreams. The realm of the dead and that of the living move
closer together, contiguous and yet separate, like the surfaces
of a die, like the two sides of a coin. There are moments of
dizzying swoon, where there is a presentiment of death in the
midst of the mechanics of the age of electricity.

Ha! le malaise d'ascenseur
m'empoigne au ventre. Je l'avais
en aéro, et même certains soirs d'été
à Paris en automobile.
C'est atroce, c'est doux, c'est mou.
Je ne suis pas d'ici, voyez-vous.
Je ne suis pas fait pour la terre.

[Ha! the elevator sickness grips me in the stomach.
I have had it in airplanes, and even some summer
evenings in Paris in an automobile. It's atrocious,
it's sweet, it's soft. I'm not from here, you see. I am
not made for this earth.]

Nervous thrills in an airplane or an elevator are more familiar
to modern man than was the lulling happiness of a canoe ride
to the Romantics. To bring such sensations to life is not affected; to contest their validity is. Technological civilization
belongs to Cocteau's poetic materials. And yet his verse is
completely free of any kind of Americanism. It is purely Gal-
lic. And it is a breath of *La vieille France*, of roses and cham-
pagne, of Angevin sweetness, of Louis XV pomp and
sparkling wit. A froth of silvery delight bubbles up over
barbed-wire landscapes:

453

Là-bas, partout, l'aube couchée,
l'aube mouillée, l'aube éreintée;
le spasme du canon meurtrit
ses cuisses roses.

[There, everywhere, the recumbent dawn, the humid dawn, the exhausted dawn; the cannon's spasm bruises her rosy thighs.]

Explosions of death—explosions of life. Cocteau has discovered the language of detonations:

Le rosier, viril en boutons,
bientôt féminin, concentre
un explosif d'odeur
qui tue les papillons crédules.

[The rosebush, virile in its buds, soon feminine, concentrates an explosive of scent that kills the credulous butterflies.]

Bursting odors. Bursting saps of joy:

Je sens avec délice en moi les folles balles
D'où tu jaillis comme un bouton d'or,
Vénus!

[With delight I feel in me the mad bubbles from which you burst like a golden bud, Venus.]

Surnaturalisme et ironie . . . : the second attribute that Baudelaire demands of the poet is also characteristic of Cocteau's verse. He shapes entire poems out of arabesques of fantastic caprice, such as *Les Anges maladroits*, which closes with the cogent critical remark:

Ce poème en dix vers, est-il beau, est-il laid?
Ce n'est ni laid ni beau, il a d'autres mérites.

[This poem in ten lines—is it beautiful, is it ugly?
It is neither beautiful nor ugly, it has other merits.]

A high-spirited, ever graceful play-instinct has inspired many poems. *Spielmann* was the name for the wandering minstrels of the Middle Ages—*joculator*; it is the same word as *jongleur*. Poet—jongleur—juggler—jester: all this was not far apart, could be united in one person. It may be possible to explain this phenomenon in terms of cultural history— but there may be more profound reasons for it as well. Perhaps the troubadour-poet contrasts with the priest-poet— the *vates*—as an eternal type. It is good and beautiful that this is so. Let us rejoice in the *gaya scienza*. Joculator of our technically rationalized world—that is one aspect of the poet Cocteau. His inner angel sometimes makes room for a harlequin whom we also know from Picasso's paintings, and who, moreover, points back to Watteau's Gilles. This jongleur is a charmer. This poet is an enchanter.

1927

William Goyen

++

HERE is the fledgling work of a young American. I have rendered it into German because spiritual currents flow through it that I should like to transmit.

A house in the remote southwest of the United States, a long-decayed house with its family relations and its fortunes, is erected here by the power of the spirit. Breath is respiration, breath is the breath of life, breath is the creative spirit moving upon the waters; it carries the word, it spans the abysses of human solitude, it builds palaces, cathedrals, worlds of ideas. Franz Werfel has expressed it in hymnic tones:

> Lausche Du, horche Du, höre!
> In der Nacht ist der Einklang des Atems los,
> Der Atem, die Eintracht des Busens ist gross.
> Atem schwebt
> Über Feindschaft finsterer Chöre.
> Atem ist Wesen vom höchsten Hauch.
> Nicht der Wind, der sich taucht
> In Weid, Wald und Strauch,
> Nicht das Wehn, vor dem die Blätter sich drehn ...
> Gottes Hauch wird im Atem der Menschen geboren.

[Listen, hearken, hear! In the night the harmony of the breath is free, breath, the concord of the bosom, is vast. Breath floats above the hostility of tenebrous choirs. Breath is the essence of the highest inspiration. Not the wind that plunges into meadow, wood, and hedge, not the blast before which the leaves dance ... God's breath is born in the breath of men.]

THE TRUTH expressed in these ten lines we shall encounter
once more in Goyen's book, and it evidently means so much
to him that he refers the reader to it in his title and harps on it
again and again through the leitmotif technique of the work.
The breath with which he builds the house of his childhood
belongs to the region outlined by Werfel's stanza.

The house of which Goyen tells is located in the small town
of Charity, Texas. Perhaps this place will one day be recorded
on those maps of the soul in which Proust's Combray as well
as Joyce's Dublin are inscribed. The house faces a meadow
(soon oil rigs will root it up). Herds graze there (before they must make way for the oil wells), giving the children of the house that intimacy with animal nature which has
been associated with the human realm since the Garden of
Eden, and which responds to the natural in man. The pasture
is sown in bitterweed; and it is as if bitterness had become a
part of the milk on which the children were raised. But sometimes its effect is like that of the enchanted grass of which
Glaucus, the Fisherman, partook (Ovid tells his story): all
of a sudden his heart was shaken and he was seized by an irresistible longing for a different element. He said farewell to
the earth, on which he would never again set foot, plunged
into the waters, and was transformed. So the adolescent Folner is transformed when the circus spreads its tent on
the meadow, with its tinsel display of wild and colorful life,
which Folner will follow into tawdriness, corruption, and
death. This magic also seduces Christy, carried out to sea or
into the deep woods. Also Sue Emma; also Berryben; also the
small boy who is the narrator of these destinies. All the children break with house and home and custom; only the old
remain to wait and watch. They are the prisoners of the
house, aging and decaying and rotting with it, until it becomes
food for the elements and for the hordes of uncannily quiet,
greedy insects.

The bitterweed meadow slopes down to the bottomlands
of the river. The river plays a generative and destructive role
in the lives of the people of Charity. It is older than man and

animals; it is the God of buried cycles of time; it is the elemental power that demands its prey and casts its spell. Immersion in it brings thrills of bliss (Novalis could speak of the "supernal bliss of all that flows" and of the "outpourings of the primal waters within us") but it also brings death. The river is one of the central characters in the book. Another is the wood on the other side of the river, or rather the woods, those endless regions of wild forest in which Christy goes bird-hunting; where death lurks and blood flows; where, if anywhere, the heart could disclose its secret— if it could find the language or the ear to listen. The wild wood of Charity conceals enigmas like the wood of Arthurian legend.

The elements of nature not only constitute the background of this book, they are also demonic participants in the action. The element of water is in it as river and sea; the element of earth as meadow and wood. Associated with them is the air as breath; as the amphibious element which belongs to both spirit and nature. Alive in William Goyen is a primal affinity with the first things of creation ("O I am leaf and I am wind and I am light"). He has the keen senses of the woodsman, whom no creak or rustle can elude. He registers the sensual qualities of natural things, and it is as though he himself had experienced, from within, the cycle of germination, budding, flowering, and withering of all created matter. We seem to be hearing the voice of an aboriginal America that is being constantly pushed back by industrial civilization and forced to languish in its big cities.

To plunge into the river and into the wilderness of the woods; to escape from the house and its ties of guilt and suffering, of bodily decay and dullness; from the spiritual corruption of the old but also from the self-destruction of the young through vice, revolt, aberration: this is the thorny path of the boy whose story is related in this book. But he struggles through, and roses will bloom for him, because he has had courage.

Courage: this means to obey the lesson of life. In order to do so we must first take life's measure completely: must reach its heights by flying like the bird; must penetrate its depths like the fish (this book cannot be understood if its animal symbolism is overlooked). We must be able to change elements like that legendary fisherman who became a sea-god. Alternation between air, earth, water; alternation between sinking and rising again: the fabric of the book is shot through with the drama of man and the elements. Otey's intact maidenhood is swallowed up by water; but her last breath sprays the body of her beloved as with a shower of diamonds. To plunge into the deadly deep; but also to bring up its treasure, shelter it and help it toward the light—this is what we recognize as the demands of life but also as the mission of art. From all the world's darkness, from all its regions of misery, the spirit rises again like the pearl diver, laden with responsibility toward its own vision of the depths. Only it must first dress its finds and shape them. What it brings to light is raw material: an amalgam of sense and soul. This booty from the deep must be fused and annealed. Art is alchemy; a higher stage of chemistry. It carries on and sublimates the process of life, which is itself a "great mysterious chemistry." Human beings react upon each other like acids, salts, and sulphur; everything acts upon everything else; in this process the stuff of human life is transformed and enhanced. It is refined in pain, in wisdom, and in love.

But first its hardness must be broken. Life, experience, guilt break the human being. Youth means the destruction of the magic of childhood; that is why it is the bitterest time of life. A broken world has been given to us to live in. That is how it presents itself to the artist, that is how he suffers it. He sifts these fragments and splinters; he sifts them, saving the most precious. These he polishes and fits together with long patience. Out of these bits of mosaic he pieces together his picture. So on his part he restores the unity and wholeness of the world.

A fledgling work—but a mature one. We are accustomed to a first novel being an eruption in which ore, slag, and ashes are whirled up together; or a so-called confession; or the reaction to the shock of growing pains on the nerves. Goyen's art is of a different sort. He has pledged himself to silence and waiting; to wait until he should find the word, "strong, small, but hard as a stone," which would utter his loneliness to the world; to wait until the breath which the house breathed in him should become speech; till this breath should take form and become matter pliant and capable of being transformed into an image. The genesis of a work of art is a two-sided process. It is the response to an inner impulse that makes itself felt as suffering and as a goad to the spirit; at the same time it responds to a demand that the unspoken existence of things makes upon the artist. "Lost time" wants to be recovered, the decayed house wants to be rebuilt. For these things the artist must find the word, the word that is both a touching and a naming. The title, *House of Breath*, comprises this polarity. The breath of lived life has merged with the breath of the artist. William Goyen had the power to attend this moment. He was able to wait because this breath was energy, an energy that wanted to be caught and directed so as to become the driving force of a power station. This energy had to be harnessed by a generator and converted into communication: communication through discourse, not through outcry or puling. Communication is something else and something more than mere "expression," which today is often considered an adequate validation of the artist. Communication means demonstration and construction of a spiritual content. The goal to which it aspires is "a full clear statement, a singing, a round, strong, clear song of total meaning, a language within language, responding each to each forever in the memory of each man."

For the artist everything depends on whether this conversion into spirit and language is successful. It is for this that he struggles and experiments, for this that he suffers and chooses the way of greatest resistance. For this he sacrifices the easy solutions and mechanical aids. This is the ordeal by which he is tested, and, if he stands the test, he wins the highest prize: he becomes real and substantial. He is redeemed from his solitude, connected with the world and the flow of its energies. And his work is the bridge to other men. He has vaulted the stream and stands now on the farther shore.

The artist must assume this burden of sorrow in an obtuse world, under a leaden sky. Not many choose this path. But those who do have the vocation.

Like all modern art Goyen's book is the testimony and result of a sincerity that refuses to draw the line at cruelty. Bodies and souls are displayed with their wounds, their scars, their disintegrating tissue, their shames. In some artists such unmasking is cynical or bitter. In some it purports to be the ultimate truth about life, art being the only exception: an art which sees its nobility in hardness of form and of heart. Flaubert, Valéry, Joyce are the saints of this kind of art. Goyen too lays bare the cancer of the flesh and of the soul; he too proclaims the passion of man. But with him suffering and torment include compassion. The tragic agony is carried through to the catharsis. The harmony with the elemental power of earth operates in this book as a stream that washes away all stains, that purifies and heals. Folner has died of the bitterweed of the Charity meadow. But he will be healed beyond death on a meadow bright with clarity. What does the river tell us once we have learned to understand its language? "Everything flows into everything and carries with it and within it all lives of its life and others' life and all is a murmuring and whispering of things changing into each other, breeding and searching and reaching and withdrawing and dying. Whatever crossing is made each over other, by boat or bridge or swimming, is to another side; and whatever drowning is dying and sinking back into a womb, and what salvation or rescue of the perishing in waters or wickedness, dead or alive, is a union of silence or rejoicing; and to drop down into any of us, into depths (in river or self or well or cellar) is to lower into truth and sorrow. But we are purged, to plunge beneath a flood is to lose all guilty stains and to rise is to be purified. And we are to keep turning the wheels we turn, we are wind we are water we are yearning; we are to keep rising and falling, hovering at our own marks, then falling, then rising." The children in this book have grown up in the ecstatic piety and otherworldly hope of the Methodist Church. Stanzas of hymns, full of nostalgia for the golden city of heaven, reverberate within them. All this turns to dust along with the dream images of childhood. But a longing for redemption, a trust remains, even if its form has been completely changed. It has been transmuted into the blowing of the breath that restores wholeness:

Gottes Hauch wird im Atem der Menschen geboren.

[God's breath is born in the breath of men.]

If I have set Goyen's novel beside Werfel's lines (which Goyen has undoubtedly never read) or beside the sibylline words of Novalis, it was in order to point out a spiritual law. There are emotional realities that can only be discovered through the poets (this is perhaps the essential function of poetry). And one of the functions of criticism might be to register such discoveries; to draw the lines connecting explorers widely separated in space, time, and culture, who knew nothing of one another and yet shaped their course for the same islands and were guided on their voyage by the same stars. Such a view of literature might, within its modest limits (yet also guided by a clear sense of responsibility), assist in the great task appointed to mankind since the Tower of Babel: the restoration of unity. Separation, division, fragmentation are evil and lead to death. Connection, completion, conjunction restore the fullness of life; they lead to goodness and love. They are two opposing principles, as separation and conjunction are two complementary operations of alchemy. The law of separation and reunion also prevails throughout Goyen's book.

It is no accident that this book recalls poetry. The element of poetry entirely pervades Goyen's novel. It is not as if it had isolated "lyrical passages." No, its very substance is poetic in nature. Everything that the author experiences presents itself to him in the aggregate state of poetry; a primary poetry in which the epic and the lyric have not yet been sundered. The mode of discourse is not descriptive but imaginative. This is already shown by the title. Mingling with the human voices is the voice of the river, the voice of the fountain, the voice of the wind. Goyen's mode of lyrical epic is related to myth and legend. The muse of the book is the blind girl sitting on a blue, rolling, cosmic sphere, bent over her lyre, and reciting her memories in a lyric lament (Greek myth makes the Muses the daughters of memory). She is a cosmogonic muse. She knows all the legends of genesis and all history. She could speak of heroic expeditions and of the founding of cities; of errant voyages and of the quest for salvation. *The House of Breath* tells us of Charity and East Texas; when it ranges farther, it only crosses the border of the neighboring state of Louisiana. And yet this book is something other than a local novel. What we are given here is not regionalism. The language and the landscape of East Texas are only the ground here of a fabric in which living and neighboring people talk and move. In the kitchen of the house at Charity hangs a map of the world. To the boy whose story is related to us the outlines of the countries and continents seemed like the organs of a human body. The articulation and conformation of the earth has impressed itself with the utmost vividness upon his child's consciousness. In the sleepy town of Charity he has had an intuitive apprehension of the wide world and known that he himself was part of it. That is why this novel of a childhood has become a book containing a universal experience.

Since 1920 the American novel has been discovered in Europe, and that is good. But since 1945 it has become the fashion, with the result that the reading public has formed a conventional idea of this branch of world literature that it now wishes to have confirmed. This notion is confused and naïve—like most of the ideas that Europeans have about America (and Americans about Europe). From the American novel we expect brutality and cynicism; intellectual over-refinement but also primeval eruptions; morbidity and neurosis. In William Goyen's book we shall find very different elements: substantive poetry (as I have already said); harmony with the deepest simplicities of existence; reunion of sexuality with love; but also an artistic discipline that is more reminiscent of Flaubert, Proust, Joyce than of Melville, Wolfe, Faulkner.

It seemed more important to me to bring out some of the personal characteristics of William Goyen than to investigate his place in American literature of the 1950s (which will be done by others). Moreover, I believe that we form an erroneous conception of American literary sociology when we apply European conditions to the enormous transatlantic community. The loneliness of the young American who indentures his life to literature, let alone to poetry, is absolutely distinct from that of his European colleague, and infinitely more cruel. To endure it requires heroism. That is why it pleases me all the more that William Goyen's first book has been favorably received in America and England, and that it can now be submitted to German readers. For as André Gide said of Charles-Louis Philippe: "Cette fois, c'est un vrai."

1952

The Ship of the

Argonauts

++

According to a widely-held opinion the Argo was the first ship to sail the seas. The poets of Antiquity like to tell of the astonishment that it aroused among gods and men. The invention of navigation was a revolutionary event, comparable to the discovery of fire in prehistoric times and the invention of flight in ours.

The legend of the Argonauts is said to reflect the earliest Aeolian voyages of colonization toward the East or Milesian trading expeditions toward the Black Sea, and appears to be pre-Homeric. But we possess no poetic version of the theme prior to Pindar's Fourth Pythian Ode. It furnished the Attic tragedians with a considerable number of subjects, the most effective being Medea. Apollonius of Rhodes turned it into an epic (third century B.C.). He was imitated by Valerius Flaccus under Vespasian, and around A.D. 400 by an unknown Greek writer, who pretended that his poem was the work of Orpheus. In all these epic and dramatic connections the Argo could occur and could be used for effects of pathos. In the prologue to his *Medea*, Euripides, who was fond of tracing tragic complications to their remote origins, has the nurse execrate the fatal ship. Would that it had never sailed through the Symplegades! Would that the pine which furnished wood for the oars had never been felled on Mount Pelion! This was imitated by Ennius:

> Utinam ne in nemore Pelio securibus
> Caesae accidissent abiegnae ad terram trabes

465

Neve inde navis inchoandi exordium
Cepisset, quae nunc nominatur nomine
Argo . . .

[Would that in Pelion's grove pine beams hewn with axes had never fallen to earth, and that the ship had never begun to be built which now is called Argo . . .]

The passage is preserved for us by the Herennius-Rhetoric as an example of a *vitiosa expositio* (erroneous exposition of the facts in the case) which is only permitted to poets (II, 22). Here we encounter the mutual interference, so frequently to be observed, of poetry and rhetoric. The exemplification by means of the Medea prologue was maintained in the rhetorical tradition of the schools.[1] In his discussion of the technique of proof Quintilian (V, 10, 83) warns against using reasons that are too farfetched: "recte autem monemur causas non utique ab ultimo esse repetendas ut Medea 'Utinam ne in nemore Pelio'; quasi vere id eam fecerit miseram aut nocentem, quod illic ceciderint 'abiegnae ad terram trabes.' "[2]

After Ennius, an Argonaut or Medea tragedy was attempted by another of Rome's archaic tragedians, Accius. Fragments of his work have been preserved by Cicero who, following Stoic models, sought to enliven scientific discourse by quoting poetry (cf. *Tusc.* II, 26). This occurs in the course of a proof in which the workings of a divine providence are inferred from the purposive arrangement of the cosmos (*De natura deorum* II, 36, 89): "utque ille apud Accium pastor,

[1] The "pine of Pelion" (Catullus, 64, 1; Ovid, *Her.* XII, 8; idem, *Am.* II, 11, 12; Statius, *Thebais* V, 336) is the standing periphrasis for the Argo in Roman poetry.

[2] "We are rightly admonished not to trace causes all the way back to their origin, as for example in Medea's speech beginning, 'Would that never in Pelion's grove,' as though her misery or her guilt were due to the fact that 'hewn pine-beams had fallen to earth' there."

qui navem numquam ante vidisset, ut procul divinum et novum vehiculum Argonautarum e monte conspexit, primo admirans et perterritus hoc modo loquitur:

> tanta moles labitur
> Fremibunda ex alto, ingenti sonitu et spiritu.
> Prae se undas volvit, vertices vi suscitat:
> Ruit prolapsa, pelagus respergit, reflat.
> Ita dum interruptum credas nimbum volvier,
> Dum quod sublime ventis expulsum rapi
> Saxum aut procellis, vel globosos turbines
> Existere ictos undis concursantibus:
> Nisi quas terrestras pontus strages conciet,
> Aut forte Triton fuscina evertens specus
> Subter radices penitus undante in freto
> Molem ex profundo saxeam ad caelum erigit."

("like that shepherd in Accius who had never seen a ship before and who, when he espied in the distance the divine and new vessel of the Argonauts from the top of a mountain, first amazed, then frightened, exclaimed:

> So huge a mass glides roaring thus from out
> The deep with mighty blare and blast! In front
> It billows rolls and swirling eddies stirs;
> Headlong it hurtles, splashing back, and back
> Blowing the sea. So came it that you would
> Believe now that a thunder cloud rolled riven,
> Now that a rock was caught and flung aloft
> By winds or storms, or whirling water spouts
> Uprose, upbeaten by the brawling billows;
> Unless it be the sea, which sets astir
> Some havoc of the land; or maybe Triton,
> Outheaving utterly a cave, his trident
> Set 'neath its roots within the billowing sea,
> Delves up a rocky mass from deep to sky.")
> [E. H. Warmington, Loeb Classics]

Accius' shepherd sees a huge mass approaching on the waves, is unable to identify it, and weighs several possibilities: is it a riven storm-cloud? A rock that has been flung up? A waterspout? A deluge devastating the earth? Or has Triton whirled up a stony underwater cave with his trident? The Roman tragedian had produced a brilliant effect the repercussions of which continued to be felt for a long time. But the invention itself may be traced back to the Attic satyr-play, as I learn from Kurt Latte. In Sophocles' "Bloodhounds," discovered in 1911, the satyrs hear a wonderful music and are informed that it is being elicited by the young Hermes from a dead animal. Now they start to guess: is the animal long, curved, short? Is it like a cat or a leopard? Does it resemble an ichneumon or a crab? Answer: it is a tortoise equipped with strings. In Aeschylus' fragment *The Fishermen* (*Diktyulkoi*), which we possess since 1933, doubts arise as to whether an object in the water is a whale, a hammerhead shark, or a chest (it is the chest of the Danaë). Finally, since 1942, we have an Aeschylean fragment (*Pap.Ox.* 18, no. 2159) in which a shepherd describes his impression of Glaucus emerging from the sea in colors very similar to those used by Accius for the Argo. Accius' direct or indirect dependence on Aeschylus is evident. But it has become visible only through the papyrus finds of the twentieth century. These finds have enabled us to extend the history of the Argos theme, or rather of an artistic device accreted onto it, backward by three hundred years. It is both curious and instructive that this particular device, which is meant to be comic and is only documented in the satyr-plays, could be adopted by a Roman of the second century B.C. for tragedy. What spiritual transformation made this possible? The accumulation of conjectural questions with regard to an unidentifiable object obviously has no fundamental connection with the Argo-theme. The transfer could take place, however, because the first ship was an occasion for astonishment and because the trial questions in the Aeschylean satyr-plays were directed toward an object sighted on the sea. This resulted in an intertwining of two motifs that persisted for an amazingly long time. It was admired by the rhetoricians of late Antiquity. Hermogenes (under the Emperor Marcus Aurelius) recommends in his *Preliminary Exercises* as a subject for an ethopoeia (character-drawing): "What would a rustic say on seeing the first ship?" (ed. Rabe, 21, 22). The famous grammarian Priscian (beginning of the sixth century A.D.), whom Dante, on the basis of a misunderstanding, consigns to his inferno,[3] translated the Greek work of Hermogenes, written in Rome, into Latin in Constantinople, thereby transmitting it to the Middle Ages.[4] He renders "ethopoeia" as *adlocutio*. The passage that interests us reads (Halm, *Rhetores latini minores* 558, 14ff.): "sunt autem quaedam adlocutiones morales, quaedam passionales, quaedam mixtae. Passionales sunt, in quibus passio, id est commiseratio perpetua inducitur, ut quibus verbis uti potuisset Andromache mortuo Hectore; morales vero, in quibus obtinent mores, ut quibus verbis uti potuisset rusticus, cum primum aspexit navem" ["Some *adlocutiones* are moral, some are emotional, some are mixed. Emotional are those in which emotion, i.e., continuous sympathy is induced; such as the words Andromache might use on the death of Hector; moral, however, those in which manners prevail, as for example the words a rustic might use on seeing a ship for the first time"].

The practice-theme of Hermogenes-Priscian is in keeping with Accius, but it could also depend on a post-Euripidean *Medea*, transmitted through Hellenistic handbooks. The continuing effect of Accius is attested by Priscian's notice (*De metris Terentii* 15; p. 424, 9 Keil): "Accius in Argonautis ex persona pastoris qui primam vidit navem." The Accius

---

[3] Cf. my book, *European Literature and the Latin Middle Ages*, trans. Willard R. Trask (New York, 1953), p. 43, note 22.

[4] Whereas in post-Constantinian Athens the *Preliminary Exercises* of Aphthonius were preferred to those of Hermogenes. Aphthonius (*Progymnasmata*, Rabe p. 35, 5) replaces "astonishment of a rustic on seeing the Argo" with "astonishment of an inland dweller on seeing the ocean for the first time." Was this an emendation?

469

fragment preserved by Cicero probably also inspired Dracontius, who composed his poetry under Vandal rule in Africa around A.D. 500 and who wrote in his *Medea*:

32 Dives apud Colchos, Phrixei velleris aurum,
Pellis erat, servata diu custode dracone.
Hanc propter pelagi temerator primus Iason
Venerat, ut rutilas subduceret arbore lanas.
Ut Scytha conspexit Graiam de littore puppim
Ire per undosum proscissis fluctibus aequor,
Expavit, nam monstra putat: quis crederet unquam
Per freta, per rabidas hominem transire procellas?[5]

(Among the Colchians was the Golden Fleece of Phrixus, guarded for ages by a dragon. For that reason Jason, the first violator of the deep, had come to steal the gleaming wool from the tree. When the Scythians standing on the shore caught sight of a Greek ship stirring the billows and gliding through the wavy sea, they quaked with fear, for they deemed it a monster: who would ever have believed that man could traverse the straits and the raging squalls?)

As I have tried to show elsewhere, there is an unbroken continuity of literary techniques from the time of the Roman Empire to the end of the seventeenth century. During this period, moreover, a constant interchange between poetry and rhetoric takes place.[6] The practice-theme transmitted by Priscian is invested with poetry once more by Calderón. How he accomplished this has been so charmingly described by Max Kommerell in his posthumously published *Beiträge zu einem*

[5] The astonishment of a seaman at the sight of Zeus ploughing the waves in the form of a bull is given by Nonnus, *Dion.* i, 92.

[6] Its beginnings go back much further, to be sure—one has only to think of Euripides. Quintilian sees in Homer a rhetorical authority. Late classical theoreticians on the epideixis cite Sappho as the model for hymeneal orations, etc. The matter has not yet been sufficiently clarified by scholarship.

470

deutschen Calderon (1946), I 21ff. [*Contributions toward a German Calderón*] that I should like to let him have the word: "The profound distinction that exists for us between a product of nature and a product of technics is inessential to Calderón. No less a favorite than the horse is the ship—for the most part a gigantic ship which man, like an elemental power, has wrought. Wonderful in itself, motion makes it a true wonder. And no matter how frequently it has been represented by all kinds of similes, it only becomes thoroughly incredible and thoroughly dramatic when men are standing on the shore and, so to speak, seeing it rise. Calderón is stating his own formula when he says in the *Príncipe constante*: 'Because distance always creates things unheard of and wonderful.' He even deprives these coastal inhabitants of their familiarity with ships, and allows a dispute to arise among them over what sort of thing is approaching, whether fish, cloud, bird, or mountain, and so forth. By this means the staggering dimension of the phenomenon is turned into a dramatic event. To give an example: As the Christian fleet was gliding toward Tangier in the morning, the people on shore believed, says Muley in the same work, that it was a bank of clouds, since their tops grazed the sky. Then it is supposed to be a stray fleet of sea monsters, Neptune's escort, for they seem to shake their wings, that is, the sails, over the waves. Drawing nearer it was a Babylon whose hanging gardens were pennons which whip the wind; then an Armada, recognizable by the silver hills that curl and the crystal caves that arch in its wake. This series of similes undoubtedly culminates in a work that is intended to embrace the wonders of three continents and that might have been decisive for Grillparzer's treatment of the Medea myth: *Los tres mayores prodigios del mundo*. Here the manner in which pure poetry of a Gongoresque splendor of imagery is fashioned into a component of drama becomes particularly evident. Dialogue between Medea, the King, Friso, Absinto, and Astrea by the seashore before Jason lands. Astonished, they listen: a mysterious sound. Can it be trumpets? But why from the direction of the sea? Triton's horns rather. Echo must have wafted the sound outward. But Echo lives only in the mountains. The thrill of horror becomes plainer as amazement steals from ear to eye. A mountain is walking on the foam. Not a mountain—that would sink; no, a cloud! Clouds descend lightly and, having drunk their fill of the sea, rise again, encumbered. So this too: in order to pour rain into the sea, it drinks the sea. Not a cloud, otherwise wind or sun could affect it. But a bird, a bird-monster—the sound is his cry. See how he shakes his white pinions! Not a bird. It would merely fly, but this thing swims. A bird does not venture so far from the mainland. But moisture is this thing's element. Conclusion: it is mountain, cloud, bird, and fish, for—and now follows the recapitulatory enumeration[7] of all the aforementioned phenomena. And yet it was none of these. Jason lands, it was a ship." That Muley in the *Príncipe constante* lacks "the shore-dweller's familiarity with the ship" can of course be explained by the fact that Calderón transferred the Argo theme to an era exceedingly well-versed in navigation. In the *Tres mayores prodigios* he restores it to the mythical age. But he enriches the motif of the shore-dweller's astonishment transmitted by Accius and Priscian with the Gongoresque motif which I should like to designate "the exchange of substances."

In the dedicatory poem of the *Soledades* the Duke of Béjar's hunting spears are presented as walls of pine and pinnacles of diamonds, the blood of the game as corals of foam. The sea in the *Soledad Primera* is a desert of waves (*Libia de ondas*) and can be regarded equally as a range of water and as an ocean of mountains (*montes de aqua y piélagos de montes*). In the *Fábula de Polifemo y Galatea* we hear that Amor is in doubt whether the color of Galatea's face is closer to snowy crimson or to red snow:

> Duda el Amor cual más su color sea,
> O púrpura nevada, o nieve roja.

---

[7] "Summation schema" (*European Literature and the Latin Middle Ages*, p. 289).

Such doubts are frequent in Góngora. They are the subjective correspondence to the objective finding that sea and mountain, spear and pinnacle, blood and coral—to say nothing of many other similar pairings—can approximate each other so closely in appearance that the one seems to pass over into the other. To elucidate this typical element of Góngora's art historically and aesthetically would be out of place here.[8] It seems to me that it has analogies in sculpture. Bernini can give marble the downy texture of feathers, the soft volutes of clouds, or even the structure of living rock.

Calderón employed the ship-theme in numerous other plays. It belongs to the ready reserve on which he draws again and again, "a stock composed of turns of phrase, figures of speech, stylistic forms, metaphors, types of scenes and characters" (Kommerell I, 34). Thus it occurs again in the auto sacramental *La Nave del Mercador* (ed. Pando y Mier I, 236):

> . . . esta trémula nave
> Que siendo pez del mar, del viento ave,
> Al impulso violento
> Del aquilón, de quien el mal proviene
> Tan nueva especie en su embrión contiene
> Que uno y otro elemento
> Duda si ave es del mar, o pez del viento.

[. . . this tremulous ship which, being a fish of the sea, a bird of the wind, under the violent impulse of

---

[8] Here too, I would suspect the influence of antique Mannerism. In a letter to the *praefectus praetorio* Abundantius, who built a fleet, Cassiodorus writes (*Variae* v, 17 Mommsen, p. 153): "obtulisti oculis nostris subito classeam silvam, domos aquatiles, exercituales pedes, qui nullo labore deficiant. . . . Hoc primum instituisse legimus Argonautas. . . . Nunc praedictis rebus armamenta procurate, vela praecipue alas navium facentia: lignum volatile. . . ." Thus ships can form a fleetwood, can be addressed as aquatic houses or the feet of armies, the sails as ships' wings or winged wood. Here applications are piled up of a schema that must have made its way from poetry into artistic prose. But when? And how? Where did Cassiodorus find models for it?

the north wind, from which evil comes, contains in embryo so new a species that one and the other element doubts whether it is a bird of the sea or a fish of the wind.]

The ingenious theoretician of Spanish Mannerism, Balthasar Gracián,[9] did not permit this *concetto* to elude him. In the *Criticón* I, 4 (ed. Romera-Navarro I, 148) Andrenio describes what he sees approaching by sea: "unas montañas que buelan, quatro alados monstruos marinos, si no son nubes, que navegan. —No son sino naves, dixo Critilo" ["some mountains that fly, four winged marine monsters, unless they are seafaring clouds. —They are nothing but ships, said Critilo"].

Not only men, but the Gods too, marveled at the Argo. According to Apollonius of Rhodes, all the Gods gazed down upon the ship; the nymphs of Pelion marveled (*Argonautica* I, 547ff.). Even though Apollonius, by reason of the "relative chronology of legend,"[10] could not allow the Argo to be accounted the first ship, he nevertheless knew how to elicit the "Argo-effect" from it; at any rate, the settlers on the Danube had never yet seen a ship. The shepherds on its banks flee with their flocks (*Arg.* III, 315ff.). During the passage through the Planctae or Symplegades[11] Thetis lays her hand on the helm; the Nereids disport themselves round about the ship, hitching up their garments and exposing their breasts for the first time to mortal eyes (IV, 930ff.). Has this erotic point been developed out of the practice, already popular with Sophocles and Euripides, of mentioning the Nereids in connection with the play of the waves? The motif per se has nothing to do with the Argo. It could be employed by Moschus in the second century B.C. for Europa's sea voyage on the back of the bull; by an anonymous poet of the first

[9] His theory of mannerism is analyzed in my previously mentioned book, pp. 293 to 301.
[10] H. Herter, *Rhein. Mus.* 91 (1942), 246.
[11] The Bosporus.

century for the ship of Isis.[12] But then Catullus connected it once more with the Argo-theme in his highly ornate poem on the marriage of Peleus and Thetis (no. 64):

> 12 Quae simulac rostro ventosum proscidit aequor,
> Tortaque remigio spumis incanduit unda,
> Emersere freti candenti e gurgite vultus
> Aequoreae monstrum Nereides admirantes.

> (Soon as the ship's beak ploughed the windy waste,
> And churned by oars the water boiled and foamed,
> Wild faces from grey depths, the Nereids,
> Looked forth in wonder at so strange a sight.)
> [Hugh Macnaghten]

Mermaids make a charming setting for the Argo. But it is not forceful enough to extract from the motif of the "astonishment of the Gods at the Argo" all the pathos of which it was capable. To do so required bringing on a greater God: Neptune, ruler of the seas. Valerius Flaccus introduces him in his epic on the Argonauts. He relates that after the Argo had been built Jason prepared a sacrifice for Neptune and asked him for a favorable journey. He was well aware, Jason confessed to the God, that he was embarking upon forbidden paths and deserved storms. He was not sailing from presumptuousness, however, but at the behest of Pelias, who wished to compass his ruin. The sacrificial flame leaps up, the seer Mopsus proclaims in great agitation (i, 211):

---

[12] The epigraphic Isis hymn of Andros was first seen and read, among more recent scholars, by Ernst Curtius in August 1838 (*Ernst Curtius. Ein Lebensbild in Briefen*, edited by Friedrich Curtius [1903], p. 165). The first usable scholarly edition came out almost a hundred years later: Werner Peck, *Der Isishymnus von Andros* (1930); see verses 152ff. Isis was the tutelary goddess of navigation. On the hymn, cf. Otto Kern, *Die Religion der Griechen* iii (1938), 138ff.— In the letter of Cassiodorus cited above Isis is credited with the invention of sails: "Isis rati prima vela suspendit, cum per maria Harpocran filium suum audaci femina pietate perquireret. Ita dum materna caritas suum desiderium festinat explere, mundi visa est ignota reserare."

Heu quaenam aspicio! nostris modo concitus ausis
Aequoreos vocat ecce deos Neptunus et ingens
Concilium. Fremere et legem defendere cuncti
Hortantur.

(Alas, what do I see! Stirred up by our boldness,
Neptune convokes all the sea gods to a mighty council. All exhort him to rage and defend the law.)

But Neptune, allowing himself to be persuaded by Juno and
Pallas, revokes his threats and sanctions the voyage. He
wards off a storm from Argo, although he foresees that many
other ships will follow her. She is a menace to mankind
(I, 648):

Miseris tu gentibus, Argo,
Fata paras.

(You are preparing death for unfortunate peoples,
Argo.)

Thetis and Nereus emerge from the placated flood. Jason
offers a libation and prays to all the marine divinities, especially the enraged Neptune, for merciful protection. He promises them "well-merited" altars (677) and even specially
commends the Tritons (679).[13] The poet's version of the
voyage of the Argonauts and, consequently, of the sea voyage
offers difficulties because it is full of contradictions. This is
because it represents a contamination of several versions. Is
the sea voyage an impiety? Jason feels that it is, and Neptune
rages. But why is the God persuaded to change his mind?
Why does he ward off a storm? And why does he accuse the
ship of bringing disaster after all? The cursing of the invention of navigation is a favorite commonplace in poetry.[14] But
on the other hand the sea gods "love to protect bold keels"
("audaces amor est servare carinas"), as Statius says (*Silvae*

---

[13] Not until late Antiquity do several Tritons develop out of Triton,
the son of Amphitrite and Poseidon.

[14] Documentation in Fr. Vollmer, *P. Papinii Statii Silvarum libri
neu herausgegeben und erklärt* (1898), p. 399.

III, 2, 1). In poems that pray for a prosperous voyage (*propemptica*), these divinities are invoked (Propertius II, 26; Statius, *Silvae* III, 2; *A.P.* VI, 349): at their head Neptune, the Dioscuri, the Nereids. Precise instructions, which probably hark back to a schema of the schools,[15] had been given by the rhetor Menandros (third century A.D.). These gods, then, derived benefits from the invention of navigation: it afforded them prayers and worship. Moreover, it had previously been rather dull at sea:

> Ante rates pigro torpebant aequora somno,
> Nec spumare Thetis nec spargere nubila fluctus
> Audebant.

> (Before there were ships, the ocean lay in sluggish sleep. Thetis did not dare to foam, nor the flood to hurl itself at the clouds.)

So Statius (*Silvae* III 2, 73), in verses for which there seem to be no parallel passages. The result is an ambivalent judgment of navigation: it is impious and brings disaster to men but it is welcome to the sea gods for reasons of worship. Valerius Flaccus clumsily combined these opposing viewpoints. The introduction of Neptune into the Argo-theme, the significance of which will later become clear, was probably suggested to him by the *propemptica*.

We review. As a poet Apollonius cannot compare— in spite of his psychological analysis of Medea's passion— with his great contemporaries Callimachus and Theocritus. But he fits in well with Hellenistic literary aspirations, which demanded of the poet erudition, a cultivated technique, and demonstrations of exquisite aestheticism. He was able to lend Virgil colors for Dido's tragic love, and Quintilian has described his work as "not contemptible." But Valerius Flaccus! "He cannot indeed wholly destroy the perennial charm of the story of the Golden Fleece, but he comes as near doing so as is reasonably possible" (J. W. Mackail). His mytholog-

[15] Vollmer, p. 395.

ical epic is just as stillborn as the historical one of his contemporary Silius Italicus, even though Quintilian says with polite restraint: "We recently lost much in the death of Valerius Flaccus." Apart from the Medea tragedies, the Argonaut material never found a poetically-winged epic treatment. This was undoubtedly also sensed by the great poet of the late efflorescence, Claudian. An animadversion on the Argonaut epic might possibly be detected in the exordium to his *Bellum Gothicum,* although here—in accordance with the custom of the panegyric style—the past must be disparaged for the sake of praising Stilicho.

Claudian also has the motif of astonishment. But with him it is not the Gods that are astonished:

> 8 ... stupuere superbae
> Arte viri domitae Symplegades.

(The proud Symplegades were astonished, subdued by the man's skill.)

The merit of the pilot Tiphys cannot compare with that of Stilicho, who preserved a kingdom—not a mere ship. Do the poets not exaggerate a little?

> 14 ... licet omnia vates
> In maius celebrata ferant ipsamque secandis
> Argois trabibus iactent sudasse Minervam....
>
> 20 Plurima sed quamvis variis miracula monstris
> Ingeminent, teneras victuri carmine mentes
> Harpyiasque truces insopitisque refusum
> Tractibus aurati custodem velleris anguem
> Et iuga taurorum rapidis exusta favillis
> Et virides galeis sulcos fetasque novales
> Martis et in segetem crescentis semina belli:
> Nil veris aequale dabunt.

(Although the poets greatly exaggerate everything and boast that even Minerva exerted herself in felling logs for the Argo. ... But although they pile

478

wonder upon wonder in order to captivate youthful minds with their song, although they tell of savage harpies, of the sleepless dragon stretched out to guard the golden fleece, of the yoke of fire-breathing bulls, the green crops of helmets and the sprouting furrows of Mars and the seeds ripening into the harvest of war: none of their inventions is equal to the truth.)

Perhaps the Argonaut material might have been forgotten had it not contained the antecedent history of the Trojan War[16] and, together with it, been handed down to the Middle Ages in the prose romance *De excidio Troiae* (beginning of the sixth century A.D.) of the fictitious Dares. Prosification is the natural end product of the epic. It satisfies the most robust of interests, the interest in content. It almost always involves —Malory's *Morte d'Arthur* is the great exception—a considerable decline in the level of excellence. But it conserves the epic material which is then given new shape and new life by a later poet. We can observe the course of this development in the mediaeval French epic, which is turned into prose in the fifteenth century and lives on in Italy both as a popular prose romance (*I Reali di Francia*) and in Ariosto's glorious Renaissance poem. Dares' prose history of Troy, too, served as a medium of transmission. As is well known, it was turned into large-scale verse romances in the vernacular languages. But it was also treated—with almost excessive virtuosity—in Latin hexameters in the *Bellum Troianum* of the Englishman Josephus Iscanus (d. 1210) or Exoniensis ("of Exeter"). The importance of this work must not be underrated. It was still widely read even in recent times, as the many reprints from the sixteenth to the eighteenth centuries attest. The last edition was published in London in 1825.[17]

[16] Heracles' conflict with Laomedon, the father of Priam, had been added on to the voyage of the Argonauts.

[17] The text of the vulgate of Dresemius (originally Frankfurt, 1620) is in a sad state. Jules Jusserand (1855–1932), later a proved scholar

Joseph Iscanus attributed the Argonauts' enterprise moralistically to the lust for gold; in so doing he was able to make use of motifs from classical poets (e.g. Tibullus I, 3, 40). The Argo is apostrophized in phrases reminiscent of Valerius Flaccus:

> 87 ... Quonam, quo, naufraga tendis?
> Quo populos in fata trahis?

(Toward what shipwreck do you shape your course? Toward what doom do you draw the peoples?)

Earth is summoned to destroy the ship by means of a cliff ("iniectae Symplegadis ictu"). Fate and Atropos are also inimical to the construction of the ship. But now comes a remarkable turn:

> 95 Plus superi quam fata queunt. Trabs Thessala divos
> Praesentes,[18] quos fecit, habet:[19] contemptus in antris
> Hippotades,[20] in aquis Triton, in carcere Corus,[21]
> Hac rate praerepta summos senuisset in annos.[22]
> Quippe deum genitore metu mens caesa creavit
> 100 Ditem imbris, coelo superos et numina ponto.
> Vix pelagi sensere minas, iamque "Aeole!" clamant,
> "Aeole tuque dato mulces qui cerula sceptro,
> Undarum Neptune potens, date numen ituris.
> Si reduces, meritis numen sacrabitur aris."[23]
> 105 Mox certant in vota dei, gaudentque vocati.

---

of English literature and diplomat, discovered a manuscript in Paris going back to the autograph of the poet and containing his own glosses. From it Jusserand published Book I of the work in 1877. Since then nothing has been done for the text. "Multi pertransibunt, et augebitur scientia."

[18] Helpful: Virgil, *Ecl.* I, 41.

[19] Argo first made gods of the gods.

[20] Aeolus.   [21] The Northwest Wind.

[22] Until their extreme old age the marine divinities would not have experienced anything: a reminiscence of the passage from Statius cited above.

[23] "meritae arae" after Valerius Flaccus, I, 677.

(The gods can do more than fate. The Thessalian vessel is favored by the gods whom it created: scorned was Aeolus in his cave, Triton in the waters, Corus in his cell; without this ship they would have grown old uncelebrated. But the deluded wit of men created gods, the products of fear: Dis in the realm of the shades, the high gods in heaven, and the divinities of the sea. Hardly had they perceived the menace of the deep when they exclaimed, "Aeolus, and you Neptune who calm the blue waves with your scepter, protect the voyagers. If they return, they will consecrate to you well-merited altars." Soon the gods vie with each other to grant the prayers, happy to have been invoked.)

So it is the Gods, the previously despised Aeolus, as well as Triton and Neptune, who favor navigation. And why? They gain worshippers and altars—but only, of course, if the seafarers return unharmed (104). This, then, is the idea with which we are familiar from Statius, though ingeniously combined, to be sure, with the rhetorical commonplace (Petronius *fr*. 27; Statius *Theb*. III, 661; Fulgentius *Myth.*, Helm, p. 17, 3): "the Gods are the products of fear"—that is to say, all the Gods. It pleased our poet to refute the heresy of Antiquity with an argument drawn from Antiquity itself (just as he also rejected the invocation to the Muses as pagan: *ZRPh* 63 [1943], 258). By this means he both "deepened" the Argo-theme, employed the fear of shipwreck for a genetic theory of religion and, finally, wove into a significant pattern the motifs which in Valerius Flaccus lack all coherence.[24] A notable achievement.

One other passage from the *Bellum Troianum* requires our attention (I, 174ff.):

[24] Joseph of Exeter and Jean de Meun have demonstrably used Valerius Flaccus. The assertion that he was not known in the Middle Ages (so most recently R. J. Getty in *The Oxford Classical Dictionary* [1949] p. 936) cannot be sustained.

Quid memorem Aesonidae duras incumbere leges
175 Aeetae imperio? quid somina iacta? quid hostes
Terrigenas Martisque boves saevique draconis
Excubias? ignis virtuti cedit et ensis:
Eripiturque emptum summo discrimine vellus.
Neptunum sensisse putes: fugientibus aequor
180 Altius intumuit fractique in litore fluctus
Intonuere simul. Procul, o procul ite profani!
Non licet in sanctum cum praeda tendere pontum.
Has Notus haud passus causas instare timoris,
Praeripuit voces nec iter concessit in aures.
185 Navigat auricomo spoliatis vellere Colchis
Praedo potens. Culpemne ratem quae prima per undas
Ad facinus molita vias atque Atropon auxit?
An causa potiore probem? Sine remigis usu
Non nosset Memphis Romam, non Indus Iberum,
190 Non Scytha Cecropiden, non nostra Britannia Gallum.[25]

(Why should I mention that a harsh decree oppressed Jason (Aeson's son) because of the son of Aeetes? That he cast the seed? Why speak of the enemies who sprang from the earth, of Mars' cattle and the fierce dragon lying on watch? Fire and sword yield to manly courage: and the fleece, purchased with the highest danger, is stolen. You would think Neptune had sensed it: the sea swelled violently under the homeward bound Argonauts and at the same time the breakers roared from the shore. Begone, profane ones! With this spoil you

[25] To elucidate, here are the essentials. —From around 1160 it becomes the practice of a certain literary school, which is still to be more precisely circumscribed, to dispose of action (battles, journeys, meals) very briefly and to emphasize this practice through the use of preterite-formulas. I have called attention to this elsewhere (in the journal *Comparative Literature* [1949]). We observe this procedure in 174–178. —182: Resumption of the motif: lust for gold as the cause of navigation. —Gloss on *Notus*, 182: "quasi diceret 'ita intonuit mare, sed vento interposito non potuit vox illa audiri'." —Gloss on Atropon, 187: "mortem."

may not traverse the sacred seas. The South wind did not suffer you to importune him with these anxious motives, he dispelled your voices and stopped his ear to them. The brutal thief sails on with the golden fleece plundered from Colchis. Shall I blame the ship which first toiled through the waves for a wicked goal and brought Atropos increase? Or shall I approve it for the sake of a higher purpose? Without the use of the oar Memphis would not have known Rome nor the Indian the Iberian nor the Scythian the Athenian nor our Britannia the Gaul.)

It is characteristic that the islander Joseph, after considering the pro and contra, does approve of the invention of navigation. But for our inquiry, the most important passage is the wrath of Neptune (179-182). It is emphasized with an emotional fervor that appeals to the sense of piety.

In contrast to Joseph Iscanus, Jean de Meun in the *Roman de la Rose* judges navigation utterly negatively. His evaluation is dependent on the description of the Golden Age that he found in Boethius (*cons.* II m.v):

> Felix nimium prior aetas
> Contenta fidelibus arvis
> Nec inerti perdita luxu,
> Facili quae sera solebat
> Jeiunia solvere glande.
> Non Bacchia munera norant
> Liquido confundere melle
> Nec lucida vellera Serum
> Tyrio miscere veneno.
> Somnos dabat herba salubres,
> Potum quoque lubricus amnis,
> Umbras altissima pinus.
> Nondum maris alta secabat
> Nec mercibus undique lectis
> Nova litora viderat hospes. . . .

(The happy former age was content with faithful fields, it was not corrupted by luxurious indolence and would break long fasts with easily-gathered acorns. Men did not know how to mix the gifts of Bacchus with honey or to dye shining silks with Tyrian purple. The grass afforded wholesome sleep, the gliding stream was their drink, tall pines gave shade. Nor did the merchant yet cleave the high seas in search of foreign shores.)

These wonderful lines present the French poet with the subject for didactic small talk:

> 9501 N'estait lors nul pelerinage
> N'issait nus hors de son rivage
> Pour cerchier estrange contree,
> 9504 N'onques n'avait la mer passee
> Jasons qui primes la passa,
> Quant les navies compassa
> Pour la toison d'or aler querre;
> 9508 Bien cuida estre pris de guerre
> Neptunus, quant les vit nagier;
> Tritons redut vis enragier
> E Doris e toutes ses filles;
> 9512 Pour les merveilleuses semilles
> Cuidierent tuit estre trai,
> Tant furent forment esbai
> Des nés qui par la mer volaient
> 9516 Si con li marinier voulaient.

[At that time there was no pilgrimage: no man went out from his own shores to search for a foreign country. Jason had not yet passed over the sea, and he was the first to do so when he organized the ships for the journey to seek the Golden Fleece. When Neptune saw the ships sailing along, he thought for certain that he was captured in war. Triton, too, had to puff his cheeks with rage; and

Doris and all her daughters, because of the marvelous tricks, thought that they were all betrayed, so greatly were they dumbfounded by the ships that flew over the sea just as the sailors wished them to.][26]

The objective content—Neptune's anger, Triton, Doris, the Nereids—might have been transmitted by Valerius Flaccus, though possibly also by Josephus Iscanus (Doris, who is not mentioned in either, was readily available to the author through his wide reading). The hostility of the sea gods is a twist of the author's, perhaps by attraction from Neptune's wrath. The theme of astonishment (9514) is thus forced into the background. Nor could Jean de Meun pass over the amorous adventures of Jason, who was a fascinating but unscrupulous seducer. He abandoned Queen Hypsipyle of Lemnos when she was already with child.[27] This led to a fatal chain of events that has left its mark on the legend of Thebes. Jason was also unfaithful to Medea, to whom he was so deeply indebted, in order to marry Creusa, the daughter of the King of Corinth. Ovid had movingly and eloquently rendered the laments of both women (*Heroides* VI and XII). Jean de Meun was following in his footsteps when he put together exempla of forsaken heroines. He relates the story of Jason and Medea in lines 13229–13262. Jean de Meun returns to the subject again when he treats of feminine wiles, which could even take in Argus (Ovid *ars* III 618 = *Roman de la Rose* 14383).

The *Romance of the Rose* was transplanted to Italy by the author of the *Fiore*, who calls himself Durante. The grounds in favor of identifying him with the young Dante were last set forth by Alfred Bassermann.[28] They are not to be dismissed casually; nevertheless, this is not the place to examine the question. The *Fiore* is a recasting of the *Romance of the Rose*

[26] Trans. Charles Dahlberg.

[27] Cf. her account in Statius, *Thebais* V, 29–498.

[28] *Dante Alighieri, Die Blume (Il Fiore), übersetzt von Alfred Bassermann* (Heidelberg, 1926).

in 232 sonnets. Argus, Jason, and Medea are touched upon in sonnets 8, 161, and 190.

Dante showed great interest in the Argonaut material. Jason appears in *Inferno* XVIII, 82ff. as a seducer. Virgil introduces him with admiration:

> E'l buon maestro, sanza mia dimanda,
> > Mi disse: "Guarda quel grande che vene,
> > E per dolor non par lagrima spanda.
> Quanto aspetto reale ancor ritene!
> > Quelli è Iason, che per cuore e per senno
> > Li Colchi del monton privati fene,
> Ello passò per l'isola di Lenno,
> > Poi che l'ardite femmine spietate
> > Tutti li maschi loro morte dienno.
> Ivi con segni e con parole ornate
> > Isifile ingannò, la giovinetta
> > Che prima avea tutte l'altre ingannate.
> Lasciolla quivi, gravida, soletta;
> > Tal colpa a tal martiro lui condanna;
> > E anche di Medea si fa vendetta."

> (And the good master, without my inquiry,
> > Said to me: "See that tall one who is coming,
> > And for his pain seems not to shed a tear.
> Still what a royal aspect he retains!
> > That Jason is, who by his heart and cunning
> > The Colchians of the Ram made destitute.
> He by the isle of Lemnos passed along
> > After the daring women pitiless
> > Had unto death devoted all their males.
> There with his tokens and with ornate words
> > Did he deceive Hypsipyle, the maiden
> > Who first, herself, had all the rest deceived.
> There did he leave her pregnant and forlorn;
> > Such sin unto such punishment condemns him,
> > And also for Medea is vengeance done.")
> > > > > [Longfellow]

Jason's youthful appearance and aristocratic beauty had already been emphasized by Ovid (*Met.* VII, 26 and 44). But Dante goes further. He endows him with regal dignity of bearing, with outer and inner grandeur. These are the traits of the ideal hero,[29] reserved by Dante for his favorite characters. According to ancient tradition, the Argo carried a band of chosen heroes: "delectos heroas" (Virgil, *Ecl.* IV, 35). In a prominent place he again has recourse to the Argonaut material. The old metaphor,[30] "poetry as navigation," is heightened by him to the sublime as his otherworldly journey takes him to the kingdom of the blessed (*Par.* 2, 1ff.). He advises the readers who have accompanied him thus far to return to their native shores: else they might lose themselves on the high seas. His summons is meant only for the "few," who early in their lives have already craved heavenly nourishment:

> 13 Metter potete ben per l'alto sale
> Vostro navigio, servando mio solco
> Dinanzi a l'acqua che ritorna eguale.
> Que' gloriosi che passaro a Colco
> Non s'ammiraron come voi farete
> Quando Iason vider fatto bifolco.

> (Well you may launch upon the deep salt-sea
> Your vessel, keeping still my wake before you
> Upon the water that grows smooth again.

[29] An anticipation, as it were, of the Burgundian romanticism about Jason. Philip the Good of Burgundy married Isabella of Portugal in 1430. For this occasion—and perhaps also as an act of homage to the best seafaring nation of his day—he founded the Order of the Golden Fleece. Its patron saints were Jason and Gideon. A miraculous fleece had also played a part in the story of Gideon (*Judges* 6:36–40). One of Calderón's sacramental dramas is called *La Piel de Gedeon* (1650); printed in the edition of Pando y Mier (1717), vol. 3; German in F. Lorinser, *Calderons geistliche Festspiele*, vol. 9. On the romanticism about Jason: George Doutrepont, *La Littérature Française à la Cour des Ducs de Bourgogne* (1909), pp. 147–176.

[30] *European Literature and the Latin Middle Ages*, pp. 128ff.

Those glorious ones who unto Colchos passed
Were not so wonder-struck as you shall be,
When Jason they beheld a ploughman made!)
[Longfellow]

Jason was "oxherd" and "farm hand" (*bifolco*, Lat. *bubulcus*) when he ploughed in Colchis with the fire-breathing bulls, protected by Medea's magic spells. Then the Colchians were astonished, the Argonauts encouraged their leader with shouts (Ovid, *Met.* VII, 120):

Mirantur Colchi, Minyae clamoribus augent
Adiciuntque animos.

Jason having stood the test,

. . . gratantur Achivi
Victoremque tenent avidisque amplexibus haerent.

[. . . the Achaeans congratulate and hold the victor in their eager embraces.]

These passages are the material from which Dante distilled his energetic compression ("s'ammiraron . . ."). The Argonauts are described, in the periphrastic manner dear to Dante,[31] as

Que' gloriosi che passaro a Colco,

words which betoken admiring respect. The myth of the Argonauts struck a deeply responsive chord in Dante's soul. Its vibrations carried over to his depiction of Jason. But it was not the person of the hero that engaged Dante's sympathy but the daring sea voyage. A *navigare necesse est!* unknown to the esteemed Virgil (*Ecl.* IV, 32) was inscribed in Dante's heart. It inspired him with the magnificent invention of Odysseus' last voyage (*Inferno* XXVI, 90ff.). It explains his relation to the Argonaut myth. When he set out upon the third and last section of his undertaking, to become the poet of supernal bliss, his own daring seemed to him as bold as that

[31] *Ibid.*, p. 277.

of the Argo voyagers; indeed, bolder. And when he had completed the work, when he had beheld this world and the celestial world for a moment in ineffable unity, he had recourse
once more to the Argo-myth (*Par.* XXXIII, 94):

> Un punto solo m'è maggior letargo
>> Che venticinque secoli a la 'mpresa
>> Che fè Nettuno ammirar l'ombra d'Argo.

> (One moment is more lethargy to me,
>> Than five and twenty centuries to the emprise
>> That startled Neptune with the shade of Argo.)
>>> [Longfellow]

This tercet expresses a unique situation in Dante's poetry;
perhaps the most solemn. In *Paradiso* II, 17 he had promised
his readers things worthier of astonishment than the wonders
of the Argonauts. By degrees of unprecedented intensity he
had carried them aloft through all the spheres into the Empyrean, had guided them as far as the illumination vouchsafed to him by the simultaneous vision of the many in the
one (*Par.* XXXIII, 85):

> Nel suo profondo vidi che s'interna
>> Legato con amore in un volume,
> 87 Ciò che per l'universo si squaderna;
>> Sustanze e accidenti e lor costume,
>> Quasi conflati insieme, per tal modo
> 90 Che ciò ch'i' dico è un semplice lume.
>> La forma universal di questo nodo
>> Credo ch'i' vidi, perchè più di largo,
> 93 Dicendo questo, mi sento ch'i' godo.

> (I saw that in its depth far down is lying
>> Bound up with love together in one volume,
>> What through the universe in leaves is scattered;
> Substance, and accident, and their operations,
>> All interfused together in such wise
>> That what I speak of is one simple light.

The universal fashion of this knot
    Methinks I saw, since more abundantly
    In saying this I feel that I rejoice.)
                                    [Longfellow]

These nine lines, by virtue of their content, their interweaving
of imagery, their precise rendering of the unseizable,
undoubtedly constitute one of the most magnificent poetic
utterances ever made. It does more than surpass the wonders
of the Argonauts. Only in verse 92 is there a slackening in the
diction, beginning with *perchè*. What then follows down to
godo, though required by the sense, could be imagined differently expressed. The effect of *più di largo* is pallid after the
enormous compression of what preceded it. This can only be
said, of course, with the grave reservation that we are here
touching the iron law that Dante forged for himself: the *terza
rima*.

The threefold rhyme is the indispensable expression for the
concatenatio rerum, the coherency of all relations in Dante's
intellectual cosmos—"la forma universal di questo nodo."
Only the implacable rigor of this rhyme scheme was capable
of welding the poetic material indissolubly together. This
rigor is sometimes strained to the point of violence. The
rhyme that matters to the poet necessarily attracts the other
two. In the tercet that now follows, *Un punto solo*, the rhyme
word first fixed for the poet is Argo. It attracts *letargo*, and
Dante then has these two vehicles of the poetic emotion prel-
uded by the everyday word *largo*. *Lethargus*, which denotes
somnolence in classical Latin, is found in Alanus ab Insulis
in the acceptation of "entrancement."[32] But what is the relevance of Neptune here? On this point Dante scholarship has
failed. Some commentators refer to Catullus' astonished
Nereids, who do not fit. Others explain it as a free invention
of Dante's own. That contradicts everything we know about
the poet's methods. In the Dante literature I find only one
useful reference: it is Parodi's (*Bullettino della Società dan-*

[32] More details in *Romanische Forschungen* (1950), 28ff.

tesca XXIII, 66) to Statius' *Achilleis*. Statius intended to relate the entire life of Achilles—"ire per omnem heroa"—, and he begins effectively with the return of the abductor Paris to Troy. Before his birth Hecuba had dreamt that she would bring forth a burning brand that would set fire to Ilium. The abduction of Helen gave this prophecy of war a menacing actuality. Achilles' mother Thetis also takes account of this situation. She foresees that this war will prove her son's ruin. The consciousness of the danger flashes through her mind as she sees Paris' oars, fashioned from the wood of Mount Ida in Troy, cleaving Hellespont's glassy flood:

> 20 Solverat Oebalio classem de litore pastor
> Dardanus incautas blande populatus Amyclas
> Plenaque materni referens praesagia somni
> Culpatum relegebat iter, qua condita ponto
> Fluctibus invisis iam Nereis imperat Helle:
> Cum Thetis Idaeos—heu numquam vana parentum
> Auguria!—expavit vitreo sub gurgite remos.

> (The Dardan shepherd sailed from the shores of Laconia, having smoothly pillaged unsuspecting Amyclae. He had fulfilled the presage of his mother's dream and was retracing his guilty path over the waves, in the depths of which Helle, who now commands the hated flood as a Nereid, was concealed: when Thetis—alas, the auguries of parents are never vain!—started with fear beneath the glassy waters at the oars from Ida.)

Statius obviously modeled this situation on the Argo-theme: an ill-omened ship, built with ill-omened timber, is perceived by a marine divinity. A new trait has been added: the ship is described from a viewpoint beneath the surface of the sea— "vitreo sub gurgite."[33] A marine divinity, catching sight of a fateful ship and being strongly affected emotionally by it—

---

[33] So Poseidon is astonished at the bull which ploughs through the ocean, carrying Europa.

expavit—: this scheme is what Statius and Dante's Argo tercet have in common. Only Dante has handled it much more concretely: he has the God perceive the Argo's shadow. And this God is Neptune, and his emotion is that of astonishment. This emotion, as we have seen, is traditionally connected with the "Argo-effect." As vehicles of this astonishment we have come to know the Olympian Gods and the nymphs of Pelion (both in Apollonius), the Nereids (Catullus), and the Symplegades (Claudian); but not Neptune, for whom the emotion of wrath was reserved. Thus Dante has melted down, as it were, three motives for pathos which tradition had kept apart and cast the fusion into a new form: the astonishment of the Gods at the sight of the Argo; the view from beneath the sea's surface of the ship gliding upon it; and finally the link "Neptune-Argo." Whether he derived these elements from Valerius Flaccus or Joseph of Exeter or Jean de Meun it will hardly be possible to determine. Dante's creative power enabled him, in this instance as at many other high points of his poem, to reshape a literary tradition composed of many strata but frequently containing little valuable ore, into a structure of the highest expressive content. In the Argo-tercet the profound emotional impact of the Argonaut myth upon Dante is manifested for the last time: Jason's voyage is the most astonishing *impresa* of all the ages. The word possesses here a heroic tone that will be modulated by Ariosto into the courtly-chivalric:

> Le donne, i cavallier, l'arme, gli amori,
> Le cortesie, l'audaci imprese io canto.

According to ancient chronology the Argo set forth on its voyage in 1263, in other words seventy-nine years before the fall of Troy. That is how Dante arrives at his twenty-five centuries. Dante's conception of history requires the perspective of millennia—as does Goethe's. A span of thirteen centuries separates Dante from Virgil, but it is bridged by their encounter. All history is raised to synchronicity.

From the view of the present Goethe moves into temporal proximity with Dante. That is not all. Like Dante he represents once again the thesaurus of European tradition. In his work, too, we encounter the Argonaut myth. As a student at Strasbourg he sees a figured tapestry which depicts the story of Jason, Medea, and Creusa: "and hence an example of the unhappiest of marriages." It hung in a festival pavilion for the reception of the royal bride Marie Antoinette. Goethe was "utterly outraged" at the choice, and the memory remained, so that forty years later he still thought it worth recounting (*Dichtung und Wahrheit* ii, 9; Jubiläums-Ausgabe 23, 178). In his exchange of ideas with Schiller he ponders whether the Argonaut expedition might provide material for an epic (Goethe, 26 April 1794; Schiller, 28 August 1798). Goethe concludes: "there are magnificent themes in it" (29 August 1798). For his preliminary studies toward the *Achilleis*, the first and only canto of which was completed in 1799 but not published till 1808, Goethe borrowed the Trojan romances of Dares and Dictys. The Goethean Achilles is mindful of "Argonautic daring" (*Achilleis*, 555). In jest, Goethe calls himself an Argonaut: "Loder has just returned from Halle, where he has rented a house. When I talk to him about his new circumstances, I am sincerely pleased that the dice fell for him as they did. What man of the world would not wish, like the rest of us strange Argonauts, to drag his own bark over the isthmuses? These are adventures of older, less skillful navigators, which modern enlightened technology smiles at" (to Schiller, 5 July 1803). In the essay *Philostrats Gemälde* (1818) various designs for pictures from the Argonaut cycle are listed. In the poet's extreme old age the myth emerges again, reaches its maturest expression, and is incorporated into the lifework. In the *Klassische Walpurgisnacht* (composed between January and June 1830) Faust begs Chiron for tidings of the heroes he has educated,[34] and is told:

[34] The Faust commentators assure us that Chiron's relation to the Argonauts was freely invented by Goethe. But Hesiod (*fr.* 19 Rzach)

7365 Im hehren Argonautenkreise
War jeder brav nach seiner eignen Weise,
Und nach der Kraft, die ihn beseelte,
Konnt' er genügen, wo's den andern fehlte.
Die Dioskuren haben stets gesiegt,
Wo Jugendfüll' und Schönheit überwiegt.
Entschluss und schnelle Tat zu andrer Heil,
Den Boreaden ward's zum schönen Teil.
Nachsinnend, kräftig, klug, im Rat bequem,
So herrschte Jason, Frauen angenehm.
Dann Orpheus, zart und immer still bedächtig,
Schlug er die Leier allen übermächtig.
Scharfsichtig Lynceus, der bei Tag und Nacht
Das heil'ge Schiff durch Klipp' und Strand gebracht.

[Of those beneath the Argonauts' bright banner,
Each worthy was in his peculiar manner.
And by the virtue of his strength selective,
Sufficed therein, where others were defective.
Castor and Pollux were as victors hailed,
Where beauty and the grace of youth prevailed:
Decision, the swift deed for others' aid,
Gave the fair crown before the Boreads' laid:
Reflective, prudent, strong, in council wise,
So Jason ruled, delight of women's eyes:
Then Orpheus, gentle, silent, brooding, lowering,
But when he struck the lyre, all over-powering.
Sharp-sighted Lynceus, who by day and dark
Through shoreward breakers steered the sacred
      bark.]
[Bayard Taylor]

---

and Pindar (*Nem.* 3, 53) already attest that Jason was educated by Chiron. In addition to him numerous other heroes, whom Xenophon (*Kyneg.* 1) enumerates, were Chiron's pupils. The objection that they could not all have lived at the same time is ingeniously met by Xenophon: Chiron's life "was long enough for all," since he was born before and died after all of them.

The Argo in *Faust!* It is called sacred here because it bore the pick of Hellenic heroes. The Greek hero, however—in contrast to the Nordic—participates in the world of the Gods, be it through descent of birth, elevation to Olympus, translation to the stars. In Goethe as in Apollonius of Rhodes (I, 151) Lynceus, whose glance, according to Greek legend, could penetrate trees and even the earth, appears as one of the Argonauts. By a bold stroke Goethe provides an *aristeia* for this hero. He is transformed into the watchman of the tower:

> 9230 Augenstrahl ist mir verliehen
> Wie dem Luchs auf höchstem Baum.
>
> [Beam of sight to me was given,
> Like the lynx on highest tree.]
>
> [Bayard Taylor]

Helena's beauty dazzles him. In the fifth act he is charged with the dramatic function of announcing a raging fire (11304 to 11337), but before that he celebrates, in four glorious stanzas, the bliss of sight. The Argonaut who became a watchman has been transformed once more. He has become the herald of a message that to the eighty-year-old Goethe signifies the ultimate epitome of his ripest wisdom. He stated it twice, both times through a mask. Such a mask is the title *Der Bräutigam* [*The Bridegroom*] which Goethe gave to a poem published in 1829. It is a midnight poem and concludes:

> Wie es auch sei, das Leben, es ist gut.
>
> [Life, be it as it may, is good.]

Such a mask is the song of Lynceus the watchman in "deep night," with its ending:

> Ihr glücklichen Augen
> Was je ihr gesehn,
> Es sei wie es wolle,
> Es war doch so schön!

[Thou fortunate vision,
Of all thou wast 'ware,
Whatever it might be,
Yet still it was fair!]
[Bayard Taylor]

Both poems express the same experience with a serenity clear as the stars, and both conceal a secret testament of Goethe's. That one of them has been put in the mouth of Lynceus possesses a profound meaning: Lynceus' sight is blissful because it is without desire, a resigned harmony with the universe. It represents the complete antithesis of Faust's insatiable striving. The poet has no need to desire, for he enjoys and lavishes inherited abundance (the boy-charioteer, son of Plutus). Lynceus is the anti-Faust. Lynceus is Goethe, the transformed Argonaut.

A glance at the Argo-theme affords an insight into the economy of literary tradition. This tradition can appear as a bewildering conglomerate of fragments. Three verses of Accius, a sentence from a long-forgotten rhetorician, fusty epics from the Rome of the Flavians and the England of the Angevines: these are but a few samples of the scanty remains we have examined. But it does seem as if they had been employed with the strictest calculation of means and the maximum of efficiency. The dry schema of a Priscian can unfold, in Calderón, into a flowering of tropical splendor. Reminiscences of Latin and French poetry are compressed by Dante into one eternal line of verse. From the fabricated histories of the mythologists Goethe selects Lynceus and entrusts him with his testament. There is an Argo in every era, as Virgil prophesied:

> Alter erit tum Tiphys, et altera quae vehat Argo
> Delectos heroas.

[Then there will be another Tiphys, and another Argo to carry chosen heroes.]

1950

Appendix

THE FOLLOWING pages appeared in 1945 in the Heidelberg review *Die Wandlung*. The manuscript of the book announced at the time was revised once more in 1946–1947 and was published with a different preface in 1948.

PREFACE TO A BOOK ON THE LATIN MIDDLE AGES AND EUROPEAN LITERATURE

TO FACILITATE the reader's understanding of this book, I believe I must say something about its antecedent history, but that means: about the course of my development as a scholar.

During my years of study with Gustav Gröber (1844–1911) in Strasbourg, I adopted the view of the tasks of Romance philology which pervaded his instruction and which, as editor of the *Grundriss* [*Outline*] of this discipline, he set down in a deliberately sober and factual manner. If Diez was the great founder of Romance philology, then Gröber may be called its great systematizer—quite irrespective of his historical, philological, and grammatical achievements, which laid new foundations in all these areas. Gröber had been trained in philosophy, and his thinking addressed itself to the entire range of the new discipline. Following a suggestion of his teacher Adolf Ebert (1820–1890), he came to regard Mediaeval Latin literature as one of the most important bases of the Romance literatures, and was the first to devote to it a full-scale scholarly treatment. This enticed me, while still a student, to take a few halting steps in this field. Even so, I still had to complete two projects in the field of French philology which had been assigned to me by Gröber himself—a new edition of the Old French *Book of Kings* (1913) and a study of the critic Ferdinand Brunetière (1849–1906), which was published in 1914. This study made it necessary for me to familiarize myself with modern French literature.

But at the same time French intellect and culture were becoming important to me in another way. My Alsatian friends were reading the *Nouvelle Revue Française*, the *Cahiers de la Quinzaine*. A whole new France was in the making. Bergson, Rolland, Péguy, Gide, Claudel were the stars discovered by my generation. On this contemporary France I gave a course at the University of Bonn in the summer of 1914. The lectures, revised, were published as a book in 1919 under the title of *Die literarischen Wegbereiter des neuen Frankreich* [*The Literary Pioneers of The New France*]. It was followed by books on Barrès (1921), on Balzac (1923), on *Französischer Geist im neuen Europa* [*The French Mind in The New Europe*]—Proust, Valéry, Larbaud, Thibaudet, *et al.*— (1925), finally an introduction to French culture, *Einführung in die französische Kultur* (1930) (English tr. *The Civilization of France*, 1930). With this latter work I felt that I had concluded my studies of modern France:—for inner reasons. A compelling psychological necessity drove me to seek a change in my field of research. I felt the need to return to older periods—metaphorically speaking I would say today, to more archaic strata of consciousness: in the first instance, the Romance Middle Ages. Beyond that I was seeking, without being precisely aware of it, the road to Rome. Ever since my first visit the city had become for me, not only on all its historical levels but rather in its spiritual essence, in other words in a sense that transcended history, the holy city; yet withal one not chosen but discovered, an ancestral homeland and a goal of pilgrimage. Every fresh sojourn in Rome strengthened this relation to my life. I knew myself bound to the *Roma aeterna*. In the course of years and decades I realized that this bond contained a secret with many layers of symbolic meaning. As my work moved away from France, a lock sprang open. The way was clear for the experience of Rome to flow into my research. What had first enthralled me in Rome was the Palatine hill. The ruined palaces of the

Caesars bespoke the eternal glory of the Empire. The Imperium became an ideal realm, a timeless reality. It held me spellbound with the magic that Stefan George has incarnated in his poem *Porta Nigra*.

During the years of my Alsatian youth, the Upper Rhine region had filled me with longing for the West (to which George's poem *Franken* gave an echo). Later, the region of the Middle Rhine afforded me the experience of that millennium of Roman-Germanic communal life in which Nadler discovered the key to the intellectual history of the German west and south and which, prior to the bombing raids on the Rhineland, was splendidly evident to the sensitive observer in Bingen, Trier, Bonn, Cologne, and in many other less prominent places. These complex and challenging experiences were to enter fruitfully, at first as fragmentary attempts, into my work.

In the 1920s, in addition to France, I became increasingly fascinated with modern Spain, as it was represented in the *Revista de Occidente* (1923–1936) and in the works of Ortega. . . . The shift in my interests since 1930 led me back to the Middle Ages in this area too. And it was here that my first fresh encounter with the Rome of the Palatine took place. In a famous Spanish poem of the fifteenth century I found the imperial idea of Rome expressed as the permanently-valid measure of mankind. I pursued these connections, which I considered to be profoundly significant.[1]

Burning issues of the day tore me away from the tranquil course of my studies. My book *Deutscher Geist in Gefahr* [*The German Mind in Peril*] (1932) was a polemic against the self-surrender of German culture, against the hatred of civilization and its sociological and political backgrounds. I was impelled to deliver this warning by a premonition of the shameful catastrophe which befell Germany shortly there-

---

[1] "Jorge Manrique und der Kaisergedanke," *Zeitschrift für romanische Philologie* 52 (1932), 129. In the journal *Romanische Forschungen* (1944) I published a translation of the poem in the meters of the original.

after. From 1933 to 1945 the German mind subsisted in a state of peril that increased from year to year, and suffered inestimable losses.

The remedy which, in 1932, I believed I could prescribe was a new Humanism, albeit one which should have little in common with that of the nineteenth century. "If it is true," I wrote at the time, "that before us lie dark centuries to be succeeded by bright renaissances, it follows that the Humanism of today must start out not from Antiquity nor from the Renaissance but from the Middle Ages. The new Humanism will therefore have to be not Classicism but Mediaevalism and the Restoration principle." I appealed to the "illustrious founders of our Western civilization from Augustine to Dante." In the years 1932 and 1933 I drew from this belief the practical conclusion of giving courses in mediaeval Latin literature. I had to work my way into the difficult material from the ground up. Soon I noticed that on this basis it was possible to acquire a deeper understanding of the monuments of Old Romance poetry (*Zur Interpretation des Alexiusliedes*, 1936). The book by the professor of English, Glunz, on *Die Literarästhetik des Mittelalters*, which appeared in 1937, proved inadequate and was criticized by me in detail in 1938. This controversy prompted me to make a thorough investigation of the Middle Ages and its influence. The result was twenty-two studies between 1938 and 1944, which were presented in scholarly journals and which furnished me with a welcome intellectual alibi during the war. They were not conceived according to a predetermined plan.[2] Beyond the pupillary stage

[2] The origin and progress of my mediaeval Latin studies I may characterize in these sentences of Gröber's: "Undirected observation, inconspicuous attempts precede the all-round comprehension of the subject. Then, traversing the space at a bound, the seeker snatches at the goal. With a scheme of imperfect ideas concerning similar subjects he seems to be able to grasp the whole before its nature and constituents are known. This rash opinion is followed by the discernment of error, only slowly by the resolve to approach the subject by small and smallest careful steps, to observe parts and particles,

there is no method in the humanistic disciplines. Or only one, which cannot be taught: the cooperation of instinct and intelligence.

Behind this condensed formula is something deeper: the essential metaphysical connection between love and knowledge, which Max Scheler has grounded philosophically. Through feeling, through preferring, in the last analysis through loving and hating, all intuition and all knowledge of value is built up. What I have called instinct is the manner in which such an emotional apprehension of intellectual values, guided by the richness and fullness of the capacity for experiencing them, presents itself to the mind of the scholarly investigator. This instinct is a function that can be refined, differentiated, and strengthened by practice. Applied to the method of scholarship, it means developing the flair for noticing that certain passages in a text are "important"—even if it is not yet clear why. Such passages must be collected and compared till the interpretation has been found. "The individual traits that matter,"—I had already written in 1925 in connection with Proust—"cannot be sought out, they must flash upon the mind. If the activity of philosophy is rooted in wonder, the premise of all criticism is that the critic should be struck by certain things. Both activities can only be accomplished by a receptive surrender to the object. . . . Reception is the essential condition for perception, and this then leads to conception." But these sentences are also valid for literary scholarship insofar as it is of the same nature as criticism. Only such a technique enables us to liberate ourselves from the mental attitudes of the present and to read ancient texts without modern preconceptions—and that also means to read them without the preconceptions of modern science. . . .

In the course of my investigations I discovered how I was gradually penetrating deeper and deeper into my chosen field

---

and not to rest until the conviction has been attained, thus and not otherwise is the matter to be understood."

of studies; how new connections and cross-connections were constantly opening up; how, in the end, a new line of continuity in the history of European culture was becoming discernible. Thus the idea arose of recasting my researches into the form of a book. . . .

In conclusion, one last point. What I have said about the personal underlying motives in my evolution as a scholar is intended to explain why I moved from Romance studies to the Latin Middle Ages. I have given an outline of the answer. The issue, however, concerns not only this book but rather a more general question, which has been raised again and again in the last decades: how are the life and the work of a scholar related? It is a problem in the "biology of the scholar." But it also has a practical significance. After the First World War we saw numerous instances of a "new science," basing itself upon "insight" or "intuition" and proclaiming its hostility to a much-cited positivism. There were those who tried to remold the great personalities of history in accordance with the dogmas of the George circle. Others brought adroit syntheses to market. History was turned now into fiction, now into "myth." These were for the most part aberrations the full extent of which can be measured only today. For they paved the way for the falsification of history on a grand scale which had been fatefully at work since 1933. "There is no objective science," was taught at the time. Science had to be affiliated with race, nation, politics. This falsehood must disappear. As surely as all important research is nourished by personal experience and personal insight—so just as surely must these be controlled by the strict discipline of self-criticism, impartiality, and wide learning. Experience must be transmuted in the fire of creation into a structure of knowledge as hard as steel. In this sense science must always remain objective.

Index